Commoi

With George Caffentzis and Silvia Federici

'We need to struggle, perhaps more than ever, given the magnitude and the character of the current destruction of everything – nature, society, culture, the very social fabric allowing us to live together. We need *compas*. We need, particularly, comrades with a clear sight and an open, affective heart. Many of us have found in George Caffentzis and Silvia Federici that company. They have led and accompanied us in many struggles, big and small, in great events and mobilizations or in small coffee talks. And here they are, to celebrate them, with an exceptional cohort of intellectuals/activists, with *compas*, who are saying today what needs to be said to continue the struggle, to resist the horror and to create a new world'.
— Gustavo Esteva, activist, 'deprofessionalised intellectual' and founder of Universidad de la Tierra in Oaxaca, Mexico

'This collection offers an extraordinary kaleidoscope of critical reflections on social reproduction and class struggle. More than that, it is fitting testimony to the inspiration and grounding that Silvia and George continue to provide for those seeking a life beyond the sway of capital'.
— Steve Wright, author of *Storming Heaven: Class Composition and Struggle in Italian Autonomist Marxism*

'No one has taught us more, and more generously, that communism is with us than George Caffentzis and Silvia Federici. Indeed, to be in their presence, to be with their writing and interviews, is to feel intimately the social wealth we are struggling to defend and expand in the face of the geocidal and genocidal plans of the policy class and its backers. That we are the sources not only of that wealth but also of the social transformations necessary to survive in abundance, this is the insight, the lifeline, the hug we receive from the greatest living theorists of commoning'.
— Stefano Harney, co-author of *The Undercommons: Fugitive Planning and Black Study*

'In this labour of love, radical theory joins passionate praxis to honour the social thought and political vision of Silva Federici and George Caffentzis, whose work together and apart offers hope that another world can be made.'
— Eileen Boris, co-author of *Caring for America: Home Health Workers in the Shadow of the Welfare State*

Commoning

With George Caffentzis and Silvia Federici

Edited by
Camille Barbagallo,
Nicholas Beuret and David Harvie

PLUTO  PRESS

First published 2019 by Pluto Press
345 Archway Road, London N6 5AA

www.plutobooks.com

British Library Cataloguing in Publication Data
A catalogue record for this book is available from the British Library

ISBN 978 0 7453 3941 2 Hardback
ISBN 978 0 7453 3940 5 Paperback
ISBN 978 1 7868 0466 2 PDF eBook
ISBN 978 1 7868 0468 6 Kindle eBook
ISBN 978 1 7868 0467 9 EPUB eBook

This book is printed on paper suitable for recycling and made from
fully managed and sustained forest sources. Logging, pulping and
manufacturing processes are expected to conform to the
environmental standards of the country of origin.

Typeset by Riverside Publishing Solutions, Salisbury, United Kingdom

Simultaneously printed in the United Kingdom and United States of America

For Eve, Azadi and Bastien

Contents

Acknowledgements

As editors our motivation in assembling this collection has been an experiment in modes of celebrating life – specifically the militant and rebellious lives, ideas and influence of George and Silvia. It is intended as a small gesture of our immense gratitude and recognition of the intellectual debt we owe to two comrades who have had such an impact on global social movements and also our lives as individuals.

In one sense, this book has multiple beginnings. The moment in 1992, when one of us picked up a copy of *The New Enclosures* for the first time. The first face-to-face encounter with Silvia and George in London in 2003 – and discovery of their warmth and openness. The days we were all lucky enough to spend in their company – and also that of many contributors to this volume – in the summer of 2008, in the Italian Apennines, at the first 'commoner convivium' – and at subsequent gatherings over the next three years.

As with all good commoner projects we would like to acknowledge all the producers, for their ideas, time and energy (and patience) in creating this project with us. In addition to the names that appear inside, we would like to also express our gratitude to those who, for one reason or another, are not represented in this book, but who nevertheless offered support and encouragement: Kolya Abramsky, Ousseina Alidou, Mariarosa Dalla Costa, Gustavo Esteva, John Holloway, Craig Hughes, Sabu Kohso, Maria Mies, Tadzio Müller, Monty Neill, Kevin Van Meter, Steve Wright. Our thanks too to David Shulman at Pluto Press, who was so enthusiastic about the book, and the other folk at Pluto: Neda Tehrani and Melanie Patrick. For invaluable assistance with translations, transcription and copy-editing, we thank Anna-Maeve Holloway, Gloria Loris and Cath Long. Emma Darbyshire of the Fitzwilliam Museum in Cambridge provided last-minute assistance with images. John Barker constructed the index, practising a form of artisanal labour too often overlooked and undervalued.

Introduction: Always Struggle

Camille Barbagallo, Nicholas Beuret and David Harvie

> ...ideas don't come from a light-bulb in someone's brain; ideas come from struggles – this is a basic methodological principle. – George Caffentzis[1]

The militant scholarship of George Caffentzis and Silvia Federici has never been more needed. Together and separately, they have, over a half-century, developed a radical political perspective and praxis. Today, activists and militants across the world are engaging more widely with their many insights and methods. The commons, the uptake of ideas of social reproduction, the integration of ecological and energy concerns with Marxist analysis, and a renewed radical critique of technology are all contemporary themes that they have helped develop over the past decades.

What connects all of these ideas and perspectives is the concept of *struggle*. There are three ways to understand struggle in George and Silvia's work: as practice, as theory and as method. The first is reflected in the *practice* of Silvia and George themselves. For more than 50 years – from the 1960s' anti-Vietnam war movement, through feminist movements, including Wages for Housework in the 1970s, various workers' and anti-colonial struggles, anti-nuke movements from Three Mile Island to Fukushima, campaigns against the death penalty, the Gulf War, the second Gulf War, to Occupy Wall Street and debtors' movements – George and Silvia have always involved themselves in social struggle of one form or another. The second is as the source of *theory* – of ideas and praxis. Theory as something that comes not only from struggle, but also from a commitment to struggle as that which drives social change. The third is to see struggle as a *method* for understanding crises, events, social and political relations, and movement.

The work of George and Silvia converges on and flows out of these interconnected understandings of struggle. More than that, they both – separately, together, with others – have worked tirelessly to expand and deepen our understanding of the terrain of struggle. Of who it is that struggles, how struggles come to matter or count, and of the significance of struggles across the social field.

This volume explores the life and scholarship – the main themes and key insights – of George and Silvia. It is a celebration of two comrades, a chance to revisit their writings and appreciate the wealth of their contribution, and at the same time a continuation of the circulation of militant ideas, theories and histories – a continuation of their own practice.

Through militant lives that became intertwined in the 1970s George and Silvia developed a particular orientation to radical politics, one that started in conversation with the Italian Marxist tradition of *operaismo*, and continued through the perspective developed by Wages for Housework. They experienced first-hand – and struggled against – the emergence of neoliberalism with the 'structural adjustment' of New York City in the mid-1970s; a little later, their experiences in Nigeria deepened their understanding of colonialism, imperialism and energy struggles, which in turn sparked an engagement with 'primitive accumulation' and a rediscovery of the commons. On returning to the United States, they became heavily involved in the emerging counter-globalisation movements; by chance arriving in Mexico at the beginning of 1994 they witnessed the Zapatistas' uprising and went on to spend considerable time in Latin America. What these examples – just a handful out of many – demonstrate is the extent to which Silvia and George have always been grounded *within* revolutionary and other rebellious movements and currents.

The concept of struggle reflects a feature of the world: there is *always struggle*. Here we understand struggle most broadly as class relations. As Werner Bonefeld reminds us in his chapter in this volume, 'history does not unfold at all. "History does nothing"'. There are just human beings, pursuing our ends – struggling. We cannot understand the development of the capitalist mode of production or other social forms without understanding the struggles of millions, and now billions, of human subjects. In this sense, George and Silvia's work is in dialogue with the insight that opens *The Communist Manifesto*: 'the history of all hitherto existing society is the history of class struggle'.

For both George and Silvia the 'Copernican inversion' of Marxist theory developed within *operaismo*, where working class struggles are understood as primary – primary in the sense that it is struggle that militants must be concerned with and theorise, and primary to capitalist development, where struggle precedes capital's transformations – marked a turning point in their own political development.

> The first set of ideas came out of the Italian *operaista* movement... We begin to look at class struggle as a field, instead of certain spots or sites – that there's this field of struggle that takes place all across the system... You look at

buildings and you begin to see not the thing itself but the processes that went on, the sufferings, the struggles that went on to make the thing. It was like an opening of the eye, really. – George Caffenzis[2]

From the Operaist movement... we learned the political importance of the wage as a means of organizing society... From my perspective, this conception of the wage... became a means to unearth the material roots of the sexual and international division of labour and, in my later work, the 'secret of primitive accumulation'. – Silvia Federici[3]

It is here that struggle becomes something ordinary, everyday. It is not a matter of unions, parties or parliaments, but of the daily actions of workers *in work* – and struggling *against and beyond* work. Within this tradition, the refusal to work figures as a key weapon of the proletariat, one through which autonomy from both capital and the state is asserted. Silvia and George have helped extend this tradition to encompass and speak to women struggling against patriarchy, people of colour struggling against racism, peasants struggling against 'progress' and 'development'. In the words of the Zapatista Ana María, 'Behind us we are you, ... behind, we are the same simple and ordinary men and women who repeat themselves in every race, who paint themselves in every colour, who speak in every language and who live in every place'.[4]

When the capitalist counter-offensive of the 1970s took hold, George and Silvia responded by staying within the struggles around them. They 'stretched' Marx and his categories in order to develop an account of the wage that foregrounded the crucial role of the *wageless* – 'housewives', peasants, students, for example – of how people devalued, made invisible or less-than-human laboured to underpin capitalist accumulation through their partial and total exclusion from the wage relation. Thus throughout their work we find an emphasis on expanding and developing our understanding of the composition of the proletariat, with this insistence that the struggles of the unwaged are as important – sometimes more so – as those of the waged. Rejecting forms of autonomist Marxism that flee the question of value, George and Silvia instead develop a current in which Marx's 'law of value' – appropriately 'stretched' of course – is as important as ever. In their expansive conception, we find a broadening of the field of struggle. This allows them – and us – to continue to pose the questions of energy, war, money and debt, and automation in a manner profoundly relevant for contemporary political debates and antagonisms around climate change, environmental destruction, automation and the role technology can and does play in shaping our world and those worlds to come.

Social Reproduction

I saw the struggle, that feminism really had a class dimension, once we understood the feminist movement as one that confronted the revolt against one of the major articulations of the capitalist organisation of work, which is the work of reproduction. – Silvia Federici[5]

It is well known that Silvia was a founding member of the International Wages for Housework Campaign as well as organising numerous other militant feminist collectives and initiatives. In connected ways, the feminist movement in general, and Wages for Housework in particular, were formative for George as well. Wages for Housework was more than the source of theoretical insight. It was both part of a struggle against capital and the state and, at the same time, a critique of the radical social movements of the time. Seeing housework and social reproduction as work, as a site of labour and exploitation, situated women as workers. It was a political praxis that generated considerable conflict within both the left and feminism. Understanding social reproduction in this way was a provocation that led to the 'opening up [of] a new terrain of revolt, a new terrain of anti-capitalist struggle directly' and no longer acting as just supporters to men's struggles.[6] These insights remain as important now as they were in the 1970s – for these struggles and tensions, within social and left-wing movements, and within feminism, continue today, albeit under different names.

Connected to the definition of reproduction as a labour process is the Marxist feminist argument that, at the same time that reproductive labour makes and remakes people, it also produces and reproduces that 'special commodity', labour-power – a process which Silvia refers to as the 'dual characteristic of reproduction'. In positing reproduction as possessing a duality, it becomes possible to both revalue this work and, at the same time, identify the practices and processes that are implicated and foundational in the maintenance of capitalist social relations. The dual characteristic of reproduction draws attention to the tensions and contradictions at the centre of the processes of social reproduction; a tension that is directly related to what reproduction does within capitalism and how it operates.

In societies dominated by capitalism, people are reproduced as workers but also, at the same time, they are reproduced as people whose lives, desires and capabilities exceed the role of worker. People are more than their economic role; they are irreducible to it. This is one aspect of why labour-power is 'special' – if we did not exceed our economic role, we would not be capable of producing surplus-value. People struggle, are involved in conflict and, frequently, resist. In this way reproductive labour can be said to have two functions: it both maintains capitalism in that it produces the most important commodity of all – labour-power – and, at the same time, it has the potential to undermine accumulation, by producing rebellious subjects.

The Commons

...when we returned to the United States – other comrades had already left the US during this period. And we all returned and had pretty similar stories to tell. So we began to work on this notion of the commons and enclosures. Being the way in which we can talk about the class struggle in this period. – George Caffentzis[7]

George and Silvia are also well known for their work on the commons. They have credited their experiences in Nigeria in the early-to-mid-1980s as being the genesis point on their thinking around commons and their antithesis, enclosures. But potentially as significant is the New York they left behind them. That city was declared bankrupt in 1975: capital's response was one of the world's first 'structural adjustment programmes', a weapon that would become well-established in neoliberal globalisation's armoury. This restructuring used the city's 'debt crisis' to enforce a series of privatisation programmes, savage cuts to the social wage and attacks on working conditions and workers' rights to organise. When George and Silvia witnessed first-hand another 'structural adjustment' in Nigeria, they could see how capital's various restructurings were in fact different manifestations of one global process, in which questions of the social wage, land and still-existing commons – in Third World as well as First – all intersected.

The transnational character of 'structural adjustment' and capital's offensive against commons led directly to an engagement with the continuous nature of what Marx called 'primitive accumulation'. George and Silvia, as a part of the Midnight Notes Collective, described these ongoing instances of primitive accumulation as 'new enclosures'.

The Enclosures... are not a one time process exhausted at the dawn of capitalism. They are a regular return on the path of accumulation and a structural component of class struggle. Any leap in proletarian power demands a dynamic capitalist response: both in the expanded appropriation of new resources and the extension of capitalist relations.[8]

Midnight Notes' work on the new enclosures covered struggles spanning the globe. It emphasised not only the central importance of land as a site of struggle and dispossession, but also debt as a mechanism of dispossession. This recognition of the tight connection between debt on the one hand and enclosure on the other forms a crucial part of George and Silvia's work on the commons. Insights developed to understand capital's creation and exploitation of an 'international debt crisis' in the 1980s continues to inform their work today, on microfinance, say, or in their involvement in the Occupy movement.

But against the capital's various mechanisms to dispossess and to enclosure, just as crucial is the recognition of the commons' role in facilitating resistance: in Nigeria, the commons 'made it possible for many who are outside of the waged market to have collective access to land and for many waged workers with ties to the village common land to subsist when on strike'.[9]

> Even when urbanized, many Africans expect to draw some support from the village, as the place where one may get food when on strike or unemployed, where one thinks of returning in old age, where, if one has nothing to live on, one may get some unused land to cultivate from a local chief or a plate of soup from neighbours and kin.[10]

Here we also have the recognition that commons may have the potential, not only to enable struggle against capital, but also provide a foundation for the creation of worlds that exist outside and beyond capital and the state.

This scholarship has directly inspired and influenced more recent theoretical work on the present-day relevance of commons and enclosures.[11] It also predates by a decade and a half David Harvey's discovery of 'accumulation by dispossession'.[12] Through it, George and Silvia have connected the 'old' Enclosures – and the struggles of English and Scottish commoners against these – to the wide range of present-day European and non-European commons that continue to be fiercely contested. But, more than this, Silvia and George present to us the commons as a political project. Commons are not *things*, but social relations – of cooperation and solidarity. And commons are not *givens* but processes. In this sense, it is apt to talk of common*ing*, a term coined by one-time Midnight Notes collaborator Peter Linebaugh.[13] Neither George nor Silvia argue that commons as projects are a panacea for the issues that beset the contemporary left, feminist, anti-racist, anti-colonial or environmental movements. However, the commons fill a lacuna in radical thought, providing a way in which we might practically work out how we are to live with each other and the world without the violence of the state or the rule of capital. That is, when we pose the question, as urgent now as ever, *What sort of world do we want to live in?* commons must surely be part of the answer.

In the chapters that follow a wide range of comrades explore and develop the themes woven above, as many other concepts and struggles that George and Silvia have addressed. We begin with George and Silvia's engagements with history. This first section opens with an interview in which they outline their own experiences – the interview both lays the groundwork for later chapters but also emphasises the role historical thought has played in their work. In Section II we turn to questions of money and value. As we noted above, George and Silvia insist on the continued relevance of value – with money as its expression – as organiser of human activity and the contributions here explore various historical and contemporary aspects of the way the 'law of value' operates – and is resisted. The subject of Section III is reproduction. The chapters in this section address the modes in which human beings are 'produced' and reproduced, and the separations between spheres of 'production' and 'reproduction'; we also include here a speculative account of the way an entire society might transition from one way of life to another – and the consequences of this. The book then turns – in Section IV – to the commons, working through both practical and theoretical engagements with the concept. Finally – and appropriately – we end – in Section V – with five chapters which engage with the idea and reality of contemporary struggles.

We cannot do justice in this collection to the extent of the contribution George Caffentzis and Silvia Federici – singly, together and in collaboration with others, such as the Midnight Notes Collective – have made to militant feminist and anti-capitalist scholarship. It goes without saying that we recommend readers explore their many writings – if they haven't already.[14] We are delighted how enthusiastically our invitation to contribute to this volume was received. This is testament to the esteem and affection with which George and Silvia are held by comrades around the world. And yet we haven't been able to *represent* the breadth and depth of their contributions over half a century, touching militants on every one of our planet's inhabited continents. All we have been able to do is *sample*. The contributions here are, nevertheless, extremely varied. In content. In style. In tone. And spanning several generations. This diversity is testament to the wide reach of the influence of George and Silvia and their care.

Notes

1. 'In Conversation with George Caffentzis and Silvia Federici', this volume.
2. 'In Conversation with'.
3. Silvia Federici, *Revolution at Point Zero: Housework, Reproduction and Feminist Struggle* (Oakland, CA: PM Press 2012), p. 7.
4. Quoted in John Holloway, 'Zapatismo and the social sciences', *Capital and Class*, 78 (2002), p. 156.
5. Part of the longer interview from which 'In Conversation with' was taken, but not included in this volume.

6. 'In Conversation with'.
7. Part of the longer interview from which 'In Conversation with' was taken, but not included in this volume.
8. Midnight Notes Collective, 'Introduction to the New Enclosures', in *The New Enclosures* (Jamaica Plain, MA: Midnight Notes, 1990), p. 1. Two other former members of the collective, Peter Linebaugh and P.M., have contributed to this volume.
9. George Caffentzis, 'Two Themes of Midnight Notes: Work/Refusal of Work and Enclosure/Commons', in Craig Hughes (ed.) *Toward the Last Jubilee: Midnight Notes at Thirty Years* (Brooklyn, NY: Autonomedia and Washington, DC: Perry Editions, 2010), p. 28.
10. Silvia Federici, 'The debt crisis, Africa and the new enclosures', in Midnight Notes Collective (eds) *The New Enclosures*, p. 11. Reprinted in Midnight Notes Collective (ed.) *Midnight Oil: Work, Energy, War 1973–1992* (Brooklyn, NY: Autonomedia, 1992).
11. One scholar who draws directly from George and Silvia and the Midnight Notes Collective is Massimo De Angelis – see his contribution in this volume.
12. David Harvey, *The New Imperialism* (Oxford: Oxford University Press, 2005).
13. George Caffentzis, 'Commons', in Kelly Fritsch, Claire O'Connor and A.K. Thompson (eds) *Keywords for Radicals: The Contested Vocabulary of Late-Capitalist Struggle* (Chico, CA: AK Press, 2016), p. 101; Peter Linebaugh, *The Magna Carta Manifesto: Liberties and Commons for All* (Berkeley, CA: University of California Press, 2008).
14. Good starting points are four anthologies: George Caffentzis, *In Letters of Blood and Fire: Work, Machines, the Crisis of Capitalism* (Oakland, CA: PM Press, 2013); George Caffentzis, *No Blood for Oil: Essays on Energy, Class Struggle, and War 1998–2016* (Brooklyn, NY: Autonomedia, 2017); Silvia Federici, *Revolution at Point Zero: Housework, Reprocution, and Feminist Struggle* (Oakland, CA: PM Press, 2012); and Silvia Federici, *Re-enchanting the World: Feminism and the Politics of the Commons* (Oakland, CA: PM Press, 2019). We also recommend Midnight Notes' *Midnight Oil: Work, Energy, War, 1973–1992* (Brooklyn, NY: Autonomedia, 1992).

I

REVOLUTIONARY HISTORIES

In Conversation with George Caffentzis and Silvia Federici

Carla da Cunha Duarte Francisco,
Paulo Henrique Flores, Rodrigo Guimaraes
Nunes and Joen Vedel

George:

The 1960s, maybe the early 1960s, was the first experience I had of a political struggle in the United States. I've always wondered what happened to me as a young person, a teenager, and why my political path was so different from the rest of my family. Because you might not know it, but Greek Americans are very conservative, in general, from the point of view of US politics. So I'm one of those rare birds. I used to joke that you could count radicals of Greek-American origin on your right hand. What led me to this path, I'm not sure. I've done some investigations, and it appears that I went to Greece in 1958. This was a breaking point. It was the first time after a long period of repression that the forces of the left came out on the streets officially, actually to protest the American bases in Greece. I'm projecting back that it was that experience – and because my family in Greece was much more on the left – that it had a profound impact upon me and I picked up that path. Of course, this is all in retrospect.

What then happened is, I begin to try to understand what a left-wing path would be in the US during the time of McCarthy and so on. I began to – in high school – read Marx, especially the young Marx, the 1844 Manuscripts and so on, that were just becoming available at that time, and I began to question the type of left-wing politics that had been available in the United States, especially the Communist Party. I got drawn into the civil rights movement at that time, because that was the place to be. I got arrested, on various demonstrations and so on. And along with that I met Harry Cleaver; he is my oldest childhood friend, if you can say that childhood goes on to 18 or 19. So we began to explore the kind of thinking that would be appropriate, politically, for this kind of period.

During the great student strike in the wake of the Kent State killings,[1] I and a number of other comrades in the movement began to think of a project that would make permanent much of the political thought that had begun to develop in the United States. And so we decided that we would write an anti-Samuelson textbook. A counter-textbook for a counter-course that would really, not only criticise the work of Samuelson and bourgeois economics, but also begin to see what this critique would lead to in terms of politics. So, I basically, with these comrades, spent three years reading Marx and criticising Paul Samuelson's work.[2] We published a four-volume book in East Germany for this counter-course that, by the time of 1973, was appealing to a movement that had largely spent its energy.

But 1973 became an important year for me. I call it my *annus mirabilis*, my year of – at least intellectual – miracles. Marvels. Because it was in that year that I met a whole group of political activists and theoreticians, one group coming from Italy, and the other group coming from the feminist movement. I began to recognise some themes that would become part of my permanent conception of how the system works and ways in which it could be overturned. Let me take them in order.

The first set of ideas came out of the Italian *operaista* movement, with the conception that capitalism is not something that is confronted and this class struggle is not something that takes place on the formal level between unions and parties and the capitalist state. That in fact the struggle takes place not only in the strike lines but also within the centres of production. We begin to look at class struggle as a field, instead of certain spots or sites – that there's this field of struggle that takes place all across the system. If you want to understand how capitalism operates, you have to see it on the micro level. That was an eye-opener, because as you walk around, you hear the voices of these struggles speaking to you in the same way as with the labour theory of value. You look at buildings and you begin to see not the thing itself, but the processes that went on, the sufferings, the struggles that went on to make the thing. It was like an opening of the eye, really. I was very pleased by this experience, because it opened up a political connection that led to the publication of a journal called *Zerowork*.[3]

Now simultaneously, almost, with this experience, came my exposure to Wages for Housework. In fact, much of this took place with Silvia, and I met Mariarosa Dalla Costa and Selma James, and began to personally understand the thinking that was taking place in the Wages for Housework movement. It was very important for me as, well, I don't know, as the patriarchal tradition was behind me. I was a young Greek-American child of immigrants and so on, and I must say, I brought from Greece much of this patriarchal bedrock, you might say, this psychological bedrock, and it needed to be blasted! I began to understand the depth of the work that was being done by Wages for Housework and it re-transformed my conception of what capitalism is.

The first edition of *Zerowork* [published at the end of 1975] was an attempt to bring together these two insights, theories, ways of seeing capitalism and our collective struggles.

So, with that there was an experience of going in the height of the Reagan reactionary period, and Silvia and I discussed our need to take a step out of the United States. So I started again to apply for jobs, all around the world.

Silvia:

The beginning of the 1980s is neoliberalism… Reaganomics, Thatcherism, this move to the right, it's the rise of the new model majority, which presents a big attack on women, you know, the attempt to recuperate against the feminist movement. It's also a time of the institutionalisation of the feminist movement, so you have together these two things. On one side, there's an affirmation of the feminist movement coming from a very institutional position – the United Nations, the American government, the more enlightened part of the government sees the possibility in using women's labour, of using women's demand for the economy, to relaunch their – to regain control of our work. To get out of the crisis – of the labour crisis – which they had faced in the 1970s. And on the other side, is this very right-wing, this moral majority, who wants to go back, let's pick up our children, let's get the women back into the kitchen. So we were confronting on one side the institutional feminists – and then on the other… so in any case, to make it short, after a while, both George and I started applying for going out of the country. We decided, let's leave! Also, it was a time, the late 1970s, where it was very difficult to organise in New York. Because [in] 1975, New York declared bankruptcy. And that began a very very tough period. New York was the first structurally adjusted country in the world.

George:

The first position that opened up was in Nigeria.

Nigeria had a profound effect on my body, and on my sociology, and on my understanding of class struggle. Because in Nigeria, in actual practice, there was an immense amount of common land that was being used for subsistence production. Everywhere I went, the idea that, for example, 'this is your property, this is state property' was often taken with a pinch of salt, because most property was communal property, and it took me a long time to understand that. I remember when I looked at this big field behind my house, and I would wonder, 'where are all these people going?' They would walk in at any time of day or night and there would be all this cultivation going on. I thought there were all these little plots that each individual owned. But in actual fact that was not the case. This large plot of land was actually being organised for subsistence production by the village. This took some time to understand. Instead of the idea that common land was a concept that was lost sometime in the sixteenth century, we began to see that actually there was a tremendous amount of communal land, at least in Africa, that was actually existing but needed to be defended.

Silvia:

George went in 1983 to Nigeria. Then in 1984 the job I had came to an end, I was ousted from my house, I was in a real crisis and I decided to go and visit him. And very shortly after that I was offered a job, and I moved to Nigeria. And for three years I was there. Nigeria opened up an amazing... you know Nigeria was another born again. I cannot explain it how powerful that experience was. As George said, Nigeria was discovering the commons, it was discovering land. Land is a key element in a struggle.

But we went to Nigeria at a time when it was under the pressure from the World Bank and IMF to adjust its economy. There we learned about the farce of the debt crisis, we saw how the debt crisis was totally engineered, and was used as an instrument of recolonisation. That actually what they called structural adjustment was used as a tool of recolonisation. Because in the 1970s they gave a lot of loans cheaply to countries like Nigeria coming out of struggles of independence, at variable interest, almost no interest but variable, then at the end of the 1970s, the Federal Reserve raises the cost of money, and the debt, of the Nigerian or Mexican country, which had been taken, which had been manageable after the point, became unmanageable, and so begin the crisis. Because then the IMF comes in, and they use the crisis to impose structural reform, the classic structural reform. Re-adjust your economy towards export, devalue your currency, the same thing they did in Brazil. Freeze wages, freeze investment in any public service, schools, hospitals, roads, everything that is for the poor. Basically disinvest in the reproduction of your workforce. Disinvest and instead bring all this money out to your coffers of the banks in New York, Geneva, Paris, London, whatever it is. This is what we saw — so we arrived in the middle of an incredible debate, especially in the schools, in the newspaper, everybody, 'IMF = DEATH!' ...

George:

Poison pill!

Silvia:

We hardly knew what the IMF was when we went there but we got edu-cated very quickly! And we saw together with the attack on the university, on the student movement, came the criminalisation of so many things. They started shooting people who had stolen things. Who had stolen some yams, stolen a keg of beer, maybe they had a machete in their hands but they didn't use it. They would have execution squads. So, to make this story short, eventually we left, we couldn't survive any longer because our cheques were bouncing. But when we went back, for a long time, our political experience in America was shaped by Nigeria.

George:

In the late 1980s we returned to the US, and began to continue the work of Midnight Notes, a collective that we founded in the late 1970s. It was in 1989 that we began the process of putting together a general issue called *The New Enclosures*. We began to see that although the wage struggle was, of course, still profoundly important, the struggle for the defence of the commons against the enclosures that were taking place was another dimension that is very important to understand. The reason being that land makes it possible for workers either to refuse work or to have more power in their negotiations with the capitalists. It's a logical point, but it has a very profound historical appearance. So this constituted my third political-intellectual discovery. Much to our amazement, after the publica-tion of *The New Enclosures* in 1990, we saw before our own eyes the Zapatista revolution in Mexico. It just so happens that Silvia and I and a number of students from our university were in Mexico at the beginning of the Zapa-tista rebellion. We arrived on the 1st January 1994 and spent the month in Mexico. Since then Midnight Notes has had a close relationship with the Zapatista and all that that means.

Silvia:

As you know I'm 74 years old, 74-and-a-half actually. So it's a long history. I like to see the development of my political trajectory from my childhood, because very early on in my life, from the time I could understand anything, and even before that, my life was profoundly affected by World War II.

The first conversation I recall from my mother was, 'what about the bombs falling on our head?' – and I was a little child. For all of my childhood, whenever my parents got together and they talked, it was always about the war. So from very early I knew that I was born in a very bad world and that it was a miracle I was alive. Many tales were told of all the times that my parents escaped, just by one hair, they escaped total destruction. When I was a young teenager we moved to the countryside because my parents were kind of refugees, because our town was bombarded all the time. Then of course I came back, we returned to the town and, in my teenage years, I grew up in a town that was a communist town. Parma, part of the Red Emiglia, which at the time was very significant, because first of all the Communist Party still had some element of contestation against the social system. They were coming from the experience of the partisans. It was also significant because in the period immediately after the war, Italy went through a tremendous repression. We were liberated into a great repression. Actually, the liberation was produced mostly by the partisans. But the official story is that we were liberated by the Americans. Immediately after the war, one of the first tasks of the new government, together with the American embassy was to ensure that any possibility of a left takeover, or even a left government in Italy, would be eradicated. So this was a period in the 1950s that had the police in the factories, in which fascists were integrated into positions, and leftists in particular, working-class people, were severely repressed. In Fiat, in the 1950s, you had police in the factories.

This was the moment of the great union between the Vatican, the political structures of the American embassy and the Christian Democratic party, that was put into place practically by our 'liberators'. Nineteen-fifty-one was the beginning of an anti-communist crusade and, because of that, to grow up in a town that was Communist was something very different. I grew up in an environment that was quite anti-clerical, and as we went to school, we were breathing a bit of a different atmosphere. Then, of course, in the end of the 1950s, in the years of high school an amazing international transformation… I was in high school when the Cuban Revolution took place… the anti-colonial struggles, I remember the stories of the Mau-Mau rebellion in Kenya. There was a sense that all over the world, despite this closure in Italy, there was a sense of forces, of the world that was changing.

I also had a great teacher, he was a mad man but a great teacher, a communist, in high school, who I think helped to form a whole generation of youth. I went to university, I studied in Bologna, and once I was finished at university, I had this desire to leave. I was really suffocated, particularly on a personal level, living at home. By this point I was in my early twenties, and I couldn't make any money. I was working hard, very hard, doing substitute teaching, going up the mountain, getting up at five in the morning, teaching kids that, you know, the only future that they would have is to be farmers. So I decided OK, I need to see the world. I started applying for all kinds of scholarships, and the first that I got was to go to the US. So, in 1967, I went to the United States. I ended up in the town of Buffalo, because I had enrolled in Philosophy. My teacher – he was a teacher in aesthetics – wanted me to go to Buffalo because Buffalo was a centre for phenomenology, and he thought this is what I was supposed to study. In any case, I went to Buffalo, and sure enough it was a centre for phenomenology, but I met something very different. I arrived to Buffalo campus, a campus in revolt, because in the summer of 1967, two things happened – a major riot in the black community, which ended up with the imprisonment of a guy who became kind of a hero. The other was the trial of the nine youths who had tried to cross the border and been arrested, the Buffalo Nine.[4] So that's how I was introduced to the campus – and for the three years I was there, from 1967 to 1970, the campus was always very active. At one point we had the police on campus every day, and we had them on the roofs, we had teargas, clouds of tear gas everywhere, constant meetings, so I got drawn into it in different ways. I started working for a theoretical journal that was called *Telos*, that was produced in the department.

* * *

Mario [Montano] and I worked an article that became 'Theses on the mass worker and social capital'.[5] It was an attempt to apply the principles of *Operaismo* to a reading of the history of the class struggle in the nineteenth and twentieth century. Mario and I spent quite a lot of time together, translating, discussing and in this process he said, 'you know, here's all these articles, and take a look, there's this one that's really interesting, by these feminists'. You know, this was Mariarosa [Dalla Costa]. So I began my encounter with the feminist movement. I was in Buffalo through 1969 and I moved to New York in 1970, in fact it was 20th August 1970, everything happened in August. The feminist movement in the United States really takes off in the fall of 1969, because in the summer of 1969, there was a famous meeting [in Chicago] of SDS [Students for a Democratic Society]; they [feminists] presented their demands, they were denied and there was a walkout. A walkout of the women and the walkout of the Weathermen, these were the two things that came out of Chicago.

So the fall of 1969 was very alive, and Buffalo was one of the liveliest campuses for the growth of feminism. There had been groups of women calling themselves feminist around Shulamith Firestone, some who called themselves radical feminists, but that was really the spark, that conference, and from that moment feminism took off very strongly. Then I went to New York in 1970 and in New York – these two speak of parallel worlds, because by 1970, before meeting the Italian comrades, by 1970 I had been involved in a few feminist activities. One had been the Women's Bail Fund, which was a broad organisation that organised around women in jail. It was an organisation that brought together different strands, it was very powerful, very interesting. There were women from the Young Lords, women from the Black Panthers, and then from the surging feminist movement. In fact, in New York, there was an organisation called WITCHes, Women's International Terrorist Conspiracy from Hell.

In 1972, after I read Mariarosa's article, for me it was like, 'this is it!', because I had all these questions, but to me it made perfect sense. So this happened in the spring, in the summer I went to Italy, and I went to Padua, at the time there was going to be a big meeting. At the end of this we had another meeting, and at the end we formed the International Feminist Collective, this was July 1972. We went separate ways with the common idea that we would all form a common network that would launch a Wages for Housework campaign in our respective countries. And that's what I did. For the next few months, when I went back to New York at the end of August 1972, I began to look for people who would want to do things. I met another woman from Switzerland, Nicole, and we started doing some stuff together, but it was only early in 1973, when Selma and Mariarosa came to the US for a political tour that the group took off. It's very easy, you know, when someone comes from outside, they come to speak, there's enthusiasm generated. So we took the enthusiasts, we started having meetings, and that's how the Wages for Housework Collective was born. We called ourselves a committee, and then by the fall of 1974 we had our first international conference. And by that time we had groups, we had a little network. We had women from Italy, from England, from Canada, from Philadelphia, some from Boston. And at the end of the meeting we wrote a manifesto: *Theses on Wages for Housework*.[6]

George:

Ideas don't come from a light-bulb moment in someone's brain. Ideas come from struggles – this is a basic methodological principle. It's when the wageless begin to speak… and let's not forget that Marxism and the interpretations of Marx have been open to many interpretations. When we say 'traditional Marxism', we only mean one strand, because Marx's texts – if we are going to take them as the origin of our discussion – Marx's texts are open and are for reconsideration. This is what makes it possible for us to continue dealing with Marx and Marxist texts, because often you are asking yourself 'Why am I dealing with this twenty-first century phenomenon using a nineteenth century theory?' It has to do with the fact that the theory that you're using has been transformed by many people in and through struggle.

The anti-colonial struggles forced us to stretch Marx's concepts. This is what [Franz] Fanon said he had to do. The reason he had to do this was because he was working with unwaged labourers. Workers who are on the verge of slavery in the colonial interior. So the colonial class struggle needed to have new categories. But not new, because the unwaged workers or low-waged workers in the colonies, and the waged workers in France or England, were connected, both materially and via capital. Also other struggles, because the anti-colonial struggle included Vietnam and that was the source of so much of our politics – a support for movements that were demanding control over their land. I think that the question of Marxism and the interpretation of Marxist texts is still very open. Because this is what's happening now, and I am very pleased to see that there has been an interest in Marx's work from an ecological perspective. Often you realise that when Marxists are saying this, it's a stretched Marx.

The question is whether the stretch breaks the rope, right? I think our interventions – the introduction of the struggle against work as a field throughout this society and the conception of the struggle of unwaged workers in reproduction of labour-power – are essential to our understanding of capitalism. The whole conception of the commons, in the capitalist sense, to enclose the commons, these are ways of restructuring our understanding of capitalism. So now we look at the chapters on primitive accumulation [in *Capital*, vol. 1], not as a distant conclusion or as a line of argument, but actually as the foundation of our understanding of capitalism, as well as of Marx's texts. This is my understanding of the story of where we are with Marx and Marxism. With these key questions, politically and textually, you have to ask yourself, why are you reading this?

Notes

The conversation took place in Rio de Janeiro, Brazil in 2016. It was transcribed by Gloria Loris and abridged by Barbagallo, Beuret and Harvie.

1. On 4 May 1970 members of the National Guards opened fire during a demonstration against the Vietnam war at Kent State University in Ohio: four students were killed and a further nine were wounded, one of whom suffered permanent paralysis.

2. First published in 1948, Samuelson's Economics was at the time the best-selling economics textbook and remains popular. The 19th edition, co-authored with William Nordhaus, was published in 2009. Samuelson once quipped: 'Let those who will write the nation's laws if I can write its textbooks.'

3. Available online at http://zerowork.org/.

4. The 1967 Buffalo riot took place over four days and nights at the end of June. The Buffalo Nine, a group of anti-Vietnam war protestors, were actually arrested in the summer of 1968. But given Buffalo's location right on the US-Canada border many young men fleeing the draft passed through the town and many of these were arrested.

5. The piece was published under the name Guido Baldi in *Radical America*, vol. 6, no. 3 (May–June 1972).

6. Reproduced in Silvia Federici and Arlen Austin (eds), *Wages for Housework: The New York Committee 1972–1977: History, Theory, Documents* (Oakand, CA: PM Press, 2017).

2

Comradely Appropriation

Harry Cleaver

Some years ago, while teaching a course on the political economy of education – created in response to demands by activist students – I experimented with an alternative to 'testing'. I asked students to write about what, if anything, of the ideas we were studying they could appropriate for their own purposes – as useful to the further elaboration of their personal trajectories, both intellectual and through life in general. I thought this rather straightforward, in as much as I had long studied in this manner.

Upon reading their first essays, however, I discovered that most were puzzled by what I was asking them to do. In response, I eventually drafted an essay on 'Learning, Understanding and Appropriating' to explain and illustrate the kind of self-reflection I had in mind.[1] Some of the illustrations were excerpted from classical autobiographies by Marcus Aurelius, Augustine of Hippo and Jean-Jacques Rousseau. But suspecting that they might be able to relate better to a more immediate example, I recounted a few of my own appropriations – from *my* school years – elementary through graduate school – in which new ideas had an impact not only on my thinking, but also on my behaviour, in some cases on my political actions. The last of those examples concerned my return to Marx after completing my PhD, because of dissatisfaction with the ability of the Marxist writings I had been using to frame my dissertation to adequately illuminate the history I had discovered while writing it. That return began shortly before encountering, evaluating and appropriating some ideas from George and Silvia in the mid-1970s. Although I have learned much from both in the years since, I describe below some of those early appropriations that led to changes in both my thinking and my political behaviour. First, some background.

George, I have known since our undergraduate years at Antioch College in the early 1960s, where we spent many a long evening listening to 'cool' jazz, debating Sartre, the Beats, imperialism and many an other subject. (Probably the most important thing I discovered through George in those days were the writings of Nikos Kazantzakis.) We also marched together in a civil rights demonstration in Yellow Springs, were arrested and shared a Greene County jail cell. Thereafter, our studies and jobs led us along different paths, somewhat parallel but distinct. I pursued graduate studies in economics at Stanford; George did the same in the philosophy of science at Princeton. We were both heavily involved in the anti-Vietnam War movement. While I was digging up dirt on Stanford's involvement in the war and helping Professor John Gurley put together his first course on Marx, George was reading Marx and collaborating with Marc Linder and Julius Sensat to prepare chapter-by-chapter critiques of Paul Samuelson's iconic textbook *Economics* – eventually published by Linder as *Anti-Samuelson* (1977). After graduate school, I went off to teach in Quebec at l'Université de Sherbrooke, while George found a teaching job at Haverford College in Pennsylvania. Our geographical paths converged in New York City in the fall of 1974 when I accepted a job at the New School for Social Research; George had found one at Brooklyn College of CUNY the year before.

Silvia, I met through George after moving to New York City. She was, at that time, a stalwart member of and important spokeswoman for the Wages for Housework Movement/Campaign. She would soon be publishing – and I would be reading – influential essays as contributions to that Campaign.

In the exciting, often urgent, back-and-forth of collective thinking and struggle, I have often found it difficult to pinpoint the unique contribution of individuals to the unfolding of ideas and political action. I first realised this during the anti-Vietnam War movement. Sustained collective efforts, I discovered, engage large numbers of people, from different backgrounds, who draw upon a variety of ideas and political orientations to undertake a wide variety of activities that contribute to the growth and effectiveness of collective action. The form and content of individuals' contributions may vary over time, shifting with collective needs – doing research at one moment, writing an article or pamphlet at another, handing them out at yet others, organising food or baby-sitting during building take-overs, participating in organisational meetings again and again. Each of these contributions is influenced by past ideas, recent reading, contemporaneous conversations and debate – all involving other people's ideas and actions, often those of many other people. True during the anti-war movement, true amongst those who supported the Wages for Housework movement, which developed in New York City in the mid-1970s.

That period was one of global crisis for post-World War II Keynesian (or Fordist) policies – a crisis caused by an international cycle of workers' struggle.[2] The capitalist response included both anti-worker austerity and monetary manipulations, foreshadowing the strategies of neoliberalism at a global level. Locally, in New York City, the crisis took the form of a 'fiscal crisis' in which city government borrowing to cope with workers' struggles, especially those of city employees and those on welfare, were suddenly cut off by its lenders, the big banks, which refused to roll over the government's debt.[3]

Against this backdrop, women organised the local Wages for Housework (WFH) Campaign, almost completely autonomously from men. Such autonomy was not new in the United States; many women had been organising autonomously since the self-organisation of second-wave feminism in the late 1960s. One implication for men who supported such efforts was to undertake their own separate organisational efforts. Amongst those with whom I began to collaborate after moving to the city, the results were two-fold. One, launched before I arrived, was Zerowork, first a collective of men located in the United States and Canada and then a journal of the same name, prepared as a political intervention into Left discussions debating the crisis of Keynesianism. The other result was the formation of militant groups, one of which called itself New York Struggle Against Work (NYSAW) that organised opposition to local austerity programmes.

Those in both Zerowork and Wages for Housework drew on ideas and previous political experience from both sides of the Atlantic, dating – I would later discover – back to the 1940s.[4] More recently, those ideas were elaborated with exceptional theoretical refinement in Italy by opponents of the policies of the main left-wing political parties and trade unions, which had been collaborating with Italian capital's efforts to rebuild after World War II. Eventually the internal gender dynamics of such opposition led to women organising autonomously from men – as had similar dynamics in the American anti-war and student movements. Central to much of that opposition were notions of the 'refusal of work' – as a strategy pitted against capitalist development – and demands by groups such as Potere Operaio that some unwaged work, such as that of students, be recognised as work-for-capital – producing their own labour-power – and be properly remunerated. That recognition flowed from a more general understanding of how capital, through social engineering, has sought to extend its management from the shop floor throughout society, turning it into one large *social factory*.

The case for capital paying wages for the housework of producing and reproducing the labour force was most clearly enunciated by women, a renewal of a demand that had been made, off and on, by previous generations of women since the early twentieth century. The key text that set out a clear Marxist analysis of the role of housework in capitalism was written by Mariarosa Della Costa for a women's group in Padua, Italy in 1971 and was titled *Donne e sovversione sociale*, usually translated as 'Women and the

Subversion of the Community'.[5] That essay became a founding document for both an International Feminist Collective and the Wages for House-work Campaign. As that Campaign spread across Europe and the Atlantic to North America, the essay also set off a firestorm of opposition.

The argument that women should fight to be paid for their labour pro-ducing and reproducing labour-power infuriated a wide range of leftists who promptly attacked both the strategy and the underlying theory. One bit of heated opposition echoed old arguments against wage struggles in general and can be summarised as 'a little more money for waged workers or a little money for the hitherto unwaged doesn't change the social rela-tionship, the one strengthens existing chains and the other creates new ones'. Flaming opposition to 'creating new chains' was particularly strong among those who defended the home as an oasis of healing and solace from the ills inflicted on waged labour and argued that to demand wages for housework amounted to inviting capital in, which would inevitably pollute that oasis. One line of theoretical attack argued against the idea that unwaged housework resulted in more surplus value. It was wrong, some claimed, to equate unwaged housework with surplus-value-producing waged labour. As you might suspect, those of us in New York Struggle Against Work read these attacks and debated their validity.

Although George and I had been friends much longer, and were both members of the New York Struggle Against Work group and contributors to *Zerowork*, I want to begin with a discussion of how Silvia's response to that firestorm of opposition offered ideas and analyses that not only NYSAW and the Zerowork Collective adopted, but that I, personally, appropriated as important new weapons in my efforts to understand and oppose capitalism.

Silvia:

In 1975, in response to those heated attacks, Silvia wrote two essays, *Wages Against Housework*, and *Counter-Planning from the Kitchen*, both originally published as pamphlets by Falling Wall Press in Bristol, England, but quickly circulated throughout the Campaign.[6] The very title of *Wages Against Housework*, as the essay explained, emphasised how the demand for wages *for* housework was not merely a demand to be paid, but a means to force recognition of the value of housework to capital and a vehicle for this hitherto unwaged mass of workers – mostly women – to be accepted as integral parts of the working class and their struggles to be valorised as every bit as vital as those of waged workers. The demand for wages for housework, she argued, was a *political perspective* on both the dynamics of capitalism and prospects for transcending it.

This perspective offered an alternative to a tendency by some on the left, ever since Citizen Weston, to dismiss wage struggles as futile,[7] and since Lenin to marginalise them as 'economistic', not rising to the level of the class interest as defined by the Party. Nevertheless, most of those who support struggles against capitalism have recognised that wage workers winning higher wages (or avoiding cuts), if they lead to new, more comprehensive demands, can be intermediate steps on the way to the revolutionary abolition of wage system and capitalism. And that, Silvia argued, was the character of the demands by the unwaged for wages. She wrote, 'To say that we want wages for housework is the first step towards refusing to do it, because the demand for a wage makes our work visible, which is the most indispensable condition to begin to struggle against it.' Making visible how housework serves capital, she argued, strikes at the heart of a fundamental vehicle through which capital controls workers – the division between waged and unwaged – and lays the basis for working class collaboration across that divide.

Unlike too many workers, Silvia and others in the WfH Campaign argued, capitalist policy makers understand the essential role of housework and their understanding has guided policies made in moments of crisis. Some such moments have followed wars, e.g. World War I, where high death rates depleted the ranks of the labour force and capital, through the state, enacted pro-natalist laws that paid women to have more children. When forced, by working-class struggle, to generalise such policies, however, those policy makers cloaked their concessions under the rubric of 'welfare' rather than admit they were paying for housework. The political problem, to which the Campaign offered a solution, was to reveal how such payments amounted to a camouflaged form of wages for procreation and child rearing, for the work of producing labour-power.[8]

This demand for making unwaged work-for-capital visible, in a way that exposes its integral role in the expanded reproduction of capital, struck me forcibly. Marx had made the point of how the wage hides the existence of exploitation. However, when he analysed the unwaged in the various ranks of the 'surplus population' or 'reserve army of labour' – he did not apply the kind of reasoning that Silvia was making in this essay. How unwaged housework in the home, or schoolwork in schools, was structured to produce and reproduce labour-power – the key commodity in capitalism, the one that makes all the others possible – was clear enough. But I came to her essays almost directly from writing a dissertation on capitalist efforts to manage the struggles of unwaged peasants in the Third World. What about *their* work? And what of the work of others in the 'reserve army'?

The theory that had guided me in studying capitalist efforts to deal with peasant unrest, at least to some extent, was appropriated from Marxist anthropology, one that framed such efforts in terms of the capitalist mode of production imposing itself on non-capitalist ones. This fit with another traditional Marxist tendency to generalise Marx's analysis of primitive accumulation in Britain in a way that led to seeing all peasants not yet proletarianised as outside of capital and their struggles marginal, doomed and irrelevant to those of waged workers. Even Mao, who discovered in 1927 that peasants had started the revolution without him, sought to subordinate them to the Party, which he thought represented the interests of waged workers. The mode-of-production framework could identify, but offered no tools to analyse, the struggles of peasants, or to situate them as moments within accumulation – understood as the accumulation of antagonistic classes in conflict.

My studies of capitalist agrarian policies in the post-World War II period had shown me the continuing relevance of Marx's location of peasants – 'those working in agriculture, not yet repulsed from the land' – in the *latent* ranks of the reserve army. At that time, partly as a result of their analysis of the 'loss of China', capitalist policy makers frequently supported land reform. Whether in Japan, South Korea, Taiwan, the Philippines, India or elsewhere, they sought, by responding positively to peasants' struggles for better access to land – by legal changes in either tenure or ownership – to stabilise the peasantry as a non-revolutionary labour reserve. Not motivated by some version of Jefferson's agrarian democracy, the objective was to keep them on the land until needed elsewhere, at which point various measures could force them from the *latent* into the ranks of the *floating* reserve, i.e. joining others actively looking for waged jobs. Within such a situation, Silvia's analysis, by focusing on the work of the unwaged, provided further insights.

Although her essay didn't discuss labour-power in exactly these terms, I found her analysis of housework a nice illustration of my own formulation of labour-power as 'the ability *and willingness*' to do commodity-producing work for capital. She pointed out how women had to be convinced to do housework – be made willing – by various means, from being taught it was in their nature to the seductions of romantic love. Like Simone de Beauvoir before her, Silvia painted a picture of how so many women have discovered, to their dismay, that the apparently rosy path to life as beloved wife led through a gloomy, dark wood to a domestic hell of endless and often thankless work – all too often including psychological and physical abuse.[9]

In the case of peasants, both their attachment to the land, often spiritual as well as material, and the satisfaction of having autonomous control over their lives, in both work and non-work, has often meant only dire necessity – forcible enclosure or the threat of starvation due to flood or drought – could convince them to search for waged jobs. Certainly, this was the case during the early centuries of capitalist development when waged jobs off the land could only be found amongst the satanic mills and teeming pauperism of capitalist cities. In more recent years, with the development of those cities and mass media portrayal of their bright lights, diverse entertainments and illusions of hopeful futures for everyone 'willing to work hard', less force and poverty has been required to seduce many young people to leave the land. What they have found, of course, has often been like the discoveries of love-besotted women, a hard-scrabble existence in barrios and favelas where good waged jobs are few, steady income hard to come by and survival dependent on integration into the networks of the so-called informal sector.

Those in the 'welfare' sector of the *latent* reserve share conditions of life similar to both those in the informal sector and job hunters. With welfare payments kept near subsistence, to remove any disincentive to move from the latent into the *floating* reserve, living on those low payments is far more work than normal housework for those with access to a decent wage. More-over, just as those seeking unemployment compensation have to provide evidence of job search, so too have those on welfare been forced to expend vast amounts of energy meeting the requirements of welfare officials.[10]

I eventually realised, in reading Silvia's essays and then discussing them with others in our New York Struggle Against Work group, that she and other feminists before her, whether thinking in Marxian terms or not, were replicating, in the case of *unwaged* housework, the kind of close analysis of both the technical division of labour *and the political composition* of factory work that had been undertaken by Marx in the nineteenth century and renewed, after World War II, by some of his followers on both sides of the Atlantic. Men such as Martin Glaberman, Matthew Ward and Paul Singer in the United States, G. Vivier and Daniel Mothe in France, Danilo Montaldi, Romano Alquati and Raniero Panzieri in Italy, had taken up, once again, Marx's efforts to analyse and understand exactly how capital imposed *waged* work on the shop floor and how worker resistance led to changes in the forms of that imposition.[11] I saw that just as these men had studied this in factories, and Silvia had studied it in bedrooms and kitchens, so too could we study, in a similar manner, every other sphere of activity of the unwaged – *throughout* Marx's 'reserve army' and beyond. The immediate implication was that his army was 'in reserve' only in relation to waged work; capital has been very busy in the years since he wrote trying to organise the activities of those 'in reserve' as work contributing to the expanded reproduction of the class relation.

All workers in the *floating* reserve, for example, face the problem of finding jobs, not just recent rural-urban peasant migrants. Looking for work is work, not just in the sense of requiring a lot of effort, but because it produces and reproduces the labour market! In a few cases, capitalists – in the form of labour contractors for low-waged positions or 'head-hunters' for high-waged ones – actually go out and search for workers. But more often, workers must shoulder the frustrating work of looking for jobs. For the most part, only the 'supply' side of the market searches; the 'demand' side sit at a desk, and wait for anxious workers to knock on factory gates or office doors and beg for a job and a wage or salary. For some, looking for work only requires local efforts; for others, it requires dangerous treks across borders, deserts or oceans, risking the violence of all those who prey upon or repress multinational workers. Those waged workers who have lost jobs and need some form of 'unemployment compensation' to carry them over while they look for a new one, often must prove that they have actively sought jobs by providing evidence from job interviews. Analysing what economists call 'job search' in the ways Silvia analysed housework reveals it to be work for capital. Usually treated as a kind of welfare, 'taking care of those willing souls who have lost their jobs through no fault of their own', 'unemployment compensation' actually amounts to payment for the work of making the labour market function.

But if everyday life for those in the *latent* and *floating* reserves involves the work of producing and reproducing labour-power, and sometimes making the labour market function, what of the *stagnant*, that third sector of Marx's 'surplus population'? Examination of his discussion of this sector in Chapter 25 of Volume I of *Capital* reveals that those he included in this sector consisted of people who were working, some waged, some unwaged, but still contributing, in one way or another, to accumulation. Indeed, the 'chief form' through which such workers were organised, he identified as 'domestic industry' – outsourced labour, working in homes or tiny workshops – what a hundred years later Italians would call *la fabbrica diffusa* or diffused factory. Workers employed in this way were only 'surplus' to the factory proper, and were *stagnant* mainly in the sense that, alienated from the higher-waged factory proletariat, they had little chance of improving their condition and could gain income only in the worst jobs at the lowest wages. Also as part of this sector, he included the *lumpenproletariat* – vagabonds, criminals, prostitutes – and those too old or too disabled to work at waged jobs.

But within the ranks of this *stagnant* reserve, Marx clearly saw resistance, e.g. the unwillingness of vagabonds and criminals to look for waged jobs.[12] Their refusal of the labour market we can see as akin to the resistance of peasants to being forced off their land – a refusal so strong as to require the 'bloody legislation' described at length in Chapter 28 of Volume I.

Shifting focus from capital's efforts to impose work on the unwaged to their resistance, reveals whole new realms of working-class struggle. In the

United States, think of the march of Cox's Army of the Unemployed in 1932, a revolt by members of the *floating* ranks of the reserve army. Or, of efforts of Welfare Rights and student movements of the 1960s, also members of the *latent* ranks demanding compensation for the work of producing and reproducing labour-power. Or, the 'EMA [Educational Maintenance Allowance] Kids' of Britain's 2010 student movement. Or, of those increasingly militant demands made by members of the Black Power and Brown Power movements, often seen as rising from the ranks of Marx's lumpenproletariat. Or, the armed peasant resistance in rice paddies, rubber plantations and jungles to forcible subordination to colonial or neocolonial exploitation. And finally, of course, the swelling revolt of women – both waged and unwaged – that gave birth to, among other efforts, the Wages for Housework Campaign and Silvia's analysis.

This shift in focus, was highlighted as the first methodological principle enunciated in the Introduction to the initial issue of *Zerowork*.[13]

First [we begin with] the analysis of the struggles themselves: their content, their direction, how they develop and how they circulate. It is not an investigation of occupational stratification nor of employment and unemployment. We don't look at the structure of the workforce as determined by the capitalist organization of production. On the contrary, we study the forms by which workers can bypass the technical constrictions of production and affirm themselves as a class with political power.

The second principle derived explicitly from the work of Silvia and others in the Wages for Housework Campaign.

Second, we study the dynamics of the different sectors of the working class: the way these sectors affect each other and thus the relation of the working class with capital. Differences among sectors are primarily differences in power to struggle and organize. These differences are expressed most fundamentally in the hierarchy of wages, in particular, as the Wages for Housework movement has shown, in the division between the waged and the wage-less. Capital rules by division. The key to capitalist accumulation is the constant creation and reproduction of the division between the waged and the unwaged parts of the class.

This explicit derivation was a clear statement of how those involved in producing *Zerowork* had appropriated the arguments in Mariarosa Dalla Costa's original essay and in Silvia's responses to critics.

My own writing of that period also made my appropriation of these ideas explicit. First, in a 1976 essay for a conference at the Sinha Institute in Patna, Bihar (India) later published in the *Economic and Political Weekly*

(Mumbai), I critiqued the results of applying mode-of-production analysis to the Indian peasantry and offered the kind of analysis laid out in *Zerowork* as an alternative.[14] Then, in a 1977 essay for the second issue of *Zerowork* on 'Food, Famine and International Crisis', I applied the analysis more or less worldwide, West and East, North and South, to understand the widespread famine and food riots of the 1970s and as an intervention into the 'food movement' that had arisen in response to famine.[13] In the years since, these ideas have informed many of my essays on various topics. The debt has been long-lasting.

George:

Because George and I both participated in the NYSAW group and in the Zerowork collective, and because of many conversations during the summer of 1975, when I was rethinking Marx's labour theory of value, through 1975–6, when I was elaborating a critique of the mode-of-production analysis to understand the relationship between capitalism and the peasantry, it is difficult for me to identify, precisely, all of George's unique contributions to the evolution of my thinking in that period. However, one set of appropriated insights, easy to point to, were plucked from George's contribution to the analysis of schoolwork and the struggle against it.

During the NYSAW struggles in New York City, and during the preparation of the first issue of *Zerowork*, George collaborated with two graduate students, Monty Neill and John Willshire-Carrera studying 'radical' economics in the Graduate Program of Economics at the University of Massachusetts at Amherst. George and the students together wrote and published a critique of education: a pamphlet, in the form of a blue book, titled *Wages for Students*.[16] Drawing on the theoretical framework of WfH, the pamphlet analysed schoolwork as work-for-capital, primarily structured to impose work discipline for the benefit of future employers. The essay critiqued the usual arguments by economists that education is both a consumption good and a good investment. The former, they argued, was patently false because schoolwork is work and gets in the way of consumption. The second was no longer true on a personal level because high unemployment in the 1970s made future payoffs less likely. Left professors' support for extra work, in the name of raising social and political consciousness, they also claimed, merely forwards capital's agenda. Pointing to how student wagelessness put a burden on parents or forced students to add waged jobs to their unwaged schoolwork, the essay argued that regular students should be paid by capital much as some corporations pay for employee training. This demand clearly echoed the one made by Potero Operaio in Italy that had influenced Mariarosa Dalla Costa's analysis and the demand for WfH. Many of the ideas elaborated in their pamphlet were incorporated into George's contribution to *Zerowork* #1: 'Throwing Away the Ladder: The Universities in the Crisis'.[17]

As with the other essays in *Zerowork*, his essay offered an analysis of concrete, historical developments in the class struggles that had brought on the crisis of Keynesianism mentioned above. In it, he traced how the crisis of education had been brought on by student struggles and how capitalist counterstrategies included abandoning the old 'career ladder' in favour of a set of precarious footstools. It was also the only essay devoted solely to the unwaged.

Having been engaged in student struggle and, like George, having become one of those ex-protestors who had found a spot teaching, his article – written before I joined the collective – was of particular interest to me. His analysis of student struggles rang true and his analysis of recent capitalist responses brought new aspects of the conflict to my attention. My appropriation of elements of his analysis – especially the emphasis on how student struggles often involved a refusal of work – quickly informed both my retrospective understanding of the struggles in which I had been involved and my teaching behaviour. Here follows a few words on each.

First, although the student movement in which I had participated often involved disrupting or walking out of classes, taking over administrative buildings, converting auditoriums from teaching arenas to collective teach-ins and seizing or shutting down research facilities, we never formulated what we were doing as a *refusal of work*. Even though we were, effectively, walking off the job or forcing administrators, professors and researchers out of their offices and laboratories, we tended to think about what we were doing either as 'shutting down school complicity' with the war machine or with capitalism more generally, or as efforts to transform schools into institutions that better met our own self-defined needs. Seeing such actions as *refusals of work* required understanding studying as work, work on par with that of waged workers who were obviously refusing work when they played on the job, faked sick leave or went out on strike. We did see a homology between such actions and our own, e.g. we spoke of 'going on strike' when we shut down campuses.[18] But, we did not have the Marxist analysis, first formulated by the Italian workerists, of our schoolwork as the work of shaping our labour-power. We understood capital's investment in what economists call 'human capital' – and our struggles included explicit efforts to undermine that investment[19] – but we lacked the theoretical tools to grasp studying as work within a comprehensive Marxist analysis of accumulation.

Appropriating insights from Potero Operaio, Mariarosa, Silvia and George, within the context of my teaching of *Capital* (first at the New

School and then at the University of Texas at Austin), led me beyond homology to formulate what I have called the 'circuit of the reproduction of labour-power':

$$LP - M - C(MS) \ldots P \ldots LP^*$$

This provides a formal representation of the processes required to reproduce the one element – labour-power – left out of Marx's own analysis of the circuits of capital in Volume II of *Capital*.[20] Labour-power must not only be sold for wages or salaries (LP – M), and then used to purchase the means of subsistence (M – C(MS)), but the consumption of MS must be organised to make sure it results in the production ($\ldots$ P $\ldots$) of labour-power (L^*). Schoolwork, like housework, is organised by capital to produce labour-power, to convert our innate spontaneous curiosity, imagination and energy into the disciplined ability and willingness to work for future employers. For students, gaining a wage LP – M may be accomplished by their parents or it may be achieved via fellowships or research or teaching assistantships, or other part-time employment – in which case they are at least partially waged, however minimally. (In my case, at the undergraduate level it was the former; at the graduate level, the latter.) For students, M – C(MS) includes not merely paying for a dorm and meal tickets, or renting an apartment and shopping for food, etc., but the purchase of text books, calculators or computers and whatever other equipment is mandated for schoolwork. When it comes to schoolwork per se, i.e. ($\ldots$ P $\ldots$), while those with fellowships may effectively be paid for all of their work at school, teaching, research assistantships and part-time jobs usually involve direct pay only for designated hours of work, e.g. 20 hours/week. Beyond those hours, time spent studying is only measured indirectly via course load and grades. For most students, lacking even such partial wages, schoolwork is completely unwaged with the amount of work determined by the conflict between the demands of administrators and professors and students' resistance. As George pointed out in his *Zerowork* article, in the 1960s that resistance was great and students were working much less than anticipated by those policy makers who supported investing tax monies in the development of 'human capital'. (In my case, I failed and had to repeat an entire year of graduate courses due to having diverted my energies into struggles against the war and against Stanford's complicity with it.)

The second effect of grasping students' struggles as involving the refusal of work was on my own teaching behaviour. It forced me to think through how my own work and struggles as a professor related to those of students. During the 1960s, the heavy lifting of the anti-war movement in universities was done overwhelmingly by unwaged students, with participation of the waged professoriate extremely limited. Having moved into the latter sector of the working class, salaried and with more control over my day-to-day work, I was forced to recognise how my 'job' was really to impose the work of producing their own labour-power on students and to consider how I might resist and subvert (i.e., *refuse*) such work. An initial consequence was sharing with my students this analysis of how work was being imposed on us all and discussing with them various forms of resistance. In each of my courses, I allocated time to examining how business had influenced both the content and form of schooling to meet its needs rather than those of teachers and students. That discussion included everything from the history of business intervention, through the content of curriculum to the physical structure of classrooms (designed to centre the attention of passive students on an active lecturer). Another result – spun off from response to a critique of my book *Reading* Capital *Politically* (1979) – was an essay on 'On Schoolwork and the Struggle Against It' (2006) spelling out my analysis of the imposition of work on both professors and students as well of modes of resistance.[21] Yet another eventual result, which I described at the beginning of this essay, was the shift to asking students to consider how they might replace capitalists' intentions with their own self-defined goals and appropriate course materials for their own purposes.

Contemplating schoolwork, both that of students and that of professors, in the light of George's essay, also led me assess the possible application to schoolwork of some other elements of Marx's analysis of waged labour. At the time, I was teaching Volume I of *Capital* chapter by chapter, and found myself undertaking such assessment repeatedly – with respect to peasants' subsistence labour, housework and schoolwork.

In the case of schoolwork, besides Marx's analysis in Chapter 6 of the production and reproduction of labour-power, the part of *Capital* whose relevance struck me most was Chapter 21 dealing with piece-wages. In piece-wages, workers are paid by the piece. This mode of organising the wage relationship not only helps hide exploitation but reduces the costs of supervision (and thus increases capitalist profits). All that is required is 'quality control' to make sure workers are not cheating by producing defective goods or services. Once you recognise students and professors as workers in the social factory, the industrial logic in the way schools are set up is clear. Both students and professors are 'paid' on a piece-work basis.

In the case of unwaged students, their 'pay' is grades (IOUs on future income) and their 'pieces' are things like tests, papers and research reports. The work of professors at the university level, unlike that of teachers at the elementary and secondary level, does not usually involve minute-to-minute supervision; it is generally assumed that university students are well-behaved in the classroom.[22] But, it *does* require quality control – checking to make sure students don't cheat and assigning grades based on the usual assumption that more work deserves higher grades.

In the case of professors, in so-called research universities, it's very much 'publish or perish'. Alongside imposing work on students, professors are supposed to do research and publish the results in peer-reviewed journals or books. In that process, their peers perform the same 'quality control' work on their submitted articles as professors do with student tests, papers, etc.[23]

In other words, professors and teachers alike are organised to *mediate* between students and capital's desires that learning be primarily devoted to the production of labour-power. That desire has been manifest both in administrators' behaviour and, as George pointed out in his *Zerowork* article, in the shifting of resources from liberal arts to professional schools. Professors are the ones directly imposing work, grading according to how much work is performed and receiving the brunt of hostility from resentful students.

In lectures – and in lecture notes that later became Chapter 5 of my book *Reading* Capital *Politically* – when I took up Marx's analysis of the general form of value, I emphasised the focus on syllogistic mediation. In the exchanges represented by $xA = yB = zC$, the relationship between commodities A and C are mediated by their mutual relationship to B, with B ultimately becoming money as the universal equivalent and mediator. Similar mediations, I pointed out, are manifest in the relations among teachers/professors, students and capital's school administrators. For example, administrators use teachers/professors to mediate their day-to-day relationship with students, to impose work and to manage discipline. Another example of mediation is how, when it helps to discipline professors, administrators use negative student evaluations of teaching quality to deny promotion or merit salary increases.

One form of struggle, therefore, has been the rupture of such mediation. Student movements, for example, have often done this by students taking their demands directly to administrators bypassing professors. (At Stanford, we followed Martin Luther's example and nailed our demands to the door of the meeting room of the university's Board of Trustees, bypassing both professors and administrators.)[24] It was partly to counter the negative use of mandated teaching evaluations that I always discussed them with my students. Constructive evaluations, whether critiques or creative suggestions, of my teaching or course content would primarily be of use to me and to future students, quite independently of whatever use the administrators might make of them. To make certain of the usefulness of their evaluations to those who would follow them, I posted their written comments – the good, the bad and the ugly – to my university website. This whole line of reasoning and actions taken derived from the appropriations outlined above.

Just a few years later, by bringing his knowledge of physics to bear on his analysis of class struggle, George added another useful framework for understanding these relationships between professors, students and capital. After the members of the Zerowork collective went their separate ways, George formed a new group called Midnight Notes. Its first interventions, in both writing and action, were in the anti-nuclear power movement. One of their essays, written by George but produced as a pamphlet by the group, was *The Work/Energy Crisis and the Apocalypse* (1980) with a nice cover featuring Albrecht Durer's splendid woodcut 'The Four Horsemen of the Apocalypse'.[25] Within that long essay is an analysis of the historical rise of thermodynamics as not just a theory of energy flows but as a reflection of capital's problems in harnessing human energy as work. In it George points out how the daemon that James Clerk Maxwell (1831–79) imagined sorting between high and low entropy molecules can be seen as incarnated in the form of capitalist personnel officers judging which potential employees are most likely to make their energy available for work and which are less likely to do so, hiring the former and dismissing the latter.

In the same vein, teachers and professors also act as incarnations of Maxwell's daemon, grading students according to their willingness to divert their energy into schoolwork and the production of their labour-power. This analysis also provides an illuminating re-reading of Marx's use of the gothic image of the vampire to describe capital's thirst for blood. What capital, via the mediation of teachers and professors do, is not just drain blood but sort and sift among potential victims for those with the most readily available blood to drain, those with the most energy available for work. By maximising the draining of this youthful sector of the working class, they help reduce the energy available for anti-capitalist or autonomous self-activity, individual or collective, the kind of activity that contributed to the crisis of the 1960s. The flip-side, of course, is the need for alternative modes of control for those less willing to make their energy available. In the case of students, elementary and secondary schools have detention/repression, and the school-to-prison pipeline. When mediation fails, university administrators call in the police or military. (Stanford administrators repeatedly called in the cops in response to demonstrations, building take-overs and the disruption of the industrial park. We were spared the military – such as the use of the National Guard at Kent State University where students were shot and four were killed.) For drop-outs or the excluded, the alternatives to passive acceptance of job search include starvation, slavery, drugs, prisons, COINTELPRO and, as Black Lives Matter has recently emphasised, murderous violence.

* * *

For almost four decades, since 1980, George and Silvia's experiences in Africa, in teaching at the University of Southern Maine and at Hofstra University respectively, and engagement in various social struggles, both within their workplaces and far afield in Europe and Latin America, have resulted in many essays and books, both individual and joint, all of which have enriched my thinking and frequently influenced my actions. While too numerous to trace here, my appropriations of their ideas and appreciation of their exemplary engagement in various struggles has been ongoing.

Notes

1. The essay can be found online at http://la.utexas.edu/users/hcleaver/Appropriation. htm.
2. This interpretation of the source of crisis was spelled out in the journal *Zerowork*, now available online at www.zerowork.org.
3. The class dynamics of the 'fiscal crisis' was analysed in Donna Demac and Philip Mattera, 'Developing and Underdeveloping New York: The "Fiscal Crisis" and the Imposition of Austerity', *Zerowork* #2, 1977, pp. 71–89.
4. The history of the influence of various political currents and ideas on *Zerowork* can be found in the online essay 'Background: Genesis of Zerowork #1' at www.zerowork. org/GenesisZ1.html. Some details of the political and intellectual background to Wages for Housework can be found in two essays, 'The Door to the Garden' (2002), and 'Statement on Selma James' (2012), both in *Women and the Subversion of the Community: A Mariarosa Dalla Costa Reader* (Oakland: PM Press, 2019).
5. Online at: http://la.utexas.edu/users/hcleaver/357k/357kDallaCostaSubversion. html as well as in the *Mariarosa Dalla Costa Reader*.
6. Both essays are in Silvia Federici, *Revolution at Point Zero: Housework, Reproduction and Feminist Struggle*, Brooklyn: Common Notions, 2012.
7. John Weston was an influential member of the International Workingmen's Association (the First International). Marx's critique of the arguments of 'Citizen Weston' concerning wages and wage struggles were later published in pamphlet form as *Value, Price and Profit*.
8. Never content to leave the work of procreating and producing labour-power up to the whims of women, capitalist policy makers have a long history of intervening to shape housework for their own ends. Prior to reading Silvia's writing, while doing research for my dissertation, I had become familiar with the efforts of the Rockefeller's General Education Board in the early twentieth century to reshape women's work and the nature of the labour force in the US South. In 1976, Herbert Gutman's *Work, Culture and Society in Industrializing America* showed how capital had faced the same problem with wave after wave of immigrant labor, often ex-peasants, in the nineteenth century. Eventually, in 2004, Silvia would

publish *Caliban and the Witch: Women, the Body and Primitive Accumulation*, that traced such manipulations, and its violence, all the way back to the birth of capitalism.

9. Another of Silvia's essays from 1975, 'Why Sexuality if Work', elaborated on this particular circle of Hell. Included in Silvia Federici, *Revolution at Point Zero*.

10. Perhaps the most vivid illustration of the work imposed by welfare agencies is Frederick Wiseman's documentary film *Welfare* (1975). The situation got much worse in the 1990s with President Bill Clinton's response to welfare rights struggles: 'reforms' that reduced payments and forced many into part-time participation in the floating reserve, a cruel increase in the work of producing labour-power by the poor.

11. For a brief description of each of these efforts, which includes links to original articles, see the 'Background: Genesis of Zerowork #1' at www.zerowork.org/GenesisZ1. html. The best English language introduction to these Italian Marxists is Steve Wright, *Storming Heaven: Class Composition and Struggle in Italian Autonomist Marxism* (London: Pluto Press, 2002), republished in 2017 in a second, expanded edition.

12. Henry Mayhew's *London Labour and the London Poor* (1851) provided ample illustrations of this resistance by vagabonds. In more recent years, another contributor to *Zerowork*, Peter Linebaugh, published a study – *The London Hanged: Crime and Civil Society in the Eighteenth Century* (1992) – that dramatically amplified our understanding of such resistance through case after case of once-waged workers choosing unwaged lives of direct appropriation in defiance of changing capitalist laws.

13. Online at: www.zerowork.org/.

14. Online at: http://la.utexas.edu/users/hcleaver/CleaverModeOfProduction.pdf. A parallel critique of the application of the mode of production approach to understanding Mexican peasants was later made by Ann Lucas de Rouffignac, *The Contemporary Peasantry in Mexico: A Class Analysis* (New York: Praeger, 1985).

15. Online at: www.zerowork.org/CleaverFoodFamine.html.

16. This essay is now available in a trilingual edition, *Wages for Students | Sueldo para Estudiantes | Des salaires pour les étudiants* (Brooklyn: Common Notions, 2016). Online at www.zerowork.org/WagesForStudents.pdf.

17. Online at www.zerowork.org.

18. In the history of student activism, this same limited understanding appears again and again. Students, who walked out of class and marched in the street, have spoken of going on strike, but not of refusing work, even when their demands included less work. This was the case in the student strike in 1911 that spread to schools in over 60 towns in the UK. It was also true in a first-person account of a high-school student strike in New York City in 1950. Examples from the 1960s are manifold. On the 1911 strike see 'The 1911 Schoolchildren Strikes', *BBC History Magazine*, September 2011. On the 1950 strike see Arthur Bauman, *Artie Cuts Out* (New York: Jaguar Press, 1953).

19. Examples of such self-conscious undermining can be found not only in the diversion of income, time and energy from job training to struggle, but in efforts to subvert the legitimacy of university-business ties that sought to normalise the subordination of learning to business needs and the disruption of research projects connected to the war machine or other overtly capitalist plans. At Stanford, this included such projects as an annual Student Guide to the university that laid out the results of our research on such ties and projects, teach-ins, the disruption of Reserve Officer Training Corps, a take-over of the Applied Electronics Laboratory (which hosted research for the Department of Defense on methods of

defending the planes that were carpet bombing Indochina from surface-to-air missiles), a campaign against the counterinsurgency research of the Stanford Research Institute to the shutting down of the Stanford Industrial Park (the nucleus of what became Silicon Valley).

20. Originally formulated for my courses on *Capital*, I first published this representation in the appendix to Harry Cleaver, 'Malaria, the Politics of Public Health and the International Crisis', *Review of Radical Political Economics*, 9(1), April 1977, pp. 81–103.

21. Online at: http://la.utexas.edu/users/hcleaver/OnSchoolwork200606.pdf.

22. Although the disruptions initiated during student movements have long been considered exceptions, the advent of laptop computers and smart phones and their use by students for purposes other than taking notes, e.g. texting, email, games, clearly provide contemporary examples of in-class absenteeism – the equivalent of showing up for your factory job but then playing or taking care of personal affairs instead of working.

23. Another quality check on the work of professors emerged with capitalist worries over 'grade inflation', i.e. the awarding of higher grades for less work – one fruit of student struggles. Campaigns against grade inflation have involved both harangues against too many high grades and attempts to measure the degree of inflation in order to sanction easy grading and reward greater discipline. In the College of Liberal Arts at the University of Texas at Austin, administrators started compiling data on each professor's grading history. Any trend toward higher grades was interpreted not as a sign of improved teaching or greater student competence but as evidence of grade inflation. Any trend toward lower grades was thus seen as manifesting the desired effort to deflate grades. One year several professors, discovered to be grade deflators, were given permanent salary increases as a reward for tightening the screws on their students.

24. That Board of Trustees was made up almost exclusively of businessmen, many of whom were involved in formulating and setting pro-business policies at the local, state, federal and international levels. As concrete personifications of capital-in-general, they were natural targets for protests and demands that challenged capitalist control over the university.

25. This essay, minus the graphic, can be found in George Caffentzis, *In Letters of Blood and Fire: Work Machines, and the Crisis of Capitalism* (Brooklyn: Common Notions, 2013), pp. 11–57.

3

The Radical Subversion of the World

Raquel Gutiérrez Aguilar

Why is Silvia Federici so popular amongst such a broad spectrum of young – and not so young – Spanish-speaking women? Why do her ideas resonate so much on both sides of the Atlantic Ocean, from Barcelona to Buenos Aires, from Madrid to Puebla? Why do they make sense to so many women with an experience of struggle, feminist or not, Marxist or not, indigenous or not? And why does this happen at a moment when such a huge number of women in struggle in different American and European countries – a diverse galaxy of women in a multiplicity of different constellations – is taking to the streets and the squares of the world over and over again, showing their indignation, making connections, building new visions of social transformation?

I choose these questions as my starting point because they not only inspire me to open a conversation with other critical perspectives, but they also allow me to highlight what women, in ever-increasing numbers and combinations, in the streets and in academia, are trying to express in dialogue with Silvia Federici.

I will answer these questions in three sections. First of all, I want to underline the relevance of Federici's contribution in establishing a starting point for critical arguments: one that does not obscure the actions, efforts, and labours – in other words, struggles – to guarantee the conditions that allow for dignity of reproduction of human and non-human life. Indeed, Federici suggests that this feminised, negated and belittled social sphere, that of the reproduction of life, is where we can start to think more radically about social transformation. This argument has a powerful impact on the experience of many women. In response to her call, we stop feeling obliged to fragment the life we live, the only one we have, between public and private times and spaces; a division that is fundamental to the processes of accumulation of capital and state power.

The second section will briefly explore Federici's theoretical capacity to articulate the plurality that fuels the contemporary movement of women in struggle. Why is it that so many of us experience Silvia's arguments as a toolbox that we can use for building bridges between different people and between their differences? And I stress the use of 'experience', because I refer to a situation that is, at the same time, intellectual and emotional, corporeal and rational. What is it that she brings to the movement of women in struggle and, by extension, to the broader movement for transformation?

Finally, I will take a brief look at the fresh horizons opened up by Federici's contributions to the women's movement, the feminist struggle, and beyond.

The Material and Symbolic Reproduction of Social Life as Starting Point and Object of the Radical Subversion of the World

In *Caliban and the Witch. Women, the Body and Primitive Accumulation,* without doubt her best-known book, Federici criticises Marx for obscuring the multiple material, emotional and psychological processes and activities that have to take place to enable the production and consumption of commodities. Once the worker has been separated from the means of existence and has entered a relation of wage labour,[1] they receive a sum of money in exchange for their labour-power and must, with this money, guarantee their reproduction. However, as some forms of feminism first pointed out decades ago, in agreement with the voices of indigenous peoples, you cannot eat money, money will not keep you warm, it will not heal you... Between the process of production and that of commercial consumption lies a great continent of efforts, actions, calculations, energies: the continent of reproductive labour, which, to some, might seem an 'invisible space' and which is largely populated by women. In her work, Federici names this place and, in doing so, grants it visibility. She explains why this place has been rendered invisible and to whom and recovers the terrible experiences that many women have had to suffer for this negation to be imposed. She reminds us of the witch hunts, she refers to the ways that the voice and capacity of many women that came before us were silenced, she unveils the brutal expropriation of an immense body of feminine knowledge. In naming and shedding light on all this, in constructing an explanation that 'makes sense to us' – as a huge diversity of women have stressed – she provides each and every one of us, individually and collectively, a renewed capacity to express what is tremendously hard to articulate without these arguments.

In this sense, *Caliban and the Witch* is one of those books that speak to us, which is how some of us women name the experience of finding a text which presents and analyses the 'missing pieces' that help us understand our realities, explain them in terms of our lived experience and, therefore, shed light on our individual and collective struggles. Sometimes, we also find a shared empathy with young men (some, not all) who have also found resonances in Silvia's arguments.

Silvia Federici's Work as a Toolbox for Building Bridges, Opening Channels and Creating Bonds

Caliban and the Witch is a book that 'speaks' to *each and every one of us* through the intimate act of reading.[2] We can immediately enter into dialogue with it, because it allows us to comprehend and clarify lived experiences that are difficult to make sense of and are usually experienced as aggression, expropriation or outright violence. Insofar as *Caliban and the Witch* enables all this, it almost automatically becomes a toolbox for expanding one's comprehension of one's own history and engaging in dialogue with the histories of others. What allows us to get to know one another? What resonances are set in motion? What new directions should be at the heart of the discussion? What limits are we feeling encouraged topush? This is the type of conversation that reading Federici's work sparks between different women.

It is interesting not only to analyse her arguments and formally discuss them; the most valuable element in Silvia's work is what she inspires in each of our own thoughts. The times and places where one can hear about her work or talk with her become something more: her words offer a bridge of dialogue that fosters new and diverse encounters. This also happens because Silvia usually prioritises working through shared concepts and elements of feminist movements without homogenising them or imposing a false unity, to reinforce the critique of what she calls 'the patriarchy of the wage', launching renewed conversations that aim, amongst others, at 'transmitting experience'. All this does not make the discussion of Silvia's arguments less interesting, but it does highlight what seems to me even more interesting: her capacity to generate collective questioning and encourage us towards the construction and nurturing of relationships and movements.

Silvia Federici's arguments spring from a rigorous and uncompromising critique of all instances of domination and they address the immediate and strategic demands of material and symbolic reproduction needed for a collective life. In recovering a critical gaze that seeks to go beyond Marx's Marxism, she does not shy away from the exploration of how human bodies suffer capitalist exploitation according to their gender. And that is also how she approaches the colonial experience. As a result, she manages to open windows to various debates at the same time: she challenges and disturbs certain critical Marxist explanations, while at the same time shakes up and unsettles established and institutional versions of feminism and suggests ways in which we can take up a radical engagement with the on-going fact of colonialism. However, there is yet another element to these contributions: Silvia does not enter a relation of 'competition' with other theories; she stands out for trying to expand our comprehension of the entanglement of domination and exploitation we inhabit in order to challenge it more profoundly and on many different fronts.

The Radicalness of the Call to Struggle

Silvia gives us a clear and explicit starting point for a critique of the current situation: the material and symbolic reproduction of life. Although in the iron grip of capital and the value regime today and threatened by all types of patriarchal violence, this reproductive space as starting point is capable of regenerating and opening new possibilities over and over again. Federici provides an interesting lens through which to look at the politicisation of broad spheres of existence which, in the context of other analytical perspectives, are neither visible nor taken into account. In setting out, above all, to stimulate dialogue between struggles that take place in different spheres, so that they can cultivate proximity and manage distance, and not entering into competition for a specific interpretation of this or that theoretical context, Federici opens up horizons of transformation guided by substantial internal coherence in *multiple spheres of existence*. Silvia and her work, developed in parallel – and at times in close collaboration – with George Caffentzis, are an invitation to engage with different struggles. Struggles against what happens in the homes and the everyday reproduction of life, whose oppressive demands almost always rely on the abusive exhaustion of feminine energies. (If in doubt, look at the workload of separated or divorced women, just to take one example visible in almost any workplace.) We are also called on to link these struggles to the flood of efforts which aim at setting limits to what governments expropriate under the title of 'austerity' and are capable of making links with heterogeneous experiences which other approaches ignore. Silvia and George embody an energy that pushes towards renewed struggles against all types of exploitation and, precisely for that reason, produce a common: a common sense of the dissidence that knits together a community. They both do it from a feminist perspective that pursues the subversion of everything, starting from the intimacy of the material and symbolic reproduction of life, which is always more than the reproduction of capital.

Between Barcelona and Málaga, March 2017

Notes

1. The 'worker' in this argument can be a man or a woman, cis- or trans- – gender is irrelevant, at this point: what matters is the space the individual occupies in capitalist social relations.
2. I found it difficult to express exactly what I wanted to in this sentence. It is an interesting case of what, in mathematics, is to define a group by 'extension' or 'by comprehension'. My first effort consisted in trying to 'enumerate' to whom Silvia's book speaks: this is the reglamentary way of establishing a group 'by extension'. However, I believe it is clearer to define it 'by comprehension': those to whom *Caliban* speaks and those to whom it does not. This is a distinction worth looking into; it would be of great interest for those to whom 'it does not speak' to ask themselves why *Caliban* remains silent before them.

4

Strange Loops and Planetary Struggles: A Postscript to Midnight Notes

Malav Kanuga

> It is said that in the period of the First World War, in a bar in Zurich, Vladimir Illich Lenin and Tristan Tzara met, without ever having associated before. The language of Lenin tried to create the world with the strength of the will, of law, of power. Tzara used language as irony, as the creation of worlds in which will, law and power were suspended. If they had understood each other, the twentieth century would have been lighter. If they had been friends, they would have undertaken the construction of small crafts able to navigate on the ocean of chaos: rafts for all the exiles who travelled away from the arid and warlike lands of late-modern capitalism. – Franco 'Bifo' Berardi, *Félix Guattari: Thought, Friendship and Visionary Cartography*

We were plunged in these first decades of the twenty-first century into the desperate darkness of seemingly permanent crisis and war. Like the beginning years of the last century, so much of how we transform our present planetary condition now depends on whether we find ways to understand the languages and experiences necessary to create worlds; on how we build crafts with which to navigate across an 'ocean of chaos' and toward one other; on what shared basis we gather among friends – 'all the exiles who travelled away from the arid and warlike lands of late-modern capitalism' – and learn from one another the arts of collective itinerancy and consistency.[1] The pall of war casts ominously over the world, but perhaps far-flung midnight illuminators can still help steady us toward a different horizon. This *Festschrift* celebrates two such lantern-bearers. How much lighter are the paths that George Caffentzis and Silvia Federici have created and shared with us in this dark world through their friendship as well as their own planetary itineraries and consistencies?

This Festschrift is also an opportunity to reflect on what kind of work seems necessary and possible in the wake of the generational 'auroras' of Silvia and George's visionary politics, whose projects have centred on ways of knowing and connecting disparate parts of our collective world and, in their attention to the shifting composition of our world's many struggles, have revealed contours of a planetary thought. George and Silvia's political work, their conceptual and methodological creations, and the ways they learned to manoeuvre reactionary and repressive counter-revolutionary advances and low periods of movement activity, are important legacies and starting points for those considering new projects in these times. For decades, they have helped us bear witness to our social body, gather essential light, consider lessons, and circulate the wisdom of our worlds-making. Importantly, they have also facilitated the converging of many languages and experiences shared by the ethnographers, poets, and plenipotentiaries of the last decades of class struggles; and they have simultaneously shared the results of these encounters in the pages of their own journals and books as well as in many other spaces such as dinner tables, convivia and assemblies.

George and Silvia are lodestars for those interested in augmenting the means of communication for the circulation of struggles. Their dedication to bringing together, preparing and sharing materials (linguistic, experiential, cartographic, affective, aesthetic) from the planetary itineraries of struggle have been ballasts in those 'small crafts able to navigate on the ocean of chaos'. In this sense, of analysing 'political currents coming from different parts of the world and different sectors of the world proletariat, each rooted in a history of struggles',[2] their example inspires us to consider how 'reading the struggles' is necessary work we must continue to develop.

Midnight Friendships

I was a longtime reader of *Midnight Notes* before I was a member of the final era of the group's formation, when it was called 'Midnight Notes and Friends'. In the summer of 2008, George invited me to a gathering at the Autonomedia loft with associates, new and old, of Midnight Notes (the original 1970s and 1980s collective; a few from the 1990s; some, like me, of the mid-2000s) to reflect on this rich history. We also came together to map an elaborate itinerary for a new phase of the collective scrawled across a large scroll that would detail the work – and the working groups – to come. Much of that work, 'to develop new material concerning present and future anticapitalist struggles' as George put it, did not come to pass. The same intimations of deepening resistance and crisis that we deliberated on in those meetings came to a head in the months following that meeting.

In 2009, members and friends of Midnight Notes published *Promissory Notes: From Crises to Commons* to look squarely at the crisis from the point of view of the 'the struggles billions have made across the planet against capital's exploitation and its environmental degradation of their lives'.[3] These struggles – manifested in financial, ecological, housing, food, governmental and migrant crises, and war – both decentred narratives of capital's internal crisis tendencies and centred urgent forms of resistance the world over. The itinerary of these movements mapped dramatically onto the cartographic vision we conjured on that scroll the previous summer and served to reinforce the ongoing necessity of our editorially ambitious if diffuse collective project. These were intimidating but auspicious times for Midnight Notes to turn thirty!

Midnight Notes hosted its final gathering at the Brecht Forum in New York City six months later, during the 'harsh winter' of a deepening capitalist crisis. This 'MN30' meeting was intended to celebrate 30 years of a collective project and, it turns out, to minister to its last rites, neither through absolution nor anointment, but sober reckoning about the present state of things and a dignified resolve to find new methods to transform them.[4] After three decades of peripatetic inquiry – in 'small crafts' determined to traverse oceans of chaos and 'long caravans' dedicated to relaying news and gather powers across the desiccated lands of conquest and enclosure – the journal ceased to be a viable place for collective work. Steadfast in its purpose to serve as a space of critical dialogue within and about the anticapitalist movement, and inventive in its many expressions, Midnight Notes surpassed its humble origins and fell short of its gargantuan ambition.

The seemingly abrupt interruption of these shared itineraries pushed me closer toward a new publishing project in 2010 that I named Common Notions. My ambition was to reciprocate the gift of friendship in the aftermath of Midnight Notes. I worked with Silvia and George to collect their writings and present them to the world in two publications, *Revolution at Point Zero* (2012) and *In Letters of Blood and Fire* (2013), and more recently in *Wages for Students* (2016). These books have circulated in a manner that has inspired even more beautiful friendships and connections around the world, and have traced many common lines of struggle, thought, care and convivial encounter in the few years since they were published. They are important indications that our work as an editorial and publishing project remains necessary.

Yet I believe we still need another collective editorial project in the wake of the ones George and Silvia sustained and animated for so long. On the day Midnight Notes gathered for the last time a decade ago, George told us: 'I know I need a site of continuous collective discussion and debate in dialogue with the anticapitalist movement in order to create a political perspective that can be expressed in a journal. However, Midnight Notes stopped being such a site a while ago. It is time to create a new and larger one.' A new project such as this has yet to emerge, though its contours can be traced in the long arc of George and Silvia's life and work. How can their experiences guide us today?

Recognise and Record

We shall simply show the world why it is struggling, and consciousness of this is a thing it must acquire whether it wishes or not. – Karl Marx, Letter to Arnold Ruge (1843)

To publish such a paper demands besides deep theoretical understanding, technical knowledge, journalistic skill, a sense of values, flexibility and firmness, combined to an exceptional degree. Some of these can to some extent be studied in isolation, but today their full application and development can only be achieved in what we have shown are the vast implications contained in the formula: to recognize the existence and record the facts of the new society. – C.L.R. James, *Facing Reality* (1958)

Ruthless criticism and abolition of the present order predicated on experience in practical struggle. That was the vision of the young Karl Marx as he shifted about Europe evading censors and state police, mingling with conspirators and collaborators, and elaborating the necessary objectives of an international journal to establish common cause among myriad workers' movements. His editorial vision in this moment was dedicated to 'the self-clarification (critical philosophy) of the struggles and wishes of the age'. He would insist that 'this is a task for the world and for us. It can succeed only as the product of united efforts'.[5]

Many autonomous paths and traditions have since emerged from Marx's call for militant 'self-clarification of the struggles'. Silvia and George's 'reading of struggles' belongs in that tradition that has thoroughly 'applied Marx to Marxism' in the analysis of capital and class, waged and unwaged work, debt and expropriation, social reproduction and the commons, and crisis and war. Their expansion of the class-struggle categories of Marxism, along with their notion that social struggles reveal the changing nature of class composition across the spectrum of class society and its many divisions and hierarchies, has moved us beyond the limits of Italian workerist thinking (and to some degree that of an earlier cohort of *Zerowork* members). At the same time it has helped develop a powerful vision of struggles and autonomy through an analysis of what they refer to as 'the manifold of work' on an international scale. Drawing on the race, class and gender perspective of Wages for Housework, this work distilled a new formulation of autonomy from the refracted light from a variety of perspectives, concepts and traditions, including heterodox Marxism, feminism, social ecology, subsistence, Indigenous, anticolonial and abolitionist. These powerful contributions to internationalist anticapitalist movements allow us to perceive a deeper structure to work and wage struggles – most notably in the land and resource reclamation struggles in Africa, India, the Middle East, and the Americas. Often these were struggles that were not *simply* looking for better wage deals with capital, but for a refusal of the orchestration of a world-destroying capitalist subsumption project inaugurated in the 1980s; struggles that did not negate wage struggles but intersected with them in new ways, and frequently surpassed strictly 'workers' struggles' in terms of mass militancy.

The swerve around Lenin is notable, not only because the Bolshevik leader was so ideologically dominant in the seventies, including in workerist circles; but also because at the time Leninism offered a widely tested strategy for writing and publishing from a workers' standpoint. The *Iskra* [*The Spark*] model, based on the first all-Russian illegal Marxist newspaper Lenin founded in 1900, was attractive to many new communist organisations throughout the seventies because it clearly articulated the role that publishing would have and the results it would yield, whether oriented toward mass readership or clamouring for infraleft self-purity. Midnight Notes strived for neither, though collecting and analysing political material from struggles were 'cardinal' and 'essential' (both watchwords in the Leninist lexicon) aspects of their militant activities.[6]

Their manoeuvres within and around the programmatic visions that Marx and Lenin inspired can also be traced to an organisational strategy that the Johnson-Forest tendency and Socialisme ou Barbarie began articulating in the 1950s, namely to 'recognize and record' the activities of the class – 'where', as C.L.R. James stated, 'the new society is and where it is going'.[7] That is, Marxist organisations should observe working-class self-activities and record them so that the class can see for itself what it is doing, to 'give the working class means of expressing itself', and the radical nature of its struggle. In the first issue of *Classe Operaia*, Mario Tronti reformed Lenin's familiar line on the role of the working-class publication in light of changes in the technical and political composition of the class. The central task would be to analyse the experiences of struggle into a general political approach that is 'the total viewpoint of the working class' as it currently expressed itself, and from this basis to 'provide a monitoring of the strategic validity of particular instances of struggle ... continually judged and mediated by a political level which can generalise it'.[8] Let's consider this articulation. Is it the responsibility of militants to *judge* and *monitor* – that is, deem correct? Or is the role of militants 'to sensitize ourselves to catch the true significance and the overtones of their statements of their problems, their aims and aspirations', as Facing Reality would suggest?

To avoid Lenin is certainly to avoid this problem. But the difficulty remains of how revolutionaries participate in and record the development of struggles, how their organisations can or will represent these struggles, and how this relates to the political work of producing revolutions (or more self-consciously, revolutionary processes that may initiate revolutions). Twenty years after the first pages of *Classe Operaia* went to print that, *Zerowork* boldly declared: 'we should never identify the working class with its organizations.' This poses questions about how certain militant organisations read, interpret, and relate to the larger social body of the working class. What do these questions mean today?

We have been tracing a path through various Marxist traditions, and their associated organs, that seek, from the many perspectives of the planetary working class, to account for specific struggles while at the same time apprehending general developments of the conditions of those struggles – what they articulate, how they might circulate, and what are the potentialities and limits of their recomposition. But where is the auto-critique? Do these journals turn their critical analysis on themselves? The basis of such an autocritique implies surpassing the limits of an older Euclidean geometry of class struggle, of measuring struggles against a Cartesian economic and political 'point zero' instead of understanding their emanating effects.

Silvia and George's work on the other hand invites us to peer into the kaleidoscope of class struggle. They teach us the strategic art of deciphering the patterns of class 'codism' from an unfixed position, of translating and rotating from specific and changeable distances and angles; and then of solving the problem of mutual transformation of distinct experiences and positions into new topologies and related processes of struggle. Even as we pay attention to our own viewpoints, the critical challenge is how we collectively create reflecting surfaces, behold, inquire, and adjust to the ever-changing patterns made visible and obscure. In this regard, the twelve issues of *Midnight Notes*, 18 bulletins of the Committee for Academic Freedom in Africa (CAFA), and several collectively edited book-length anthologies are some of many channels that deserve more study. Nearly four decades of midnight writing offer testimony to the enormity of the task.

Strange Loops

Glimpses of this orientation of class struggle appear in interesting, though harder-to-trace textual strategies and editorial decisions, alongside certain political concepts. One such concept is the 'strange loop'. This notion appeared in early issues of Midnight Notes to describe the ways in which various class sectors 'recognize and record' other sectors, dispersed differently but in common in an international division of labour, and thereby make connections between and among themselves, in turn creating the conditions to circulate struggles beyond the limits of technical composition and expand the threshold of their political composition.

What is a strange loop? Douglas Hofstadter describes Godel's mathematics, the disorienting visual landscapes of M.C. Escher, and the fugal structures developed by Bach as all comprised on the phenomenon of the strange loop. Such loops occur 'whenever, by moving upwards (or downwards) through the level of some hierarchical system, we unexpectedly find ourselves right back where we started'.[9] We complete a journey, yet are compelled to start all over again. At the same time, what is strange is not only the seemingly inevitable return. A particular kind of phenomenon is at work in which there is 'an interaction between levels in which the top level reaches back down toward the bottom level and influences it, while at the same time being itself determined by the bottom level'.[10]

Midnight Notes provides this imagery as a way to understand the shifting class and political composition from the 1980s onward. A strange loop defines relationality amongst sectors of the planetary class when those on the lowest levels of the wage/nonwage, patriarchal, racial, colonial hierarchy reach up toward the top levels and influence them, while at the same time being structurally, psychologically and socially determined by the topmost levels. The strange loops along *hierarchical* lines of power and the lines of escape from them also require us to think of *horizontal* strange loops, those of becoming-in-encounters of sectors of the class who find ways to relate to each other despite manifold operations of separation and division wrought by the sorting functions of capital and its war machines. These strange loops are what Midnight Notes invoke in their reading of struggles and in their pronouncement that effective political composition of any sector of the class can only come from an overthrow of planetary divisions of the social body.

Midnight Notes' use of the concept of 'strange loops' also conjures the near dreamlike spatiotemporal combinations of struggles that emerge in ciphers and surprising tongues, across seemingly disparate territories and times, through resonances of energies, desires, demands, languages, gestures. Let's not discount in the interests of a 'hard' fidelity to struggles that surreal gestures can also guide us through the secrets of a world, many worlds, in profound transformation. Grave and uncertain times so often unmoor the dream vessels of prophetic surrealist sensibilities as well as fervent class desires. But they demand either new experiences of understanding the world that bring forth new interpretive prowess or therapy for the traumas of defeat and decomposition.

George suggests the hidden potential of Lenin's communication strategy (read clearly against the grain of Lenin's legacy as a strategist whose vision is trained on the arrangement of forces on a field of battle) in understanding the composition of struggles and the possibility of new loops when directed to the planetary proletariat. Lenin's insistence on the need for putting the proletarian body in touch with all its members, actions and powers, and his sober assessment of the need to have activists capable of outwitting a concerted police strategy of illusion- and ignorance-creation has even greater resonance today when revolution must be planetary or nothing. For the key to understanding class struggle now is not rooted in the nation state: organisations that can circulate and communicate struggles world-wide are crucial for an anticapitalist politics of social transformation. 'As if to confirm Marx's dubious adage about humanity's propensity to ask the questions that it is ready to answer, there has arisen a world-wide set of organizations devoted to circulating and coordinating struggles against capital on a planetary basis.'[11]

The core of this work is creating lateral channels of revolutionary and revelatory communication of the self-expression of proletarian struggles to other proletarians. This is one of many lessons to divine from the legacy of George and Silvia's editorial-organisational work and offers much to draw from in terms of how we today might decode the planetary cipher of struggles as well as create and encrypt the very lateral channels of communication necessary for them to circulate.

Planetary Inversions

Our new approach starts from the proposition that, at both national and international level, it is the specific, present, political situation of the working class that both necessitates and directs the given forms of capital's development. From this beginning we must now move forward to a new understanding of the entire world network of social relations. – Mario Tronti, 'Lenin in England' (1964)

'Struggle' is more than a geographic and philosophical term, and it exceeds notions of 'international' and 'global'. For Wallerstein, it is world capitalist coordination that serves as the pivot that connects the 'world-system'; it is the hyphen, which is meant to 'underline that we are talking not about systems, economies, empires of the (whole) world, but about systems, economies, empires *that are* a world (but quite possibly, and indeed usually, not encompassing the entire globe)'.[12] The differential spatiotemporal zones of a world-constituting system suggest a capitalist paradigm comprised by a number of contradictory 'political and cultural

units' each interacting, competing, rising, and decomposing; but nevertheless a differentiated and distinctive capitalist topos. Tronti made the
mistake of politically analysing an international working class assumed to
be more or less homogenous since its very homogeneity is what necessitates the worldwide capitalist coordination against it (though he admits
'the only way to prove this unity is to start organising it').[13]

Silvia and George's work, in contrast, has been much more carefully
concerned with the level of differentiation of both capitalist and working-
class compositions as mediated by an axial division of labour, with
core-like and peripheral-like production and reproduction processes, that
determine how class power does or does not emerge from struggles. Their
use of the term *planetary* provides an enlarged worldview of the Copernican revolution in the reading of class antagonism that accompanies
a many-pronged tradition of autonomism inspired by the inversion in
Tronti's *Operai e Capitale*.

In West Africa in the mid-1980s, George and Silvia had observed
firsthand how structural adjustment and neocolonialism more broadly
constituted a class attack on both communal subsistence and workers'
rights across African society. On their return to the United States in 1987, a
politically sharpened vision of the planetary body emerged in the purview
of their collective writings. In this period they helped prepare and assemble
a diverse set of writings in *The New Enclosures* (aka *Midnight Notes* 10,
1990), and, with Ousseina Alidou, organised themselves and other scholars
into the Committee for Academic Freedom in Africa. Besides the bulletins
mentioned above, which they used to organise students and academics for
over a decade, CAFA also produced the anthology *A Thousand Flowers*.[14]
In these writings, we find the expanded 'Copernican' inversion of the development of international capitalist power (and specifically an inversion from
a pan-Africanist perspective in CAFA). This new planetary perspective
was an essential move for understanding the fault lines and the divisions
internal to a planetary social body, to developing ways of seeing the new
entanglements of what was unfolding and how to refuse the separations
imposed. *The New Enclosures* details the antagonistic dynamic at the centre
of planetary class relations at the time of a worldwide reorganisation of
class deals, from the breakup of national Keynesianism-Fordism-welfare
in the North Atlantic, through inflation, deindustrialisation, and urban
'deconcentration', to new forms of imperial developmentalism through the
globalisation of austerity, precarity, privatisation, and structural adjustment.
As they state, this 'must operate throughout the planet in differing, divisive
guises while being totally interdependent'.[15]

As their work has so powerfully shown, there have been different 'deals'
that enable and repress developmental paths for different sectors of the

working classes. These deals are not limited to the wage and social wage but are also manifest in regimes of racial domination and violence against women. Divisions accumulate through a *planetary* social body that is internationally divided, lumpenised, repressed, disciplined, abandoned, devalued, incarcerated and brutalised in an era when all 'national' and 'world-regional' deals are off and each continental moment of enclosure and class attack is predicated on the elaboration of others.

This is central to understanding the inseparable forces of globalisation and war.[16] The enclosure processes Midnight Notes detailed in the early nineties provided a means for understanding the new era of enclosures unfolding in Iraq's oil fields with some of the most incisive, if marginal, critiques of the limits of the antiwar movement.[17] Midnight Notes assists in framing an anticapitalist perspective on war today by recognising the capitalist strategy to discipline (neoliberalise) the oil and energy sectors and the permanence of territorial control for the planned development of capital at a number of scales through command of infrastructures and logistics located in built environments, energy, and various resources. This project has found many new articulations and yet has not been fully realised in the collective and shared reading of struggles.

At the same time, the paradoxical stabilisation of state-forms despite ongoing crises has occurred through increased policing and subsumption of differentiated populations, and the intensification of exploitation through regimes of work, disciplining of spatial stratas, sexual orders, hierarchies of wages enforced in a range of labouring processes, and precarious cultural realms of reproduction. This planetary crisis, inaugurated some decades ago, now seems to be a permanent condition, one that is increasingly policed through wars that have now all but criss-crossed the 'peace' deals that brokered the temporary compromises of post-war Atlantic class forces and retrenched the rest of the world's victories against colonialism. The concept of 'class deals' first detailed this condition, if in generalised fashion. Our task remains to map the efflux, fissures and possibilities, continuations and ruptures, in a planetary framework.

Our ability to follow such coordinates depends upon developing a committed reading of a longer and fragmented history of domination and refusal, whose contemporary manifestations are perhaps increasingly becoming consolidated into a planetary regime governing life and the circulation of struggles against it. This management of surplus is a specifically important point of investigation for us as it connects disparate classes and social castes as well as distinct societies into zones of salvation and sacrifice. We can identify from a planetary perspective what are increasingly differentiated populations: those stripped of rights, those for whom rights are rendered meaningless by the legalities of nation-states in the wake of ecological catastrophes and other forms of transcendent terror, those whose rights are repackaged as market privileges, those for whom allegiance to ruling class values is the preferred aspirational avenues toward safety and security, those who are repressed for dreaming to exist otherwise, or for abandoning or assaulting the apparatus.

New Auroras

We still need editorial political projects that can bring together a planetary perspective on the condition of our social body in a time of crisis and war, and its resonances and dissonances across struggles. These are projects that continue to stretch and expand, as Silvia and George have, Marxian concepts and anticapitalist analyses rooted in both contemporary struggles and everyday life amongst 'the enslaved, the colonized, the world of the wageless', for autonomy and self-reproduction.[18] Insofar as these struggles pose the question of coordination and synchronicity, of their own collective awareness beyond any international organisations, they reveal a planetary logic already at work in struggles that requires more analysis if they are to become the basis of a shared project of world transformation.

We need such projects that are committed to revealing the secrets of and wishes of our time, to reviving and interrogating lessons from the movements that articulate them, to exposing the limits they face, and transforming them into possibilities for new openings. To understand the strategies currently at play within planetary and territorial refusals of the imposition of work and death through the divisions and hierarchies within our planetary body, we need help to communicate across great distances from various viewpoints necessary to unmoor us from cycles of defeat. One task that clearly remains is to develop strategies to resist the interference operations of the 'detection state' (what Lenin terms the 'political police') whose function, as George described, is to 'keep the struggle secret and the strugglers confused'.[19] Midnight Notes was one experiment. Its lessons needed to be learned.

To reveal the public secrets of revolutionary impulses and initiatives is to help a multitudinous proletarian body *focus* on what it can do next by animating (bringing back to the body) what it already *is* doing. There is poetic power in the paradox of this work, its dual sensibilities and temporalities that speak and listen; traffics in both kinetic and potential energy; reveals secrets as it cloaks itself in anonymity; shocks orthodoxies and surprises revolutionaries; and constitutes itself as a *spectre* openly haunting the world with 'an unspectacular goal: circulating the news of struggles'.[20] Its expressions are fit to a song. Recall the stanzas that close issue 10 of *Midnight Notes* (*The New Enclosures*):

Midnight
No Light
No Time
No Work
Midnight
Secret
Surprise
Power
Midnight

The interpretation of cosmologies and the surveying of geographies are part of the same militant fold and indeed, are essential to each other. Many questions remain for our caravan as it looks to the sky and ponders the earth:

What kinds of arrangements will effectively bring together struggles and dynamics in different spatiotemporal dimensions across planetary plateaus?

Is bringing together understandings, experiences, perceptions, and intuitions emerging from struggles the same as bringing struggles together?

Is a meta-struggle (totality) necessary or superfluous to revolution? Given the differentiated nature of working-class composition, the uneven and contradictory terrain of class struggle, and given that political expressions of class often form cross-currents of understandings, is a meta-struggle even possible or desirable?

How will we test the means by which we bring understanding and perception of these struggles to each other?

Will they enable new topographies of struggles to exist? Will they be limited by existing spatiotemporal geopolitics?

How will these movements and alignments help us to understand state and capitalist dynamics and hinder their projects?

The answers will be found in the secret transmissions crossing the planet in the coming years and decades. We still need late-night readers and editors, writers and dreamers, to take notice and array them into midnight notes.

Notes

1. Franco Berardi (Bifo), *Félix Guattari: Thought, Friendship and Visionary Cartography* (London: Palgrave Macmillan, 2008), p. 140.
2. Silvia Federici, *Revolution at Point Zero: Housework, Reproduction, and Feminist Struggle* (Oakland, CA: Common Notions/PM Press, 2012), p. 6.
3. Midnight Notes Collective and Friends, Promissory Notes: From Crisis to Commons (Brooklyn NY: Autonomedia, 2009), p. 2.

4. Manual Yang suggests the alchemy of Midnight Notes: '[they] decoded partially the evanescent but no less real flickers of this capitalist winter's end. In times of deracination, that is a praiseworthy task to undertake, worth of emulation but not imitation – for the midnight hour from the second Cold War to the latest moment of neoliberal financial crisis, which bookended MN's history, is coming to an end and new languages, new poetics and prophetic energies must be sought out and woven from the ongoing struggles today.' 'Elegy for Midnight Notes?' In *Toward the Last Jubilee: Midnight Notes at Thirty Years* (Washington, DC and Brooklyn, NY: Perry Editions and Autonomedia, 2009), pp. 69–70.

5. Karl Marx, 'Letter to Arnold Ruge' (1843; Letters from the Deutsch-Französische Jahrbücher) in Marx Engels *Collected Works* Vol. 3: *Marx and Engels: 1843–1844* (London/New York: Lawrence & Wishart/International Publishers, 1975), p. 145.

6. Lenin answers his own question, 'Where to begin?', with the following: 'In our opinion, the starting-point of our activities, the first step towards creating the desired organisation, or, let us say, the main thread which, if followed, would enable us steadily to develop, deepen, and extend that organisation, should be the founding of a political newspaper…without [which] we cannot conduct that systematic, all-round propaganda and agitation, consistent in principle. . .' He goes on to suggest the creation of a newspaper for the circulation of struggles is 'the cardinal and most essential sector of our militant activities.' V.I. Lenin, 'Where to begin?' *Iskra*, No. 4 (May 1901), in *Lenin Collected Works*, Vol. 5 (Moscow: Foreign Languages Publishing House, 1961) pp. 20–2.

7. C.L.R. James, Grace C. Lee and Pierre Chaulieu, *Facing Reality: The New Society: Where to Look for It & How to Bring It Closer* (Chicago, IL: Charles H. Kerr, 1975; originally Detroit, MI: Bewick Editions, 1958), pp. 131, 148.

8. Mario Tronti, 'Lenin In England', *Classe Operaia*, No. 1 (January 1964), republished in *Operai e Capitale* ('Workers and Capital') (Turin: Einaudi, 1966), pp. 89–95, under the heading 'A New Style of Political Experiment'.

9. Douglas R. Hofstadter, *Godel, Escher, Bach: An Eternal Golden Braid* (New York: Basic Books, 1999), p. 10.

10. *Ibid.*, p. 10.

11. George Caffentzis, 'Lenin on the Production of Revolutions', in Werner Bonefeld and Sergio Tischler (eds) *What is to be Done? New Times and the Anniversary of a Question* (Aldershot: Ashgate, 2002), p. 163.

12. Immanuel Wallerstein, *World-Systems Analysis: An Introduction* (Durham: Duke University Press, 2004), pp. 16–17.

13. Mario Tronti, *Lenin In England*, in Classe Operaia Issue No.1 (January 1964) (republished in Operai e Capitale [Turin: Einaudi, 1966], pp. 89–95).

14. Ousseina Alidou, Silvia Federici and George Caffentzis (eds) *A Thousand Flowers: Social Struggles Against Structural Adjustment in African Universities* (Trenton and Asmara: Africa World Press, 2000).

15. Midnight Notes Collective, *The New Enclosures* (Brooklyn, NY: Autonomedia, 1990), pp. 2, 3.

16. During the height of academic debates and theories about globalisation (culturalist and constructivist; dependency and world-system theories; neo-Gramscian; postmodern, etc.), Midnight Notes cleared a path many have followed in the years following the publication of The New Enclosures. The issue delivers a sweeping range of simultaneously occurring social realities and phenomena, to clarify and politicise the real movements of social struggles otherwise obscured by terms such

as 'new international division of labour', 'accumulation by dispossession', 'neocolonialism', 'financialisation' and 'privatisation', which often obscured the violence
that was driving globalisation.

17. See, for instance, *Midnight Notes, Midnight Oil: Work, Energy, War*, 1973–1992
     (Brooklyn, NY: Autonomedia, 1992).

18. Federici, *Revolution at Point Zero*, p. 7.

19. Caffentzis, 'Lenin on the Production of Revolutions', p. 152.

20. *Ibid.*, p. 162.

II

MONEY AND VALUE

5

Cogito Ergo Habo:
Philosophy, Money and Method

Paul Rekret

...from the abstractions of philosophy to who'd put the kettle in the work-house. – Peter Linebaugh, *The London Hanged*

Money on the Mind

What relationship is there between thought and money?[1] The question is an awkward one, at least where philosophy is concerned. The very ideal of the love of wisdom implies that philosophical activity be pursued as an end in itself, having no bearing on the philosopher's quest for survival. Indeed, philosophy's ideology of autonomy, inherited from the Greeks, has disposed it to tend to neglect its material conditions; whether slavery in Ancient Athens or intensifying commodification of higher education and publishing in the present. Of course, one might insist upon the exclusion of such concerns from philosophical inquiry proper, restricting them instead to the less lofty domains of the sociology of knowledge. But such a claim would betray a rather narrow conception of philosophy, for where the structures of social relations are discernible at the level of the concept, the question also recoils back upon theoretical inquiry in any event.

One formulation of the affinity of philosophy to its context – the categories of capitalist society in particular – is implied in this essay's title, itself a phrase drawn from C. George Caffentzis's study of John Locke. Caffentzis employs it there to indicate a certain reciprocity between subjectivity and property emergent in late seventeenth century Britain.[2] Of course, he is not altogether unique in delineating an exchange between money and philosophy, but he is noteworthy nonetheless for the intricacy by which he characterises that relationship; one defined ultimately by the exigencies of class struggle. Indeed, while the dominant strains of the philosophy of money have tended either towards positing the identity of philosophy and money or, in contrast, their complete autonomy from one another, Caffentzis has sought instead to trace out, in some historical detail, instances in the work of specific philosophers where money and conceptual thought intersect, and the terms upon which they do so.

By way of comparison, take Georg Simmel's *Philosophy of Money*. In seeking to formulate money's transcendental conditions, Caffentzis notes, Simmel 'dichotomises' philosophy and money, so the possibility of their intersecting becomes unthinkable.[3] By pursuing the conditions of money as such, the argument goes, Simmel not only leaves philosophy independent of it, but in addition, abstains from assessing how philosophical interventions have transformed understandings of money. At the opposite pole, in *Intellectual and Manual Labour*, Alfred Sohn-Rethel implies a formal identity between philosophy and money, one where the latter is afforded temporal priority. That is, in Sohn-Rethel's reasoning, the abstraction that occurs in acts of exchange between commodities precedes and conditions abstractions in the human mind.[4] This is a point to which we will return, but it bears pointing out here that Sohn-Rethel posits a relation between money and thought that runs along a single temporal vector, whereby the circulation of coinage enabling conceptual abstraction pervades the history of Western epistemology; money functions as an independent variable from the moment of its emergence. Yet whether philosophy and money are identified (as in Sohn-Rethel) or dichotomised (as in Simmel), an anachronistic understanding of money tends to prevail.

Caffentzis evades this Scylla or Charybdis of identity or dichotomy between philosophy and money by abandoning the project of *the* philosophy of money altogether. Instead, he restricts the scope of his enterprise to the study of specific philosophers – Locke, George Berkeley and David Hume to be exact – whose work, in engaging in questions of policy, 'constitutes and subsumes a monetary act'.[5] Doing so allows Caffentzis to attend to the more restricted, historically refined terrain of how particular epistemological, ontological and political formulations inform monetary ones. Equally, it reveals a level of contextual specificity that permits him to suggest how particular social relations, and monetary debates more narrowly, have shaped philosophy. This is, I think, what Caffentzis has in mind in referring to his approach as 'ampliative', one which finds conceptual architectures first averred in a work of philosophy, later refracted in policy proposals, or the obverse.

It is notable that putting philosophy in its place in this way involves viewing it as a capitalist class project. Money, after all, as the mediator between people and their means of subsistence in a capitalist society, is a form of command. Moreover, this makes it, to borrow Harry Cleaver's formulation, an 'essential moment in capitalist class relations' where life is lived as labour.[6] And it is with this basic function in mind that we might understand Caffentzis's delineation of his object of study to the oeuvres of Locke, Berkeley and Hume, poised as they are at crucial junctures of capitalism's development in the seventeenth and eighteenth centuries; each faced with urgent questions around the generalisation of exchange relations and the compulsion to wage labour. The state's role in money's creation and management and the social employment of money in the imposition of a universal form of value are especially important for Locke; overcoming resistance to capital's generalisation is particularly crucial for Berkeley; and money's civilising function as a spur to industriousness and entrepreneurial behaviour is central to Hume's project.

But attending to the *reciprocity* of philosophy and money, as I have suggested Caffentzis's philosophical oeuvre does, entails a further move: the examination of the ways these problematics are shaped by and come to shape theoretical inquiry. Thus, in *Clipped Coins*, his study of Locke, Caffentzis reveals a philosophy mobilised by the problem of the universal-isation of money in the late seventeenth century, along with the ways this relates to the criminalisation of pre-capitalist forms of survival and the legitimation of enclosure and indefinite capital accumulation, underpinned by a metaphysical notion of personhood and a conception of knowledge as a mode of labour.

If Locke can thus be said to be 'the philosopher of primitive accumula-tion', then Berkeley is the theorist of 'import substitution' and economic diversification.[7] For while Locke's fundamental concern was the generali-sation of a mode of property that would subject the whole of the world to the impersonal power of the market, Berkeley's conundrum, framed by his experience as Bishop of Cloyne, is centred upon compelling his recalcitrant Irish flock into wage labour all while inducing the Anglo-Irish gentry's investment in Ireland. It is through this problem of needing to 'excite' or stimulate productive activity that Caffenztis reads Berkeley's defence of a specieless currency: given his setting in an under-developed economy, for Berkeley the function of money does not rest with its capacity to store value as it does for Locke but with its potential to stimulate and regulate behaviour. In other words, it is the 'monetisation' of life itself that Berkeley seeks. And it is in these terms that Caffentzis interprets the development of the conception of 'notion' in the Irish philosopher's later work: here is a referent to volitional impulse inseparable from the view of money as a reflection of the 'spirits' that guide it.

While his efforts are focused upon the rebellious Scottish Highlands rather than Ireland, Hume's monetary programme emerges from a problem analogous to Berkeley's: the process of expropriation associated with Locke, it turns out, is insufficient as a compulsion to wage labour. Yet while Berkeley calls for a temporary withdrawal for Ireland from the world market as a means of transforming social relations along capitalist lines, Hume proposes complete integration into the national and world market as a means of 'civilizing' Scotland's aboriginal cultures.[8] Hume's defence of a metallic money standard is therefore not a sign of regressive essentialism as is often assumed, but, Caffentzis shows, a response to the promiscuous issuing of promissory notes widespread in eighteenth century Scotland, along with the balance of payments crisis that results. Read through the frame of Hume's functionalist ontology, his defence of a metallic standard for money is centred upon a moral argument against paper money's ability to sever the 'barbaric' Scottish Highlanders from a gift economy to the capitalist discipline of frugality, work, and investment.[9]

Together then, these three studies, (a monograph on Hume remains unpublished), offer an expansive examination of the intersections of biography, philosophy, and monetary policy. In doing so, they illustrate not only how the function of money as an equaliser between different objects and activities is crucial to the imposition of capitalist command but, broader still, show philosophy's concepts to be inextricable from their class content.

The patience and clarity characteristic of Caffentzis's style render a fuller reconstruction of this philosophical project redundant. Despite the accessibility of the work however, it is all too often overlooked where study of the history of philosophy is concerned. Even if we restrict our gaze to the more widely referenced book on Locke as I will for the remainder of this essay, it is apparent that undue neglect of the rich theoretical terrain it opens has entailed unnecessary enigmas in the English philosopher's contemporary reception. Caffentzis's work, I hold here, merits further consideration.

Admittedly, situating Locke's philosophy in the context of an emergent global capitalism in late seventeenth century Britain is not in itself a unique proposition. At least since C.B. MacPherson's formative study of *Possessive Individualism*, leftist readings of Locke have been premised upon his place in the rise of market society and the theoretical priority given to the individuals who inhabit it.[10] The exception of *Clipped Coins*, in other words, does not merely rest with the contention that there is an inherent relationship between Locke's philosophy and capitalism. Rather, it sits with the argument that a peculiarly capitalist ontology of money, at a decisive moment for modern social relations, acts as the hinge around which both Locke's political theory and his epistemology revolve. Such a claim, as we will see, not only resolves a host of tensions in the reception of Locke, it offers important insights into the history of modern thought more broadly. Looking primarily to Caffentzis's study of Locke in what remains then, this essay seeks to evince the fecundity of that project. In doing so I hope to persuade the reader of the significance of Caffentzis's philosophical project for understanding both the origins of capitalism and the conceptual architecture through which we examine it.

Between Nature and Convention

Money is poised ambiguously between being a natural substance and a social convention. This ontological axiom is, as far as Caffentzis sees it, key to unlocking the manifold tensions and uncertainties pervading Locke's work. Caffentzis first discerns this notion through what ends up as the winning case in a polemic that has come to be known as the 'recoinage debate', and it bears a bit of unpacking here. Having become severely undervalued relative to the price of silver on the world market by the 1690s, it had become highly profitable to trade English silver coins on world bullion markets for their silver content alone. This not only produced a severe shortage of coins – exacerbated by rampant counterfeiting and the clipping of coins for bullion – but, in turn, led to chronic price inflation.[11] While broad agreement existed for the minting of new clip-proof coins, the dispute hung over whether to set the current market price for silver at London Mint parity or to instead keep the official Mint parity unchanged. Tasked with drafting a recommendation, Secretary of the Treasury William Lowndes proposed devaluing English coinage by re-minting coins at a lower silver content all while maintaining their nominal value. Opposed to this deflationary strategy, Locke instead proposed re-minting coins at their formal silver content while simultaneously bringing all-out discipline and justice upon counterfeiters and clippers.[12]

Although it is often viewed as fetishising metal money, Caffentzis instead reads Locke's proposal as reflecting the need for a stable measure of value to underpin contracts and transactions upon a burgeoning world market. On this view, Lowndes's inflationary proposal, effectively deflating the value of money from its metal content, threatened trust in both money and the state. Not only would Lowndes's plan threaten world trade by failing to impose a spatial and temporal identity upon contracts, but it would enrich hoarders and manipulators of bullion while also effectively transforming the state itself into a coin clipper. Certainly, with Locke's re-minting plan deflation would occur, but this would only be the case when viewed from the relative myopia of a British idea of value and not from the perspective of a global market dealing in the objective value of silver coins.[13] As we will see, the question of the relation of value to substance brings monetary policy immediately into the ambit of epistemic questions regarding the universality of knowledge.[14] For if experience is essential to knowledge, as Locke holds, then where the relation between money's metal content and its value is severed, ideas of money become deprived of coherence.

Here lies the key to Locke's 'mercantilist prejudice'; while money is subject to convention, it is only through its substantial qualities that it is assured a level of objectivity beyond subjective intention.[15] This is a claim that will bear further examination, but suffice it to say that holding the universality of money as of a higher order than the nation-state, as Locke does, extends beyond local questions of inflationary policy to underlie the issue of the dominance of capital on a world scale.[16]

The priority attending the universality of money in Locke's position in the recoinage debate, especially insofar as it conceives money ambiguously between subjective convention and its objective qualities, is reflected in the role money is assigned in the account of the origins of political society presented in the *Second Treatise on Government*.[17] In fact, as Caffentzis shows, not only does the introduction of money function as 'efficient cause' of the social contract but moreover, money's ambiguous ontological status between convention and nature forms the basis for Locke's programme of political reform. Before examining the consequences of this claim for conventional readings of Locke, let us see in more detail why this is the case.

As is well known, in the *Second Treatise* Locke establishes 'life, liberty, and estate' as rights that are temporally and logically prior to civil government. Where Robert Filmer and other defenders of absolutism hold property in biblical terms as a royal inheritance from Adam, to whom the Earth was given, Locke's argument sets off from the claim that everyone is a 'proprietor in his own person' and in the products of his labour.[18] 'I labour on X, therefore X is part of me', as Caffentzis puts it.[19] While the notion of self-ownership allows man to inscribe property in the natural commons, Locke further insists on a natural law to 'preserve God's creation', implying moral limits to appropriation.[20] A so-called 'spoilage limitation' restricts property to what can be used before it spoils, while a 'sufficiency limitation' means that one is dutybound to 'leave enough and as good' for others.[21] Only with the invention of money and men's mutual consent to put a value upon it are both limitations overcome so that man may 'fairly possess more land than he himself could use the product of'.[22] In other words, money's capacity to store value frees the subject from moral limits to appropriation of that with which he mixes his labour or, implicitly, frees him to sell his labour for a wage. Property ceases to encroach on anyone's natural rights from this moment since the universal consent conferred upon the value of money amounts to a universal consent to the 'disproportionate and unequal Possession of the Earth' it engenders.[23]

So far this is a relatively orthodox account of Locke's theory of property. The potency of Caffentzis's explanation, and the conception of money upon which it rests in particular, only truly becomes evident where it resolves some of the tensions and aporia that have plagued reception of the 'Second Treatise'. This is apparent if we take up the so-called 'religious turn' that has dominated Locke scholarship in recent decades. Taking Locke's Protestant belief as crucial to understanding his political philosophy, John Dunn, Quentin Skinner, Peter Laslett, James Tully and others have read the invention of money against the grain of MacPherson's influential framing of Locke as *the* philosopher of market society, in viewing it through a biblical lens that sees it as a fall from natural grace.[24] Contra MacPherson's view of Locke as erecting a capitalist economy as a natural state of affairs, in situating money as a wholly conventional phenomenon, scholars of the religious turn foreground the moral limits Locke places upon acquisition and in doing so, seek to rescue an egalitarian spirit from his work.

Drawing upon *Clipped Coins*, Onar Olus Ince has shown that this sort of theological interpretation offers little means to explain why Locke doesn't simply call for the eradication of money instead of invoking the state to manage its effects.[25] Equally, Ince argues, to view Locke as naturalising capitalist social relations as MacPherson has it, only works by awkwardly discarding the limits Locke ascribes to property. Implicit in the conventional left reading rests the assumption that Locke is not deeply invested in giving moral foundations to property. But if this were the case then he would have no reason, Ince continues, to insist upon the *right* to property even where 'disproportionate and unequal Possession of the Earth' occurs.[26]

The point here, drawn from Caffentzis, is that the tension between a natural and conventional view of money cannot be overcome since, for Locke, the very being of money oscillates between them. On one hand, Locke is explicit that the use of money is based on consent and thus, is not to be viewed as wholly natural, as MacPherson's interpretation suggests. Still, *pace* Ince, it is only insofar as the consent to recognise the value of money is understood by Locke to be a universal yet pre-political event that precedes the constitution of the commonwealth, can he morally defend accumulation without making the dubious claim that inequality is a religious commandment.[27] Money, it turns out, is neither wholly natural nor political and moreover, it is only on this basis that it can become universal.

Likewise, if we follow *Clipped Coins* to that moment in the 'state of nature' where men consent to the use of money, the outlines of a further moral economy central to Locke's political theory becomes apparent. On the one hand, man's chief moral obligation is 'the preservation of God's creation' such that the central purpose of labour and the appropriation it engenders is to 'improve [the Earth] for the benefit of life'.[28] On the other hand, Locke says 'land that is left wholly to nature, with no improvement through cultivation [. . .] is rightly called "waste"'.[29] Only given its enclosure through social relations founded upon money as a mechanism for preserving things that would otherwise perish and be wasted, is land improved.[30] Not only therefore, does private property trump common possession, it is redefined away from webs of local use-rights specific to individual manors, professions and communities to discrete units of abstract value.[31] Such a transformation thus poses a dual injunction against those not working for a wage and against land not being worked by wage labour; 'idleness' becomes viewed as a criminal disposition that fails to engage in 'improvement'.[32]

Money and Criminality

This brings us to the close relation discerned in *Clipped Coins* between money and criminality in Locke's political philosophy. As Koshka Duff argues, Locke's dual moral economy of improvement and waste was 'instrumental in delegitimating those uses of nature he finds undesirable, and criminalising the people engaged in them'.[33] Locke's notion of criminality implied a policy of enclosing the English commons since, it was widely held, if left unimproved the commons would generate an idle and disorderly mass while profits would be lost.[34] It further entailed support for the colonial enterprise since indigenous American failure to use money meant land was allowed to lie waste. Expropriations of land and trade made independent survival all but impossible insofar as they eradicated access to grazing, hunting and gathering along with attacks upon customary entitlements to workplace materials. In fact, so extensive was the criminalisation of subsistence beyond the wage in Locke's time that Silvia Federici has described life lived outside the capital relation as 'always one step away from the whip and the noose'.[35] In a similar vein, in a reference to the widespread use of capital punishment, Peter Linebaugh refers to the epoch as a 'thanatocracy'.[36] For, as Locke argues in the 'Second Treatise', while the end of government is the protection of 'life, liberty, and estate', he who transgresses against them might 'deserve death'.[37]

On one level, the relation between money and criminality is quite patently self-evident: if the imposition of money wages and prices was necessary to compel labour to be sold to capital, this in turn required the state to both control the creation of money and to impose it as a universal measure. But Caffentzis's argument extends further, not merely to underline money as the theoretical mechanism by which the whole of the Earth is viewed as potential profit, but as the device by which, to borrow a turn of phrase from Duff once more, 'subsistence beyond the wage is excluded from the body politic'.[38]

At this point the intimate relationship between Locke's ontology of money and his conception of criminality ought to be apparent. Ultimately, for Caffentzis, it hinges upon the peculiar temporality of money. For while money's relative permanence overcomes the moral limitations to appropriation in the state of nature, it only does so, as Caffentzis maintains, by introducing a hiatus between the acts of appropriation and consumption. Accordingly, if money preserves property and makes unlimited accumulation possible, it also bears the corollary of an insecure temporal space characterised by 'fears and continual dangers' and populated by criminals.[39] To begin with, the point here merely revisits money's ambiguous state of being between nature and convention. Metal content exerts a certain 'power of objectivity', yet unlike any other substance direct knowledge of the real essence of money is unattainable. Accordingly, though it affords a certain permanence to property, money nonetheless generates a new temporal site of 'dangers' and uncertainty that, in turn, demands exiting the state of nature to form a civil compact.

In this context Caffentzis presents us with a further thesis regarding the relation between money and criminality that begs further unpacking. As we have seen, the state's function is to preserve money from criminality or, to use Locke's expression: the 'corruption and viciousness of degenerate men'.[40] While the sources of such degeneracy are only ever fleetingly referenced in the 'Second Treatise', by referring us to the *Essay on Human Understanding*, Caffentzis gleans an account of crime that coheres quite seamlessly with Locke's ontology of money. For in that text we discover that crime results from a temporally bounded rationality which leads the subject to fail to defer the satisfaction of his pleasure and thus, to transgression of natural law. As Locke puts it, '[f]or though he will be always determined by that which is judged good by his understanding, yet it excuses him not; because a too hasty judgement of his own making, he has imposed on himself wrong measures of good and evil'.[41] Money, it would appear on this reading, stimulates the 'evil' of easy gratification. If in the pre-monetary state of nature the satisfaction of pleasures is immediate, once a money economy generates a moral law of endless improvement then crime amounts to a failure to live according to the temporal discipline of the logic of property and accumulation.

This brings us back to the question of the state. For on this account it is only upon the mutual consent to money, along with the scarcity and deferral of pleasure it entails, that it becomes necessary to exit the insecurity of the state of nature to form a civil compact. Its ultimately in this sense that the account of the state presupposes criminality, as Locke's widely cited formulation implies: '[t]he great chief end therefore, of men's uniting into commonwealths, and putting themselves under governments, is the *preservation of their property*'.[42]

Returning to the debate with Lowndes, its apparent that Locke's defence of a metallic money standard, along with his desire to tackle counterfeiters and clippers, rests with the premise that money generates the social contract in the first place.[43] Of course this theory of the state, anchored upon property grounded in individual labour, obfuscates the history of legally constituted violence of theft and punishment.[44]

Subjectivity and Property

The peculiar temporality ascribed by Locke to the money-form does more than condition criminal subjectivity, by Caffentzis's account. As it turns out, Caffenztis argues, the abstract conception of property that appears in the 'Second Treatise' already presupposes a metaphysical notion of personhood and identity. This is insofar as the indefinite circulation of commodities presupposes continuity in the identity of their owners. That is, in order for what is mine today to be mine tomorrow 'I' must continue to be the same person; I must be the 'proprietor of my own person', as Caffentzis ventriloquises.[45] The contention here insinuates a formal affinity between the notion of self-ownership reflected in Locke's notion of 'property in the person' grounding the 'Second Treatise' and the account of memory in chapter 2 of *An Essay on Human Understanding*. The latter text presents memory as acts of appropriation of past action by present consciousness. Identity, it would seem, consists in the continuity of a claim to ownership of one's self or, at least, this appears to be what Locke has in mind: 'consciousness always accompanies thinking and it is that which makes everyone to be what he calls self [...] and as far as this consciousness can be extended backwards to any past action or thought, so far reaches the identity of that person'.[46]

Caffentzis sees the intersection of subjectivity and property further refracted through Locke's theory of language. There Locke ascribes words the function of transporting ideas from a private self so they may be 're-privatised' by an interlocutor or preserved for a future self against oblivion.[47] In this light, the conclusion drawn by Caffentzis rests with the notion that Locke in fact transforms the Cartesian deduction of the self into a deduction for the creation of property in the self along with private property more broadly: *cogito ergo habo*, as Caffentzis puts it.[48]

This is a bold claim, for conceiving the subject as a form of self-ownership in this way entails a reformulation of the conventional history of modern philosophy: the Cartesian philosophy of consciousness is recast by Locke's notion of self-appropriation into a conception of identity persisting across time. Nevertheless, Caffentzis is not entirely isolated in conveying such an argument. Indeed, he anticipates Étienne Balibar's study of the English philosopher a decade later. Not unlike the assertions in *Clipped Coins*, Balibar discerns the constitution of identity in Locke's philosophy as an act of self-appropriation. On his reading, this is mobilised through a linguistic contradiction whereby the self divides its unity in the process of its self-naming. 'I speak about myself', Balibar says, 'therefore about my "self"'.[49] Like Caffentzis then, Balibar also detects an unstable equivocation underlying the Lockean account of subjectivity; one that lies between the categories of identity and property. There exists an 'anthropological doublet' between consciousness and language grounded upon an unstable relation between 'being' and 'having', between the 'self' and the 'own'.[50]

While the recognition of the intersection of personhood and possession in Locke's philosophy goes back as far as MacPherson's designation of Hobbes and Locke as philosophers of 'possessive individualism', Balibar argues that the tendency among historians of political thought has been to view property as an external condition of, or barrier to, subjective freedom.[51] Not only is this to subordinate anthropology to positive law, it obscures the way identity itself becomes a form of property in Locke's philosophy.[52] Balibar's contention here aligns closely with Caffentzis's interpretation. For where the labour theory of property 'projects the privateness of the person into the ontological transformation of the earth', as Caffentzis puts it, property and freedom are of the same ontological order.[53] Moreover, just as MacPherson understands property as external to subjectivity, so too does he assess its function too narrowly, as a mere limit upon the state rather than the very condition of its power. This in turn belies a narrow view where capitalism is concerned; one centred upon individual wealth rather than the indefinite accumulation of capital implied by Locke's theories of property and money. Contra MacPherson, Caffentzis thus holds it to be more apt to describe Locke's philosophy as a 'possessive universalism', denoting the generalisation of the commodity form and the global domination of market principles Locke has in mind, rather than the 'petit bourgeois shopkeeper' that he discerns as the central figure in MacPherson's narrative.[54]

This argument for what I have called a formal affinity between subject and property can be made to stand in as a tangible philosophical manifestation for a broader account of the historical co-emergence of abstract conceptions of property and of abstract will. For while common law systems tend to apprehend contractual relations as occurring between concrete persons, this acts as a barrier to systems of exchange.[55] To follow a line of argument put down by Evgeny Pashukanis, the indefinite circulation of commodities becomes possible only where an abstract 'free' will – a 'purely social function' – is established through the continual transfer of rights in the market.[56] It is through this process that the bearers of these rights come to appear as independent and substitutable: they become abstracted from any concrete bond. In capitalism therefore, as Marx avers, 'private property has become the subject of will', the will survives only as 'the predicate of property'.[57] Nowhere are these intersections clearer perhaps, than in Locke's theory of property.

Commodity and Concept

This account of the social function of property brings Caffentzis's study of Locke into dialogue with other assessments of him as bourgeois partisan, most notably, the work of Neal Wood and Ellen Meiksins Wood. Ellen Wood is particularly significant in this regard insofar as, in a number of books, she has contested dominant currents of thought in political theory that postulate the relative autonomy of Locke's discursive context from the categories of capitalism. Partly under the sway of hermeneutic methods imported from continental philosophy, Anglo-American scholarship – under the guise of the 'Cambridge School' especially – has sought to isolate Locke's work from the forces of the commodity form by situating his oeuvre within the historical horizons of the Grotian tradition of natural law.[58] While Ellen Wood has convincingly eschewed such claims along with the deeply atomised view of history they entail, Neal Wood's studies of Locke, in reading the bourgeois concepts plainly perceptible in the 'Second Treatise' back into the *Essay on Human Understanding*, complement the assessment offered in *Clipped Coins* and so deserve further scrutiny.

Seeking to situate Locke's political theory as an articulation of the institutional architecture necessary for the cultural renewal proposed by his epistemology, Neal Wood locates the peculiarly bourgeois character of his philosophy of knowledge across four distinct themes: a Baconian natural history of the psyche that implies a commitment to social reform; a celebration of independent reason against conformity; a self-directed industrious subject; and empiricism as a meritocratic form of philosophy where intellectual or moral inequality is a result of circumstance.[59] In discerning the work of bourgeois ideology at the level of Locke's concepts themselves, Wood's theoretical enterprise is not at odds with Caffentzis's. But while Wood perhaps risks the reductionism that accompanies a mostly linear causative relation between politics and philosophy, the 'deep coherence' between philosophy and money discerned in *Clipped Coins* and elsewhere is less reducible to a determinist logic.[60]

In this regard, it is instructive to examine more closely the intersections identified by Caffenztis between Locke's famous doctrine of primary and secondary qualities and his ontology of money. As is well known, in the *Essay* Locke gives ontological primacy to what he takes to be the objectivity of the 'primary' qualities of substances (such as solidity, extension, motion) over 'secondary' qualities (such as colour, taste or heat) since the latter promise to be explained on the basis of the former. That is, while absolute knowledge of the essence of natural substances is unattainable, it is nonetheless possible to acquire knowledge on the basis of experience and observation.[61] Even if human organs do not directly observe bodily motion or structure, sensory ideas are still generated by a determinate corpuscular world. In short, even if human knowledge is by definition incomplete, nature provides it with objective limits.

It's possible to assert here, along with Neal Wood, that in freeing knowledge from innate ideas by grounding it in sensory experience, Locke liberates it from the fetters of superstition.[62] Moreover, one might further speculate that the social force of the distinction between primary and secondary qualities reflect a modern capitalist experience of nature as an abstract object of production, whereby labour and land are increasingly reduced to the qualities of number, weight, and measure in order to be exploited and exchanged. However, in *Clipped Coins* the argument goes further, to locate a formal affinity between the philosophy of primary and secondary qualities and capital at the level of the form of value itself. It is here that the intimate connection between concept and commodity in Locke's work becomes especially apparent. For if the value of money is to be universally established as Locke wants, it cannot be wholly embodied in the sensuous qualities of the commodity, nor in the primary qualities of precious metals. As a measure of value, money is conventional; its existence hinges upon consent. Yet, as we have seen, the preservation of value across time and space demands its stability. Accordingly, what Caffentzis refers to as the 'bond between convention and nature' represented by metallic money amounts to a unique synthesis of primary and secondary qualities.[63]

The point becomes even clearer when we see how this view of money further coheres with Locke's taxonomy of ideas. Where ideas of substances are concerned words are said to merely 'tag' an already coalesced idea and so are not subject to whim. Since substances are discovered and not invented, their names are 'passive and external'.[64] Conversely, insofar as they lack a natural external standard, abstractions are not confronted by reality, and thus are said to bear an inherent indeterminacy. There is a continuity discernible here between Locke's ontology of money and a 'mercantilist' conception of language where words give stability to ideas so they may be smoothly exchanged.[65] As Caffentzis suggests, while for Locke a coin signifies both the particular idea that is produced upon its appearance *and* the abstract quality of gold or silver it represents, it is only the corpuscular metallic nature of the coin that assures its bearer that the abstract idea of value will have a continuous objectivity in the world, and therefore, preserve property through money's 'power of objectivity'.[66]

Conceived as marking a particular intersection of the commodity and the concept, Caffentzis's study is thus not restricted to detecting the bourgeois desire motivating his philosophy as other historical materialist accounts have sought to demonstrate, but rather to show how 'the abstractions to which capital submits social life', to employ Alberto Toscano's formulation, are uncovered at the level of the history of ideas.[67] What is more, this insinuates the potential for the arguments discussed above to offer a wider contribution to discussions, often revolving around the work of German philosopher Alfred Sohn-Rethel, on the material sources of mental abstraction. Not unlike Caffentzis to some degree, Sohn-Rethel's theoretical venture centres upon the attempt to locate the conditions of cognition in the exchange of commodities and so, merits a brief detour through his argument in order to further glean the significance of Caffentzis's contribution.

Money and Abstraction

Sohn-Rethel's philosophical project begins with the premise that posing an equivalence between two different objects necessarily involves abstracting from their physical qualities. This entails what he calls a 'real abstraction', for while the subject of exchange thinks of the qualitative properties of the object, the practice of exchange takes place in terms of the form of the exchange value of the object. In other words, abstraction in the mind is preceded by abstraction in practice.[68] Drawing on this basic premise, Sohn-Rethel seeks to trace the development of conceptual knowledge from antiquity through the medieval period to the rise of merchant capital and finally, to the development of industrial capital. Of course, the crucial juncture in this narrative occurs with the emergence of capitalism, since here the separation of manual from mental labour becomes stark. Sohn-Rethel's contention is that the epistemic project of modern science and philosophy is inseparable from capital's need to posit a mental labour autonomous from manual labour since it permits the imposition of abstract knowledge over labour and so, control by automation over artisanry.[69] In this expansive reading, the dualism of mind and world inaugurated by Descartes and later presented as a transcendental necessity by Kant reflects a dualism inherent in a society wherein social control is grounded upon a knowledge of nature based in intuition and whose sources are non-sensuous.[70]

Sohn-Rethel is widely regarded as contributing to a truly historical materialist account of conceptual abstraction insofar as he locates the sources of the latter in the practices of class societies. Yet in taking the consumer's relation to the product as the source of abstraction, it is argued he obscures what Marx views as the specific basis of abstraction in capitalism, namely, the commodity form of abstract labour. As both Anselm Jappe and Moishe Postone have suggested, Sohn-Rethel seems to presume capitalism to be defined only by the sphere of exchange, circulation and distribution of commodities, while labour in production is seen as a neutral activity not alienated by its commodification.[71] Moreover, given the priority he accords to abstraction in exchange rather than in labour, Sohn-Rethel's historical narrative centres upon the gradual expansion of exchange from Ancient Greece to modern capitalism, culminating with Galileo's concept of inertial motion as the founding gesture of a truly capitalist form of knowledge no longer derived from nature but deduced from abstractions that are themselves derived from the 'pattern of motion contained in the real abstraction of commodity exchange'.[72] This is an account that cannot but fail to provide any meaningful distinction between a situation of widespread commodity production and a capitalist society where social reproduction is dependent upon the market.

Abjuring the sort of historical narrative espoused by Sohn-Rethel, the scope of Caffentzis's study of Locke does not extend to setting out the sources of mental abstraction as such. At stake is not merely a question of analytic scope but also a methodological proposition. Or, at least, this seems to be the case, where a more detailed historical perspective suggests a crucial transformation in early modernity in the philosophical understanding of thought from a form of activity to a form of labour.[73] That is, where Sohn-Rethel sees a continuous division of mental and manual labour running from Ancient Greece to eighteenth century Europe and culminating in industrial capital's taking direct control of the labour process, Caffentzis insists that only with Locke is the idea conceived as property or chattel and thus, it is included in the ontological order of the products of labour.[74] For Plato, for instance, thought consists in contemplation of and participation in ideal forms; its products could not be alienated. Similarly, if for Aristotle thought is distinct from labour, this is so to the extent that labour has a telos while thought is an end in itself.[75] In either case, an unequivocal gulf in the being of master and slave classes, between thought and labour, excluded any discourse between absolutely distinct ontological orders. Despite subscribing to Sohn-Rethel's (and indeed, Federici's) view of Descartes as inaugurating a separation of mind and world as a reflection of capital's view of the world as a mechanism to be mastered, Caffentzis indexes the modern rupture with the Platonic separation of knowledge and property to Locke since it is only with the latter that the equation of subjectivity with property extends to the level of thought itself.[76]

This much becomes apparent if we take Locke's philosophical enterprise as centred upon a critique of the notion of innate abstract ideas, for it appears particularly clearly from this perspective as a project, as Caffentzis suggests, grounded upon a conception of knowledge as effort and of ideas as the objects of labour. As a matter of fact, Locke views the exercise of mental labour as a moral compulsion; asserting in the *Essay* that, 'God having fitted men with faculties and means to discover, receive and retain truths, according as they are employed'.[77] The activity of thought, it would seem, coheres perfectly with the labour theory of property.[78] That is, while Locke holds the mind as passive in the reception of simple ideas, he nevertheless obliges it to act upon them not unlike the requirement to labour upon the commons in order to transform it into private property. What Locke calls the 'workmanship of the understanding' therefore, seems to amount to a sort of 'improvement' in the realm of ideas.[79] It is thus that thought becomes a form of appropriation and its products come to be potential commodities. *Cogito ergo habo* indeed.

I have suggested, however, that given the constraints Caffentzis places upon the scope of a given history of thought, this accounting of Locke's philosophy of money is not the last word, nor does it account once and for all for philosophy's relation to the commodity. In this light, Locke's philosophy is read as an attempt to assert the priority of capital over the state and the imposition of a universal form of value upon labour. Locke's project thus differs from Berkeley's attempt to monetise the everyday life of a resistive peasantry or Hume's desire to break the Highlanders' gift economy. We might discern echoes in these projects of Keynesian, neoliberal monetary policy or whatever might supersede it, but all in all, the point is that, if we understand money as a form of command, this implies that where the philosophy of money is involved so too are the coordinates of struggle. George Caffentzis has given us a method for mapping their conceptual history and its reverberations in the present.

Notes

1. I owe a debt of gratitude to Jonathan Martineau, Koshka Duff, and Nicholas Beuret. I'm especially grateful to Bue Rubner Hansen along with the editors for comments on earlier drafts of this essay.

2. C. George Caffentzis, *Clipped Coins, Abused Words, and Civil Government: John Locke's Philosophy of Money* (New York: Autonomedia 1989), p. 50.

3. Georg Simmel, *The Philosophy of Money*, translated by Tom Bottommore and David Frisby (London & New York: Routledge, 1978); George Caffenztis, 'Locke, Berkeley and Hume as Philosophers of Money', in Silvia Parigi (ed.) *George Berkeley: Religion and Science in the Age of Enlightenment* (London and New York: Springer, 2010), p. 62.

4. Alfred Sohn-Rethel, *Intellectual and Manual Labour: A Critique of Epistemology* (London: Macmillan Press, 1978).

5. Caffentzis, 'Locke, Berkely and Hume as Philosophers of Money', p. 62.

6. For a longer account of money as command see Harry Cleaver, 'The Subversion of Money-As-Command in the Current Crisis', in Werner Bonefeld and John Holloway (eds) *Global Capital, National State and the Politics of Money* (London: Palgrave MacMillan, 1996).

7. George Caffentzis, *John Locke: Philosopher of Primitive Accumulation* (Bristol: Bristol Radical History Group, 2008); C. George Caffentzis, *Exciting the Industry of Mankind: George Berkeley's Philosophy of Money* (London & Dordrecht: Kluwer, 2000), p. 118.

8. C. George Caffentzis, 'Hume, Money, & Civilization: or, Why Was Hume a Metallist?' *Hume Studies*, 27(2) November 2001, pp. 301–35; C. George Caffentzis, 'Civilizing the Highlands: Hume, Money and the Annexing Act', *Historical Reflections/Réflections Historiques*, 31(1), 2005, pp. 169–94.

9. George C. Caffentzis, 'On the Scottish Origin of "Civilization"', in Silvia Federici (ed.) *Enduring Western Civilisation: the Construction of the Concept of Western Civilisation and its Others* (Westport & London: Praeger, 1995), pp. 13–36.

10. C.B. MacPherson, *The Political Theory of Possessive Individualism: Hobbes to Locke* (Oxford: Oxford University Press, 2011).

11. The Locke literature has only very recently begun to focus on this debate in earnest. See for instance Daniel Carey, 'Locke's Species: Money and Philosophy in the 1690s', *Annals of Science*, 70(3), 2013, pp. 357–80; Douglas Casson, 'John Locke, Clipped Coins, and the Unstable Currency of Reason', *Ethica & Politica*, XVIII, 2016, 2, pp. 153–80; Patrick Kelly, "Monkey' Business: Locke's 'College' Correspondence and the Adoption of the Plan for the Great Recoinage of 1696', *Locke Studies*, 9, 2009, pp. 139–65. Rather outrageously, this literature rarely cites Caffenztis's pioneering work, with David McNally as a rare exception. See David McNally, 'The Blood of the Commonwealth: War, the State, and the Making of World Money', *Historical Materialism*, 22(2), pp. 3–32.

12. See John Locke, *Locke on Money*, P.H. Kelly (ed.) (Oxford: Clarendon Press, 1991).

13. On this point see David McNally, 'The Blood of the Commonwealth'.

14. Caffentzis, *Clipped Coins*, p. 28.

15. Caffentzis, *Exciting the Industry of Mankind*, p. 186.

16. McNally, 'The Blood of the Commonwealth', p. 20.

17. see John Locke, *Two Treatises of Government*, Peter Laslett (ed.) (Cambridge: Cambridge University Press, 1988).

18. John Locke, 'Second Treatise on Government', Sections 27, 44.

19. Caffentzis, John Locke: Philosopher of Primitive Accumulation, p. 3.

20. John Locke, 'Second Treatise', Section 6.

21. John Locke, 'Second Treatise', Sections 31, 34.

22. John Locke, 'Second Treatise', Section 50.

23. John Locke, 'Second Treatise', Section 50.
24. See John Dunn, *The Political Thought of John Locke* (Cambridge: Cambridge University Press, 1969); Quentin Skinner, *Liberty Before Liberalism* (Cambridge: Cambridge University Press, 1998); James Tully, *A Discourse on Property: John Locke and His Adversaries* (Cambridge: Cambridge University Press, 1980); Peter Laslett, 'Introduction', *Two Treatises of Government*.
25. Onur Ulas Ince, 'Enclosing in God's Name, Accumulation for Mankind: Money, Morality, and Accumulation in John Locke's Theory of Property', *Review of Politics*, vol. 73, 2011, pp. 29–54.
26. John Locke, 'Second Treatise', Section 50; Onur Ulas Ince, 'Enclosing in God's Name'.
27. Onur Ulas Ince, 'Enclosing in God's Name'.
28. John Locke, 'Second Treatise', Section 32.
29. John Locke, 'Second Treatise', Section 42.
30. I draw here on a series of studies of the relationship between accumulation and the concept of waste in Locke. See in particular Onur Ulas Ince, 'Enclosing in God's Name'; Mark Neocleous, 'War on Waste: Law, Original Accumulation and the Violence of Capital', *Science and Society*, 75(4), 2011, pp. 506–28; Jesse Goldstein, 'Terra Economica: Waste and the Production of Nature', *Antipode*, 54(2), 2013, pp. 357–75; Ellen Meiksins Wood, *The Origins of Capitalism: A Longer View* (London: Verso, 2002); Ellen Meiksins Wood, *Liberty and Property: A Social History of Western Political Thought from the Renaissance to Enlightenment* (London: Verso, 2012).
31. See Mark Neocleous, 'War On Waste'; Jesse Goldstein, 'Terra Economia'.
32. See Koshka Duff, The Criminal is Political: Real Existing Liberalism and the Construction of the Criminal. PhD dissertation, University of Sussex, December 2017.
33. Koshka Duff, The Criminal is Political, p. 36.
34. Mark Neocleous, 'War on Waste', pp. 510–12; Ellen Meiksins Wood, *The Origins of Capitalism*, p. 276; Jesse Goldstein, 'Terra Economia'.
35. Silvia Federici, *Caliban and the Witch: The Body and Primitive Accumulation* (New York: Autonomedia, 2004), p. 85.
36. Peter Linebaugh, *The London Hanged: Crime and Civil Society in the Eighteenth Century* (2nd edn) (London: Verso, 2006).
37. John Locke, *Second Treatise*, Section 182, Locke writes: 'for though I may kill a thief that sets on me in the highway, yet I may not (which seems less) take away his money, and let him go: this would be robbery on my side'. The protection of property seems to trump human life here.
38. Koshka Duff, The Criminal is Political, p. 16.
39. John Locke, 'Second Treatise', Section 123; Caffentzis, *Clipped Coins*, pp. 69–72.
40. John Locke, 'Second Treatise', Section 128.
41. John Locke, *An Essay on Human Understanding*, P.H. Nidditch (ed.) (Oxford: Clarendon Press, 1979), Book II, Chapter XXI, Section 56.
42. John Locke, 'Second Treatise', Section 124 (emphasis added).
43. Caffentzis, *Clipped Coins*, p. 71.
44. The state must, by definition, be estranged and abstracted from society where a regime of work and property exists since such a society can have no common interest except, as Lucio Colletti writes in a discussion of the young Marx's critique of the liberal state, 'by dissociation from all contending interests'. This is even though, as Colletti notes, the state is nothing but a reflection of those very

interests. See Lucio Coletti, 'Introduction', *Karl Marx: Early Writings*, translated by Rodney Livingstone and Gregory Benton (London: Penguin, 1975), p. 35.

45. Caffentzis, *Clipped Coins*, p. 101.
46. John Locke, *An Essay on Human Understanding*, Book II, Chapter XXVII, Section 9. Quoted in Caffentzis, *Clipped Coins*, p. 53.
47. Caffentzis, *Clipped Coins*, p. 101.
48. Caffentzis, *John Locke*, p. 4; Caffentzis, *Clipped Coins*, p. 52.
49. Étienne Balibar, 'My Self and My Own: One and the Same?' in B. Mauer and G. Schwab (eds) *Accelerating Possession: Global Futures of Property and Personhood* (New York: Columbia University Press, 2006), p. 322.
50. See Balibar, 'My Self and My Own'; Étienne Balibar, *Identity and Difference: John Locke and the Invention of Consciousness* (London: Verso, 2013), pp. 23, 32. Balibar seems to reject the standard reading of Locke that equates his conceptions of consciousness and memory, a kind of empirical unity persistent across time and instead understands consciousness in Locke as a 'proto-transcendental' conception of consciousness as immanent to the structure of mind. In doing so, Balibar echoes Caffentzis in positing a reciprocity between the theory of consciousness and theory of property inherent to Locke's philosophy. While there are some important tensions between Balibar's and Caffentzis' readings, this falls outside the scope of this chapter.
51. C.B. MacPherson, The Political Theory of Possessive Individualism; Balibar, *Identity and Difference*, p. 72.
52. Balibar, *Identity and Difference*, p. 72; Stella Sanford 'The Incomplete Locke: Balibar, Locke and the Philosophy of the Subject' in Étienne Balibar, *Identity and Difference*, pp. xi-xlvi.
53. Caffentzis, *Clipped Coins*, p. 50.
54. Caffentzis, *Clipped Coins*, p. 118.
55. Caffentzis, 'On the Scottish Origin of "Civilization"'.
56. Evgeny Pashukanis, *General Theory of Law and Marxism*, translated by Dragan Milovanovic (New Brunswick & London: Transaction Publishers, 1978), pp. 115, 112, 127.
57. Karl Marx, 'Contribution to the Critique of Hegel's 'Philosophy of Right" in *Karl Marx: Early Writings*, p. 175. Marx makes an analogous claim in *Capital*, Vol. 1 where he argues that in order for commodities to be exchanged 'their guardians must place themselves in relation to one another as persons whose will resides in those objects, and must behave in such a way that each does not appropriate the commodity of the other, and alienate his own, except through an act to which both parties consent. The guardians must therefore recognise each other as owners of property'. Karl Marx, *Capital: A Critique of Political Economy, Volume 1*, translated by Ben Fowkes (London: Penguin, 1976), p. 178.
58. See Ellen Meiksins Wood, *Citizens and Lords: A Social History of Western Political Thought From Antiquity to the Middle Ages* (London: Verso, 2008), pp. 1–27. I owe the methodological insight in part to Jonathan Martineau, 'Ellen M. Wood and the Social History of Political Theory', paper delivered to Historical Materialism Conference, London, November 2016.
59. Neal Wood, *The Politics of John Locke's Philosophy: A Study of An Essay Concerning Human Understanding* (Berkeley: University of California Press, 1983), pp. 180–1.
60. The phrase 'deep coherence' is used by Caffentzis to refer to the relation of philosophy and money in Berkeley's work but it applies equally to his reading of

Locke. See Caffentzis, *Exciting the Industry of Mankind*, p. 3. Stella Stanford makes an analogous claim with regards to Wood's work in 'The Incomplete Locke: Balibar, Locke and the Philosophy of the Subject' in Étienne Balibar, *Identity and Difference*, pp. xi–xlvi.

61. Caffentzis, *Clipped Coins*, p. 109.
62. Neal Wood, *The Politics of John Locke's Philosophy*; Joanne Faulkner, 'Innocents and Oracles: The Child as a Figure of Knowledge and Critique in the Middle-Class Imagination', *Critical Horizons*, (3)2, pp. 323–46.
63. Caffentzis, *Clipped Coins*, p. 116.
64. Caffentzis, *Clipped Coins*, p. 81.
65. Caffentzis, *Exciting the Industry of Mankind*, p. 193.
66. Caffentzis, *Exciting the Industry of Mankind*, p. 187; Caffentzis, *Clipped Coins*, p. 110; Caffentzis, 'Locke, Berkeley and Hume as Philosophers of Money', pp. 64–5.
67. Alberto Toscano, 'The Open Secret of Real Abstraction', *Rethinking Marxism*, 20(2), pp. 273–87.
68. Alfred Sohn-Rethel, *Intellectual and Manual Labour: A Critique of Epistemology* (London: Macmillan, 1978), pp. 28–9.
69. Sohn-Rethel, *Intellectual and Manual Labour*, pp. 113, 122, 141, 179–80.
70. Sohn-Rethel, *Intellectual and Manual Labour*, pp. 77–8 and passim. The claims made here are largely reproduced from Paul Rekret and Simon Choat, 'From Political Topographies to Political Logics: Post-Marxism and Historicity', *Constellations*, 23(2), June 2016, pp. 281–91. It deserves mentioning that Sohn-Rethel's claim here is echoed by Silvia Federici who has suggested understanding the Cartesian institution of an ontological division between the mental and the physical domains along with the mechanical conception of the body it implies, in terms of the suppression of pre-capitalist social relations. From this perspective the central accomplishment of the age of reason entailed posing the body as intelligible and thus, as an object that could be subordinated to uniform and predictable modes of behaviour. See *Caliban and the Witch*, pp. 138–55.
71. Anselme Jappe, 'Sohn-Rethel and the Origin of 'Real Abstraction': A Critique of Production or a Critique of Circulation?' *Historical Materialism*, 21(1), pp. 3–14; Moishe Postone, *Time, Labour and Social Domination: A Reinterpretation of Marx's Critical Theory*, pp. 177–8, p. 156; n. 90.
72. Sohn-Rethel, *Intellectual and Manual Labour*, p. 128.
73. George Caffentzis, 'Marx, Turing Machines and the Labor of Thought', *In Letters of Blood and Fire: Work, Machines and the Crisis of Capitalism* (Oakland & Brooklyn: PM Press, 2013), p. 165.
74. Caffentzis, 'Marx, Turing Machines and the Labor of Thought', p. 192.
75. Caffentzis, 'Marx, Turing Machines and the Labor of Thought', p. 168.
76. Sohn-Rethel, *Intellectual and Manual Labour*, p. 123; Silvia Federici, *Caliban and the Witch*, pp. 138–55; Caffentzis, 'Marx, Turing Machines and the Labor of Thought', p. 167.
77. John Locke, *Essay*, Book I, Chapter IV, Section 22.
78. Caffentzis, *Exciting the Industry of Mankind*, p. 199.
79. Locke, *Essay*, Book III, Chapter XIII, Section 13.

6

Thomas Spence's Freedom Coins

Peter Linebaugh

'Don't take any wooden nickels', witty uncles used to instruct the children, testing the filthy lucre between their teeth. Next to stones, metal coins have been the historian's most perdurable source of knowledge. Early in the historian's apprenticeship one learns of the trade routes along the Volga, of Teodor Mommsen and the *Corpus Inscriptionum Latinarum* with its 16 volumes of Roman history, of Henri Pirenne's thesis, 'Charlemagne, without Muhammad, would be inconceivable'. All depended on the evidence of coins.

The Lincoln penny is so common as to be a nuisance, even in the penny jar. Perhaps the most valued of all US presidents, now on the coin of littlest value. Washington's on the quarter. The Roosevelt dime is proverbially thin. Then the Indian head nickel signifying the appropriation of the native Americans. The Sacagawea dollar coin never took hold, too much like the quarter in size and weight. Still, it signified more conquest. All the quiz questions – who's on the dollar bill, the 5-dollar bill, the 20, the hundred? – are answered, generally, with presidents. 'Have an Indian killer', my Wobbly friend from Chicago used to say as he handed a 20 over to the waitress. What will he say when Harriet Tubman replaces Andrew Jackson on the 20-dollar note – 'welcome to the underground'?

So, one purpose of coin design is the assertion of sovereignty. 'Coining', Marx wrote, 'is the business of the State'.[1] The second goal in coin design is singularity. Its image, its material, its technique must be inimitable or able to confound the skilled counterfeiter. Bank notes, exchequer bills, many paper instruments performed monetary functions in the eighteenth century. And with each new instrument came possibilities of forgery, and with these possibilities came new laws, and with the new laws, death. Coins signified the power of the state and the geographies of commerce. George Caffentzis wrote, 'The accumulation process and the state are preconditioned on the monetary system; should it breakdown so will they. Mistakes with money are fatal'.[2] With John Locke, the English philosopher of the seventeenth century, George Caffentzis taught us that money and the death penalty go together in the logic of property and sovereignty. With George Berkeley, the Irish philosopher of the eighteenth century, George Caffentzis taught us that money goes with motion and the proletariat as the value-creating social class.

Recently, it has been proposed to see money as art. J.S.G. Boggs was the artist famous for his money designs. The artist mastered the intricacy of imagery, design, materials and technique. Not quite facsimiles, they were works of art rather than currency. He would exchange them for other goods and ask for a receipt which he would then sell, leaving it to the buyer to track down the person who had accepted the work of art in a barter exchange. He calls them performances not transactions. His mother's name – Marlene Dietrich Hildebrandt – already suggested some artistry; she joined a carnival as 'Margo, Queen of the Jungle'. His first English pound note exhibited in 1986 at the ICA was called, imitating the pinched voice of the English very-upper class, *Pined Newt*.[3] The subject invites wit, paradox, and many subconscious spillings, surreal uproar and supernatural stupidities. 'In God We Trust' was added to American currency only after it went off the gold standard, the monotheistic supplanting the metallic. Shakespeare's *Timon of Athens* put its paradoxical powers this way:

> Gold, yellow, glittering, precious gold!
> Thus much of this will make black white; foul fair;
> Wrong right; base noble; old young, coward valiant.

Shakespeare forgot to add 'life death'. The gallows is never far. Seeking subsistence, not art, poor James Wooldridge, an anvil maker, actually did forge a pound note and hanged for it in January 1801.

Interpretations based on numismatics and antiquarian researches are easily available; my comments depend upon them.[4] One might explore the violence specific to money in the *Proceedings at the Old Bailey* which are available online. Coining, forgery and counterfeiting offences became numerous. Here's how a typical indictment reads.

> James Royer, James Smith, and Edward Ivory were indicted for that they, not having the fear of God before their eyes, but being moved and seduced by the instigation of the Devil, on the 14th of September last [1790], at the parish of St. Luke, one piece of base coin resembling the current coin of this kingdom, called a six-pence, falsely, deceitfully, feloniously, and traitorously did colour, with materials producing the colour of silver.

They were sentenced to death.[5]

Caffentzis explained that in the eighteenth century tickets, counters, tokens, tallies and marks were not all the same, and each provided a different monetary function.[6] Diogenes, the slave, went to Athens in order to debase the coinage leaving it to the sages of subsequent centuries to puzzle out why. Thomas Spence (1750–1814), the radical and advocate of common land, did not so much debase as deface the coinage.[7] Alan Judd has found and described these altered coins.[8] These were used to counter mark the coin of the realm, largely halfpennies and farthings (a quarter of a penny) which carried an image of the monarch. Spence created a number of stamps which, when pressed upon the coin, permanently marked them. This challenged his ability to compress his message into a word or two. He did this either with positive terms, such as

LAND
LIBERTY
PLENTY
FAT BAIRNS
FULL BELLIES

reaching an apex of positivity with

OURS.

Or, he would countermark with negative terms such as

YOU FOOLS
STARVATION
LANDLORDS
YOU ROGUES

or in pure, terse negation,

NO.

To the extent that this coin circulated Saturday night at the public house when wages were paid over beer and trouble, or at the shop counter where the maidservant sought to buy a pretty ribbon, or at the market stall where the countryman brought fruits and veg, to the same extent basic challenges were conveyed to the foundations of the society. The wage is irrational inasmuch as it conceals the production of surplus-value. Marx regarded this insight as his original contribution to political economy, or we should say, his contribution to economics, rather than to political economy, because from the standpoint of the political it was not so much irrational as simply oppressive. Spence made coins to turn the image of the political world upside down – people replaced kings.

The crisis of the 1790s arose from the revolt of the slaves in San Domingue; it arose from the opposition to conquest in the subcontinent of India; it arose from the London 'mob'; it arose from the fast-developing United Irishmen; it arose from the commoners who were being fenced, hedged and enclosed from their land; and it arose from the regime in north America facing slave revolt and Indian warfare. The crisis took a monetary form with the suspension of gold payments on banknotes that occurred early in 1797, just a few months before the mutinies in ships of the Royal Navy. Payment to sailors was one of the largest single demands on currency and money of the English state. The situation seemed unprecedented. The Bank of England was forced to issue paper notes in lieu of hard, metallic cash. This was one part of the monetary crisis. The other part of it was the severe shortage of copper coin for wage payments and for the retail business of the nation of shop-keepers, as Adam Smith called it in *The Wealth of Nations*. All kinds of people produced tokens to enable local exchanges, among them the vegetarian, communist and spelling reformer, Thomas Spence.

The 1790s began the last phase of European craft labour. It was skilled, often hand work, digitally complex and domestic. Thomas Spence was such a craftsperson, a 'Geordie' from Newcastle-on-Tyne, the major port for the export of coal to London, the largest market for coal. Here is one of Spence's coins, called 'Coal & Tyne', showing a fanciful depiction of single-masted collier as the ships were known perhaps with a fire smoking on deck and a helmsman aft, or perhaps it is a river barge known as a 'keel'. That smoke has not gone away. It is there still messing up the

Coal & Tyne
Image: courtesy of Spink

atmosphere and poisoning the air we breathe, as the geological Anthropocene approaches!

Thomas Spence loved Newcastle. His auntie lost a cow when the town commons was enclosed. Enclosure with its consequent loss of possibilities of subsistence destroyed the domestic economies and forced people into the factory regime. Silvia Federici writes, 'to see the house and housework as the foundation of the factory system, rather than its other', is to understand how unpaid labour of the home makes wage-labour possible.[9] Spence was furious at his auntie's loss but powerless to stop it. Instead, he delivered a plan to the Philosophical Society of Newcastle, 8 November 1775, in which he declared that the land is a common for the people. The coal miners of the region, like Spence himself, held themselves proud. You can see it in this sailor and slop (sailor's clothes) seller, 'J. Spence, Slop Seller, Newcastle', with his open jacket, sailor pants and jaunty hat. 'J. Spence, Slop Seller, Newcastle' was Thomas's younger brother, Jeremiah.

J. Spence, Slop Seller, Newcastle
Image: © The Fitzwilliam Museum, Cambridge

Spence's coins functioned as money rather than as medals. Thousands lay about in heaps in his shop. Nowadays, 158 different coins are attributed to him, mostly halfpenny and farthing dies. He may have owned the dies, or he may have owned a press. He used the coins as propaganda for his plan to abolish private property in land. His policy was to diffuse agitation by song, pamphlet, graffiti, newspaper and coins!

Thomas Spence was a member of the London Corresponding Society founded in 1792 shortly after he arrived in London. The goal of the society was to link together, by correspondence, radicals and reformers in different parts of England; London and Sheffield, for example.

They had been encouraged by the French Revolution and by Olaudah Equiano, the former slave and leader of the growing abolitionist movement in England. Spence designed a coin, 'Before the Revolution', showing an imprisoned man shackled to the wall and with his mouth padlocked. Between loss of commons and compulsion to factory discipline lay the condition of pauperisation and what Federici calls the 'criminalization of the working-class.'[10] Prison and the wage become two sides of the same coin.

On the obverse side of the coin, 'After the Revolution', he rendered a leafy tree with three men on one side holding hands and dancing, and on the other side of the tree a man sitting at a table enjoying a glass and meat (in Spence's day the word 'meat' referred to food generally and not to flesh as it does in our day).

Before the Revolution
Image: © The Fitzwilliam Museum, Cambridge

After the Revolution
Image: © The Fitzwilliam Museum, Cambridge

The theme is repeated with men dancing around the 'Tree of Liberty'. These were planted all over France and soon became an international fixture. Besides France, England, Ireland, Scotland and the United States planted trees of liberty. The custom is seriously needed today for shade from the heat, sunlight in the winter, nuts and fruits, numerous wooden uses and oxygen to breathe.

Tree of Liberty
Image: © The Fitzwilliam
Museum, Cambridge

In 1790 Edmund Burke wrote *Reflections on the Revolution in France* where he claimed 'our manners, our civilization, and all the good things which are connected with manners and with civilization have, in this European world of ours, depended for ages upon two principles; and were indeed the result of both combined; I mean the spirit of a gentleman, and the spirit of religion'. They kept learning alive, he said, but not for long. With the French Revolution 'learning will be cast into the mire, and trodden down under the hoofs of the swinish multitude'. Oink! Oink! Oink! Oh, how the London proletariat squealed with delight! So, Thomas Spence began publishing a weekly, one-penny newspaper called *Pig's Meat; Or, Lessons for the Swinish Multitude* which is here advertised by a coin sporting the revolutionary cap of liberty on the top and a pig trampling on the headwear – the mitres and coronets – of kings and bishops below.

The reformers appealed to a tradition that Spence satirises in 'A Free-born Englishman'. Here we see him handcuffed, gagged and shackled.

The revolutionary theme of 'the true-born Englishman' goes back to the seventeenth century. Spence and all of his literate, plebeian comrades would know about Mr Money-love, the school mate of Mr By-ends, taught by Mr Gripe Man, a schoolmaster in Love-gain which is a market town in the County of Coveting. The 'school master taught them the art of getting

Pig's Meat
Image: © The Fitzwilliam Museum,
Cambridge

A Free-Born Englishman
Image: courtesy of Spink

either by violence, cousenage, flattery, lying or by putting on a guise of Religion…' John Bunyan's allegory of *Pilgrim's Progress* was written in jail and published in 1678. He was a tinker, that is, a man who repaired pots and pans. In prison he made shoelaces.

Spence quoted John Milton who also wrote in prison and who turned Christianity to revolutionary purposes. 'Man over Man he made Not Lord', Milton wrote in *Paradise Lost* and Spence quoted first in *Pig's Meat* and then on a coin depicting a man and a woman in loving, naked, equal, entanglement.

'The End of Oppression' shows two men exulting over a bonfire of title deeds, legal papers and that parallel paper world of private property, the

Man Over Man He Made Not Lord
Image: © The Fitzwilliam Museum,
Cambridge

commodity, etc. Scenes like this were widespread in the summer of 1789 among the *émeutes* (means both riot and emotion) of the French peasantry. Such fires have a long history in England too, going back at least to the Peasant's Revolt of 1381. In Spence's time the legal apparatus sought to de-legitimise common rights. Defence of the commons sometimes required fire.[11]

The End of Oppression
Image: © The Fitzwilliam Museum,
Cambridge

The fabulous wealth of the British ruling class – its palaces and jewels, its stocks and gold, its green lawn and Rolls Royces – came from conquest, enclosure and slavery. So Spence struck a coin with the abolitionist image of the supplicating slave, 'Am I Not a Man and a Brother?'

As for conquest he was fully aware of the wars against the native Americans. In fact, he wrote a pamphlet about their superiority of life where subsistence is available to all owing to the absence of landlordism: *The Reign*

Am I Not a Man and a Brother?
Image: © The Fitzwilliam Museum,
Cambridge

If Rents I Once Consent to Pay My Liberty is Past Away
Image: © The Fitzwilliam Museum,
Cambridge

of Felicity, Being a Plan for Civilizing the Indians of North America Without Infringing on Their National or Individual Independence. He also struck a coin: 'If rents I once consent to pay my liberty is past away'.

Popular voices of criticism fired up by the French Revolution threatened both the wealth taken from native Americans and the wealth produced by Afro-Americans. War and slavery were accompanied by mechanisation, and this applied to everything including the coinage. Erasmus Darwin, the grandfather of Charles, the evolutionist, understood the danger of popular sovereignty. He wrote to a correspondent in October 1792, 'Now Mr Pain [sic]', the author of *Rights of Man,* 'says that he thinks a monkey or a bear, or a goose may govern a kingdom as well, and at much less expense than any being in Christendom, whether idiot or madman or in his royal senses'.[12] But Erasmus also comprehended the knowledge of life forms that enclosure and conquest had appropriated from commoners. He expressed his comprehension in poetry. *The Botanic Garden* (1791) expressed in traditional couplets (the most conservative of verse forms) and organised in a series of cantos, Rosicrucian style, by Salamanders of Fire, Gnomes of Earth, Nymphs of Water, and Sylphs of the Air. The science of it is verified by long footnotes.[13] He describes the rolling mill and stamping press of copper coin production:

> With iron lips his rapid rollers seize
> The lengthening bars, in thin expansion squeeze;
> Descending screws with ponderous fly-wheels wound
> The tawny plates, the new medallions round
> Hard dies of steel the cupreous circles cramp,
> And with quick fall his massy hammers stamp.
> The Harp, the Lily and the Lion join,
> And George and Britain guard the sterling coin.

The humble copper coins are stamped with King and Government, and the symbols of England, Ireland and France. His footnote provides the relationship between mechanisation, criminalisation and child proletarianisation.

> Mr. Boulton has lately constructed at Soho near Birmingham, a most magnificent apparatus for coining, which has cost him some thousand pounds; the whole machinery is moved by an improved steam-engine, which rolls the copper for halfpence finer than copper has before been rolled for the purpose of making money; it works the coupoirs or screw-presses for cutting out the circular pieces of copper; and coins both the faces and edges of the money at the same time, with such superior excellence and cheapness of workmanship, as well as with marks of such powerful machinery as most totally prevent clandestine imitation, and in consequence save many lives from the hand of the executioner; a circumstance worthy the attention of a great minister. If a civic crown was given in Rome for preserving the life of one citizen, Mr. Boulton should be covered with garlands of oak! By this machinery four boys of ten or twelve years old are capable of striking thirty thousand guineas in an hour, and the machine itself keeps an unerring account of the pieces struck [just in case one of the boys should be tempted to pocket one or two].

But even the proud wearer of the civic crown could not unlock that connection between mechanisation and criminalisation. About the same time a carpenter in Manchester came to the White Horse public house last Christmas [1800] 'to share his Club money'. He met Boulton's night watchman and they hatched a plan to rob the manufactory at Soho, on a Tuesday night, because the men were paid on Wednesday. They found 'a quantity of Guineas'. They were joined by 'Bromwich' George who had previously robbed Boulton of a great deal of copper. Wall surrounded the works and William Fouldes escaped over it but took a bad fall and a wagon ran over his arm breaking it.[14] The physician turned him in. Wherever you look at enclosures you will find 'crime'. I put quotation marks around the word 'crime' only to remind us that common people commoned well before they thieved.

Political philosophy tells us that state power monopolises money and force. Erasmus Darwin showed us money, now for force.

Since the European Renaissance cannon was the weapon of choice on land or sea because besides killing people it could knock down walls, demolish cities or destroy ships. Artillery conquered the world. For the English empire cannons were made at the Carron Works in Falkirk, Scotland, where its infernal iron blast furnaces lit up the sky. In the 1770s the works were enclosed behind a wall 'to make them secure against theft and petty pilfering'.[15] In 1787 Bobbie Burns tried to enter but was turned away. He wrote a poem comparing the place to Hell and its keeper to Satan. Pilfering continued. Watchmen were employed to patrol it constantly day and night. Despite frequent whippings, Scots workers would not work. Hundreds were employed. The Scottish miner was bound for life to his coalmine in a form of slavery. The company took pauper boys from the poor house in even yet another form of coerced labor. The owners even paid the hangman. One of the workers here, injured on the job, made his way to London and the founding of the London Corresponding Society.

Everything was done in the midst of war that had commenced in February 1793 against the French republic which had recently put King Louis XVI to the guillotine. Devastation in the Ohio Valley as settlers burned villages and massacred natives; arson in County Armagh where the Orange Order threw peasants out of their cottages which they then burnt; on the continent of Europe huge armies fed themselves by foraging and robbing whole villages. 'One Only Master Grasps the Whole Domain' is a chilling rendition of a devastated village. The phrase is quoted in his newspaper, *Pig's Meat*, and comes from the Irishman, Oliver Goldsmith, whose poem *The Deserted Village* (1760) showed that what happened in the colonies was prologue to what would happen in the metropolis: sports are fled, the tyrant governs supreme, desolation covers the green, the river is choked, the children flee as refugees. Spence wrote in 1801, 'they would make us believe that the more they rob us the better we thrive... and still the cry is work – work, ye are idle – ye are idle'.

Only One Master Grasps the Whole Domain
Image: © The Fitzwilliam Museum, Cambridge

Spence's coin of the shepherd is an idyll of supine relaxation; there is no anxiety here, under a tree gazing across the meadow to the highlands beyond. This is the opposite of our usual images of the period, unrelieved toil and moil, misery and hell. Spence and the poor and humble people once upon a time had a life to live. Now such posture was reserved for the upper class, the class of idlers.

Reclining Shepherd
Image: © The Fitzwilliam Museum, Cambridge

Take such a man and put him to war leaving a widow behind, and you have the theme of the Romantic poetry of the period. The soldier's craft is death: kill or be killed. Some resisted war, others mutinied in the midst of it. 'Who Know Their Rights and Knowing Dare Maintain' refers to a long tradition in which rights included freedom from unthinking obedience and freedom to participate in decisions risking life. Such rights could be found in law but in times of popular sovereignty when laws became democratic they might be found in the will of the people. Spence quotes a poem, 'Ode in Imitation of Alcaeus'.

What constitutes a State?...
Men, who their *duties* know,
But knowing their *rights*, and knowing, dare maintain.

**Who Know Their Rights and
Knowing Dare Maintain**
Image: © The Fitzwilliam Museum,
Cambridge

A government spy informs us that Thomas Spence took up the pike himself, and practised with others upstairs in his High Holborn book stall. A blade as long as your forearm and sharper than your nails was attached to a pole, sometimes sixteen feet long. Many of them anchored in the ground and held at an angle could repel a cavalry charge. It was the people's weapon. John Oswald, the vegetarian and Edinburgh artisan, developed the theory and practice of the people's weapon among the sans-culottes of Paris. 'A pike in de 'tatch' became proverbial among Irish cottagers. London radicals talked to soldiers where they were quartered in public houses. Later the authorities built barracks to isolate soldiers from civilians to prevent them talking with each other.

'We are also the people.' This phrase comes from the famous 15th chapter of Volney's *Ruins of Empire*, a book more influential even than Thomas Paine's *Rights of Man*. The white supremacist culture of the United States has ignored it because it puts the origin of civilisation in Africa instead of Europe. To Volney society is divided between the privileged class and the labouring class. The military steps forward to explain the justice of the arrangement, 'The people are timid, let us menace them; they only obey force. Soldiers, chastise this insolent rabble!' The people reply, 'Soldiers! You

We Also Are the People
Image: courtesy of Baldwin's of
St. James's

are of our own blood; will you strike your brothers?' And the soldiers, grounding their arms, said to their officers, 'We are also the people.'

The fleet of war, the fleet of commerce, the coastal fleet – indeed, the sailing vessels of other nations all depended on 'Jack Tar', the British sailor. He was the most international of the proletariat and, like the people of west Africa, he was not 'recruited' but kidnapped by gangs of uniformed bullies who impressed him into His Majesty's service. The press-gangs snatched you off the street. Sailors hoisted the red flag of battle in the spring of 1797, signaling the largest mutiny in British history. It went on for a considerable time. While it ended violently with more than 30 hanged, at least there were permanent victories, including 16 ounces in the pound instead of fewer to favour the ship's purser. Here is Spence's treatment of the press-gang, 'British Liberty displayed'.

British Liberty Displayed
Image: © The Fitzwilliam Museum,
Cambridge

The exercise of strength, stamina, speed and skill is always a joy to behold, and contests of such have been part of games and sport for millennia. At first they may have been necessary to the hunt; then they became part of training for war. In the 1790s however they became not so much an adjunct to the craft of soldiering as a gladiatorial celebration of cruelty and an amusement for the aristocracy, as pointed out in 'Fashionable Amusement'.

Fashionable Amusement
Image: courtesy of Knightsbridge Coins

Without gloves and no holds barred, boxing matches were one of many blood sports, including bear baiting and cock fighting. Mutual pummelling then, as ever since, was one of the only ways a man could grasp the next rung up the ladder in these lands of opportunity where the ladders of social success depended on crushing those below. Thus, in a country that was anti-Irish, white supremacist and anti-Semitic, preceding the Irishmen and African-Americans as the champion boxers of the day were Jews – and 'Daniel Mendoza' was their champion, opening a school about 1787. Brutalised as it was, this proletariat could take a punch.

Erasmus Darwin dedicates *Phytologia; Or, The Philosophy of Agriculture and Gardening* (1800) to Sir John Sinclair, President of the Board of Agriculture, the advocate, promoter and theorist of enclosure. He also wrote to Boulton concerning the enclosure of Needwood forest. His last book was called *The Temple of Nature; Or, The Origin of Society* (1803). He divided bodily action into four classes – irritation, sensation, volition and association. Under volition he includes credulity which is endemic to 'the bulk of mankind' with its fears of poverty, death and hell; superstitious hope (*spes religiosa*), a 'maniacal hallucination' and *orci timor* or the fear of

D. Mendoza
Image: © The Fitzwilliam Museum, Cambridge

hell. Language, tools and money are the defining characteristics of human nature.

> Thy potent acts, VOLITION, still attend
> The *means* of pleasure to secure the end;
> To express his wishes and his wants design'd
> Language, the means, distinguishes Mankind;
> For *future* works in Art's ingenious schools
> His hands unwearied form and finish tools;
> He toils for money *future* bliss to share,
> And shouts to Heaven his mercenary prayer.

After the Two Acts were passed in December 1795, one of which prohibited assemblies of people without prior authorisation from the magistracy, the other putting a gag on such speech or print which the government deemed subversive, Spence in characteristic simplicity coined 'Mum'.

Mum
Image: © The Fitzwilliam Museum, Cambridge

These Acts merely joined the encrustations of the ancient apparatus of law which was slow, expensive and partial to the interests of the propertied, and so Spence styled himself in court as 'the unfee'd advocate of the disinherited seed of Adam'. Spence's reaction was sarcastic, 'If the law requires it we will walk thus'.

If the Law Requires It We Will Walk Thus
Image: courtesy of Baldwin's of St. James's

Proletarians had become beasts of burden. Their labours carried product from one point of the earth's surface to another, or from beneath the surface on upto the top of it! They also were exploited via money rents and taxes. In 'I was an ass to bear the first pair' the panniers are labelled 'rents' and 'taxes'. Indeed, these were effective tools of proletarianisation: how else can you get money without risk of hanging?

I Was an Ass to Bear the First Pair
Image: courtesy of A.H. Baldwin's & Sons/Courtney Buckingham

Capitalist accumulation is told to London children as a feline fable of fortune. It goes like this. Dick Whittington, a poor orphan, works as a kitchen scullion for a cruel master in Leadenhall. One day Dick escapes and walks north with his cat to Highgate Hill but changes his mind when he hears Bow Bells ringing and seeming to say, 'turn again, turn again'. So Dick returns and, with his cat, ventures on one of the cruel merchant's ships. The cat keeps the ship's rat population down and in Istanbul preserves a feast from vermin. When it is discovered that the cat is pregnant, the Moors buy her for a huge amount of gold, worth much more than the entire cargo of the ship. In consequence, back in London Whittington finds himself rich beyond imagining. He becomes Lord Mayor and does good works such as re-building Newgate Prison. It would be amusing to know how Thomas Spence would re-tell this story about London, city of gold and prisons, and Istanbul, city of bridges and cats. Spence loved animals, so he must have had a cat and probably a good ratter. A cat which was a predator, silent and graceful, 'My freedom I among slaves enjoy'.

My freedom I among slaves enjoy
Image: © The Fitzwilliam Museum, Cambridge

Notes

1. Karl Marx, *Capital*, vol. 1, chapter 3, section 2, subsection c.
2. C. George Caffentzis, *Clipped Coins, Abused Words & Civil Government: John Locke's Theory of Money* (New York: Autonomedia, 1989) p. 163.
3. Lawrence Weschler, *Boggs: A Comedy of Values* (Chicago: University of Chicago Press, 1999) and William Grimes, 'J.S.G. Boggs, artist, dies at 62; he made money. Literally', *New York Times*, 27 January 2017.
4. R.H. Thompson, 'The Dies of Thomas Spence (1750–1814)', C.E. Blunt *et al.* (eds), *The British Numismatic Journal*, 38 (1969), pp. 126–62.
5. The Old Bailey, *Proceedings*, 27 October 1790.

6. C. George Caffentzis, *Exciting the Industry of Mankind: George Berkeley's Philosophy of Money* (Dordrecht: Kluwer Academic Publishers, 2000) p. 286.

7. After neglect and scholarly put-downs Thomas Spence is at last coming into his own. See the webpage of the Thomas Spence Society (www.thomas-spence-society.co.uk/), and also the important collection of essays in Alastair Bonnett and Keith Armstrong (eds), *Thomas Spence: The Poor Man's Revolutionary* (London: Breviary Stuff, 2014).

8. See his article, 'Spence's Countermarked Tokens', which is reproduced on the Spence Society webpage.

9. Silvia Federici, *Revolution at Point Zero: Housework, Reproduction, and Feminist Struggle* (Oakland: PM Press, 2012), p. 6.

10. Siliva Federici, *Caliban and the Witch: Women, the Body, and Primitive Accumulation* (New York: Autonomedia, 2004), pp. 75–80.

11. I personally am grateful to those who destroyed by fire the Media, Pennsylvania draft records during the 1960s.

12. Desmond King-Hele, *Doctor of Revolution: The Life and Genius of Erasmus Darwin* (London: Faber & Faber, 1977), p. 229.

13. *The Botanic Garden* consists of two books published earlier, *The Economy of Vegetation,* and *The Loves of Plants.*

14. Birmingham Central Reference Library. Boulton & Watt MSS. 'The Examination of William Fouldes', 10 April 1801.

15. R.H. Campbell, *Carron Company* (Edinburgh: Oliver and Royal, 1961), p. 38.

7

Standardisation and Crisis:
The Twin Features of Financialisation

Gerald Hanlon

Much has been written about financialisation's restructuring of the economy. Different schools of thought attempt to explain this alteration. Organisationally the shift in corporate priorities towards shareholder value is responsible.[1] Others suggest speculative manias where exuberance, and the following pessimism, are left uncontrolled.[2] Still others point to the realignment of class forces central to capitalism's development.[3] That the world is more financialised seems beyond doubt – Greta Krippner evidences it from 1970 as value is extracted through financialisation not production. This is so noticeable, the Bank of England's Chief Economist has accused corporate elites of 'eating' corporations.[4] All suggest a transition in capitalism. Support for this is located in the demise of Chandlerian organisational models where managers dominated organisations. The managerial revolution[5] where ownership and control were separated and firms focused on internal capabilities, R&D, secure employment strategies, and savings-derived financing is over. It has been replaced by the assertion of shareholder value through insecure employment, stock repurchases, open innovation, acquisition of new technology, etc. Although there are dissenting voices,[6] this financialised economy is often associated with a return to rent and the impossibility of measure.[7]

Like other elements of my recent work, this chapter owes a lot to the interventions of Silvia Federici and George Caffentzis. In particular, I argue that standardisation via the deskilling of work and the concentration of knowledge within management systems allows for new sources of labour to be exploited via financialisation. As such, although it is focused on what might narrowly be perceived as a white working male history, the chapter chimes with the issues Federici and Caffentzis consistently pushed scholars and activists to examine. They argued for the inclusion of a multiplicity of voices – female, non-white, colonised, enslaved, young and old – and practices – primitive accumulation, the ongoing importance of unglamorous activities such as agricultural and factory work, the centrality of reproductive labour – to broaden our understanding of the complexity of capitalism. This chapter embraces these themes by linking financialisation with older processes of exploitation which are fundamental to their analyses – appropriation of knowledge, deskilling, the centrality of a global and historical perspective, primitive accumulation, global proletarianisation, the ongoing power of elites, etc. to argue that standardisation, the recomposing of the division of labour, and the social forces it unleashes partly set the stage for the success (or not) of what today we call financialisation. In so doing, it concurs with calls for more attention to be paid to labour processes within financialisation.[8] It seeks to demonstrate the Marxist critiques of financialisation are not without empirical evidence.[9] It does so by examining how class forces were realigned to create, and then undo, an earlier period of financialisation – the era prior to the Great Crash. Significantly it is influenced by Thorstein Veblen's 1904 book *The Theory of the Business Enterprise.*[10] The date is central because it emerged in the slipstream of the 1898–1902 merger wave that gave us modern corporations and monopoly capitalism.

Veblen discusses what he calls the 'machine process' and the 'business enterprise'. He suggests contingency, irregularity, craft, are anathema to the machine process as it networks like a contagion. Standardisation grows because producers seek it in internal production, administrative, and supplier systems and they themselves, as suppliers, must supply to standards. Thus, through science, technology and planning, standardisation penetrates the whole economy. This generates a real subsumption of labour to capital and changes the organic composition of capital.[11] However, also important in Veblen's analysis is the 'business enterprise'.[12] Perceptively, he highlights how capitalism altered to demand firm size increases. This growth creates an increasing separation between the machine process and the business enterprise. Crucially, the business enterprise becomes more concerned with investment and less with the direct surveillance of labour. Thus, the business enterprise prioritises finance and separates business strategy from day-to-day management. Indeed, as the post-merger separation of ownership and control heightened, industrial capital emerges as an intermediary between employees and financiers in ways which resonate today.[13] Often this is done by credit-based finance which shifts resources out of production into finance.[14] One witnesses this ownership/control separation in Rockefeller's management of the Colorado Fuel and Iron Company. Rockefeller only paid attention to labour issues after they became politically problematic – prior to that, local management had a free hand in labour matters provided targets were met.[15] Such freedom was blamed for the

Ludlow massacre by company militia. At the time, like today,[16] many commentators pointed to the separation of ownership and management as a structural problem leading to social conflict.[17] Indeed, this separation is evident in J.P. Morgan's US Steel reorganisation – as David Brody expressed it.

But the task (of merging firms into US Steel) required not merely uniting the warring factions but also overseeing a pacified industry. J.P. Morgan and Company announced to investors that it would itself determine the 'Plan of Organisation and Management' of the steel corporation. The house of Morgan put its own partners on the board of directors, appointed much of the top management, and passed on the remainder. The imperious Morgan reserved for himself ultimate, if distant, authority.[18]

Through monopoly power, Morgan controlled the increasingly wide spectrum of the organic composition of capital within steel. He sought to dominate all firms – from large capital-intensive firms to smaller suppliers – to extract profit in an (ideally) pacified industry.[19] One manifestation of this plan was the profit sharing schemes allowing employees to subscribe for preferred stock, pay in instalments, receive dividends, and gain $5 per share after five years – all of which 'embodied the aims of the financial men'.[20] General Motors and Du Pont also had executive and non-executive schemes.[21] Elements of finance's rise emerge in John J. Raskob's career, a senior executive in General Motors and Du Pont, who, leading up to the Great Crash, championed stock investment for ordinary workers. As such, Raskob was an early advocate of Thatcher's 'shareholder democracy'.[22]

Returning to the machine process, Veblen argued standardisation meant production became a 'concatenation of industrial processes' embedded in a uniform comprehensive mechanical field.[23] This also implied that when imbalance set into the concatenation, the shrewd business took short term advantage and entrepreneurially invested where it saw the greatest disequilibrium and hence most profit. Here arbitrage and differentials between individuals, groups, units, firms and mechanical processes, rather than direct labour management, were preyed upon to extract value. In ways that are contemporary, Veblen argues capitalists became increasingly interested in disequilibrium, in crisis and chaos within the economy. Disequilibrium encourages a declining direct interest in labour management and even an interest in restricting production and productivity.[24] Business relations between groups, rather than directly managing industrial sectors, grow in importance, further divorcing financial capitalists from stability as they exploit 'the vertical spectrum of organic composition possibilities'.[25] Here, capitalists and society are increasingly at odds because capitalists pursue arbitrage profits and rents.[26] Central here is the merger wave itself, because it recasts ownership to ensure owner-managers increasingly become a

thing of the past; instead ownership emerges as control through investment or divestment in a variety of corporations and/or opportunities.[27]
Capitalists – like 'Captains of Industry' such as Rockefeller, J.P. Morgan, or
the Du Ponts – move from production to finance. This world is shaped by
churn because businessmen shift resources from one venture to the next
in search of higher profitability – it is only passive small shareholders 'that
hold(s) permanently to a given enterprise'.[28] Here, contra the idea that
value is not measurable,[29] financialisation implies a hyper-measuring as
short term profit is pursued. I argue this financialisation tendency is a central feature of capitalism unless checked by other social forces. I examine
this transition through tracing the birth of the mechanical process,
analysing the business enterprise, describing how this first period of
financialisation collapsed because of the refusal of mass industrial workers,
and the increasing necessity of states to plan the economies. Finally, I
conclude to comment on contemporary financialisation and recent class
realignment.

Craft, the Inside Contract and Standardisation

Capitalism's pursuit of standardisation is a long affair. As with organisational discipline, supply chains, and strategy, standardisation too traces its
origins in the military.[30] In the 1760s the French army sought to rationalise
arms production with standardised inter-changeable parts. Pursuing
uniformity would ensure weapons were easily replaced or restored with
standardised elements, making repair quicker, cheaper, and enabling further military effort. These ideas were influential in the United States.
Thomas Jefferson promoted them to key people. With different levels of
determination post 1800, the US military sought standardised inter-
changeable parts for its equipment over 50 years.[31] Whilst initially the military pursued repair efficiencies on battlefields rather than cost savings,[32]
as a process, standardisation represented a conflict over knowledge between
craft workers and capitalists.[33]

The struggle over who controls factories was a key battleground in nineteenth century social restructuring. Like all social struggles, standardisation
was of its time, but it also laid the foundation for conflicts around financialisation because, as we will see, without standardisation, imagining
Veblen's business enterprise is difficult. In its uniformity, standardisation
facilitated the growth of wealth, development of tangible products and
production systems upon which intangible assets such as brands, goodwill,
or intellectual property rights could emerge as sources of monopoly/
oligopoly, and become major forces for the distribution of value.[34] Was
mass production possible without this struggle over knowledge? Certainly

Chandler emphasises marketing and distribution more than labour control (something Veblen saw as creating oligopoly and rents from intangible assets). For example, Singer, which was always more interested in marketing than production, retained craft labour and annually mass produced 500,000 sewing machines into the 1880s.[35] But, as Veblen highlighted, standardisation became necessary if factory goods within the same (or different) organisations were to be made inter-changeable and hence regularised. Thus, Singer's push to build overseas factories along its US lines led to standardised machine tools, gauges and other devices.[36] This was not simply driven by labour costs (which were cheaper in Scotland than the United States), but by the desire for standardisation which emerged because organisations and markets experienced a 'concatenation of industrial processes'. This spreading of the machine process increases as economies develop[37] and hence continually alters the composition of capital. In this view, early twentieth century globalisation is partly the internationalisation of the machine process and so imagines the division of labour within firms and oligopolistic markets that allow corporations to coordinate value extraction practices as a 'new imperial system'.[38] Here capitalist standardisation appears inevitable. However, this is an appearance because its development emerged through conflict with a key labour group – craft workers[39] who were favourable to markets but not necessarily to standardisation, or profit maximisation or, indeed, finance.

This craft antagonism to capitalist development arises in worker petitions to the Commonwealth of Massachusetts directed against an application to establish the Amherst Carriage Company. The logic for this opposition was their view that incorporated companies were a danger to the public because they were protected from liabilities and offloaded risk to communities.[40] Others echoed these charges, claiming corporations crushed small establishments and, whilst journeymen workers 'relinquish' part of their earnings to the master craftsmen who train them, this did not pertain to businessmen who are 'inexperienced', simply 'take from us the profits of our art', and 'compel us to wear out our days in the service of others'.[41] Here was the strong tradition of independence central to craft workers and bound up with their adherence to labour theories of value[42] – an adherence that was an obstacle to capitalism's development. This antagonism mattered because in 1825, 50 per cent of New York's workforce were in crafts[43] and, as a group, were often supportive of markets but hostile to capitalist owners and profit maximisation.[44] Thus, one major social struggle was between craft workers and capitalists.[45]

This conflict is perhaps most evident in the struggle over the Inside Contract system.[46] The Inside Contract is the name for the production regime that emerged and helped generate US proto-mass industrial production.[47] It was a compromise production system based on tensions between capitalist owners who had finance, but no or limited knowledge of production, and a group we might think of as the original knowledge workers – craftsmen. In this system, capitalists had minimal understanding or direct control of labour/labour process. One sees this in perhaps the original American corporate industry, the Lowell textile industry, where financial men had little understanding of labour processes or management.[48] The Inside Contract system existed in the United States' leading industries e.g. steel, copper, tobacco, arms manufacture.[49] Unlike the 'putting out system' where employers dispersed raw materials to people's homes and then collected the finished product, the Inside Contract brought workers into the factory. It did so because rising production costs encouraged master craftsmen into factories. Within the system, craftsmen selected and hired labour, decided on production processes, disciplined and managed staff and importantly, innovated production processes in order to reduce costs and hide savings from owners to better preserve their negotiating position for the annual discussion on costs and profits.[50] Here knowledge empowered craftsmen against owners who 'represent(s) a new breed of entrepreneur in the firearms industry'[51] – one with capital, but without technical knowledge.

The system created tensions around who got the lion's share of the value. These were often expressed as class antagonisms. For example, Williamson speaks of contractors wearing 'frock coats, and sporting diamond stickpins, spats, and gloves'; Arnold[52] refers to the 'haughty machinist'; and Roland discusses how contractors were 'a power which must obviously be treated as an equal, although actually occupying the anomalous position of a belligerent inferior'. Being unable to control craftsmen, Taylor[53] characterised them as lazy and Arnold called for their replacement by technology, the reshaping of their attitudes, deskilling tasks, and rejected the idea their skill was an 'art' in favour of viewing it as an adjunct to 'selling' and hence profit.[54] These pronouncements argued wealth distribution was to be directed away from knowledge/craft towards ownership. One way to do this was to systematically undermine craft[55] and reorganise work by 'exerting pressures for change that would benefit management'.[56]

Through focusing on the disadvantages of the system for owners, Chandler presents a functional analysis of its demise.[57] Chandler's explanation downplays the fact the system innovated and mass produced. For example, the Winchester New Haven Arms Company was nearly bankrupted because of owner lack of knowledge. However, B. Tyler Henry (a mechanic), developed the new, mass produced, standardised 'Henry rifle' which, with its ammunition, was subsequently patented. The rifle's success enabled Winchester to unsuccessfully bid for a $1.8 million US arms contract.[58]

Despite losing that contract, the firm made $171,335.31 from other government contracts. In 1874, it renewed its patent and, as part of its bid, suggested Henry give up his job to become the firm's first Inside Contractor. This allowed him a 100 per cent salary increase as he moved from a $1500 per annum to earn $15,000 over five years.

Although Henry was earning a huge income for the time, in 1874 alone the New Haven Arms Company net profit was $265,000. Technical skills were a paramount resource central to profitability, but they belonged to empowered craftsmen who 'were excellent and ingenious mechanics who operated their own machine shops and had enough time to experiment'.[59] This knowledge, combined with capital's smaller and weaker scale, meant craftsmen negotiated from a position of strength. Furthermore, the system also mass produced. Winchester produced 26,000 guns in 1880 and 225,000 in 1904. Colt made 73,000 guns in 1861 and 188,000 just two years later. Singer manufactured 181,260 sewing machines in 1871 and 431,167 in 1879.[60] Thus, a functional argument that mass production, distribution and/or innovation were causes of the system's demise, seems inaccurate. What was at work here is not a Smithian model of market driven change,[61] but a Marxist analysis focusing on the necessity of controlling labour and redistributing wealth and power upwards. The end of the Inside Contract is based in capitalist social relations located in the desire of capital to intensify production processes, standardise and valourise. What informs the push to both Taylorise and technologise production is skilled labour's knowledge, power and (limited) refusal of capitalist social relations.

The Pursuit of Standardisation and the Bureaucratic Organisational Form

Bureaucracy is central to standardisation.[62] Creating gauges, tolerances and machines precise enough to repeatedly produce the same cut, joint, product, etc. requires bureaucratic forms.

> The goal of inter-changeability, still very elusive, Lee believed, became an exacting exercise that imposed a bureaucratic system upon the armoury (in 1820) in its attempt to prevent any deviation from the standard pattern.[63]

Anticipating assembly lines, this pursuit led to the aligning of machines that facilitated sequential production and flows to virtually eliminate hand labour. For example, US Steel emerges less than two decades after the infamous Homestead strike which reshaped power relations in favour of owners.[64] This strike, and its reshaping of relations, occurred just as the industry standardised production to empower capital to win the conflict.[65] Thus, as the business enterprise detached leading capitalists – like

J.P. Morgan – from production, the machine process ensured labour was simultaneously subjected to planned, bureaucratic authority designed to enhance control from above. Furthermore, the organisational form changed as a result of management developments post 1890.[66] Stone suggests modern bureaucratic organisations developed out of such struggles. So dominant was this form to become, Chandler suggested the 'basic organisational structure and the basic techniques of coordinating and controlling their operation have changed little'. Central here is the transferring of production knowledge from workers to management, the emergence of semi-skilled workers, the development of internal labour markets, the new importance of promotion and career paths, the increased use of technology, the rise of the problem of motivation, the attempted individualising of the work place, and the increased use of formal education to hire management cadres. The struggle over the steel industry between 1890 and 1920 is key to the modern corporation. It is also a place where finance capital became entrenched.[67]

The Homestead strike restructured steel and ended previous relations between capital and labour – it announced a changing organic composition of labour. In the ensuing thirty years the industry was radically transformed through a machine process involving a minute division of labour.[68] The industry underwent three changes – one, new technology altered production and job structures; two as a result of this, new job structures emerged creating new problems and solutions for motivating and disciplining a labour force no longer capable of self-organising production; and three, capital pursued lasting control over the entire labour process. Steel accepted costs, new problems, new management layers, and it restructured work to destroy worker self-organisation and control of knowledge – the knowledge worker was to be stamped out, made dependent and the division of labour would allow for new a University/College trained, elite led authority.[69] What emerges is the bureaucratic organisational form.[70]

Within this transition, despite increasing productivity per worker, skilled workers' pay declined. For example, a Homestead Roller in 1899–92 could expect $14 per tonnage, yet by 1908 he could expect $4.75. Hence, steel broke the connection between productivity and wages[71] or 'labour-time expended and the price of commodities sold'[72] – a connection that was re-established as a central block of the New Deal[73] and the dismantling of which is so important to contemporary financialisation[74] Within this transition, labour's composition also changed. From 1890–1910 the total labour force grew by 129 per cent. However, native born skilled white workers only grew by 55 per cent and immigrants from Germany and the British Isles (where overseas skilled workers generally originated) declined by 18 per cent. In contrast, Afro-Americans grew by 165 per cent. Most remarkably,

Southern and Eastern Europeans expanded by 227 per cent, so whereas in 1890 they made up less than 10 per cent of the workforce, by 1910 they were nearly half of it.[75] By pulling in new, non-industrial sources of labour (a form of primitive accumulation),[76] steel shifted from skilled and unskilled to semi-skilled labour, creating the mass industrial working class.

This deskilling of tasks meant workers became increasingly homogenised and hence more likely to experience collective grievances and see themselves as a mass. Taylor – who advocated simultaneously standardising and individualising workers – raised concerns such a process might massify labour. The solution proposed by management involved using calculative, norm-inducing piece rates to individualise pay, thereby pitting worker against worker.[77] This created an internal labour market with elongated promotion ladders designed to stoke desire, develop certain potentialities and inhibit others, and entrench a world of competitive individualism.[78] These tactics were designed to suggest workers were competing with one another and that their individual interest and the company interest were the same, even, or especially, as workers themselves became standardised, inter-changeable and dependent – the US Steel, General Motors, Du Pont and Rasbok sponsored schemes should be viewed in this light. These systems simultaneously sought to generate discipline and individualisation – they were trying to create disciplined organisations now workers had finally been stripped of control, independence and access to their means of production outside of wage dependency – Edwards called it a totalitarian organisation. At the heart of the machine process is the idea – key to Smith's pin factory – that labour can be deskilled, made dependent, compared and measured.[79]

Class Composition and the Realignment of the Machine Process and Business Enterprise

One reaction to craft labour's monopoly of knowledge was scientific management.[80] Following Tronti's[81] argument that the emergence of the capitalist class as a class is forged in labour's resistance to the discipline of the production process, workers generated change and redeveloped the capitalist class through insubordination. It is in this light we should understand standardisation. Making things and people inter-changeable and standardised enables ease of management via the concentration of knowledge in management systems, technologies and the capacity to measure within a 'concatenation of industrial processes'. As Daniel Bell expressed it:

The meaning of industrialisation did not arise with the introduction of factories, it arose out of the measurement of work. It's when work can be measured, when you can hitch a man to a job. When you can put a harness on him and measure his output in terms of a single piece and pay him by the piece or by the hour that you have got modern industrialisation.[82]

Taylorism epitomises the capitalist tendency towards more and greater standardisation, bureaucracy, and planning[83] – capitalist planning grows as the economy becomes more complex. It does so through bureaucracy, technology, labour management, science, etc. Veblen too, and in a contemporary setting, Nolan[84] and Hymer, emphasise the use of bureaucracy, science, technology, organisation, marketing and brands to create the real subsumption of labour to capital and 'planned' monopolies and oligopolies. Planning allows the machine process to grow production and, upon this, it enables finance to act as strategic investment. As such, although de-coupled, both are tied.[85]

Once standardisation emerges as a powerful corporate force, planning becomes necessary because having deliberately weakened craft capacity to self-organise production, capitalism massified the working class.[86] This brought two problems in its wake. Firstly, the process of massification created the industrial working class on a larger scale, which allowed it a certain autonomy. Secondly, because of its new centrality to consumption and production, this industrial class produced future development. The altered class composition of monopoly capitalism brought about by the new relations of (mass) production, became evident with the Great Crash and destroyed laissez-faire capitalism. Keynes highlighted this. He rejected the Versailles Treaty's destruction of the German economy because it undermined demand and risked pushing Germany east towards the Soviet Union with potentially dire consequences for capitalism. Keynes saw the UK 1926 General Strike as a moment of shifting class forces that demonstrated the capacity of the working class to challenge capitalism and/or preserve it through consumer demand, and to thereby act as the source of capitalism's development.[87] Intervention, not laissez-faire, was capitalism's future because the state became 'the most important' entrepreneur.[88] State intervention was not new, e.g. Bismarck had used it to weaken the left in Germany. However, this new intervention acknowledged the working class as the driver of the economy. A central feature of this was the belief that insecurity – a mainstay of neo-liberal financialisation[89] – was no longer viable as the motor of economic change.[90] Echoing Veblen, Keynes highlighted uncertainty and disequilibrium as 'enabling great inequalities of wealth to come about' thereby threatening capitalism, and called for states to direct economies. The power of the industrial working class to shift class forces lay in its necessary consumption and ability to disrupt production.[91] The working class could demand that the business enterprise and the machine process were realigned to challenge rentiers[92] and the untrammelled rights of property.[93]

The New Deal/Keynesianism recognised these changed class forces precisely to pursue stability and a new form of equilibrium located in the primary economic actor – the state. One sees this in New Deal legislation directed at the banks blamed for the crisis. This legislation split investment from commercial banking; enabled the Federal Reserve Bank to tightly regulate bank loans for investing (speculating) in securities; introduced interest ceilings on time and savings deposits via Regulation Q, partially removed housing from the market; and provided economic stability by limiting the boom and bust of speculation.[94] A constellation of class forces aligned to support such limitations to laissez-faire financialisation. Equilibrium was further achieved through full employment, sufficient demand, higher incomes, and a propensity to consume within the working class (partly to manage working class political autonomy).[95] This militated against the crisis and disequilibrium prioritised by the business enterprise. The balance of class forces moved away from the business enterprise towards the machine process. The massification of the working class through the destruction of craft and standardisation first encouraged financialisation, but then undermined it.

Class Composition and the De-coupling of the Machine Process and the Business Enterprise

By the 1960s the New Deal was unravelling. The development of inequality in the 1960s/1970s enabled an inter-class alliance of owners, top management, and a subordinate passive class of salaried earners to create a two-tier capitalism. This broke the Keynesian compromise.[96] As Veblen predicted, and Hymer demonstrated, by the 1970s, US capital was altered through a global division of labour that enabled corporations to increase profitability by re-routing the machine process and planning production across ever increasing spatial terrains to pursue cheap labour, new markets, pliable states and value extraction.[97] This shift weakened labour in its core heartlands but, primitive accumulation-like, it also opened up new sources of labour and new fields of exploitation.[98] Capital, via the international division of labour, could force the 'interstate federalism' advocated by Hayek at the height of the New Deal. States and supra-state agencies altered regulation systems e.g. the US New Deal system was dismantled.[99] Individual states also undermined organised labour through legislative changes, economic policies, globalisation, direct attacks on rights, etc.[100] And finally, organisations downgraded collective bargaining and unions in a variety of ways through individualised management forms, new public management, human resources, etc. All of this enabled capitalist social relations to colonise new spheres of society, allow increases in public and private debt, empower finance capital, and undermine democracy.[101] One outcome was the rapid rise in social inequality as working-class gains were rolled back and society returned to levels of inequality comparable to the early twentieth century.[102]

These forces disorganised relations between the machine process and business enterprise to allow a new era of financialisation and create the disequilibrium or crises which Veblen suggested were beneficial to finance. For example, echoing Rockefeller management of the Colorado Fuel and Iron Company, Rossman and Greenfield highlight how investment fund owners of companies such as Gate Gourmet, the airline food provider, disavow any obligation to manage labour/labour processes by arguing they merely invest in companies that others manage and are responsible for. Nolan calls this 'a new "separation of ownership and control" in which the boundaries of the firm become blurred'. This disorganisation disempowered (elements of) labour. It did so by shifting much of the machine process overseas in search of new labour[103] and/or disembowelling labour so much that industries which were once shipped overseas could make a return to core cities, e.g. textiles. The return to financialisation emerges in the wake of the machine process and consolidation movements Veblen discussed. Nolan highlights how Western firms consolidated and concentrated to take control of global markets in key industries. They now act as 'systems integrators' which dominate suppliers and firms within their global value chains to squeeze value via what he calls the 'cascade effect'. We should not see the firm as its legal entity, but as one that increasingly plans and coordinates the activities of others firms though its oligopolistic power (as Morgan did with US Steel).

Banks are central to this change.[104] Between 1997 and 2006 of the biggest 1000 banks, the share of total assets of the top 25 banks increased from 28 per cent to 41. This concentration was intensified post 2008 financial crisis so that by 2009, the figure was 45 per cent. Within asset management – a key element of financialisation and its relationship to labour[105] – globalisation also led to concentration. Total funds under the Global 500 grew from $25 trillion to $62 trillion between 1997 and 2009 but within this the top 50 management funds accounted for 61 per cent (up from 57 percent). Much of this is US dominated – although potentially less tied to the nation-state than the past.[106] Since the rise of the crises of the New Deal – social, fiscal and legitimation – the power of financialisation has grown rapidly so that financial sector profits represent more than 40 per cent of US total profits in 2001 – which is an underestimation because it does not include the financialised activities of non-financial corporations, like GE or Ford.[107] Financial profits squeezed out productive profits so that organisations are administered solely to benefit property owners who see value extracted elsewhere come to them. These changes arose with the reconfigured class relations of the post-1970s. Class re-composition has allowed financialisation to return (albeit different to the past).

Conclusion

This chapter demonstrates how standardisation of the (labour) machine process and the (financialised) business enterprise connect depending on how class (re)composition impacts financialisation. These relations centralise and subordinate knowledge of the production process to capitalist valorisation. Without control of the division of labour, financialisation cannot succeed because it feeds off disequilibrium and crises generated through standardisation: investors need to be able to say we can get a good return here but even better there. Financialisation is the enacting of this prioritisation of capital over any other need or activity. The re-composition of class in the old industrial heartlands means the end of financialisation will not emerge anytime soon. Indeed, what we have witnessed with this crisis, unlike the great Crash, has been an intensification of financialisation.[108] However, given the globalisation of the machine process and the business enterprise, it seems safe to say the only solution to rising inequality and crises driven by financialisation's lop-sidedness, is global. This is some way off and hence social, economic and political instability seems likely to be with us for the long term.

Notes

1. William Lazonick and Mary O'Sullivan, 'Maximising Shareholder Value: A New Ideology for Corporate Governance', *Economy and Society*, 29(1), 2000, pp. 13–35.
2. Greta R. Krippner, *Capitalizing on Crisis: The Political Origins of the Rise of Finance* (Cambridge: Harvard University Press, 2011).
3. Gérard Duménil and Dominique Lévy, 'Neoliberal Income Trends', *New Left Review*, 30, Nov/Dec 2004, pp. 105–33.
4. Andrew G. Haldane, 'Who Owns a Company?' Speech given to University of Edinburgh Corporate Finance Conference, 22 May 2005. At www.bis.org/review/r150811a.pdf.
5. James Burnham, *The Managerial Revolution: What is Happening in the World* (Westport Connecticut: Greenwood Press Publishers, 1941).
6. For example, Ismail Erturk, Judy Froud, Sukdhev Johal, Adam Leaver and Karel Williams, *Financialization at Work* (London: Routledge, 2008).
7. Michael Hardt and Antonio Negri, *Empire* (Cambridge, MA: Harvard University Press, 2000); Christian Marazzi, *Capital and Language: From the New Economy to the War Economy* (South Pasedena, CA: Semiotext(e), 2008); Christian Marazzi, *Capital and Affects: The Politics of the Language Economy* (South Pasedena, CA: Semiotext(e), 2011).

8. Jean Cushen and Paul Thompson, 'Financialization and Value: why labor and the labor process still matter', *Work, Employment and Society*, 30(2), 2016, pp. 352–65.
9. Krippner, *Capitalizing on Crisis: The Political Origins of the Rise of Finance* (2011), pp. 10–14.
10. Thorstein Veblen, *The Theory of the Business Enterprise* (Mansfield Center, CT: Martino Publishing, 2013), p. 11.
11. Karl Marx, *Capital: A Critique of Political Economy*, Vol. 1 (Harmondsworth: Penguin, 1976), pp. 975–1060.
12. Veblen, *The Theory of the Business Enterprise* (2013), pp. 16–37; Veblen, 'On the Nature of Capital: Investment, Intangible Assets, and the Pecuniary Magnate', *The Quarterly Journal of Economics*, 23(1), 1908, pp. 104–36.
13. Veblen, *The Theory of the Business Enterprise* (2013), pp. 131–4; Peter Rossman and Gerard Greenfield, 'Financialization: New Routes to Profit, New Challenges for Trade Unions', *Labor Education, the quarterly review of the ILO Bureau for Workers' Activities*, 1/2006 (No. 142), 2006, pp. 1–10.
14. Veblen, *The Theory of the Business Enterprise* (2013), pp. 58–9.
15. Howard Gitelman, *Legacy of the Ludlow Massacre: A Chapter in American Industrial Relations* (Philadelphia, University of Pennsylvania Press, 1988).
16. Wolfgang Streeck, Buying Time: The Delayed Crisis of Democratic Capitalism (London: Verso, 2014).
17. Gitelman, *Legacy of the Ludlow Massacre: A Chapter in American Industrial Relations* (1988), p. 160.
18. David Brody, *Labor in Crisis: The Steel Strike of 1919* (Chicago: University of Illinois Press, 1987), p. 19.
19. On this spectrum, see George Caffentzis, 'Immeasurable Value? An essay on Marx's Legacy', *The Commoner*, 10, 2005, pp. 87–114.
20. Brody, *Labor in Crisis: The Steel Strike of 1919* (1987), p. 22.
21. Richard T. Holden, 'The Original Management Incentive Schemes', *Journal of Economic Perspectives*, 19(4), 2005, pp. 135–44.
22. John K. Galbraith, *The Great Crash 1929* (Harmondsworth: Penguin Books, 1954), pp. 77–9.
23. Veblen, *The Theory of the Business Enterprise* (2013), p. 14.
24. Veblen, 'On the Nature of Capital: Investment, Intangible Assets, and the Pecuniary Magnate', (1908), pp. 107–9. This is not to say that industrial relations or the labour problem disappeared – far from it, the early twentieth century was a period of historic industrial unrest [see Brody, *Labor in Crisis: The Steel Strike of 1919* (1987); David Montgomery, *The Fall of the House of Labor*] (New York: Cambridge University Press, 1987).
25. Caffentzis, 'Immeasurable Value, an Essay on Morx's Legacy', p. 105.
26. Tawney, 'Against the Rentier and Financier' (2008), in Ismail Erturk, Judy Froud, Sukhdev Johal, Adam Leaver and Karel Williams (eds), *Financialization at Work* (London: Routledge) pp. 55–62.
27. Veblen, *The Theory of the Business Enterprise* (2013), pp. 18–20; Veblen, 'On the Nature of Capital' (1908).
28. Veblen, 'On the Nature of Capital' (1908) p. 192, note 7.
29. Hardt and Negri, *Empire* (2000), pp. 353–9.
30. Alfred D. Chandler 'The American System and Modern Management' in Mayr, O. and Post, R.C. (eds), *Yankee Enterprise: The Rise of the American System of Manufactures* (Washington DC: Smithsonian Institution Press, 1981), pp. 153–70.

31. David A. Hounshell, *From the American System to Mass Production, 1800–1932: The Development of Manufacturing Technology in the United States* (Baltimore, MD: Johns Hopkins University Press, 1984).

32. Eugene S. Ferguson, 'History and Historiography' in Mayr, O. and Post, R.C. (eds), *Yankee Enterprise: The Rise of the American System of Manufactures* (Washington DC: Smithsonian Institution Press, 1981), pp. 1–23.

33. Gerard Hanlon, *The Dark Side of Management: A Secret History of Management Theory* (London: Routledge, 2016); Montgomery, *The Fall of the House of Labor* (1987).

34. Veblen, 'On the Nature of Capital' (1908), pp. 115–18; Veblen, *The Theory of the Business Enterprise* (2013), pp. 30–6, 84–6.

35. Hounshell, *From the American System to Mass Production, 1800–1932: The Development of Manufacturing Technology in the United States* (1984), p. 89.

36. Hounshell, *From the American System to Mass Production, 1800–1932: The Development of Manufacturing Technology in the United States* (1984), p. 97.

37. Veblen, *The Theory of the Business Enterprise* (2013), p. 14.

38. Stephen Hymer, 'The Efficiency (Contradictions) of Multinational Corporations', *American Economic Review*, 60(2), 1970, pp. 441–8; Folker Fröbel, Jurgen Heinrichs and Otto Kreye, 'The New International Division of Labor', *Social Science Information*, 17, 1978, pp. 123–42.

39. Michael Hardt and Antonio Negri (eds), *Labor of Dionysus: A Critique of the State-Form* (Minneapolis: University of Minnesota Press, 1994), pp. 23–52.

40. Commonwealth of Massachusetts, *Remonstrances Relating to the Amherst Carriage Company*, House of Representatives No. 38 (1837).

41. Commonwealth of Massachusetts, *Petitions and Remonstrances Relating to the Amherst Carriage Company*, House of Representatives No. 33 (1838), p. 10.

42. Montgomery, *The Fall of the House of Labor* (1987); Hanlon, *The Dark Side of Management: A Secret History of Management Theory* (2016); Stephen Wilentz, *Chants Democratic: New York City & the Rise of the American Working Class, 1788–1850*, Twentieth Anniversary Edition (New York: Oxford University Press, 2004).

43. Wilentz, *Chants Democratic: New York City & the Rise of the American Working Class, 1788–1850*, Twentieth Anniversary Edition, p. 27, ft. 13.

44. Wilentz, *Chants Democratic: New York City & the Rise of the American Working Class, 1788–1850*, Twentieth Anniversary Edition, p. 26.

45. Importantly, craft workers themselves were at least partially capitalists and were often involved in creating corporations thus there was intra-craft conflict between those craft workers seeking to maintain traditional working patterns and craft-capitalists intent on destroying these (see Wilentz, *Chants Democratic: New York City & the Rise of the American Working Class, 1788–1850*, Twentieth Anniversary Edition). Indeed, Marx comments on it on numerous occasions e.g. Irish journeymen bakers seeking to resist the intensification of work and, more substantially, in his analysis of the formal subsumption of labour to capital. See Henry Roland, 'Six examples of Successful Shop Management V', *The Engineering Magazine*, XII (1897), who suggests craftsmen exploited those they controlled, but also see those who argue craftsmen often protected junior staff from the vagaries of markets (see John Buttrick, 'The Inside Contract', *Journal of Economic History*, 12(3), 1952; Ernst J. Englander, 'The Inside Contract System of Production and Organization: A Neglected aspect of the History of the Firm', *Labor History*, 28(4), 1987.

46. Roland, 'Six examples of Successful Shop Management V', *The Engineering Magazine*, XII (1897), pp. 994–1000.

47. Dan Clawson, *Bureaucracy and the Labor Process: The Transformation of US Industry, 1860–1920* (New York: Monthly Review Press, 1980); Ferguson, 'History and Historiography' (1981); Chandler 'The American System and Modern Management' (1981); Hounshell, *From the American System to Mass Production, 1800–1932: The Development of Manufacturing Technology in the United States* (1984).

48. John Buttrick, 'The Inside Contract', *Journal of Economic History*, 12(3), 1952, pp. 205–21; Hanlon,. *The Dark Side of Management: A Secret History of Management Theory* (2016).

49. Chandler, 'The American System and Modern Management' (1981).

50. Roland, Buttrick, Alfred D. Chandler, 'The American System and Modern Management' (1981).

51. Harold F. Williamson, *Winchester – The Gun That Won The West* (New York: A. S. Barnes and Company Ltd, 1952) p. 21.

52. Horace L. Arnold, Horace L. 'Modern Machine-Shop Economics: The Newer Types of Metal Cutting Machines', *The Engineering Magazine*, XI, April-September (1896) pp. 883–904.

53. Frederick W. Taylor, 'Shop Management', *ASME Transactions* 24, (1903), pp. 1337–480.

54. see also Horace L. Arnold, 'Modern Machine-Shop Economics: The First Principles in the Management of Men', *The Engineering Magazine*, XI, April-September (1896), pp. 1089–96.

55. Katherine Stone, 'The Origin of Job Structures in the Steel Industry', *Radical America* 7(6), 1973, pp. 19–66; Montgomery, *The Fall of the House of Labor* (1987); Brody, *Labor in Crisis: The Steel Strike of 1919* (1987).

56. Ferguson, 'History and Historiography' (1981), p. 10.

57. Englander, 'The Inside Contract System of Production and Organization: A Neglected aspect of the History of the Firm' (1987), pp. 429–46.

58. Williamson, *Winchester – The Gun That Won The West* (1952), pp. 30, 395, note 3.

59. Williamson, *Winchester – The Gun That Won The West* (1952), p. 89.

60. Hanlon, *The Dark Side of Management: A Secret History of Management Theory*, (2016), p. 99.

61. Chandler, 'The American System and Modern Management' (1981).

62. Clawson, *Bureaucracy and the Labor Process: The Transformation of US Industry, 1860–1920* (1980).

63. Hounshell, *From the American System to Mass Production, 1800–1932: The Development of Manufacturing Technology in the United States* (1984), p. 35 – date added.

64. See Montgomery, *The Fall of the House of Labor* (1987) on craft labour's power prior to this.

65. Brody, *Labor in Crisis: The Steel Strike of 1919* (1987), p. 18.

66. Stone, 'The Origin of Job Structures in the Steel Industry' (1973); Montgomery, *The Fall of the House of Labor* (1987), p. 41, ft. 99, acknowledges the influence of Stone's essay, but suggests she 'seriously overestimates both the pace and extent of the steel industry's adoption of a job hierarchy based on "scientific management" principles'. Nevertheless, what Stone does highlight is the emergence of many of the management tactics and organizational strategies which dominated much of the twentieth century.

67. Brody, *Labor in Crisis: The Steel Strike of 1919* (1987).

68. Stone, 'The Origin of Job Structures in the Steel Industry' (1973).

69. Williamson, *Winchester – The Gun That Won The West* (1952), pp. 136–7.

70. Richard Edwards, *Contested Terrain: The Transformation of the Workplace in the Twentieth Century* (New York: Basic Books, 1979); Clawson, *Bureaucracy and the Labor Process: The Transformation of US Industry, 1860–1920* (1980).
71. Brody, *Labor in Crisis: The Steel Strike of 1919* (1987), p. 15.
72. Caffentzis, 'Immeasurable Value, an Essay on Marx's Legacy', p. 105.
73. Michel Aglietta, *A Theory of Capitalist Regulation: The US Experience* (London: Verso, 2000).
74. Rossman and Greenfield, 'Financialization: New Routes to Profit, New Challenges for Trade Unions' (2006).
75. Montgomery, *The Fall of the House of Labor* (1987), p. 42.
76. Sylvia Federici, *Caliban and the Witch. Women, the Body and Primitive Accumulation* (New York: Autonomedia, 2004), pp. 63–4.
77. Marx, *Capital: A critique of Political Economy*, (1976), pp. 692–701.
78. Taylor, 'Shop Management' (1903), p. 1415.
79. Arnold, 'Modern Machine-Shop Economics: The First Principles in the Management of Men' (1896), and Arnold, 'Modern Machine-Shop Economics: The Newer Types of Metal Cutting Machines'.
80. Gerard Hanlon, *The Dark Side of Management: A Secret History of Management Theory* (2016), pp. 89–124.
81. Mario Tronti, *Strategy of Refusal* (1965). At: http://operaisoinenglish.wordpress.com/2010/09/30/strategy-of-refusal/ (retrieved January 2013).
82. Quoted in Herbert Marcuse, *One Dimensional Man: Studies in the Ideology of Advanced Industrial Society* (London: Routledge, 1964), p. 29. Importantly, this increasing rise in the capital intensity of the organic composition of capital is predicated on the countervailing need to access new areas of surplus value and labour in the form of primitive accumulation (see Caffentzis, 'Immeasurable Value, an Essay on Marx's Legacy', p. 107; Federici, 'Caliban and the Witch. Women, the Body and Primitive Accumulation' (2004).
83. Hymer, 'The Efficiency (Contradictions) of Multinational Corporations' (1970).
84. Peter Nolan, *Is China Buying the World?* (London, Polity Press, 2012).
85. Veblen, *The Theory of the Business Enterprise* (2013).
86. Hardt and Negri, *Empire* (2000).
87. Ibid.
88. John Maynard Keynes, *Essays in Persuasion* (New York, Classic House Books, 2009), p. 67.
89. Friedrich A. Hayek, *Individualism and Economic Order* (London: Chicago University Press, 1948).
90. Hardt and Negri, Empire.
91. Gerard Hanlon, *The Dark Side of Management: A Secret History of Management Theory* (London: Routledge, 2016).
92. Keynes, *Essays in Persuasion* (2009).
93. Tawney, 'Against the Rentier and Financier' (2008).
94. Krippner, *Capitalizing on Crisis: The Political Origins of the Rise of Finance* (2011), pp. 60–3.
95. Hardt and Negri, Empire.
96. Duménil and Lévy, 'Neoliberal Income Trends', *New Left Review*, 30 (Nov/Dec 2004).
97. See Alain Lipietz, *Mirages and Miracles: The Crisis of Global Fordism* (London: Verso, 1987).

98. Caffentzis, 'Immeasurable Value, an Essay on Marx's Legacy', and Caffentzis, 'Crystals and Analytic Engines: Historical and Conceptual Preliminaries to a New Theory of Machines'.
99. Krippner, *Capitalizing on Crisis: The Political Origins of the Rise of Finance* (2011), 27.
100. Aglietta, 'A Theory of Capitalist Regulation: The US Experience' (2000).
101. Streeck, 'Buying Time: The Delayed Crisis of Democratic Capitalism' (2014).
102. Duménil and Lévy, 'Neoliberal Income Trends', *New Left Review*, 30 (Nov/Dec 2004).
103. Caffentzis, 'Immeasurable Value, an Essay on Marx's Legacy'.
104. Nolan (London: Polity Press, 2012), pp. 110–13.
105. Peter Rossman and Gerard Greenfield, 'Financialization: New Routes to Profit, New Challenges for Trade Unions', *Labor Education, the quarterly review of the ILO Bureau for Workers' Activities*, 1/2006 (No. 142) (2006).
106. Nolan, *Is China Buying the World?* (London: Polity Press, 2012), pp. 46–8.
107. Krippner, *Capitalizing on Crisis: The Political Origins of the Rise of Finance* (2011).
108. Nolan, *Is China Buying the World?* (London, Polity Press, 2012).

8

Reading 'Earth Incorporated' through *Caliban and the Witch*

Sian Sullivan

In the 1990s, millionaire Maurice Strong – Secretary General of the 1992 UN 'Earth Summit' in Rio de Janeiro and simultaneously initiator of the CEO-led network the World Business Council for Sustainable Development – asserted in a series of widely quoted lectures that 'global sustainability' can only be achieved through applying the principles of business. Formerly an entrepreneur in the Alberta oil patch and president of the Power Corporation of Canada, as well as Secretary General for the 1972 UN Stockholm Conference on the Human Environment, Strong proclaimed that:

> In addressing the challenge of achieving global sustainability, we must apply the basic principles of business. This means running 'Earth Incorporated' with a depreciation, amortization and maintenance account.[1]

This sentiment has become almost a truism in environmental governance. It is associated with a growing primacy of expertise in business, accounting and finance as core to the management of environmental health, coupled with the creation and calculation of new exchange values for units such as certified carbon emissions reductions, species banking credits and biodiversity offset scores. Underlying this transformation is a consolidated framing of the natural environment as a provider of 'ecosystem services' that should be paid for, and as a 'bank of natural capital' whose assets should be invested in and may be leveraged financially.[2]

In combination, these innovations are underscoring new processes of enclosure of beyond-human natures as they become conceptualised and calculated as privatised and tradable units to which monetary forms of value can attach and accrue. I have understood this process to be a 'financialisation of nature' in a manner akin to evocation of the 'financialisation of the social' effected through impact investing and other extensions of venture capital into social welfare.[3] Regardless of how much money may be made in the variously financialised creating of 'Earth Incorporated', its world-making significance is profound. It entails a creeping extension of accounting and financial discourse, expertise and valuation practices to the natural world, such that vast swathes of land and habitat, as well as the communities that dwell there, become (further) enmeshed in corporatised business in which 'only production-for-market... [is] defined as a value-creating activity'.[4]

In this chapter I celebrate Silvia Federici's *Caliban and the Witch* (2004) for the role it played for me some years ago in disentangling the dissonance of assertions that an extension of marketised forms of value will curtail the environmental degradations engendered by marketised forms of production, exchange and consumption. Specifically, I remember sitting in a café in Glastonbury – not far from localities claimed in local lore to be some of the last meeting places for English 'witches' of the Middle Ages – scribbling pages of notes as Federici's clarification of primitive accumulation and of modernity's new techno-statistical divisions of both nature and the body came into focus. Her electrifying integration of the insights of Marx and Foucault encouraged in me a resistant analytical response to the new enclosures becoming naturalised as Earth Incorporated seeks to accumulate from nature's conservation, as much as from its productive transformation. In this chapter I outline the contribution of Caliban to my understandings of contemporary 'primitive eco-accumulation' and the calculations of nature that are thereby required, particularly in two pieces – 'The environmentality of "Earth Incorporated"' and 'Banking nature?' – on which I draw heavily here.[5] I close with some reflections on the positioning and potential of struggles in a moment of populist politics in which women's bodies and the natural world are once again experiencing intensified capture, violation and erasure.

Primitive Eco-Accumulation: Enclosing the World's Body as 'Earth Incorporated'

Primitive accumulation in Marx denotes the acts of possession necessary for the creation and capture of all subsequent capitalist relations of production and exchange.[6] For Marx, the two critical enclosures are of land as property and human activity as labour, the creation of which required an historical rift of each from the other to effect a disembedding of people from land-entwined social relations, as Karl Polanyi later put it.[7] Federici and other scholars highlight additional historical forms of primitive accumulations as integral to the capitalist strategy of bending nature *in situ*, as well as human life and bodies, to the commodity form. Michael Perelman, for example, understands the eradication of scores of annual religious 'holy-days' throughout the Middle Ages as primitive accumulation.[8] The removal of these days from the annual calender further released an increasingly individualised and disciplined labour force for capital, both by increasing the number of work days annually and by eroding collective solidarities consolidated through the celebration of Saints' Days.

In *Caliban* Federici clarifies two further key enclosures in the service of capitalist primitive accumulation. First, women's wombs and reproductive labour were accumulated as a free service through systematic destruction of women's productive autonomy, linked with the terrorising 'witch-hunts' in Europe in the sixteenth and seventeenth centuries in which some two-hundred thousand women[9] were murdered by emerging European states. Secondly, Federici traces an amplified self-disciplining of the body's urges in its refashioning as 'body-machine' as enabling the primitive accumulation of commoditised labour to supply the homogenised and increasingly automated organisation of capitalist industrial production.

All such accumulations of productive forces not *a priori* manufactured for sale require dramatic, albeit subsequently naturalised, conceptual transformations. The conversion of land into private property, which underscores the current wave of financialised ecology-commodity creation, thus requires the rejection of prior values, access or use rights so that land itself becomes capital that can be owned for most intents and purposes absolutely. Its abstracted monetary price, linked with associated resources and amenities, is then able to rise and fall in relation to other commodities, and its deterritorialised exchange is able to occur at a distance with money as symbolic medium and measure of 'value'. In combination, it is the transformation of land and human activity from subject to object that permits their reification as marketable commodities.[10] This is a process that disregards and makes strange the myriad other practices of relationship, value and ethical requirements enacted by people in relation to natures-beyond-the-human.[11]

Marx states additionally that '[a]s soon as capitalist production is on its own legs, it not only maintains this separation [of labour from the means of capitalist production], but reproduces it on a continually extending scale'.[12] As Federici maintains, 'primitive accumulation has been a universal process in every phase of capitalist development', re-launching 'similar strategies in the face of every major capitalist crisis'.[13] Massimo De Angelis thus refers to primitive accumulation as the *ontological*, as opposed to historical, condition of capitalist production.[14] Many other authors have stressed this ongoing nature of primitive accumulation, from Rosa Luxemburg writing in 1913, to David Harvey writing in 2010. As such, recent analyses frame the process as 'continuous',[15] 'permanent'[16] and 'contemporary'.[17]

The current proliferation of new nature values and tradable commodities for environmental conservation can be understood as a similarly productive wave of primitive accumulation. They are structuring ostensibly untransformed and variously restored nonhuman natures into reified and potentially exchangeable commodity forms in previously unthought ways,[18] at the same time as creating additional ways of bringing diverse peoples into the global market as producers-consumers of these new commodity forms. Primitive 'eco-accumulation' in this reading is the engine driving a series of expansionary and overlapping intensifications in the commodification of life itself, so as to more fully saturate and subsume 'the eco-socius'[19] – despite the resistances afforded by affected communities and the immanent diversity and liveliness of beyond-human materialities.

In creating Earth Incorporated the 'reproductive capacities' of the body of the earth are becoming conceived, measured and alienated in terms of productive labour or service-work. Unlike the unpaid reproductive labour of women, however, in Earth Incorporated nature's 'labour' should be paid for: through 'payments for ecosystem services' and associated initiatives instituted at varying scales of exchange. There is an additional parallel here with Federici's exploration of the medieval commutation to money payments of rent for land,[20] in that 'payments for ecosystem services' discourse and practice similarly effects a commutation to money payments of the generative capacities of beyond-human nature. As in the former commutation, any payments arising from the latter commutation also go to those able to assert ownership over the services that are thus produced. Indeed, the stated intention in 'payments for ecosystem services' discourse and policy is to enhance resource rents on owned land, such that these rents will out-compete alternative land uses. Through delineating ecosystem service units and creating possibilities for enhancing tradable value – for example, by bundling[21] and stacking 'multiple, spatially overlapping credits representing different ecosystem services' such that these units can be 'sold separately to compensate for different impacts'[22] – new sources of income are thereby able to accrue to alienated land. Simultaneously, new motivations are created for the alienation of land as well as of any new exchange values abstracted for so-called 'ecosystem services' and 'natural capital assets'.

A 'growing multibillion-dollar international market in carbon, habitat, and water-quality credits'[23] is thus set within multiple assertions that so-called 'natural capital' 'represents an undeveloped, but emerging private sector investment opportunity of major proportion.[24] This new metaphorical framing and fabrication of nature-as-capital is in fact a brilliant subversion of the biological metaphors through which eighteenth and nineteenth century economists understood capital, and particularly its interest-generating capacity. In *Capital* Marx observed the tendency to see '... a property of money to generate value and yield interest, much as it is an attribute of pear trees to bear pears'; such that '[a]s the growing process is to trees, so generating money appears as innate in capital in its form as money-capital'.[25] The metaphor of 'natural capital' turns this conception on its head to state instead that the generative capacities of 'nature' are akin to those of the interest-bearing capacities of capital. In doing so, conceptions and materialities of 'the natural world' are wrapped further into the logic and values of capitalist market economy, in paradoxical disregard to the manner in which marketised exchange thrives on the dissociative impetus underscoring the degradations that 'natural capital thinking' is apparently intended to redress. Indeed, fantastical notions of 'decoupling' economic activity from ecological materialities and generating 'no net loss' of biological diversity, even though losses to populations and habitats have taken place, extend this splitting impetus into arguably pathological conceptualisations of possibility.[26]

Coupled with amplified 'land grabbing' in the global south in recent years, in part as a response to financial crisis, the acquisition of land for the commoditised 'green' economic values it might produce has been variously termed 'green grabbing', 'accumulation-by-conservation' and 'accumulation-by-restoration'.[27] Market-based conservation technologies are celebrated by some as a means of amplifying possibilities for local peoples to assert claims to new sources of income.[28] They have also been linked, however, with evictions from land,[29] the disempowering of local decision-making structures[30] and heightened counter-insurgency tactics,[31] alongside amplified reach and wealth extraction by private sector investors. As such, contemporary primitive eco-accumulation can be understood to offer new impetus for old processes whereby capital creates and appropriates new commodity fictions from which surpluses can accumulate.[32] As Federici writes for the creation of the mastered labouring body that was central to the success of earlier accumulation regimes, this extension of the techno-calculative grid of economic value-making into previously uncalculated domains fabricates the natural world as a 'work machine' to make possible new forms of 'green enclosure'. It is to this dimension of the making of 'Earth Incorporated' that I now turn.

Calculating 'Earth Incorporated'

Primitive eco-accumulation has involved innovations in the ways that nature is calculated, effecting techno-statistical divisions of 'the world's body' so as to bind nature to capital in previously unforeseen ways.[33] In foregrounding the calculative practices fabricating and mastering the body as a work-machine whose labour can be sold as an alienated com-modity, Federici's *Caliban* again offers insights into the conceptualisations, practices and mechanisms by which this calculative and governing impetus is taking hold in environmental management. Here she shifts from Marx to Foucault (amongst other authors) in examining the 'philosophical debates' and 'strategic interventions' transforming 'the individual's powers into labor-power'.[34] Her insights and analysis are potent for considering the similar processes in application in the conceptualisation and trans-formation of nature's diverse powers into labour-power that can be paid for.

As Federici summarises, in *Discipline and Punish* Foucault analysed how new regimes of governance are structured and bolstered by new social sciences, which recursively and productively reinforced new disciplining techniques of management and administration. Foucault made much of the accompanying presence of a novel spirit that partitions, makes distinc-tions, classifies, codifies and calculates as central to the rise of the bourgeois class and the Age of Reason in Europe.[35] Foucault was talking about the body, and about the emergence of new social sciences that helped to construct, master and accumulate the body as a utility-maximising 'body-machine', as well as to rationalise and administer bodies as popula-tions. Federici extends this structural analysis to affirm that '[t]he product of this alienation from the body ... was the development of individual *identity*, conceived precisely as 'otherness' from the body, and in perennial antagonism with it'[36] – a point to which I will return below.

The contemporary era of primitive eco-accumulation accompanying neo-liberal environmental governance is infused with a similarly intensified extension of subjectification practices to alienated socio-ecological domains. Just as the new sciences of demography, nutrition, etc. made possible the administrations of the modern era through the application of *accounting* to social relations,[37] ecosystem service science today is effecting the application of accounting to socio-environmental relations as 'natural capital accounting', also in service to particular administrative regimes.[38] In further transforming and accumulating 'Nature's' exceeding immanence into 'work powers', the animated, embodied and sentient world that may be experienced by non-capitalist rationalities is of necessity erased. Nature's operations are made 'intelligible and controllable', 'void of any intrinsic teleology'[39] or agency.[40] As such, human nature is rendered deaf but in apparent authority over a mirroring mute and intractably distinct beyond-human nature.

This reading of Earth Incorporated views beyond-human natures as being disciplined and mastered through a conceptual transformation that seeks to catch them 'in a [new] system of subjection', whereby diversely productive characteristics can be further 'calculated, organized, technically thought' and 'invested with power relations'.[41] Like the human body, and the body-politic of populations, conserved nature as service-provider and store of capital is being entered into 'a machinery of power that explores it, breaks it down and rearranges it' to productively bend and release its immanent forces towards economic utility.[42] Through 'ecoinformatics' and natural capital accounting, ecological and economics data are connected and entrained so as to create 'value' at various ecosystem scales, in a process that mirrors the 'accumulation by molecularisation'[43] made possible through capital investment in bioinformatics at the scale of molecular biology. These infiltrations of capital at both large and small scales of nature are 'amplifying power's effects within a wider economic field of calculation'[44] by consolidating claims to unforeseen domains and inventions of life.[45] The micro-physics of power operating in the capillaries and institutional apparatuses of ecosystem service science thus strategically reshapes socio-environment relations such that they are those of 'Earth Incorporated'. The reign of money's sign over all aspects of the natural world has come to occupy centre stage in ongoing proliferations of financialised eco-control.

In later work, Foucault elaborated this intensification as biopolitical governmentality effected by the 'truth regime' of the market under neoliberalism, requiring work to create the governing incentivising and regulatory structures permitting the 'free market's' need for 'frugal government'.[46] As Martin O'Connor has also noted,

> The logic of the marketplace states plainly that all capitals will realize their 'full value' only by insertion within the sphere of exchange value. Under the doctrine of utility maximisation, their best use will be signaled by price: they should always go to the highest bidder.[47]

Muradian et al. describe how this naturalisation of capitalist 'free markets' in environmental domains is also rationalised by a Coasean institutional economics that assumes the emergence of social and environmental optima through the incentivised bargaining of those with private property allocations.[48] These contexts conspire to produce a 'governmentality' that ironically requires significant government and public engagement to facilitate the construction and regulation of the incentive structures that discipline individual and corporate behaviour to conform with the logic of the 'free market'. This, as Noel Castree notes, is 'the paradoxical need for 'free' markets to be managed'.[49] In understanding neoliberalism to take hold as governmentality – i.e. to be both reinforced and hybridised through multiplicitous yet patterned acts and practices of governance, participation and resistance – it becomes possible to notice how similar practices are unfolding as the 'truths' of contemporary environmental governance.

Extending this conceptualisation to environmental arenas thus engenders an 'environmentality'[50] whereby all environmental phenomena are rendered intelligible and governable through insertion into financial(ised) logics. Current rationalisations and monetisations of nature in terms of the disaggregated, commodified and banked services 'it' provides, thus constitute a new mechanisation of nature management to satisfy discourses of efficiency in the realm of environmental conservation, whilst maintaining accumulation as 'the engine which powers growth under the capitalist mode of production'.[51] As such, these proliferating economising rationalisations can be regarded as variously productive power effects, which permit the repositioning and territorialisation of vast regions of the world as sites for capitalised global ecosystem services conservation and supply.[52] By further secularising beyond-human nature and human-with-nature relationships they constitute a massive rendering mute[53] of the nature knowledges and value practices associated with non-capitalist ways of living. The displacement effects of this restructuring range from so-called 'green land grabs' for conservation[54] to the more subtle erasure of knowledges, values and commons that constitute an 'outside' to the logic of this financialising impetus,[55] mirroring the capture and denigration of women's bodies, experiences and capacities noted above. In 'Earth Incorporated', 'nature's agency' is further desacralised and discounted, continuing the processes documented in *Caliban* that discipline frequently feminised human and beyond-human bodies into master-slave or doctor-patient relationships.

A Concluding Comment on Continuing Enclosures and Erasures

Reading *Caliban and the Witch* over the years has engendered a range of experiences for me. I have felt relief at the clarity of thought and analysis connecting the appropriation of women's bodies and reproductive labour with anti-feudal struggles, colonialism, slavery, and capitalised land appropriation in Europe, the 'New World' and the contemporary 'global south'. I have been shocked to learn more of the obsessive vilification and violent taming of women during the witch-hunts of especially the sixteenth and seventeenth centuries, and the ways this control ushered in a new sexual differentiation of spaces and bodies that historically instituted women's loss of social power.[56] And I have been inspired with recognition as the calculative and capitalising impetus directed now towards 'the world's body' came into focus through Federici's insights into the centrality of the calculative practices for mastering the immanently productive body as controllable 'work-machine'. As I re-read *Caliban* today, however, and given a global moment wherein the bodies of women and the natural world appear to be experiencing renewed capture, violation and erasure, I find myself with new questions concerning new/old enclosures and erasures, as well as possibilities for new/old struggles.

Federici's text positions the historical 'transition' to capitalism as the unfortunate outcome of the multiplicitous anti-feudal struggles she outlines for Europe and the colonial 'New World'. Fueled by the appropriation and mining of resources from slaves to silver, the mercantile interests of the Middle Ages, in combination with the protection of their patrons in emerging modern European states, comprised the ultimately successful 'counter-insurgency' of the day. Today, neoliberal capitalism is the new political economic normal, despite the vibrant global movements of the 1990s and early 2000s contesting neoliberal values and policies.[57] Indeed, privatised capture of both public provision and public assets is being intensified in the current moment of populist 'post-truth' politics. What, then, are the implications now for a longer-lasting social impetus for change linked with contemporary contestations over the capitalisation of nature as Earth Incorporated and of human bodies as (re)productive labour?

Recalling Federici's critique[58] above of the antagonisms to the body wrought as individual identity becomes conceived as alienated from the body, the populisms of the contemporary moment appear to deepen such antagonisms to human and beyond-human bodies. A dissociative discourse of decoupling economy from ecology in the quest for green economic growth empowers a strand of ecomodernist thought directing techno-fixes to solve environmental degradation and climate change that are described as 'delusional' by some analysts.[59] A similarly dissociative discourse of 'being born in the wrong body' provides new impetus to an objectifying approach to the body focusing on making the body – as object – have the properties so desired.[60] A disassembling and reconstruction of bodies in service to identity choices, realities, and as a consciously directed attack on 'the myth of the natural'[61] thus guides trans-humanist,[62] gender reassignment and cosmetic surgery industries, and perhaps also some consumer choices regarding reproductive technologies. Taken together, these splitting impulses and the enclosures and foreclosures[63] they articulate may invite resistant anti-capitalist 're-embodiments'.[64]

Caliban clarifies further that the separations and divisions effecting capitalist enclosure during the anti-feudal struggles took place during a time of 'escalating misogyny'.[65] Ultimately the period claimed the lives of hundreds of thousands of women categorised as witches in Europe, resulting from 'a true war against women clearly aimed at breaking the control they had exercised over their bodies and reproduction'.[66] More recently, Federici describes the contemporary moment as characterised by a similarly staggering increase in violence towards women globally. It includes a rise in misogynistic identification and sequestration of especially older women as witches in 'witch-camps', which Federici interprets as linked with neoliberal structural adjustment policies that destabilise community structures – including those around gender.[67] Federici writes further that,

> ...the capitalist class *is determined to turn the world upside down* in order to consolidate its power, which was undermined in the '60s and '70s by anti-colonial, feminist, and civil rights struggles, particularly the Black Power movement. ... we are witnessing an escalation of violence against women, especially women of color, because 'globalization' is a process of political recolonization, *intended to give capital uncontested control of the world's natural wealth and all human labor*, and this cannot be achieved without attacking women, who are directly responsible for the reproduction of their communities.[68]

This currently escalating misogyny is entangled with an equally staggering increase in extractive industry and violence towards the earth that is 'greenwashed' precisely through the marketised environmental governance technologies that have formed the focus of this chapter.[69]

These phenomena that have tended to attack feminised bodies[70] are occurring in a moment shaped additionally by new theoretical, political and pragmatic destabilisations of universal(ising) categories of 'male' and 'female', as well as 'men' and 'women'.[71] From a capitalist-critical perspective, an understanding that capitalism is 'deeply invested in the compulsory two-gendered system as it guarantees maximum efficiency and control in the production and reproduction of labor power and the harnessing of bio-power', means that '[r]efusal to cooperate with the two-gendered system [becomes] a radically resistant action played out variously by different bodies'.[72] In intersecting with patriarchal structures of power and accumulation, however, it is not exactly clear how 'queered, resistant Bodies'[73] of contemporary modes of contestation can in and of themselves subvert rather than reproduce these structures, particularly given 'repetition within commodity culture where 'subversion' carries market value'.[74] It is also unclear how any essentialising of a 'two-gendered system' as core to capitalism might intersect with, and/or delimit,[75] the makings of masculine and feminine in cultural contexts that have otherwise proved resistant to modern state and capitalist forms of organisation.[76] As Judith Butler writes, 'feminism' needs to continue 'to be careful not to idealize certain expressions of gender that, in turn, produce new forms of hierarchy and exclusion'.[77] Remembering the subtitle of *Caliban* ('Women, the Body and Primitive Accumulation'), then, my suggestion here is that Federici's materialist analysis of the historical accumulation of female bodies and reproductive labour – and of the particular sexualisations of bodies, spaces and identities associated with these processes – might offer fresh insights for theorising newly normative gender troubles of the contemporary moment.[78]

In particular, *Caliban and the Witch* retains relevance for understanding the depth of historical context whereby the variously sexualised, racialised and objectified bodies of women, people of colour and beyond-human natures have been silenced and exploited in tandem as classes of pacified beings-becomings. Contemporary circumstances demonstrate that the struggle for the rights of these classes, as well as for recognition of their/ our realities, remains critical, if increasingly complex, today. Federici helps us to see additionally that the creation of divisions that implode solidarities has long been a key strategy of capital and the sustained power of the ruling class.[79] Relational solidarities that reach beyond individualised identities clearly remain critical if struggles are to refract the alienations required for capital to further subsume psychological, social and ecological experience.

Acknowledgements

Thank you to David Harvie for the encouragement to contribute this chapter and to be able to express my gratitude to Silvia Federici for her inspiring, if necessarily unsettling, work.

Notes

1. See, for example, www.mauricestrong.net/index.php/speeches-remarks3/34-asia; www.mauricestrong.net/index.php/speeches-remarks3/79-korea-econom-ic-policy; www.mauricestrong.net/index.php/speeches-remarks3/46-scenarios (all last accessed 20 July 2018).
2. See Sian Sullivan, 'Green capitalism, and the cultural poverty of constructing nature as service-provider', *Radical Anthropology* 3, 2009, pp. 18–27; Credit Suisse and McKinsey Center for Business and Environment, *Conservation Finance. From Niche to Mainstream: The Building of an Institutional Asset Class* (2016); available at: www.credit-suisse.com/media/assets/corporate/docs/about-us/responsibility/ banking/conservation-finance-en.pdf (last accessed 21 May 2016) and, for a discussion, Sullivan, 'Making nature investable: from legibility to leverageability in fabricating "nature" as "natural capital"', *Science and Technology Studies* 31(3), 2018, pp. 47–76 and Sullivan, 'Bonding nature(s)? Funds, financiers and values at the impact investing edge in environmental conservation', in Sarah Bracking, Aurora Fredriksen, Sian Sullivan and Philip Woodhouse (eds), *Valuing Development, Environment and Conservation: Creating Values that Matter* (London: Routledge, 2018).
3. E. Chiapello and G. Godefroy, 'The dual function of judgment devices: why does the plurality of market classifications matter?', *Historical Social Research* 42(1), 2017, p. 153; see also D. Harvie '(Big) society and (market) discipline: the financialisation of social reproduction', *Historical Materialism* 27(1), 2019, pp. 92–124.

4. Federici, S., *Caliban and the Witch: Women, the Body and Primitive Accumulation* (New York: Autonomedia, 2004), p. 74.
5. 'The environmentality of "Earth Incorporated": on contemporary primitive accumulation and the financialisation of environmental conservation' (2010). Online https://wordpress.com/post/siansullivan.net/375 (last accessed 20 July 2018); 'Banking nature? The spectacular financialisation of environmental conservation', *Antipode* 45(1), 2013, pp. 198–217.
6. See especially chapter 16 of *Capital*, Vol. 1. Federici (*Caliban*, p. 117) points out that for Marx 'primitive accumulation' was 'so-called' to signal his rejecting of the earlier ahistorical usage of the term by Adam Smith and the implication that accumulated inequalities 'just happened', as if in the absence of the ongoing and intentional class-based appropriations emphasised by Marx as essential to the concept.
7. *The Great Transformation: the Political and Economic Origins of Our Time* (Boston: Beacon Press, 2001 [1944]).
8. 'The secret history of primitive accumulation and classical political economy', *The Commoner*, 2 (September 2001), at www.commoner.org.uk/02perelman.pdf.
9. I understand 'women' in the subtitle of *Caliban* to refer to adult female human beings whose experience was caught in and patterned by the historical moment of the shift from feudalism to mercantile capitalism. In this reading, Federici's analysis in *Caliban* is concerned with how the bodies and experiences of adult female human beings were targeted in particular – through the 'primitive accumulation' of women's wombs and reproductive labour enabled by systematic erosion of women's productive autonomy, linked with the 'witch-hunts' precipitated by this historical moment. This is not the same as saying that all women had (or have) the same experience or the same bodies; or that many others – as signalled by 'Caliban' in her title (and discussed further in this chapter) – did not experience similar violations. But it *is* to affirm that Federici's analysis draws into focus how women as a class of human persons were subjected to particular patterns of subjection and accumulation, often accompanied by particular forms of violence.
10. See Massimo De Angelis, 'Marx and primitive accumulation: the continuous character of capital's "enclosures"', *The Commoner* 2 (September 2001), p. 7, at www.commoner.org.uk/02deangelis.pdf.
11. Discussed further in Sullivan, 'On "natural capital", "fairy-tales" and ideology', *Development and Change* 48(2), 2017, pp. 397–423.
12. Marx, *Capital*, vol. 1 (trans. S. Moore and E. Aveling) (London: Lawrence and Wishart, 1974 [1867]), p. 668.
13. *Caliban*, pp. 16–17, 104.
14. De Angelis, 'Marx and primitive accumulation: the continuous character of capital's "enclosures"' (2001).
15. De Angelis, 'Marx and primitive accumulation: the continuous character of capital's "enclosures"' (2001).
16. Werner Bonefeld, 'The permanence of primitive accumulation: Commodity fetishism and social constitution', *The Commoner* 2 (September 2001), at www.commoner.org.uk/02bonefeld.pdf; David Harvey, 'The geography of capitalist accumulation: a reconstruction of the Marxian theory', *Antipode* 7(2), 1975, pp. 9–21.
17. Jim Glassman, 'Primitive accumulation, accumulation by dispossession, accumulation by "extra-economic" means', *Progress in Human Geography* 30(5), 2006, pp. 608–25.
18. N. Kosoy and E. Corbera, 'Payments for ecosystem services as commodity fetishism', *Ecological Economics* 69(6), 2010, pp. 1228–36.

19. *Cf.* J.T. Nealon, *Foucault Beyond Foucault: Power and its Intensifications since 1984* (Stanford: Stanford University Press, 2008).

20. *Caliban*, pp. 28–9.

21. S.A. Bekessy and B.A. Wintle, 'Using carbon investment to grow the biodiversity bank', *Conservation and Policy* 22(3), 2008, p. 510.

22. M. Robertson, T.K. BenDor, R. Lave, A. Riggsbee, J.B. Ruhl and M. Doyle, 'Stacking ecosystem services', *Frontiers in Ecology and the Environment* 12(3), 2014, pp. 186.

23. *Ibid.*, p. 186.

24. Center for Business and Environment, *Conservation Finance. From Niche to Mainstream: The Building of an Institutional Asset Class* (2016), p. 3.

25. Marx, *Capital*, vol. 3 (trans. S. Moore and E. Aveling) (London: Lawrence and Wishart, 1974 [1894]), pp. 392–3). See also the discussion in Michael T. Taussig, *The Devil and Commodity Fetishism in South America* (Chapel Hill: University of North Carolina Press, 2010 [1980]), pp. 31–3.

26. This is discussed further in Sullivan, 'What's ontology got to do with it? On nature and knowledge in a political ecology of "the green economy"', *Journal of Political Ecology* 24, 2017, pp. 217–42.

27. J. Fairhead, M. Leach and I. Scoones, 'Green grabbing: A new appropriation of nature?', *Journal of Peasant Studies* 39, 2012, pp. 237–61; B. Büscher and R. Fletcher, 'Accumulation by conservation', *New Political Economy* 20, 2015, pp. 273–98; A. Huff and A. Brock, 'Accumulation by restoration: degradation neutrality and the Faustian bargain of conservation finance', *Antipode Intervention*, online at https://antipode-foundation.org/2017/11/06/accumulation-by-restoration/ (accessed 10 July 2018).

28. See, for example, G. Van Hecken, V. Kolinjivadi, C. Windey, et al., 'Silencing agency in Payments for Ecosystem Services (PES) by essentializing a neoliberal "monster" into being: a response to Fletcher & Büscher's "PES Conceit"', *Ecological Economics* 144, 2018, pp. 314–18.

29. C. Cavanagh and T.A. Benjaminsen, 'Virtual nature, violent accumulation: the "spectacular failure" of carbon offsetting at a Ugandan National Park', *Geoforum* 56, 2014, pp. 55–65.

30. S. Chomba, J. Kariuki, J.F. Lund and F. Sinclair, 'Roots of inequity: how the implementation of REDD+ reinforces past injustices', *Land Use Policy* 50, 2016, pp. 202–13.

31. A. Dunlap and J. Fairhead, 'The militarisation and marketisation of nature: an alternative lens to "climate-conflict"', *Geopolitics* 19, 2014, pp. 937–61; A. Brock and A. Dunlap, 'Normalising corporate counterinsurgency: engineering consent, managing resistance and greening destruction around the Hambach coal mine and beyond', *Political Geography* 62, pp. 33–47; J. Verweijen and E. Marijnen, 'The counterinsurgency/conservation nexus: guerrilla livelihoods and the dynamics of conflict and violence in the Virunga National Park, Democratic Republic of the Congo', *The Journal of Peasant Studies* 45, 2018, pp. 300–20.

32. Rosa Luxemburg, *The Accumulation of Capital* (London: Routledge, 2003 [1913]).

33. For detail, see for example, L. Lohmann, 'Toward a different debate in environmental accounting: the cases of carbon and cost-benefit' *Accounting, Organizations and Society* 34, 2009, pp. 499–534; M. Fourcade, 'Cents and sensibility: economic valuation and the nature of "nature"', *American Journal of Sociology* 116(6), 2011, pp. 1721–77; V. Ehrenstein and F. Muniesa, 'The conditional sink: counterfactual display in the valuation of a carbon offsetting restoration project', *Valuation Studies*

1(2), 2013, pp. 161–88; I. Lippert, 'Environment as datascape: enacting emission realities in corporate carbon accounting', *Geoforum* 66, 2014, pp. 126–35; A.P. Asiyanbi, 'Financialisation in the Green Economy: Material Connections, Markets-in-the-making and Foucauldian Organising Actions', *Environment and Planning A*, 5(3), 2018, pp. 531–48; L. Carver and S. Sullivan, 'How economic contexts shape calculations of yield in biodiversity offsetting', *Conservation Biology* 31(5), 2017, pp. 1053–65.

34. *Caliban*, p. 33.
35. Michel Foucault, *Discipline and Punish: The Birth of the Prison* (trans. A. Sheridan; London: Penguin, 1991 [1975]), pp. 137–8.
36. *Caliban*, p. 151, emphasis in original.
37. *Caliban*, pp. 84–5.
38. For an analysis of natural capital accounting in the UK, see S. Sullivan and M. Hannis, '"Mathematics maybe, but not money": on balance sheets, numbers and nature in ecological accounting', *Accounting, Auditing and Accountability Journal* 30(7), 2017, pp. 1459–80.
39. *Caliban*, p. 139.
40. V. Plumwood, 'The concept of a cultural landscape: nature, culture and agency in the land', *Ethics and the Environment* 11 (2006), pp. 115–50.
41. Foucault, *Discipline and Punish: The Birth of the Prison* (trans. A. Sheridan; London: Penguin, 1991 [1975]), pp. 24–6.
42. *Ibid.*, pp. 138, 170.
43. D. Nally, 'The biopolitics of food provisioning', *Transactions of the Institute of British Geographers* 36, 2011, pp. 37–53.
44. J.T. Nealon, *Foucault Beyond Foucault: Power and its Intensifications since 1984* (Stanford: Stanford University Press, 2008), p. 27.
45. S. Prudham, 'The fictions of autonomous intervention: Accumulation by dispossesssion, commodification and life patents in Canada', *Antipode* 39(3), 2007, pp. 406–29.
46. M. Foucault, *The Birth of Biopolitics: Lectures at the Collège de France 1978–1979* (trans. G. Burchell; Basingstoke: Palgrave Macmillan, 2008 [1979]).
47. M. O'Connor, 'On the misadventures of capitalist nature', in O'Connor (ed.) *Is Capitalism Sustainable? Political Economy and the Politics of Ecology* (London: Guilford Press, 1994), p. 141.
48. R. Muradian, E. Corbera, U. Pascual, N. Kosoy and P.H. May, 'Reconciling theory and practice: an alternative conceptual framework for understanding payments for environmental services', *Ecological Economics* 69 (2010), pp. 1202–8.
49. N. Castree, 'Neoliberalising nature: the logics of deregulation and reregulation', *Environment and Planning* A 40, 2008, p. 144.
50. T.W. Luke, 'On environmentality: Geo-power and eco-knowledge in the discourse of contemporary environmentalism', *Cultural Critique* 31(II), 1995, pp. 57–81; R. Fletcher, 'Neoliberal environmentality: towards a poststructural political ecology of the conservation debate', *Conservation and Society* 8(3), 2010, pp. 171–81.
51. Harvey, 'The geography of capitalist accumulation', 9.
52. S. Sassen, 'A savage sorting of winners and losers: contemporary versions of primitive accumulation', *Globalizations* 7(1), 2010, p. 30.
53. P. Curry, 'Nature post-nature', *New Formations* 64, 2008, pp. 51–64.
54. J. Fairhead, M. Leach and I. Scoones, 'Green grabbing: A new appropriation of nature?', *Journal of Peasant Studies* 39 (2012).

55. F. Berkes, *Sacred Ecology* (London: Routledge, 1999); Sullivan, 'On "natural capital", "fairy-tales" and ideology'.

56. *Caliban*, pp. 100–1.

57. See, for instance, *Notes From Nowhere (eds)* We Are Everywhere: The Irresistible Rise of Global Anticapitalism (London: Verso, 2003); B. Maiguascha and C. Eschle (eds), *Critical Theories, World Politics and 'the Anti-globalisation Movement'* (London: Routledge, 2005); S. Böhm, O. Reyes and S. Sullivan, 'The organisation and politics of Social Forums', ephemera: *Theory and Politics in Organization* 5(2), 2005, pp. 98–442; D. Harvie, K. Milburn, B. Trott and D. Watts (eds), *Shut Them Down!: The G8, Gleneagles 2005 and the Movement of Movements* (Leeds: Dissent! and Brooklyn, NY: Autonomedia, 2005); T. Mueller and S. Sullivan, 'Making other worlds possible? Riots, movement and counterglobalisation', in M. Davies (ed.) *Disturbing the Peace: Collective Action in Britain & France, 1381 to the Present* (Basingstoke: Palgrave Macmillan, 2016) pp. 239–55.

58. *Caliban*, p. 151.

59. United Nations Environment Programme Working Group on Decoupling, *Decoupling natural resource use and environmental impacts from economic growth* (2011), at www.gci.org.uk/Documents/Decoupling_Report_English.pdf; J. Ward, K. Chiveralls, L. Fioramonti, P. Sutton and R. Costanza, 'The decoupling delusion: rethinking growth and sustainability', *The Conversation* 12 March 2017, at https://theconversation.com/the-decoupling-delusion-rethinking-growth-and-sustainability-71996; both accessed 27 September 2018.

60. K. Stock, 'Sexual objectification', *Analysis* 75(2), 2015, pp. 191–5.

61. J. Rose, 'Who do you think you are?', *London Review of Books* 38(9), May 2016, pp. 3–13.

62. I am evoking here the 'corporeal embrace of new technologies' (D. Trippett, 'Transhumanism: advances in technology could already put evolution into hyperdrive – but should they?', *The Conversation* 28 March 2018 https://theconversation.com/transhumanism-advances-in-technology-could-already-put-evolution-into-hyperdrive-but-should-they-92694, last accessed 24 January 2019) signalled by an optimistic orientation towards prosthetic futures in which the human body is radically altered and engineered through the application and incorporation of sophisticated technology [S. Lilley, *Transhumanism and Society: The Social Debate over Human Enhancement* (New York: Springer, 2013)].

63. *Cf.* J. Butler, *Gender Trouble: Feminism and the Subversion of Identity* (London: Routledge, 2006 [1990]), p. 21.

64. R. Pellicer-Thomas, V. de Lucia and S. Sullivan (eds), *Contributions to Law, Philosophy and Ecology: Exploring Re-Embodiments* (London: Routledge, 2016).

65. *Caliban*, p. 73.

66. *Caliban*, 88, also p. 164.

67. Federici, 'Women, Witch-Hunting and Enclosures in Africa Today', *Sozial Geschichte. Online* 3, S: 10–27, at https://duepublico.uni-duisburg-essen.de/servlets/DerivateServlet/Derivate-24612/03_Federici_Women.pdf, (last accesssed 6 December 2018); also I. Epure, 'The women of Ghana's witch-camps', *Broadly Vice*, 1 February 2016, at https://broadly.vice.com/en_us/article/3dxg4v/the-women-of-ghanas-witch-camps, (last accessed 12 December 2018).

68. Federici, 'Undeclared war: violence against women', *Artforum* (Summer 2017), at www.artforum.com/print/201706/undeclared-war-violence-against-women-68680 (accessed 10 July 2018); emphasis added.

69. In addition to sources already cited, see S. Sullivan, 'After the green rush? Biodiversity offsets, uranium power and the "calculus of casualties" in greening growth', *Human Geography* 6(1), 2013, pp. 80–101; M. Hannis and S. Sullivan, 'Mining the desert', *The Land* 22, 2018, pp. 46–9.

70. C. Merchant, *The Death of Nature: Women, Ecology and the Scientific Revolution* (San Francisco: Harper & Row, 1980); V. Plumwood, Feminism and the Mastery of Nature (London: Routledge, 1993).

71. *Cf.* J. Butler, *Gender Trouble*; Rose, 'Who do you think you are?', *London Review of Books* 38(9) (May 2016); S. Hines, *Is Gender Fluid? A Primer for the 21ʳᵗ Century* (London: Thames and Hudson, 2018).

72. subRosa, 'Useless gender: An immodest proposal for radical justice', in J.P.-M. Tsang and subRosa (eds), *Yes Species* (Chicago: Sabrosa Books, 2005), p. 57.

73. *Ibid.*, also see S. Sullivan, '(Re)embodying which body? Philosophical, cross-cultural and personal reflections on corporeality', in R. Pellicer-Thomas, V. de Lucia and S. Sullivan (eds), *Law, Philosophy and Ecology: Exploring Re-Embodiments* (London: Routledge, 2016), pp. 119–38.

74. *Cf.* J. Butler, *Gender Trouble*, p. xxiii.

75. *Ibid.*, pp. 18–9.

76. P. Clastres, *Society Against the State: Essays in Political Anthropology* (New York: Zone Books, 1990 [1974]); C. MacCormack and M. Strathern, *Nature, Culture and Gender* (Cambridge: Cambridge University Press, 1980); C. Knight, *Blood Relations: Menstruation and the Origins of Culture* (London: Yale University Press, 1991); Taussig, *The Devil and Commodity Fetishism in South America* (Chapel Hill: University of North Carolina Press, 2010 [1980]).

77. *Cf.* J. Butler, *Gender Trouble*, p. ii.

78. Hines, *Is Gender Fluid? A Primer for the 21ʳᵗ Century* (London: Thames and Hudson, 2018).

79. *Caliban*, p. 106.

III

REPRODUCTION

9

WTF is Social Reproduction?

Nic Vas and Camille Barbagallo

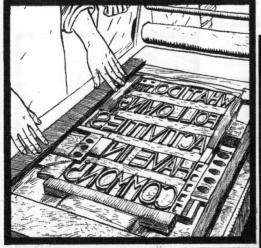

SOCIAL REPRODUCTION IS HOW
WE MAKE AND REMAKE PEOPLE.

WITH REPRODUCTIVE WORK WE *MAKE* & *REMAKE* PEOPLE ON A DAILY BASIS.

BUT ALSO *INTER-GENERATIONALLY*. HAVING BABIES IS JUST ONE PART OF IT.

Benetton we worth more then $1 million

REPRODUCTIVE WORK IS *WORK*. AND LIKE MOST THINGS *UNDER CAPITALISM*, THIS WORK INVOLVES *CONFLICT, VIOLENCE, STRUGGLE, EXPLOITATION* ...

AND IT BREEDS TENSION AND CONTRADICTIONS. BECAUSE *PEOPLE* ARE *NOT* PRODUCED AND REPRODUCED IN A *NEUTRAL* OR *ABSTRACT* WAY.

UNDER CAPITALISM, WE *REPRODUCE OURSELVES* AS LABOUR POWER, WORKERS & *CLASS SUBJECTS*.

DISCIPLINED, EDUCATED, SKILLED...

...TO KNOW OUR PLACE.

TO RULE.

TO MANAGE.

AND *WORK LIKE DOGS*.

JUST LIKE RACE, GENDER AND SEXUALITY. THESE ARE *SOCIAL CONSTRUCTIONS*, NOT BIOLOGICAL CHARACTERISTICS. THROUGH THESE *RELATIONSHIPS*, REPRODUCTIVE LABOUR TEACHES US *WHO* AND *WHAT WE ARE*. WE LEARN ABOUT, REPRODUCE AND BECOME SUBJECTS OF THESE RELATIONSHIPS THROUGH *PRACTICES OF SOCIAL REPRODUCTION*. *& IT INVOLVES A LOT OF FUCKED UP PROCESSES!*

ALL OF THEM CENTRAL TO THE REPRODUCTION OF *CAPITALISM* AS A *SYSTEM* OF EXPLOITATION AND DOMINATION: ONE THAT *DEMANDS* DAILY AND GENERATIONAL *VIOLENCE & STRUGGLE*.

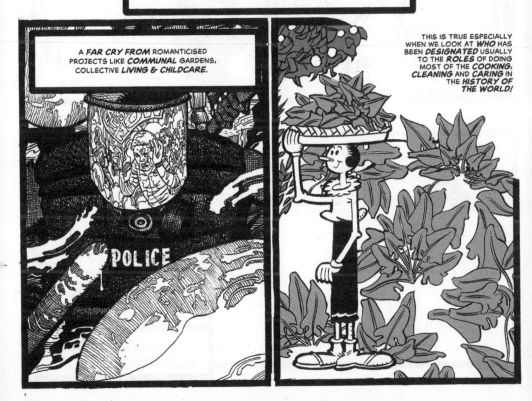

A *FAR CRY FROM* ROMANTICISED PROJECTS LIKE *COMMUNAL* GARDENS, COLLECTIVE *LIVING & CHILDCARE*.

POLICE

THIS IS TRUE ESPECIALLY WHEN WE LOOK AT *WHO* HAS BEEN *DESIGNATED* USUALLY TO THE *ROLES* OF DOING MOST OF THE *COOKING, CLEANING* AND *CARING* IN THE *HISTORY OF THE WORLD!*

HISTORY HAS CONSISTENTLY AND STRUCTURALLY DEVALUED THE WORK OF (RE)MAKING PEOPLE. IT IS NOT EVEN 'REAL' WORK.

MANY SCHOLARS STATE THAT IT DOESN'T CREATE VALUE. IT OFTEN DOESN'T EVEN ATTRACT A WAGE! AND WHEN IT DOES, IT IS POORLY PAID. THIS IS NATURALISED TO THE POINT THAT REPRODUCTIVE WORK IS CONSIDERED ONLY FOR THOSE WHO HAVE 'NATURAL' SKILLS OF BEING CARING –

– WITHOUT MUCH REGARD PAID TO HOW SOME PEOPLE CAME TO POSSESS SUCH SKILLS, WHILE OTHER'S DIDN'T. THIS LABOUR HAS BEEN MADE INVISIBLE, WRAPPED UP IN LOVE, OBLIGATION, HIDDEN BEHIND CLOSED DOORS.

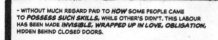

OUT OF SIGHT.

REPRODUCTIVE WORK ONLY BECOMES VISIBLE WHEN IT ISN'T DONE. JUST THINK OF YOUR DISHES, PILED UP IN THE SINK... THAT IS THE ABSENCE OF REPRODUCTIVE LABOUR. AND THE SAME CAN BE SAID ABOUT CHILD CARE. THE AMOUNT OF LABOUR IT ENTAILS GOES UNNOTICED UNTIL THE CHILD IS NEGLECTED.

REPRODUCTIVE WORK HAS BEEN DEVALUED, MADE INVISIBLE AND FEMINISED. IN THE HISTORY OF HUMAN REPRODUCTION, IT'S WOMEN WHO HAVE BEEN THE GREAT REPRODUCTIVE WORKERS OF CAPITALISM!

AND THIS WORK HAS ALWAYS BEEN GENDERED, RACIALISED AND CLASSED. IT IS WORKING CLASS WOMEN AND WOMEN OF COLOUR WHO HAVE DONE THIS WORK. AND CONTINUE TO DO SO.

WHICH BRINGS US TO ANOTHER KEY CONCEPT OF REPRODUCTION.

RICH WOMEN HAVE RARELY DONE THEIR OWN DISHES, CARED FOR THEIR OWN CHILDREN, OR EVEN FUCKED THEIR OWN HUSBANDS!

THERE'S A *VAST* AND OVERWHELMING *AMOUNT* OF REPRODUCTIVE *WORK* NEEDED TO KEEP THE WORLD FED, CLEAN, HEALTHY, EDUCATED AND READY TO WORK. ALL THESE *ACTIVITIES* ARE FORMS OF *LABOUR* THAT WHILST ARE *OFTEN UNWAGED*, THEY *ALSO EXIST AS WAGED FORMS OF REPRODUCTIVE LABOUR.*

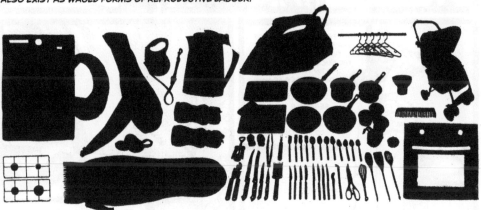

IN FACT, IN OUR POST-INDUSTRIAL *NEO-LIBERAL ECONOMY*, WE NO LONGER MAKE THINGS. WHAT THE BRITISH ECONOMY MAKES IS PEOPLE, AND FINANCE. WE *MAKE AND REMAKE PEOPLE* THROUGH A DAZZLING ARRAY OF *SERVICES.*

IF YOU HAVE THE *MONEY.*

REPRODUCTIVE LABOUR INVOLVES ALL THE **WORK** & ACTIVITIES NEEDED TO **MAKE** & **REMAKE** PEOPLE, KEEPING US **HEALTHY** & **WELL-FED**.

WITH AN **ARMY** OF WAGED REPRODUCTIVE **WORKERS** READY TO **SERVE** YOU.

WITH A **SMILE**.

DEDICATED **PEOPLE** WHO ARE **PASSIONATE** ABOUT DOING YOUR NAILS, MAKING YOUR LATTE OR CLEAN **YOUR SHIT**.

THIS REQUIRES A SOCIAL & HISTORICAL **CONSTRUCT**.

WITH THE **DESTRUCTION** OF THE **MALE FAMILY WAGE** THAT ONCE REPRODUCED THE **NUCLEAR FAMILY** – IT **NOW** TAKES AT LEAST **TWO WAGES** TO HAVE SOME MONEY IN YOUR POCKET TO **BUY** THE **SERVICES** THAT YOU **NO LONGER** HAVE THE TIME NOR THE DESIRE TO DO **YOURSELF**.

REPRODUCTIVE LABOUR HAS A LONG **HISTORY**. ONE AS IMPORTANT AND **PROFITABLE** AS FACTORIES AND COMMODITIES.

THIS WORK IS OFTEN LOW OR UNWAGED, **PRECARIOUS**, OF LOW STATUS AND USUALLY **INVISIBLE**.

THE STUBBORN **LOW STATUS** OF IT **DERIVES** FROM ITS **FEMINISATION**. **IT IS WOMEN'S WORK**.

BUT REPRODUCTION HAS A DUAL CHARACTERISTIC.

IT PRODUCES AND REPRODUCES US AS WORKERS, MAINTAINING CAPITALISM.

BUT IT ALSO PRODUCES LIFE, AUTONOMOUS HUMANS WITH THE CAPACITY AND POTENTIAL TO RESIST AND CREATE CHANGE.

COLECTIVO DE MUJERES INDIGENAS ZAPATISTAS EN RESISTENCIA

BECAUSE WE MAY BE WORKERS, BUT WE ARE NOT REDUCIBLE TO THE ROLE OF THE WORKER, *WE EXCEED SUCH SUBJECTIFICATION!*

TO PUT IT PLAINLY, WITHOUT REPRODUCTIVE LABOUR THERE IS NO EXITING CAPITALISM.

SO WE FIND OURSELVES IN A MOST COMPLEX OF *CONTRADICTIONS.*

DAMNED IF WE DO...
DAMNED IF WE DON'T...

WHEN WE BRING REPRODUCTION TO THE CENTRE OF ANALYSIS WE FIND A CLUSTER OF LABOUR THAT IS KEY TO CAPITALISM'S MAINTENANCE. PARADOXICALLY, *THOSE SAME PROCESSES* CONTAIN THE *POSSIBILITY* OF NOT ONLY HUMAN LIFE BUT ALSO OF *REVOLUTIONARY CHANGE.*

IN THIS WE TRUST

TO BRING REPRODUCTION TO THE CENTRE OF THIS ANALYSIS HOWEVER IS *NOT TO DE-PRIORITISE* SO-CALLED *PRODUCTION.* IT IS TO SEE *HOW* THESE TWO TERRAINS INTERACT, HOW THEY *CONFLICT* AND *HOW* THEY *REPRODUCE EACH OTHER.*

THERE IS AN IMMENSE AMOUNT OF SO CALLED PRODUCTIVE WORK IN THE WORLD THAT CAN AND NEEDS TO BE REFUSED, ABOLISHED EVEN. BUT THAT IS ONLY HALF THE STORY. BECAUSE *SOCIAL REPRODUCTION* CAN BE THOUGHT OF AS PART OF THE PROBLEM. IT IS CLEARLY *IMPLICATED* IN THE PRODUCTION AND REPRODUCTION OF *LABOUR POWER.*

IT'S KEY FOR THE GLOBAL REPRODUCTION OF CAPITALISM.

EQUALLY, THERE IS MUCH ABOUT HOW REPRODUCTIVE LABOUR IS *ORGANIZED* THAT NEEDS TO BE RADICALLY *TRANSFORMED*, SOME OF IT EVEN *REFUSED*. BUT HOW DO WE *DECOMMODIFY* OUR REPRODUCTION *WITHOUT* PUSHING THAT WORK BACK INTO THE REALM OF *NATURALISED DOMESTIC WORK?*

THIS PRESENTS A *PROBLEM*, BECAUSE WHO WANTS THE WORK OF MAKING & REMAKING PEOPLE TO BE *ABOLISHED?* AND WOULD WE WANT IT TO BE FULLY AUTOMATED, OR *PERFORMED BY* ROBOTS OR MACHINES?

WHERE WOULD THE WORK OF REPRODUCTION TAKE PLACE THEN?

INSTEAD OF *TECHNO FIXES* CONTRIBUTING TO THE *DEVALUING* OF REPRODUCTION BY CONSTANTLY SEEKING WAYS TO *MINIMISE* THE *WORK* INVOLVED IN IT.

THE TASK IS TO *RADICALLY* REORGANISE THE WORK, TO *REVALUE* IT, TO BRING IT TO THE CENTRE OF OUR LIVES AND STRUGGLES.

TO IDENTIFY ALL THAT IS WRONG WITH THE CURRENTLY EXISTING REPRODUCTION AS MUCH AS IT IS TO RECLAIM ALL THAT IS NECESSARY.

RECLAIM OUR IMAGINATION!

AND *FIGHT* EVERY INCH OF THE *POSSESSIVE INDIVIDUDUALIST* NARRATIVES OF *POWER* AND SUCCESS.

TO *LEAVE CAPITALISM* BEHIND, WE NEED AN *EXIT STRATEGY* THAT PAYS AS MUCH AS *ATTENTION* TO THE HISTORICAL *HIERARCHIES* OF HOW WAGE AND GENDER HAVE BEEN PRODUCED...

...BUT ALSO TO THE *SYSTEMS* OF POWER AND EXPLOITATION THAT HAVE PRODUCED THE *URBAN* AND THE *RURAL BUILT* OF *COLONIALISM* AND *SLAVERY EVERYWHERE*, AS WELL AS THE *CONSTRUCTION* OF THE *ECOLOGICAL WORLD* AS A *RESOURCE TO PLUNDER, EXPLOIT & PROFIT* FROM AS IF THAT COULD BE MANAGED SEPARATELY FROM HUMAN LIFE. BUT CRUCIALLY HERE *WE MUST UNDERSTAND HOW THE OPPRESSION OF WOMEN HAS HISTORICALLY SERVED THE ORGANIZATION OF CAPITALISM.*

'WTF IS SOCIAL REPRODUCTION?'

WRITTEN AND DRAWN BY CAMILLE BARBAGALLO & NIC VAS, 2015.

THIS IS A COMIC-ESSAY THAT ATTEMPTS TO EXPLAIN THE IDEA OF SOCIAL REPRODUCTION.
TO MAKE IT, WE COLLECTED IMAGES THAT REPRODUCE WAYS IN WHICH DOMESTIC LABOUR, OPPRESSION, EXPLOITATION, RACISM, PATRIARCHY BUT ALSO HOW
RESISTANCE TO THOSE HAVE BEEN VISUALISED IN MAINSTREAM AND UNDERGROUND COMICS AS WELL AS GRAPHIC ART FOR PROTEST AND ORGANISING.

DRAWN REFERENCES IN ORDER OF APPEARANCE

BOF AND BUZZ BY LEANNE FRANSON
MAFALDA BY QUINO
PALESTINIAN WOMAN BY TALLER TUPAC AMARU
POWER TO THE PEOPLE BY EMORY DOUGLAS
KLAN FIGURES BY PHILIP GUSTON
AUNT MAY BY GIL KANE
HOTHEAD PAISAN BY DIANE DIMASSA
OLIVE OYL BY E. C. SEGAR
GIRL MAGAZINE (UK), ARTIST UNKNOWN
JOE PALOOKA BY HAM FISHER
LUBA BY GILBERT HERNANDEZ
MAMMY TWO SHOES BY WILLIAM HANNA AND JOSEPH BARBERA
SNOW WHITE BY WALT DISNEY
CAPITALISM ALSO DEPENDS ON DOMESTIC LABOUR BY THE SEE RED COLLECTIVE
WAGES FOR HOUSEWORK CAMPAIGN POSTER
MARY'S ASSHOLE BY HANAKO YAMADA
HANDALA BY NAJI AL-ALI

THIS MATERIAL HAS BEEN COMPILED AS PART OF A COLLECTIVE RESEARCH INTO SOCIAL REPRODUCTION.
IT HAS BEEN PRODUCED AS AN INFORMATIVE AND PEDAGOGICAL TOOL. THE COPYRIGHT OF ORIGINAL
CHARACTERS AND MATERIAL BELONG TO THE ARTISTS, AUTHORS AND/OR THEIR PUBLISHERS.
FOR THE CREATION OF THIS ESSAY THE IMAGES WERE HAND-DRAWN. WE ARE VERY GRATEFUL TO CEDOZ
(CENTRO DE DOCUMENTACION SOBRE ZAPATISMO) WHO KINDLY AGREED AND MADE AVAILABLE THE
ONLY ORIGINAL MATERIAL REPRODUCED HERE. THESE ARE IMAGES OF MURALS, FOUND ON
PAGES 7 AND ABOVE THESE LINES.

THE COMIC WAS ORIGINALLY PUBLISHED IN B A M N #2 BY PLAN C (UK) IN 2015.

Extending the Family:
Reflections on the Politics of Kinship

Bue Rübner Hansen and Manuela Zechner

For centuries the work of reproduction has been a collective process. It has been the work of extended families and communities, on which people could rely, especially in proletarian neighbourhoods, even when they lived alone, so that old age was not accompanied by the desolate loneliness and dependence that so many of our elderly experience. It is only with the advent of capitalism that reproduction has been completely privatised, a process that is now carried to a degree that it destroys our lives. This we need to change if we are to put an end to the steady devaluation and fragmentation of our lives. – Silvia Federici[1]

It is easy to hate or long for the family, much easier than to create durable relations of care. When Silvia writes of the extended family, she is not inviting us to romanticise precapitalist family forms, but to seize hold of a memory in this moment of loneliness and exhaustion. This encounter with historical difference raises the question of how we might rethink the extended family today, beyond patriarchy and the reproduction of capitalist relations. In this text, we want to follow and extend Silvia's questioning, starting from the care of children, a matter that preoccupies us increasingly since the arrival of our daughter.

Care and reproduction, and the experiences of loneliness they are often accompanied by in neoliberal societies, are in fact the 'norm': the stuff our lives rest on, always and still. There is nothing more common, more shared and omnipresent, than the struggles and strategies that people and communities develop to survive and create better life-worlds. Yet these struggles and experiences are drowned out by the noise of lifestyle and productivity, hidden from view in spaces of representation and competition. Carolina del Olmo describes the problem poignantly in *Where is my tribe?*, a book about maternity and childrearing in an individualist society:

The arrival of a child makes us violently aware of the intrinsic fragility of human beings, and also their social and relational character, of the impossibility of individualism in its extremes. Our fantasies of independence and autonomy crumble. If we were lucky with our health and economy, we enjoyed the fiction of being autonomous and self-sufficient for a few years, while we were young and handsome.[2]

Of course, having a child to care for is only one way of realising this contingency: in this text it's our starting point. This leads us to the question of families: what are they, in neoliberal capitalism? Most neutrally put, they are becoming ever more crucial for our survival. As Melinda Cooper shows, neoliberal capitalism is not built on the individual as much as on individual family units; Thatcherism and Reaganism were also reactionary movements to 'restore' or 'save' the nuclear family.[3] But the fact that kinship is necessary for our reproduction also means that it can't be abandoned. It is necessary to invent other ways of responding to the crisis of social reproduction – because otherwise conservatives will hegemonise the field of responses, both real and imaginary.

How then are we to go about building other, more sustainable kinds of relations, and other kinds of families to raise children within? What's the role of the will and what's the role of the body in the building of such relations? Do we need to insist more, or indeed to persist more? With parenting, all these questions are lived in the flesh, in merciless immanence. It's a luxury to have the time to spell them out. We want to ask here: since we know that the nuclear family is painfully unable to give the care and conviviality we need, and is an often oppressive and limiting fantasy and reality, how can we imagine extensions of the family towards other shores? We know there is no salvation in 'destroying' the family in general, though of course some particular constellations must be escaped; we will not escape contingency overall. Maybe we can extend the family, both by creating new extended families, and by pushing the limits of the nuclear family to the point of it becoming something else.

For many of us, those extended families are not only built on biological but also on social bonds, such as networks of friends and comrades that care for and about one another. Often we end up weaving our most intimate care relations into these networks – one way or another, our children grow up within them. These bonds, mixing different kinds of kinship, can save us from the loneliness of nuclear families and of precarious mobilities. As comrades, friends, neighbours and family, and particularly when subsisting across changing diasporic arrangements, these kin can ground us in the world and keep us from getting too anxious or being ground down. The difficulty lies in making these other kinds of kinship work: while there is no universal formula for this, mutual support and cultures of shared care are crucial for enabling this.

But exploring these rich relations and the intertwining of different kinds of kinship is often barred by a categorisation, at once political and anthropological. Is your family bound together by blood or by free election? Many conceptions of kinship are bound up on this contrast. On the one hand, the involuntary and 'natural' or 'traditional' ties of the blood family; on the other, the voluntary, 'free' and 'modern' ties of elective kinship.

Conservatives defend heterosexual marriage as the route through which individual choice – affirmed in the marriage contract – can become ties of blood, giving rise to the family as an enclosed system, more or less extended, but bounded by genetic code. On the other side, there is an attempt to replace conservative families with intentional communities of care – to make family not a matter of conserving or preserving blood-ties, but to make it an open and changing space of cohabitation. Queer families make virtue out of necessity and invent radical models of caring, parenting and living together. In the one mode, kinship is conceived of as a matter of fate; in the other, of choice.

For many people of course, that binary does not hold. What was chosen grows into fate, and what appeared as fate, fades away or is broken by choice. Love can tear us apart, no matter how firm our commitment or how much blood we share. And no matter how strong our will to build alternative families, it's often not possible to find available or willing elective kin, or only for short periods of time. What makes kinship continue – whether we like it or not – lies beyond the dialectic of fate versus choice, of volition versus destiny.

Silvia and George remind us, quite crucially, that kinship is held together by reproductive labour. But the concept of reproductive labour itself can easily be subsumed by the fate/choice couplet. We see this in political assessments of specific forms of reproductive labour, in questions such as: Is our labour merely reproductive of a certain normative kinship-form and of human bodies – is it a mere enactment of 'fate' – or is it radical, militant, queer – established around a will to break with stifling and oppressive kinship forms? The reason that reproductive labour is easily assessed according to the fate/choice binary lies in the very notion of labour itself, and its Aristotelian definition as the goal-directed activity of a subject, whether collective or not. In this model, the immanent organisation of labour is not considered, except in so far as it can be seen as a means to realise an aim, that is to produce a product out of necessity or choice. While waged labour is always employed with an object or objective in mind – a product and a profit – the meaning of reproductive labour exceeds the capitalist *telos* of reproducing labour-power.

To understand this 'more', it is useful to shift from the Aristotelian logic of labour to Silvia and George's concept of commoning. Commons exist through communing, not merely as commoning's product or aim, but as the organisation of relations of commoning itself. And as many of us know from experience, *both the will and the need to common* are painfully insufficient for creating a practice of commoning. Commoning requires something beyond a collection of individual needs and wills. It requires a common as well as relations and a practice of commoning, which are not so much about coincidences of individual aims (as in contract or exchange), nor about the subsumption of individual aims under collective ones, but rather a transindividual game of means, irreducible both to the subject, aim and product.

We propose how we might think about relations of kinship as a game forming around *partial subjects*, and how this enables the ongoing reproductive labour of kinship. Our hope is that, starting from this narrow focus on child-rearing within relations of kinship, we can develop some concepts that will enrich the understanding of commoning and what it might mean to extend the family.

This is the problem, somewhat theoretically formulated. But rather than seek a theoretical solution, we are interested in remembering, re-narrating and reflecting on experiences and examples of belonging and becoming of kinship. The idea is not to theorise partial subjects in general or abstractly, but to develop the concept from concrete examples, such as the birth of a baby, life on the compound, relating to the land, and to Silvia and George themselves. To reflect different positions and moves in the game of kinship, irreconcilable into one general voice, we decided to write this text as a dialogue.

Pregnancy, or a Ball Starts Rolling

Manuela:

I'd like to take this up from an unusual starting point and propose some thoughts about reproduction and belonging ... as starting from the body and pregnancy. I think it's worth trying to weave some body-experiences together with the collective processes we refer to when talking of social reproduction.

While pregnant with my daughter, looking for some orientation, I reread a text by Brian Massumi, called 'The political economy of belonging and the logic of relation'.[4] I'd been compelled to revisit it because of the way Massumi questions how we think of who or what is a subject and object, and how we come to belong. It's a text about football (soccer) in fact, a kind of parable for collective movement and becoming.

How does movement come about in football? Who moves what, what moves whom? According to Massumi, on the one hand, the goals are 'inducers' of movements, the poles that hold the game in tension, like magnets. The ball is the catalyst, that which animates the actual game. It's key to understand that the ball is not the object but a subject or partial-subject of the game; Massumi defines the subject as the point around which movement tendentially unfolds. 'The ball moves the players. The player is the object of the ball. [...] When the ball moves, the whole game moves with it. Its displacement is more than a local movement: it is a global event.'[5] When I thought about what it might mean for this child to come into our lives, it struck me that it is a bit like the ball in a soccer game. It moves a whole field, without however intervening in it wilfully or interventionistically, shifting and transforming (with) it subtly. Reproduction and difference, to say it with a Deleuzian pun. The pregnant belly, or rather the subject-in-becoming in it, is the ball, the community is the team and society the playing field.

Massumi insists that the football player's movements are necessarily reflexive and not reflective, driven by affects and orientations that aren't based in language, because once the players become self-conscious they lose the drive or gist of the game. This collective movement-action is a play with potential, a potential of becoming or actualising (of winning, scoring). And here it comes: it's in that play that belonging happens. Not belonging rooted in identity (the tricot) but in collective movement. 'In becoming is belonging', says Massumi.[6]

I found myself thinking about the kinds of belonging that come with reproduction as lived process. More often than not, the matters of reproduction are not down to our conscious willing, rather they are like movements we make in the everyday, trying to avoid bad moves intuitively and sometimes analytically (in relation to capitalism, the patriarchy, etc.). While there is virtuosity in those movements, they function more like a flow than a plot. In them, becomings emerge in ways we had not imagined, we build relations that were not on our ideological game-plan, we come to depend and share in ways unforeseen. Parenting has been like this so far, lifting us out of certain social bubbles while opening onto new kinds of isolation, and opening onto constellations and alliances we could never have foreseen. We are being propelled into new relations that are not of our choosing.

With Massumi's parable, I couldn't help but think of the ball in relation to my pregnant belly. That roundness created a powerful dynamic around me and us (as a more or less extending family), a whirlwind of new becomings, all happening in the context of the becoming and reproduction of this new life, in its world. Reproduction and becoming aren't so far apart after all. The child, in utero but also once born, is a ball, a partial subject: anonymous and silent, subtle in its becoming though ever more explicit in its kicks and screams and babbles. This subject-in-becoming catalyses a whole field of relations around it, and as such enables a large and long process of collective becoming – particularly as this partial subject is articulated with all kinds of dispositifs, institutions, groups and people.

There's a force that comes with this becoming-belonging, and the name of it is care. The key aspect of that catalysing potential is care, which assures that a becoming is possible, and with it a belonging. 'The family' as such is not biologically determined nor is it a matter of names and deals, but a moving field that roots us in the world across all kinds of differences and distances. That reproduces us and that we reproduce, grow into and out of, that morphs with people coming and going, that transforms around different partial subjects.

The Child that Names You

Bue:

For me, playing football is a belonging in the sense that you become a part of the game, you inhabit and live it and breathe it, and this suspends your belonging elsewhere for its duration. And isn't this also an aspect of belonging – that there is a limit to how many places, processes, people, you can find belonging in or with at once? And the field is necessarily bounded, keeping it from dissipating, but also meaning that any player who might want to escape it will become individualised in the process and lose the connection to the game. Is any belonging a temporal and spatial suspension of other belongings? Another interesting thing about using football as a relational model for thinking about kinship and commons is that it is inherently agonistic: within the common field and common rules, there are different teams with opposed orientations and aims, composed of different players with different skills and roles. This is the 'labour' dimension in the Aristotelian sense we mentioned above, the question of individual and collective subjects, and the articulation of their aims into products of collaboration, in this example scoring and defending, with the final aim of victory by scoring the most goals. But what Massumi provides is a way to think about the fluid organisation of both teams around the same partial subject, the ball. The relational movements around and with the ball are the essence of the game, its becoming and belonging. When these movements don't work, the rules seem oppressive, the pitch limiting, the opponent overwhelming. And similarly, what makes kinship operational, inhabitable, and fulfilling is not the reproductive labour, or the common space that hosts it or the ethical and moral codes that regulate it – though they are important conditions – but the care, empathy and playfulness that emerges in our relational movements around that for which we care, for instance a child.

I think this example is fascinating, because it shows that becoming beyond contract and identity, beyond volition or fate, exists even in codified team sports such as football. This means we can begin to imagine the importance of such becoming not only in more informal and changing relations and forms of organisation, but also in often rule-bound and identity-making relations such as 'the family'. We can understand the dynamic of care created by a baby without reference to logics of marriage contract and bloodline, and how it catalyses a belonging and becoming that it would be stale and reductive to call 'family' in common sense of that term.

We are used to thinking about the birth of a child in terms of belonging. Even before it is born, the child is inscribed into a family, a lineage, a bloodline, a nation. From its first days this belonging is established through the family name and citizenship. The production of the familial and con-tractual subject of modern capitalism begins at birth, neatly intertwining the 'private' belonging to the sphere of reproduction with its 'public' belonging to the nation through the simple question: to which parents does this baby belong? We are used to noticing how care becomes subsumed by capitalist and national reproduction, so let us ask another question: how might it instead rip the ties of belonging-as-property?

I come to think of how my parents were named after me when we lived in a town in rural Tanzania in the 1980s. Following custom, they became known as Mama and Baba Bue. For among friends, family and neighbours in Tanzania, naming is not just marking the belonging of the child to the parents, but the becoming of the parents through it. Most adults are simply known as mama so-and-so or baba so-and-so, rather than the name they were given by their parents or, as it often happens, their grandparents. This shift in appellation marks the transition from being merely a child-of to becoming a parent-of, but it is also a feature of life in scattered settlements where the circulation of groups of playing children bind houses together, and parents build and maintain relations through them. Unlike a patronym or juridical name, the filionym is not stable, but dependent on context. If the neighbours do not know the eldest child, the parents will be named as the mama and baba of the second child, and so on.

In this context, parenting was practically and symbolically articulated with the extended family and neighbours, rather than in an individualised relation with the state. Roaming the paths of the town of Ifakara, the homes of my friends became an extension of mine; often, we would simply eat where we were when dinner was ready. In this part of the world, childcare is not the responsibility only of the biological parents (the baba and mama), but of all the other mamas and babas, *shangazi* and *wajomba* (aunties and uncles) and *wabibi* and *wababu* (grandmothers and grandfathers), roles that can be given or taken by neighbours and other people outside familiar bloodlines. Relying less on marriage contracts and individualised reproduction, extended families organise themselves around partial objects such as the food and children. As long as there are members of the extended family and community who have suffered a bad harvest, the surpluses of an individual household's plot of land are not considered a surplus. Food and money circulate towards those in need, and children often circulate to live with those family members who can best provide for them.

In this context, the naming of parents after their child can be taken as an index of the continued disjunction between the juridical subject and the members of extended families, and of a village or neighbourhood. People relate not as co-citizens, but as co-inhabitors of a territory of care and self-reproduction: caring for a common ecology, for the crops and animals of their neighbours, and for the co-inhabitation of in these dispersed settlements, criss-crossed by paths rather than fences. Today, this is changing. Fences are errected, unevenly and reversibly.

Care, Reproduction and Belonging

Manuela:

What you say about Mama and Baba makes me think of our daughter Mila and how as she started to babble, she said not only mama and baba but also bama and maba (and mamba, amma, etc.). In the beginning, these are just syllables. Eventually they become mapped onto relations. (A side note on that: when Brigitte Vasallo refuses to be called mother by anyone but her own child, insisting that motherhood should be understood as a relation and not a social role, I think she's onto something too. Though for me part of the point is that these relations are also recognised and taken seriously by others, without of course reducing a person to that role.)[7] For a child, any relations and roles it grows up with are normal, so there is plenty of scope for also having a Maba or a Bama, and so on. As Mila grew up a bit, she called both of us parents 'mama', as well as extended family and even strangers sometimes: 'mama' meant something like 'hey' or 'I need'. It took her ages to get the idea of 'mama' versus 'papa'. Many parents follow their kid's guidance (and insistence) in naming: I think of how the first child of some friends called his second mother 'Pouma' (nothing to do with her name, phonetically) and his parents went with it for years. Is Pouma a name or a role? I'm unsure whether to capitalise here or not: Pouma/pouma, bama/Bama, mama/Mama: this tension between singular name and role can be very fruitful, if one takes the performative potential of children's ways of relating seriously.

There is a certain poverty in our given vocabulary of care: we could also draw more on 'co-mothers' or 'allomothers'; and start applying the terms auntie, uncle, granny, grandpa, or even mama and papa to people who we feel merit being called that. Many people do that. In fact I think this might be more common in more working-class, migrant and precarious families, where these other relations take on more force out of necessity, where relations can't be contained as they are in the nuclear bourgeois family. Caring roles are invented not because of a will to creativity but precisely out of pragmatism in everyday life, and so all kinds of families grow. That's one of the beautiful things about extended families for me, to think of those as spaces of invention where biology and choice, reproduction and care, and need and desire become blurred and remixed constantly.

For me, reproduction and care go together in this sense. They are the perhaps most powerful tools we have to subvert patriarchal, capitalist and colonial power structures, because this subversion hinges on us being able to build and imagine new ways of relating.

This also concerns our collective becoming in militancy, in organising and collective practice. The point is to stop seeing those as fundamentally different from a thing like bodily reproduction and generational processes, and instead become a bit more open to seeing the many interdependences and partial subjects that move us. It's not just that the personal is political or that the political is personal, but that our becoming is neither pure volition or fate. Undoing the liberal idea of the sovereign individual, free to choose and opposed to the primitive and bad contingencies of the natural world, is going to take lots of hard feminist, decolonial and ecological work. In social movements too.

Women, traditionally put in charge of becoming-belonging, as well as migrants and all those put in charge of care services by colonialism and neoliberalism, have a lot to share and teach when it comes to this labour of subverting and interweaving.

Justice and Violence

Bue:

The extended family in rural Tanzania appears socially regressive to many urban dwellers and non-Tanzanians, with its subsistence production and patriarchal family structure. This is not too different from the way kinship-based subsistence farming has been seen as a hallmark of underdevelopment from the modernist and modernising perspective shared by classical Marxists, developmentalists and liberals alike. In the progressive NGO sector of which my parents were a part, the narrative has long been that underdevelopment was reproduced not just by colonialism and neo-colonialism, but by the extended family, which would work as a constant drain on the savings of industrious individuals, blocking the formation of local capital. Needless to say, various projects of of economic development from cash crops to microcredits have continued the processes begun under colonialism: the privatisation of land, the growth of the landless population and the erosion of the extended family.

The radicality of Silvia and George's work on this point is to suggest that the extended family – this supposed marker of underdevelopment – might be conceived as a form of social self-defence against patriarchal and capitalist relations. The extended family does not only stand in the way of national autonomy as conceived by developmentalism, it stands for women's autonomy. As Silvia explains, women have generally been able to refuse wage labour, because they 'either through their families or their husbands ... always had fields of their own, their own crops, and controlled the income they earned from the sale of the produce they farmed'.[8] Elsewhere she points to how subsistence agriculture is surviving because women lead their community struggles against the 'encroachment of capitalist relations', from outside and within the family itself.[9] Women play this role, not only because they undertake the major part of the subsistence work (in 2002 producing up to 80 per cent of all foodstuffs in sub-Saharan Africa according to the Food and Agriculture Organization), but also because they are more dependent on and active in the family and kin structures of care and reproduction.

Women's struggles are crucial for maintaining an economy of sharing, co-responsibility and care, which give households a partial and often highly significant autonomy from both labour and commodity markets. As Silvia writes, such women's struggles are not just a question of equality, but of survival, autonomy and fighting capacity:

> These struggles show that egalitarianism is for commons a question of survival, for unequal power relations within them open the way to outside intervention and expropriation. In particular, they show that gender-based disparities generate dynamics that consolidate the dominance of the market over agricultural relations for they weaken the solidarity between women and men in front of the siege to which the commons are subjected by state business, and international institutions.[10]

But this mechanism is constantly threatened by the alliance between the state, foreign capital and male family heads. The key to this alliance is to shift the organising principle of the extended family from mutual aid to property and production, or, to put it metonymically, to organise the family around the full subject of the father, rather than around the shifting partial subject of whoever needs care – the poor cousin, the orphaned niece, the infant, the grandmother – or to transform rice from a partial subject around which the extended family is stabilised into a simple commodity. One central institutional mechanism that achieves this shift is the transformation of the husband's customary claim to the land into a legal title ascribed to his juridical name. Silvia quotes Judy Adoko and Simon Levine from the Land and Equity Movement in Uganda:

> The fact that customarily a woman gained access to land via her husband is now confused (deliberately) confused with notions of individualized ownership. Men are now claiming rights that under customary law they never had, in particular to sell land without consulting the family, to disregard a wife's need for land...[11]

As the work of Silvia and George has highlighted, the emergence of the modern contractual individual through such transformation of male family leadership into 'possessive individualism' played a crucial role in European history, ignored by intellectual histories such as C.B. Macpherson's *Possessive Individualism*.[12] When land, as the playing field on which kinship relations are organised, is made into individual property, so kinship is transformed into patrimony. Instead of an extended kinship network, you have the formation of separated families and lines of inheritance. Instead of networks of co-dependence (whether patriarchal, matriarchal or other) you have nuclear families, and the creation of an inside/outside, relationally as well as spatially and architecturally: individual houses begin to be separated by fences or hedges. Where the patriarch of an extended family is merely a central node in the family network, the patriarch of a nuclear family monopolises access to the outside world, and thus autonomy. Reproductive labour becomes auxiliary to productive labour, the labour that sustains the productivity of the 'bread winner'. The question is if women and the youth find another model of freedom than that of this 'autonomous' individual, forever organised by money, forever devaluing the labour of care and game of kinship. It seems to me that as long as we equal kinship with patriarchy, we remain enamoured by a mode of life that can neither be universalised nor sustained.

Beyond the Sovereign Individual

Manuela:

One of the biggest flaws of the way the political subject is defined in law and philosophy, starting from the enlightenment and the very processes of primitive accumulation mentioned above, is that the generic subject is assumed to be an *autonomous* individual. The basic unit of law and political thought is this kind of free-floating person, modelled on unbound, white, well-off men as it were. That kind of subject is the exception rather than the rule in our world, yet it's inscribed everywhere as the norm. Feminists – particularly in recent arguments on how notions of care, interdependency or heteronomy should determine how we think about economics, society and law – have refused to accept this definition of what a 'normal' subject is. In practice, to struggle against this normativity is of course deeply difficult, for we are all shaped by habits of moving and acting within this template of being political, being a subject of rights.

There are many experiences that have the power to subvert these habits, all of them both troubling and empowering. Most of them are to do with experiencing and living agency in less individualised and sovereign ways, of being inserted into the world via other logics, other ties. Returning to pregnancy, there is an interesting lesson – it seems like the most obvious thing to say, but it's quite something to understand this in an embodied way: we are not all individuals. We split in two, or more, in absolutely crazy ways. We are 'dividuals'[13] not only from the viewpoint of our social reproduction and subjectivities: most living beings are also bodily used to becoming-more, and indeed also becoming-another. Beyond essentialism, this means that another political, economic and legal subject is possible. One that builds on thinking and living interdependency, dividuality, becoming, rooted in embodied processes. As feminists we needn't be afraid of exploring generations and reproduction, or indeed limits, we can valourise those without being deterministic or essentialist: our current ecological predicament requires us to do that.

Societies Against Capital

Bue:

The myth of the sovereign individual is articulated with other myths, such as the idea that capitalist development is something that ultimately benefits everyone. This 'everyone' that ultimately benefits is the sovereign individual. The language sometimes appears in subtle form, like in the suggestion that rural Tanzanian society has been 'unable' to give rise to local capital formation, when those that have been unable to do so are *individuals* in rural Tanzania, not the extended family, which tried to do something altogether different.

To think about this difference without thinking of it as a lack, it is useful to go back to the writings of the anthropologist Pierre Clastres. In *Society*

Against the State he showed how the social structures of indigenous peoples in the Americas are arranged to actively block the development of centralised power and wealth. Such societies are not egalitarian by nature, but by design: they are organised around mechanisms that constantly block the development of inequalities.

One central mechanism that blocks the formation of a power separate from society is that generosity is considered a key aspect of authority. Thus the chief is submitted to a 'continuous looting' that deprives him of the ability to command others through possession of scarce resources.[14] We might say the chief is turned into the 'parent' of the whole community, exercising no executive power, but rather the reproductive power of care and unconditional sharing. The effect of this mechanism is that political leadership is blocked from becoming more than moral and spiritual leadership. The essential role of the chief is not to command, but to inspire, to be a mediator and peace-maker, as well as an orator articulating the common good. Clastres describes such societies as 'societies against the state'. Unlike the indigenous Americans of Clastres' account, leadership-as-command has been common in pre-colonial, colonial and post-colonial African societies. But might we adapt Clastres to describe the way the extended family has served as an effective block of the formation of both capital and labour-power? Could we, in other words, describe societies built up around extended family structures as 'societies against capital'?

Without being able to answer this question here, it does point to the revolutionary horizon of the reconception of kinship and commons that Silvia and George have played such a big part in. But it is a horizon that has been steadily receding in age of neoliberal capitalism. Before any such horizon can open again, networks and games of kinship will have to be constituted in struggle with the kinship forms of new social conservatism. That entails the creation of communities of child care, but also the presence of generous 'chiefs', spiritual leaders without formal authority, whose stash of knowledge can be continually pillaged by the rest of us.

Presence, Elders and Collective Memory

Manuela:

We learned much from Silvia through her work on women's bodies, capitalism, colonialism and primitive accumulation, but also through her presence in social-movement circles. I have experienced Silvia's presence as firm but subtle and generous, listening; and her work and voice as a partial subject, that catalyses a collective process without centring all attention on her persona. I perceive Silvia as an elder who listens, tells and advises, with a lot of care – something we need so desperately in social movements, for living memory and being connected across times and places. There's a feeling of family, of belonging in these encounters that is nothing to do with identity or ideology but that's about how and what we become together. This kind of presence is also constitutive of a feeling of family, of continuity and care and safety, even if this presence is often only felt from afar, and encounters like that happen only every so often.

I remember sitting in the garden of a social centre in Bratislava, with Silvia talking from the base of a skateboarding ramp that had been turned into a humble podium, telling of her experience in feminist movements in Italy and the United States. There was a sense of becoming-belonging across the people there, who came from many places and collectives but mostly didn't know each other. Not a big event, nothing was set up, no declaration issued, no network created, but the encounter gave us all energy and inspiration. I have seen her presence and stories spur a dynamic between people in this way several times – both listening and telling, letting things pass through her while also sharing a wealth of knowledge. In an interview about sad and joyful militancy, Silvia reflects on her generous and positive style and tone of engagement:

> 'It's partially a consequence of growing old. You understand things that when you're younger you didn't see. One thing that I've learned is to be more humble and to hold my judgement of people until I know them beyond what I can make out from what they say, realizing that people often say foolish things that they do not really believe or have not seriously thought about. It also comes from recognizing that we can change, which means that we should stress our potential rather than our limits.'[15]

To have elders like that around grounds us as people and movements and enables the kind of becoming-belonging that's crucial to creating self-reproducing movements, as movements that can reproduce themselves not just in space but also across time. This emphasis on pedagogy rather than polemics, on possibilities rather than limits, departs from the recognition of people's vulnerabilities and limitations and tries to give answers or inspirations in situated ways, with the bigger picture in mind. David Vercauteren speaks of this in terms of a need for a 'culture of precedents' in movements, for memory and knowledges to be passed across generations and cycles of struggle.[16] Silvia speaks of the importance of knowing one's history, to see systemic recurrence in capitalism and be able to anticipate the next moves of ruling elites; and she always tells those histories through the struggles of people, the many layers and forms of resistance that make up what she has called the capitalist counter-revolution (to collective power). We need this memory, both long-term (all the way back to the middle ages, as in *Caliban and the Witch*) and short-term as relating to the struggles that come directly before and after us, as well as our own.

Extending the Family

When we speak of how extended families might arise through partial subjects – babies, resources, spaces – we want to stress how material and messily social this process is. It's not a matter of a bunch of sovereign individuals coming together in a covenant around shared interests and fears (a model so common from Hobbes to contemporary communes). More often than not, building extended families is about taking what we can get and holding on to it cautiously and carefully, minding the possibility of it extending our world outward. Extending our worlds outward, in ways that build sustainable ties, is one of the biggest challenges in the face of the great loneliness and alienation that neoliberalism bestows upon us. Our starting point is not a Tanzanian village and or an Amazonian common, but intersecting individualised yet dividual lives. Reproduction is the challenge of living with partial subjects, of building lives and worlds from those – in accordance with our environments, our homes, our differences.

What Silvia and George propose is a course beyond the blackmail of heteronomy versus autonomy, public versus private, focusing on what we have and hold in common. And the notion of kinship as a game helps us to conceive of how kinship is irreducible to and capable of going beyond bonds of blood, tradition and family obligation. This insight is not just an academic or historical lesson, but an act of collective pedagogy and care for a common world, for this generation and others to come. So the problem of creating self-reproducing movements is not separate from that of families or belonging. The dichotomy of biological versus elective kinship becomes irrelevant in the face of the need to create sustainable and caring ties. Building self-reproducing movements is about learning to flow with the often unfinished, unclear, unspectacular aspects of our everyday relations, in such a way that we can depend differently and more – rather than less – on one another.

Notes

1. Silvia Federici, *Revolution at Point Zero* (Oakland: PM Press, 2012), p. 146.
2. Carolina Del Olmo, *Dónde está mi tribù? Maternidad y crianza en una sociedad individualista* (Madrid: Clave Intectual, 2013). Translation ours.
3. Melinda Cooper, *Family Values: Between Neoliberalism and the New Social Conservatism* (Cambridge, MA: MIT Press, 2017).
4. In Brian Massumi, *Parables for the Virtual: Movement, Affect, Sensation* (Durham, NC: Duke University Press, 2002), pp. 68–88.
5. *Ibid.*, p. 73.
6. *Ibid.*, p. 76.

7. 'The family is dead. Long live the family'. Conversation between Orna Donath, Brigitte Vasallo, Maria Llopis and Bel Olid at CCCB Barcelona, March 2017. At www.cccb.org/es/multimedia/videos/kosmopolis-17-la-familia-ha-muerto-viva-la-familia/227156.

8. Silvia Federici, 'Women, Land-Struggles, and the Reconstruction of the Commons', *WorkingUSA – The Journal of Labor and Society*, 14(1) (March 2011), p. 45.

9. Silvia Federici, 'Women, Land-Struggles and Globalization: An International Perspective', *Journal of Asian and African Studies*, 39(1–2) (April 2004), pp. 47–62. At https://doi.org/10.1177/0021909604048250.

10. Federici, 'Women, Land-Struggles, and the Reconstruction of the Commons', p. 42.

11. Judy Adoko and Simon Levine, *Land rights: Where We Are and Where We Need to Go* (Kampala: LEMU – Land and Equity Movement in Uganda, 2005), p. 11. At www.land-in-uganda.org/assets/Land-rights-in-Uganda-%20where-we-are-now-and-where-we-need-to-go-Sep-2005.pdf.

12. C.B. Macpherson, *Political Theory of Possessive Individualism: Hobbes to Locke* (Oxford University Press, 1962). For a corrective see Carole Pateman, *The Sexual Contract* (Stanford, CA: Stanford University Press, 1988).

13. As Gerald Raunig also asserts, albeit in a different sense. Gerald Raunig, *Dividuum* (Vienna: Transversal Texts, 2015).

14. Pierre Clastres, *Society Against the State: Essays in Political Anthropology* (Cambridge, MA: Zone Books, 1989), p. 30.

15. Silvia Federici, Carla Bergman and Nick Montgomery, 'Feeling Powers Growing: An Interview with Silvia Federici', in Bergman and Montgomery, *Joyful Militancy: Building Thriving Resistance in Toxic Times* (Chico, CA: AK Press, 2017). Available athttps://joyfulmilitancy.com/2018/06/03/feeling-powers-growing-an-interview-with-silvia-federici/.

16. David Vercauteren, *Micropolitiques des Groupes. Pour une Écologie des Pratiques Collectives* (Paris: HB Éditions, 2007).

11

They Sing the Body Insurgent

Stevphen Shukaitis

Defending one's doctoral dissertation is a strange moment. It's one where what often starts as a collective process of inquiry and the social production of knowledge is enclosed by the legitimating apparatuses of the academy. Something is gained for the individual upon whom a mark of academic is granted, but also something is lost within that process: the individual benefits, but often to the neglect of the flows of social and collective creativity from which their work draws. This is perhaps especially the case in forms of research and inquiry based around describing and theorising political organising, social movements and radical politics. The edufactory has no problem in valuing searching out authentic moments of political discourse as data collection. What it finds troublesome are more participatory forms of research going beyond analysing movements as data. Attempts to break down the positions of researching-subject and researched-objects are looked on with much greater scepticism, if not outright dismissal.

But what if it was otherwise? What if rather than a moment of professionalising enclosure of knowledge, it was made into a moment for collective reflection and celebration of the collective creativity from which research draws? This would perhaps be to harken back to the origins of the doctoral degree as the *ijazat attadris wa 'l-iftta* ('license to teach and issue legal opinions') in the training of Islamic law, but rather with the difference that guiding focus is not the formation and constitution of the law, but rather the constituent processes that guide and continually compose social movements.

This is what I had in mind when I invited Silvia and George to join to me a having a 'movement viva'[1] when I finished my dissertation. It would be a small form of breaking these very academic enclosures, attempting to bring back some of what I had discovered in my research into forms of collective imaginations and class composition. And importantly, to bring that back into the circulation and reproduction of the very networks and spaces from which I had learned and drawn from so much. And while officially such an event does not matter, it mattered to me perhaps even more than the official evaluation, particularly as I was (and continue to be) inspired by both Silvia and George's work – not just in what they've written and said, but also in the way they have spent their entire lives working to break down enclosures of collective knowledge. My doctoral research, which was published in book form as *Imaginal Machines*, explored the formation of shared radical imaginaries in autonomous social movements, from organising against precarious work conditions to a range of activist art projects. When Silvia and George pressed me on various aspects of the work it was not from a perspective of how it measured up in relationship with 'the field' or a discipline, but rather how it was useful, or could be useful, to ongoing struggles. In the time I've known Silvia and George I've learned as much through discussions around dinner tables and kitchens with them as I have from reading their work, with many ideas and questions that still demand being followed up on.

For years now, when asked what my main influences are I always say, only half-jokingly, that it's 'Brooklyn autonomia'. When saying so I do not mean the section of Autonomia that moved from Italy to the Brooklyn neighbourhood of Bedford-Stuyvsant.[2] Rather I mean the particular constellation formed around the radical media project Autonomedia, based near the Williamsburg Bridge, a few blocks north of Bed-Stuy, to which both George and Silvia have been connected since its founding in the early 1980s. If Autonomedia embodies something like a Brooklyn autonomia it would be through bringing together autonomist Marxism into conversations with radical media theory, feminism, experimental arts, anarchism, and counterculture. This, too, is a key kind of disruption of academic enclosures, refusing to let ideas and insights be kept within particular disciplinary boxes. And you can see this across the range of both Silvia and George's work, drawing from wide ranges of sources, and organising against attempts to enclose them, for instance by setting up the Committee for Academic Freedom in Africa in response to struggles in universities in Africa around structural adjustment programmes.[3]

Near the end of my movement viva, which took place at the 16 Beaver arts and event space in downtown Manhattan, Silvia mentioned to me that she had once also worked on questions of art and aesthetics. This surprised me, as this was not an aspect of her writing I was familiar with. But I managed to track down a copy of her unpublished dissertation, on 'The Development of [György] Lukács' Realism', which she completed at SUNY Buffalo in September 1980. And so, I think a fitting way to pay a small tribute would be to return the gift, to offer a few reflections on this underappreciated aspect of Silvia's work. Her main argument involves an exploration of the formation of the Hungarian thinker's approach to realism, which has been foundational in the formation of Marxist approaches to aesthetics. Commonly it is assumed that there is a break in Lukács' work, separating his earlier 'pre-Marxist' writings on the novel and aesthetics from his later (and more influential) writings on class consciousness and reification. Contrary to this, Silvia argued that through his continued focus on realism there is no break in Lukács' work, no point where he clearly shifts from 'pre-Marxist idealism' to a properly Marxist phase. Instead she suggests he continues to utilise categories of bourgeois thought, bringing them into Marxist framework, though this is not readily apparent.

Reading this at first I was surprised that there appeared to be no discussions of feminism, autonomism,[4] or any of the various campaigns that Silvia was heavily involved in during her time in the 1970s as a PhD student. Why was that, I wondered? Are there no overlaps between the feminist struggles, aesthetics, and social reproduction? That couldn't be the case.[5] Rather it seemed more likely that academic decorum and expectations of that time made it much more difficult to bring those elements more directly into her work at the time. But what overlaps could have been made if that was attempted? One could easily start with *Nightcleaners*, the documentary film made by the Berwick Street Collective from 1972 to 1975.[6] Although it was originally conceived of as form of media production to raise awareness of the low pay and harsh conditions of women cleaning offices on the overnight shift, it is better known as an avant-garde experiment with form breaking of narrative realism. Drawing on Brecht's approaches to breaking narrative structures it is now thought of as an important example of collective and feminist film-making. Or one could easily find points of resonance with Mierle Laderman Ukeles's practice and concept of maintenance art, where the manifold activities and labour of social reproduction are turned directly into forms of approach production.[7]

In these two brief examples (as well as many others one could find) there is a commonality intersecting with Silvia's work: rupturing the assumed frames of realism. The connection might not be obvious at first, but this is precisely what Marxist feminists were arguing for around questions of gender and social reproduction, undermining any approach (including those held by comrades Marxist or not) that fell back on assumptions of who 'naturally' should be involved in any particular task.

Walt Whitman might have sung the body electric, but what can be seen through both Silvia and George's writing for many years is the singing of a body insurgent. It is a body, and a body of writing, that struggles to break free of attempt to enclose and control it, whether in the form of new forms of primitive accumulation, flexible exploitation, neoliberal academic governance or fixed assumptions about who should be caring, organising and struggling – and what it means, or could mean, to be involved in social movements. Perhaps Lukács could not completely separate himself from bourgeois categories and assumptions, but that does not mean the answer to such dead ends is found through better or more clever philosophy. Rather it points us to the ever-renewing forms of commons that are formed by bodies struggling, and dancing joyously, together.

Notes

1. Viva is short for 'viva voce' or 'oral examination.' Academia is permeated by Latin phrases.
2. Though some participants from Italian Movement of 1977, including Franco 'Bifo' Berardi and other people involved with Radio Alice, moved to the Lower East Side of New York in the early 1980s while fleeing from state repression.
3. For more on the Committee for Academic Freedom in Africa (including digitised versions of their newsletters) see https://libcom.org/library/newsletters-committee-academic-freedom-africa-1991-2003. CAFA materials are also available through May Day Rooms in London: http://maydayrooms.org/archives/committee-for-academic-freedom-in-africa (last accessed 6 March 2019).
4. As far I can tell the term 'autonomism' was not used as a term during the 1970s. Typically its coinage is attributed to Harry Cleaver's 1979 *Reading Capital Politically*, though in that text Cleaver uses the terms 'autonomist' and 'autonomist Marxism', not 'autonomism'.
5. This is not entirely true. Within the text of Silvia's dissertation there are several references to the work authors who would commonly be regarded as autonomist thinkers, including the literary critic and former comrade of Mario Tronti, Alberto Asor Rosa. Though very little of his work has been translated into English, although the situation has more recently slowly started to be addressed.
6. For more on the Berwick Street Collective see https://lux.org.uk/artist/berwick-st-collective (last accessed 6 March 2019).
7. For more information on Mierle Laderman Ukeles the best source is the catalogue produced by Queens (published by Prestel) for 2016 retrospective exhibition "Mierle Laderman Ukeles: Maintenance Art". More information can be found at www.queensmuseum.org/2016/04/mierle-laderman-ukeles-maintenance-art (last accessed 6 March 2019).

12

The Separations of Productive and Domestic Labour: An Historical Approach

Viviane Gonik

The question of the conciliation of family life and work, the so-called 'work-life balance', is much discussed nowadays.[1] In order to understand what is at stake today, it is important to examine the history of this separation. Two implicit presuppositions underlie this suggested conciliation: first, that this problem has emerged with a relatively recent entry of women into the workforce; and second, that domestic work has always, almost naturally, been the role of women. In this chapter, I wish to demonstrate historically that these two presuppositions are social artefacts, as the sexual division of labour, 'at once the object and the expression of the sexual balance of power, is not a fixed phenomenon, historically'.[2]

With an historical analysis of this separation, I aim to show that first, the process entailed important resistances and suffering; and second, that the separation is inherent to capitalist production and directly serves capitalist productivity. The demonstration is mostly based on two sources: Silvia Federici's *Caliban and the Witch: Women, the Body and Primitive Accumulation*, and *Le Travail et la Vertu: Femmes au Foyer, une Mystification de la Révolution Industrielle*, by Katherine Blunden.[3]

The separation between paid work and unpaid domestic work – or, in Marxist terminology, between productive and reproductive labour – began gradually during the end of feudalism and the early times of capitalism. It really developed during the nineteenth century, with industrialisation, but only concerned a part of the population. The great majority of male and female workers, peasants, domestics and artisans continued to live and work in the same spaces and temporalities.

In Western societies, women have almost always worked. In agriculture first of all – which occupied 80 per cent of the population until the nineteenth century – as artisans, in the mines and first factories, and of course as domestics. Even in the aristocracy, when men were often at war far from home (during the crusades, for example), women often managed the domain.

Silvia Federici's *Caliban and the Witch* explores the beginnings of capitalism, during the Middle Ages, in the light of the struggles between peasants and workers, on the one hand, and the feudal aristocracy and the Church, on the other. Already in the tenth century, important peasant movements rebelled against serfdom, imposing customary limits on their obligations which permitted their families to retain a large part of their production and to continue to have free access to the commons: forests, rivers and pastures. These struggles left a trace in the legend of Robin Hood, an 'outlaw' who hunted illegally in a royal forest. (A judicial document of 1228 mentions the imprisonment of a certain Robin Hood for non-payment of a debt or fine.) In France, Germany, Italy and England a vast movement of villages emerged, parallel to that of urban communes, to put limits to the demands of the dominant classes and to impose an autonomous management of resources. Women were as present as men in these struggles. One can cite the famous words of John Ball (died 15 July 1381): 'When Adam delved and Eve span, who was then the gentleman?'[4]

The dramatic demographic decline caused by the great plague of the fourteenth century provoked profound social change. The peasants found themselves in a position of strength, able to obtain new advantages. In reaction, a counter-revolution followed, profoundly restructuring the European economies through the colonial slave economy and the privatisation (enclosures) of the commons; the latter provoked the expulsion of masses of peasants, forced to seek waged labour. One can cite, as an early example, the Ordinance of Labourers of 1349 and the Workers Statutes of 1351, laws proclaimed in England by Edward III.[5] The Ordinance forbade paying salaries higher than those in effect before the Black Death. It also made work mandatory for all men or women in good health under the age of 60 and imposed heavy fines on the idle. An extremely harsh discipline was progressively imposed on the European workforce: the 'bloody laws' concerning vagrancy in England, forced labour in workhouses, deportation, galleys, etc.

The majority of the victims of these policies were women and, in addition, they were the targets of several specific attacks. The increased impoverishment of women expelled from their land[6] had the effect of reinforcing the domination of men over women. In addition, the elites – alarmed by the demographic decline provoked by poverty and the plague – criminalised traditional contraceptive and abortive techniques, and sought to put midwives under their own control, transforming them into the spies of their natalist policy. These persecutions were part of a more general stigmatisation of women, which theorised their natural inferiority, unbridled sexuality, and so on. During two centuries, witch hunts tortured and burned hundreds of thousands in Europe, helping to discipline the bodies and lives of women, assigned above all to child bearing. Thomas Hobbes, for instance, considers sorcery to be a superstition, but writes that witches 'are justly punished' because 'if these superstitions were eliminated, "men would be more fitted than they are for civil obedience"'.[7]

Gender relations are thus profoundly remodelled, the gradual exclusion of women from the public sphere coinciding with the emergence of capitalist productive relations. For Federici, primitive accumulation was concomitant with several phenomena: 'the development of a new sexual division of labour subjugating women's labour and women's reproductive function to the reproduction of the work-force; ... the construction of a new patriarchal order, based upon the exclusion of women from waged-work and their subordination to men'.[8]

The idea that women should not work outside the household, and that they should only participate in 'production' as their husbands' aides appears everywhere – in courts of law, fiscal documents, the ordinances of guilds. Even women's production for the market was not considered 'work' if it was done in the household. Thus women were re-defined as 'non-workers', an ideology that was practically established by the end of the seventeenth century. Suffering from the competition with the first capitalist manufacturers, the guilds and corporations thought to defend themselves by excluding women from their organisations. New laws subordinated women legally to men, even their salaries being paid to their husbands. One can recall here that in Switzerland, the right of women to work without an authorisation from their husbands dates from the modification of the law concerning marriage, adopted through a popular initiative in ... 1985! 'The physical enclosure operated by land privatisation and the hedging of the commons was amplified by a process of social enclosure, the reproduction of workers shifting from the open field to the home, from the community to the family, from the public space (the common, the church) to the private.'[9]

In the nineteenth century, the growing productivity of the industrial revolution made possible the appearance of a significant middle class: accountants, foremen, notaries, clerks, etc., whose salaries sufficed to support their whole family (wife and children). As Katherine Blunden notes, 'The division between the active and inactive populations could thus no longer run only between social classes, but also within a class and within a family. The division could henceforth be sexual'.[10]

A discourse developed – propagated by the church, the medical profession, manuals and moralists of all kinds – to justify and stabilise this new configuration, sanctifying the woman guardian of the household and its values, who thus enables her husband to confront the difficulties of his work. The sermon of a clergyman in 1871 offers a good example: 'Women must endeavour to make their household ... a little corner of brilliant sky – serene and joyous ... Women, whose hearts are an unceasing source of courage and inspiration for the man hard-pressed ... who every morning send forth their husband or brother with renewed forces to their struggle.'[11]

All the education of the young women of this social class is centred on the marriage market and their preparation for the role of 'inactive' women. A number of elements prescribe how this role should be held, including the shaping of the body and appearance: delicate traits, white skin, a high and infantile voice signal their lack of productive abilities. Similarly, dress fashions (crinolines, narrow skirts, corsets, bustles, leg-of-mutton sleeves) are all signs that they don't work (at least not in paid work) and that they depend on their husband's income. Women and children share the same exclusion from the economic sphere, the same juridical subordination, the same dependency.

Productive labour in industry is constituted as distinct from reproductive labour, the latter assigned solely to women. The organisation and the temporality of work in the factory assumes the separate existence of domestic work: it is full-time and uninterrupted, making a maximum demand on the worker's (imagined implicitly as male) physical and mental capacities, since he will be able to rest when he gets home. The temporality of productive work is thus organised for men liberated from all family or domestic tasks – despite the fact that from the start of industrialisation women (and children) are also employed. The same logic will later be applied to social security (designed for full-time and uninterrupted employment), for work health programmes (with their gender biased categories of professional illnesses) and even to popular institutions such as the unions.

Although the household is detached, spatially and in time, from the centre of production, it must remain useful to the latter. The housewife's role is to assure that her mate will return to work physically and psychologically prepared for another day of labour: to reproduce the workforce. Systematic methods of housework, patterned on industrial methods, are popularised through publications such as Maria Eliza Rundell's *A New System of Domestic Economy* (early 1800s) and in courses of 'home economics', which teach how to manage a budget, to sort, file or to organise one's agenda.

Through these methods, it is in final analysis, the workers' lifestyle which is controlled. Danièle Linhart recalls, in *La Comédie Humaine du Travail, de la Déshumanisation Taylorienne à la Sur-Humanisation Managérielle*,[12] the programmes of Henry Ford, at the beginning of the twentieth century. In order to stabilise his workforce, he both greatly increased their salary and took measures to ensure that they would return to work in prime condition.

He thus created a department of inspectors whose role was to verify in his workers' homes the respect of conditions of hygiene, morality and economy.

Ford intended to standardise his workers' lifestyle just as he did the quality of the parts involved in production. He writes, 'for production to go well, one must dispose of clean tools, a clean factory, accurate gauges and precise methods', but that the workers' domestic life must also go well, due to 'clean thinking, clean living and square dealing'.[13] The wife assures the adaptation of the new worker to his job by controlling his habits, feeding him appropriately and good management of the family budget.

This model of the housewife, first developed in the middle class, becomes the model for families of all social classes. The middle class also imposes its models with respect to housing, children's education and leisure activities. The archetype of the housewife is thus imposed as somehow in the 'nature' of women. After the war economy, which mobilised women in production to replace the men at the front, particularly in the United States, women returned to the workplace in great numbers during the 1960s, but the stereotypes created by the sexual division of labour remained strong.

Research in which I was involved illustrated this in various sectors.[14] In reality, the professional sphere remains a largely segregated universe, men and women generally practising different skills and functions, often in distinct spaces. Concerning the organisations of different skills, one observes a horizontal segregation. Women are most often limited to those 'derived' from domestic work: care, work with young children, cleaning or the manipulation of small objects. In industry, working women are often assigned to quality control, packaging or meticulous tasks, and to tasks involving little movement within or outside the enterprise; whereas men are more likely to be in charge of repairs and upkeep, machine adjustment or after-sales services outside the enterprise. One observes also a sexual discrimination concerning professional qualifications: most tasks for women are considered 'unqualified', the skills involved not being taken into consideration, since they are considered innate.

Housework and salaried labour are not two separate entities, but form a system. Professional and domestic life are articulated one to another because they share the same logic concerning the relations between sexes. The professional career of men and/or women, and the course of their domestic lives, reveal themselves to be closely related both to the dominant conceptions concerning the relations between men and women in a society, and to the economic relations imposed by capitalism.

Notes

1. This piece was first published in French in *La Revue Economique et Sociale*, Lausanne, 2017.

2. Céline Schoeni, *Travail Féminin: Retour à l'Ordre! L'Offensive Contre le Travail des Femmes Durant la Crise Économique des Années 1930* (Lausanne: Antipodes, 2012).

3. Silvia Federici, *Caliban and the Witch: Women, the Body and Primitive Accumulation* (Brooklyn, NY: Autonomedia, 2004); Katherine Blunden, *Le Travail et la Vertu: Femmes au Foyer, une Mystification de la Révolution Industrielle* (Lausanne: Payot, 1982).

4. Cited by Chris Harman, *A Popular History of Humanity. From the Stone Age to the New Millenium* (London: Verso, 2008), p. 151.

5. Rodney Hilton, *Bond Men Made Free: Medieval Peasant Movements and the English Rising of 1381*, 2nd edn (Abingdon, OX: Routledge, 2003).

6. Women were more dependent materially on the commons.

7. Silvia Federici, *Caliban and the Witch* (2004), pp. 143–4, and citing Hobbes, *Leviathan*.

8. *Ibid.*, p. 12.

9. *Ibid.*, p. 84.

10. Blunden, *Le Travail et la Vertu* (1982).

11. Cited by Blunden, *Le Travail et la Vertu* (1982).

12. Danièle Linehart, *La Comédie Humaine du Travail, de la Déshumanisation Taylorienne à la Sur-Humanisation Managérielle* (Toulouse: Eres, 2015).

13. Cited by Linehart, *Ibid.*

14. Viviane Gonik, Laura Vonèche, Benoit Bastard, Malik von Allmen, *Construire l'Égalité, Femmes et Hommes dans l'Entreprise* (Geneva: Georg, 1998).

Another Way Home:
Slavery, Motherhood and Resistance

Camille Barbagallo

Four of us were in a car on our way to a radical student conference, it was the very late 1990s and the WTO protests in Seattle had just hit the national papers. We had driven straight through from Brisbane to Sydney, nine hours with your foot flat to the floor. We arrived sweaty and tired and sort of tumbled out of the car and into the front garden of a huge run-down student house in inner Sydney. A woman I had not met before, Natasha, was at the front door. Noting my then boyfriend, she spat, 'So, you're a breeder then'.

Standing there in the harsh morning sunshine, the word breeder did the job it was intended to do: producing a connection between my 19-year-old body, its assumed capacity for biological reproduction, patriarchy and normative heterosexual sex. A little taken aback, I mumbled something in response while looking at my feet and spent the rest of the week thinking about what breeder sex would be like.

The word breeder stung in part because my 19-year-old self didn't dream of having children. By the time I reached the age of 19 I had discovered feminism and it enabled me to imagine being a woman that did not include breeding. I swapped babies for a wage of one's own. It wasn't that I didn't want to have children; it was more that I wanted be set free from the potential – that very gendered assumption that one day I would, of course, want to have kids. I even went to see a doctor about getting sterilised. He suggested I see a shrink. I laughed in his face and carried on working hard and earning nothing.

Though, it turns out that Natasha was right, I was a breeder. Around a year and half after my first child was born, I had what can only be described as a crisis of motherhood. I was not suffering from post-natal depression nor was I exclusively at home with the baby. I was one of the so-called 'lucky' mothers whose partner did more than just 'help'; he washed, cared, cleaned, cooked and worried with me about high temperatures or strange looking vomit. My problem wasn't the baby, or breastfeeding, or not getting enough sleep. All those things were certainly hard. But, as I lay sobbing, panic ripping through my body, it was motherhood, my newly acquired identity that came spilling out as the problem.

It wasn't that I couldn't find a version of motherhood to fit my lifestyle or a bundle of commodities to consume to affirm my status. It was more profound than that, it was an unnerving realisation of having birthed capital: all that blood and dirt. And that the work of wiping the snotty noses, cleaning up the shit and teaching them to be on time, it all still pretty much fell to women and yet more women, no matter how you rolled the dice. Added to that enormity was the fact that, while my nice radical reconfiguration of family was a much-needed little refuge within the horror show, it was not a way out.

Breeding

In *Caliban and the Witch*, Silvia Federici explores the historical processes that reconfigured the female body 'into an instrument for the reproduction of labour and the expansion of the work-force, treated as a natural breeding-machine, functioning according to rhythms outside of women's control'.[1] This reconfiguration of some women into 'breeders' is a story that, as Hortense Spillers reminds us, cannot be deciphered without tripping over other female narratives.[2] It is a history that asks us to consider how the reproduction of labour-power is valued, what it costs and who pays the bill. The encounter that opens this chapter begins with the profoundly racist and sexist concept of *breeding* as a uncomfortable departure point in which to unravel some of the contradictions and tensions that exist between slavery, women's bodies, motherhood and reproduction.

Through an investigation of how the concept of breeding was constructed in relation to slave women, I am interested in the political economy of reproduction under slavery and the construction and organisation of gender, race and class relations inside and outside of waged labour. My focus in this chapter is on some of the ways that motherhood and biological reproduction were reorganised, revalued and contested through the reorganisation of reproduction that accompanied the emergence of capitalist production. The history of capitalism is, of course, a history of slavery and of colonialism. Shifting from the colonial to the post-colonial context, it is a history that has continued, and has been shaped fundamentally by migration from Britain's former colonies to the 'motherland' during reconstruction in the post-war era and one that continues today with global migration from the global south to the north.

There are vast inequalities and disparities in how different racialised and gendered subjects experience the labour of making and remaking people under capitalism. The gaps and silences, as well as and the spaces of difference, have long and complex histories. One heavily contested site that emerges is that of the slave household, a site not only of exploitation and oppression but also of resistance for slave communities and slave women in particular. The complexities of the domestic lives and family structures under slavery challenge tendencies within feminist theory that assume a universal or 'shared' experience of home, motherhood and the domestic sphere. If the home is not essentially repressive, the question becomes how some homes can be sites of significant resistance while others are sites of domination. This opens up a pragmatic and operative conceptualisation of *home* as site of domination/resistance. Furthermore, where social structures block the establishment of patriarchal masculinity, there is the potential for the home to mean something else.

In the analysis that follows, the concept of 'breeding' refers in the first instance to the specific period in the history of the transatlantic slave trade in the eighteenth century in which slave labour 'was plentiful, [and] it was considered more profitable to work slaves to death than to provide the basic human requirements which would have prolonged [their] working lives'.[3] I am interested in interrogating how it was more profitable for slave owners to buy humans than it was to allow or force their existing slaves 'to breed'. This moment of economic calculation, one that is grotesque in its measurement, is revealing in so far as it makes visible the actual costs associated with reproduction – costs that are often obscured, taken for granted and occur in the background of economic considerations.

Connected to the enslavement and exploitation of African slaves in the colonies is the history of how the making and remaking of labour-power in Britain was reconfigured to be a white woman's 'natural' and 'proper' destiny. Through this move, women's labour was stripped of value, narrowed in meaning and confined to the domestic sphere. Framing this in another way, the construction and function of motherhood and women's naturalised domestic role in Britain relied on and was made possible only through the exclusion and disciplining of certain bodies, specifically those of women of colour, working mothers and slave women on the plantations.

An investigation into the political economy of reproduction makes it clear that it is crucial for feminists to pay close attention to the constructions and experiences of race and class alongside that of gender. In doing so, such a politics demands that we abandon the claim to a universalised motherhood and the domestic sphere as an always-already degraded terrain of oppression and domination. The desires of some women, overwhelmingly white middle-class educated women, to escape the home and strive for change in the world of employment has certainly dominated the story of reproduction in the last forty years. However, this desire of escape from domesticity and for a certain notion of freedom has obscured other narratives of the domestic sphere and motherhood, as well as concealing on both a local and global scale the layers of dependency that are involved in the making and remaking of people and workers under capitalism.

Dependencies

When we articulate reproduction as a political problematic connected to the histories of the Transatlantic Slave Trade, colonialism and the development of industrial capitalism in Europe, particularly Britain, it becomes possible to grasp how certain activities and bodies became sexually and racially differentiated. Reproductive activities have been not only differentiated but also devalued and, in many instances, made invisible through an evocation of the 'natural'. This long historical process involved violent separations that we need to contextualise alongside the enclosure of commons and other mechanisms of capital accumulation that connect the emergence of industrial capitalism in Britain with the colonial project and enslavement of African workers.

The vast concentrations of wealth, resources and capital that flowed into Europe, especially Britain, from the seventeenth to the nineteenth century have led many scholars to conclude that the plantation production system and the trade in African slaves played a fundamental role in the emergence of capitalism. Extending this argument, in *Black Marxism* Cedric Robinson presents the histories of race and racialism as existing prior to the emergence of capitalism and demonstrates the necessarily racist character of capitalism as an expression of European civilisation. He cautions against a narration of the history of capitalism that defines slavery and slave labour as processes of primitive accumulation relegated to an historical stage somewhere between feudalism and capitalism. He argues that 'slave labor, the slave trade and their associated phenomena ... profoundly altered the economies of those states directly or indirectly involved in colonization and production by slave labor'.[4] To stress the point, Robinson describes the 'associated phenomena' of slavery as including 'markets for cheap commodities; ship building and outfitting; mercantile and military navies; cartography; forestry; banking; insurance; technological improvements in communication, industrial production'.[5]

The extreme violence and brutality of the slave trade is often washed away in the official tales of capitalism's birth, and the scale and depth of connection between the geographies of the British Empire rarely gets acknowledged. Plainly put, to do so would give voice to uncomfortable questions as to how some people came to possess the wealth they do and why others remain dispossessed and trapped in so-called cycles of 'poverty' and 'underdevelopment'. In 1944, Eric Williams outlined the specific role England played in the 'triangular trade' between Europe, Africa and the 'New World': 'by 1750 there was hardly a trading or a manufacturing town in England which was not in some way connected with the triangular or direct colonial trade. The profits obtained provided one of the main streams of that accumulation of capital in England which financed the Industrial Revolution'.[6]

The centrality of slavery to the emergence of capitalism was one that transformed not only the landscape of the colonies, but also Britain. The immense accumulation of labour and capital that was made possible through the enslavement, forced labour and death of millions of African workers on the slave ships, plantations and colonies produced many of the economic and social conditions that enabled the separation of production from reproduction in the transition from feudalism to capitalism in Britain. In this instance, to speak of the separation of production from reproduction is to articulate the processes that ensured workers' dependence on the wage and their inability to reproduce themselves independently of capitalism. As Silvia reminds us, the significant reduction in the cost of reproducing labour-power (i.e. reproducing workers) in Britain that was made possible through the production of cheap commodities using slave labour in the colonies, prefigures capitalism's contemporary use of 'cheap' migrant labour and the production of consumer commodities in the so-called Third World.[7]

The production of commodities such as sugar, rum, tea, tobacco and cotton – the most important commodities (apart from bread) in the making and remaking of workers in Europe – did not reach large-scale production in the colonies until slavery had been institutionalised after the 1650s. Maria Mies makes the point that before production was transformed with African slave labour, the privileged European elite who could afford them consumed the 'luxury' items stolen, looted or traded from the colonies.[8] However, once production in the colonies was expanded through the use of slave labour, one direct consequence was a reduction in the costs of the commodity basket necessary to reproduce labour-power during the emergence of industrial capitalism in Britain. In other words, one of the connections established through the slave trade was between the profitability of production in the colonies and the reduction in costs associated with keeping workers alive and fed in the industrial metropolis. As Silvia argues, the expansion of colonial commodity production and the use of slave labour restructured the reproduction of industrial workers and, conversely, the costs associated with reproducing labour-power on an international scale and 'the metropolitan wage became the vehicle by which the goods produced by enslaved workers went to market, and the value of the products of enslaved-labor were realized'.[9]

The emergence of industrial capitalism in Britain was an uneven, contested and violent series of interlocking processes and events. The accumulation of labour and capital that slavery made possible assisted in forging the 'free' labourers of Britain – workers who were and often remain free to starve without the wage. The 'freedom' of capital's industrial workers was, following Marx's analysis, a double freedom. It was a freedom that enabled not only specific class relations, but also specific gender relations, that while being uneven and continually contested, separated men and women in Britain into distinct spheres of work and influence: on the one hand, that of (male) waged productive work in the factory/public sphere; on the other, (female) unwaged reproductive work in the home/domestic realm.

Separations

The centrality of slavery to the development of capitalism in Britain does not exist only within the realm of the economic. In addition to the immense monetary wealth that slavery produced for Britain's ruling class, we must also add the techniques of disciplining, policing and controlling workers that were exported from the colonies back to England and into the factory system. In additional to Robinson's list of 'associated phenomena' it is necessary to add that slavery was central to the construction of capitalist gender relations and to the separation and sorting of men and women into two distinct spheres of influence and work. Part of this process involved imagining some (white) women as 'good' mothers: bell hooks makes the point that 'the shift away from the image of white women as sinful and sexual to that of white women as virtuous lady occurred at the same time as mass sexual exploitation of enslaved black women'.[10]

The Transatlantic Slave Trade and slave economy was one in which slaves were defined as chattel and this definition of people as 'profitable labour-units' or as property to be bought and sold applied to women as much as it did to men. Angela Davis argues that slaves 'might as well have been genderless as far as the slaveholders were concerned'.[11] On the defeminisation of women slaves, the fugitive slave Williamson Pease recounted that, 'women who do outdoor work are used as bad as men'.[12] Hortense Spillers makes the point that 'under these conditions, we lose at least gender difference in the outcome, and the female body and male body become a territory of cultural and political manoeuvre, not at all gender-related, gender specific'.[13] This loss of gender difference is evident in the conditions of labour of fieldworkers that (the majority of) slaves experienced: girls and women were,

> ...assigned to work the soil, pick the cotton, cut the cane, harvest the tobacco ... [and] ... that judged by the evolving nineteenth-century ideology of femininity, which emphasized women's roles as nurturing mothers and gentle companions and housekeepers for their husbands, Black women were practically anomalies.[14]

Despite the 'equality' of exploitation that slave women experienced (vis-à-vis male slaves) in the conditions of their work, they also suffered in different and gendered ways in so far as they were victims of sexual abuse, rape and other violence that is preserved for and inflicted upon the bodies of women. Furthermore, by analysing the labour conditions of (female) slaves involved in production and the differentiated ways that (white) women in Britain came to be seen as inhabitants of a sphere that was separated from the realm of productive work and synonymous with 'mother' and 'housewife', it is important to note that 'among Black slaves, this vocabulary [of 'mother', 'housewife'] was nowhere to be found'.[15] Davis argues that the gendered role assigned to female slaves was one in which they were conceived of 'as "breeders" – animals, whose monetary value could be precisely calculated in terms of their ability to multiply their numbers ... [and] since slave women were classified as "breeders" as opposed to "mothers", their infant children could be sold'.[16]

In sharp contrast to the emergent gender ideology that attempted to naturalise, feminise and, crucially, privatise the processes of reproduction of 'industrial' workers in Britain, the explicit understanding of the costs and work of reproducing the slave population is revealed by the calculations that the slave traders and planters undertook. In many instances, the cost of reproduction was so considerable that during the operation of the international slave trade it was 'cheaper' to purchase a new slave than to 'breed' one on the plantation. In *The Sociology of Slavery*, Orlando Patterson draws attention to a report in which 'Henry Coor, a Jamaican millwright, estimated in the *West Indian Reporter (March 1831)* that the cost of rearing a slave to the age of 14 was £112 in Jamaica, £165 in Trinidad, £109 in Barbados, and £122 in Antigua'.[17] At this time the comparative market price of a field slave was £45 in Cuba.[18]

In reference to the metrics that informed the plantation owners' calculations, Hall outlines that 'during and after pregnancy, the slave is useless for several months, and her nourishment should be more abundant and better chosen. This loss of work and added expense comes out of the master's pocket. It is he who pays for the often ineffective and always lengthy care of the newborn'.[19] The considerable differences in how reproduction was constructed and valued are stark. In the colonies with regard to slaves there was visible and measurable monetary value associated with the activities of reproduction; in industrial Britain these processes were becoming more and more obscured, naturalised and devalued.

The emergence of the 'domestic ideology' in eighteenth and nineteenth century Britain was an uneven process, constantly being broken apart at the same time as it was being constructed. Nevertheless, and despite this contestation, transformations occurred and, over time, women and men began to be conceived as existing in separate spheres – and their work gendered and valued or devalued accordingly.[20] Drawing together the twin processes of the emergence of the trade in slaves and the subjugation of women, Silvia argues that 'starting in the mid-16th century, while Portuguese ships were returning from Africa with their first human cargoes, all the European governments began to impose the severest penalties against contraception, abortion and infanticide'.[21]

In her analysis of the historical dynamics and processes that led to the devaluation of women's reproductive labour, Silvia stresses the importance of the witch trials, the criminalisation of women's control over procreation and the degradation of maternity to a relative and literal position of forced labour. However, like many other feminist scholars, she also characterises the dynamic that was gaining momentum in eighteenth century as one that assigned men and women to separate spheres of influence and work and one that particularly designated women to the domestic sphere and privatised family structure. Silvia argues that the historic changes in the social location and power of women – that peaked in the nineteenth century with the creation of the full-time housewife – redefined women's position in society and in relation to men.[22]

It was within the emergent bourgeois 'middle-class' that the family and the household were first defined as separate from the sphere of production. Leonore Davidoff and Catherine Hall argue that the construction of women's naturalised domestic role within the family was key to the bourgeois assertion of cultural authority and political power, enabling the middling classes to relocate the idea of virtue, honour and morality away from the inherited form of aristocratic noblesse oblige, into the domestic sphere.[23] As guardians of morality, middle-class women were also the bearers of bourgeois cultural hegemony and, as Davidoff and Hall demonstrate, middle-class women themselves played an active role in the production of domestic ideology, just as their domestic labour made a vital contribution to middle-class economic production. Not only did middle-class women, along with the enormous amounts of work of their female servants, perform the reproductive labour upon which all the now differentiated 'productive' labour of men depended, but as consumers of an ever-increasing range of household commodities – soft furnishings, ornaments, cleaning products – they were also central in shaping new forms of commodity capitalism and colonial economies, while actively creating a new middle-class identity.

It is within this context that McClintock argues that imperialism and colonialism were not something that happened 'elsewhere – a disagreeable fact of history external to Western identity'.

> Rather, imperialism and the invention of race were fundamental aspects of Western, industry modernity [... that] became central not only to the self-definition of the middle-class but also to the policing of the 'dangerous classes': the working-class, the Irish, Jews, prostitutes, feminists, gays and lesbians, criminals, the militant crowd.[24]

She makes a similar claim with respect to the cult of domesticity as neither simply trivial nor belonging only to the private, 'natural' realm of the family. McClintock argues that the cult of domesticity was a crucial, if concealed dimension of male, as well as female identities, and an indispensable element both of the industrial market and the imperial enterprise.

The domesticated family structure that came to dominate middle-class homes mediated between the public and private spheres and, importantly, connected the emerging market with the domestic sphere. Davidoff and Hall's analysis of gender subjectivities of middle-class men and women highlights the class and gender formations that both constructed, and were constructed by, the creation of this domestic sphere. In particular, their work draws attention to the role of the middle-class home, a space that can be said to have been built on the expropriation of the labour of both working-class men and women, whether in the public world of the workplace (factories) or the private workplace of the home, with 'service' being an industry that employed upwards of one-third of all working-age women by the nineteenth century.[25] Of course, this expropriation was also only made possible by the immense amount of wealth produced by slave labour on the plantations.

Thus, the bourgeois household emerges from and is wholly integrated into the 'triangular trade'. As a home and workplace of millions of working-class servants, as well as middle-class wives, it is the site of consumption of commodities produced both in the colonies and in Britain's factories. The factories, for their part, produced commodities and value, and simultaneously consumed both raw materials from the colonies and labour-power, the latter that was 'replenished' by means of 'cheapened' (in that they were produced by slave labour) commodities from the plantations. In other words, slave plantations produced materials that reproduced workers in both the public and the private realm. This interconnected and complex picture of the boundaries that demarcated private from public emphasises the fact that the public was not really public, nor the private really that private. Furthermore, despite the powerful imagery and discourse of the separate spheres of work and home, both the private and public are ideological constructs with specific meanings that are the product of a particular historical time, constantly being contested and under revision.

Separate spheres for men and women reflected, justified and made sense of the reorganisation of society brought about by the development of industrial capitalism. Within bourgeois middle-class discourses of work, gender and the family, the potent combination and intersection of the constructions of labours of leisure (the housewife) and labours of invisibility (servants) served to further conceal and deny the economic value of women's domestic work. The defeminisation of women slaves and the measurable cost of reproduction under slavery effectively excluded female slaves not only from constructions of motherhood but also, more generally, from being imagined as women.

Labour

In the British Empire, the relative 'cheapness' of slave labour declined when the trade in slaves was made illegal in 1807, prompting plantation owners to adopt a slave breeding policy. Slavery itself – as opposed to the *trade* in slave – wasn't abolished in the British Empire for another 26 years. Writing specifically about the histories of slavery in the United States – where slavery remained legal until the end of the Civil War in 1865 – Davis argues that when the abolition of the international slave trade began to threaten the expansion of the young cotton-industry, 'the slaveholding class was forced to rely on natural reproduction ... [and that] ... during the decades preceding the Civil War, Black women came to be increasingly appraised for their fertility (or for the lack of it)'.[26]

The 'turn' to a reliance on biological reproduction, as opposed to the slave trade, has been debated and analysed by numerous scholars and 'much has been made of the slaveholders' definition of the Black family as a matrilocal structure'.[27] In *The Black Family in Slavery and Freedom*, Herbert Gutman presents evidence of developed and complex family structures that existed during slavery. These were not the infamous matriarchal family,[28] but rather families involving wife, husband, children and frequently other relatives, as well as adoptive kin.[29] Undeniably slave families were separated and disrupted, however Gutman also argues that slaves adhered to strict norms regulating their familial arrangements.

Patricia Hill Collins further develops Gutman's argument, suggesting that, 'enslaved Africans were property and one way that many resisted the dehumanising effects of slavery was by re-creating African notions of family as extended kin units'.[30] She argues that this slave community stood in opposition to a White-man controlled public sphere of political economy. Connected to modes of resistance against dehumanisation was the relative security that often accompanied motherhood, where 'child-bearing was a way for enslaved Black women to anchor themselves in a place for an extended period and maintain enduring relationships with husbands, family, and friends'.[31] Collins also argues that, within the ele-vated status of motherhood, the refusal of slave women to bear children and cases of Black infanticide can also be read as acts of resistance to the system of slavery and its dependence on the bodies of slave women.

Collins also outlines the various mechanisms involved both in calcu-lating the costs (to slave-owners) of reproduction and in encouraging reproduction. These included: 'assigning pregnant women lighter work-loads, giving pregnant women more attention and rations, and rewarding prolific women with bonuses'.[32] Deborah Gray White writes that, 'slave masters wanted adolescent girls to have children, and to this end they prac-ticed a passive though insidious kind of breeding'.[33] Gutman also notes that, especially after the abolition of the overseas slave trade, a high premium was placed on females who began early to bear children. Of course, slaves and owners measured the birth of a child differently: 'the owner viewed the birth of a slave child primarily as an economic fact but the slave viewed the same event primarily as a social and familial fact'.[34]

It is within the complex conceptualisation of equality in exploitation and enslavement and the valorisation of a limited, yet present, domestic life, that Davis adds another dimension to the story of slavery and gender: Black women 'also asserted their equality aggressively in challenging the inhuman institution of slavery'.[35] Female slaves engaged in various acts of resistance. For example, they 'poisoned their masters, committed other acts of sabotage and, like their men, joined maroon communities and frequently fled northward to freedom'.[36] Two of the better-known slave women, Sojourner Truth (c.1797–1883) and Harriet Tubman (c.1822–1913) were both born into slavery in the United States and subsequently escaped and lived as 'free' women. Both were prominent abolitionist and women's rights activists. In 1828, Truth won a landmark lawsuit to recover her son Peter who had been illegally sold into slavery in Alabama, becoming the first black woman in the United States to take a white man to court and win. After escaping in 1849, Tubman was involved in rescuing hundreds of enslaved friends and family using the network of antislavery activists and safe houses known as the Underground Railroad.[37] Yet, not every slave was a Sojourner Truth or Harriet Tubman. Strength, as White argues, 'had to be cultivated. It came no more naturally to them than to anyone, slave or free, male or female, black or white. If [slave women] seemed exceptionally strong it was partly because they often functioned in groups and derived strength from numbers'.[38] Davis also notes that slave women's resistance was often also subtle and included, for example, the clandestine acquisition of reading and writing skills and the imparting of this knowledge to others.

An analysis of slaves' social and domestic lives helps to foreground a crucial antagonistic space within slavery, a space where slaves performed, according to Davis, 'the only labor of the slave community which could not be directly and immediately claimed by the oppressor... Domestic labor was the only meaningful labor for the slave community as a whole'.[39] She argues that the domestic life of slaves took on an over-determined importance as it provided them with the only space 'where they could truly experience themselves as human beings ... Black women, for this reason – and also because they were workers just like men – were not debased by their domestic functions in the way that white women came to be'.[40] According to Davis the special character of domestic labour during slavery, its centrality to men and women slaves, involved work that was not exclusively female. While women typically cooked and sewed, men did the gardening and hunting, this sexual division of domestic labour was not organised hierarchically: men's tasks were not considered superior to the work performed by women and this division was not always rigorous.

Home

Although the home may offer a potential space for resistance and renewal, it is a contested space. It is a space that resists simplification and, crucially, destabilises claims to universal experiences of womanhood and motherhood. In the essay, *Homeplace*, bell hooks argues that 'attempts to critically assess the role of black women in liberation struggle must examine the way political concern about the impact of racism shaped black women's thinking, their sense of home and their modes of parenting'.[41] In a similar vein, Collins argues that critiques of motherhood and the family from feminists in the 1970s and 1980s overwhelmingly reflected white, middle-class women's experiences and typically lacked an adequate race and class perspective. On the question of motherhood, specifically the experiences and construction of black motherhood that have so often been absent from feminist discourse, Collins is critical of what she terms the controlling image of the 'superstrong Black mother' that 'praises Black women's resiliency in a society that routinely paints us as bad mothers'.[42] Her point is that, 'to remain on their pedestal, these same superstrong Black mothers must continue to place their needs behind everyone else, especially their sons'.[43] hooks is also clear that that the tradition of 'black mother worship', though positively motivated, 'extols the virtues of self-sacrifice while simultaneously implying that such a gesture is not reflective of choice and will, rather the perfect embodiment of a woman's "natural" role'.[44]

Speaking directly to the prevalent discourse within second-wave (white) feminism that indentified the family as the source of women's oppression, Hazel Carby argues that 'we need to recognize that during slavery, periods of colonialism, and under the present authoritarian state, the black family has been a site of political and cultural resistance to racism'.[45] Her point is that for some women (and also men and children) the home operated historically as (and continues to offer the possibility to be) an important site of resistance to institutional and structural racism and white supremacy.

Drawing similar conclusions to Carby, hooks argues that, within the context of the historical experiences of African-American women, 'homeplace' is a site of resistance to dominating and exploitative social structures. 'Historically, African-American people believe that the construction of a homeplace, however fragile and tenuous (the slave hut, the wooden shack), had a radical political dimension'.[46] Furthermore, hooks contends, 'black women resisted by making homes where all black people could strive to be subjects, not objects, where we could be affirmed in our minds and hearts despite poverty, hardship, and deprivation, where we could restore to ourselves the dignity denied [to] us on the outside in the public world'.[47] In this way, *homeplace* is conceived of as existing beyond the idea of home as a property. It is instead both a space which one can retreat to and recover in, and also a place of labour, specifically of *resistant reproduction* that teaches 'dignity [and] integrity of being'.[48] hooks is clear that the tasks and labours undertaken by black women in making homeplace cannot be reduced simply to a matter of black women providing service. On the contrary, 'it was about the construction of a safe place where black people could affirm one another and by so doing heal many of the wounds inflicted by racist domination'.[49]

The construction of homeplace as a site of resistance differs from the home as a place of paid work. It is useful to circle back briefly to the notion of service, specifically the histories of certain women (working-class, women of colour and migrants) providing domestic services as paid workers (domestic worker, cleaners, nannies and elder care workers) in other people's homes. hooks speaks to the 'tension between service outside one's home, family and kin network, service provided to white folks which took time and energy, and the effort of black women to conserve enough of themselves to provide service (care and nurturance) within their own families and communities'.[50] The experience of home as a site of paid work, experiences that overwhelmingly occur in other people's homes, opens up another line of resistance in relation to the home. The labour struggles that transformed 'service' in Britain from a form of employment that had historically been a live-in job to one that was part-time and live out, can be read as women's resistance to the conditions of isolation, domination and exploitation of paid domestic work. It is the construction of the home as belonging to the privatised sphere and, therefore, what goes on inside as somewhat concealed, out of bounds or at least out of view, that produces a specific mode of exploitation for those who labour within it.

In so far as it is useful to assert that there are many multiple experiences and, at times, contradictory meanings of home, it is also crucial to not be seduced by notions of the home as a space that is inherently good, stable or natural. The conceptualisation of home as a radical site of resistance is not inherent. Instead it is a political orientation that seeks to revalue and reconfigure the home as site of counter-power and one that must confront the construction and maintenance of patriarchal masculinity and capitalist social relations. In locating and making visible home as a potential and lived place of resistance, it is also necessary to remain attentive to experiences of home as a place of exploitative waged and unwaged work and sensitive to the experiences of many people, many of them women for whom the home is a space marked by violence, isolation and unhappiness. Indeed the task is to confront the contradictory constructions of home, so as to make clear the social structures that perpetuate it as a site of domination. The challenge in confronting the home and reproduction as a problematic is to make sense of the various structures, histories and processes that have produced the traditional white nuclear family as the normative family structure.

Conclusion

As Chandra Mohanty so forcefully argued, the relationship between 'Woman' a cultural and ideological construction and 'women' who are real material subjects of our collective histories is one of the central questions that feminism seeks to act upon.[51] Insofar as women have multiple histories, they are histories that always intertwine but which are also frequently in conflict: working-class women, who are required to be both workers and mothers; middle-class women, many of who were historically 'just housewives' but who are also now mostly working mothers; women of colour, who have been excluded from discourses of 'good' motherhood and have traditionally always worked, as slaves, as bonded labourers and today overwhelmingly in badly-paid and low-status jobs.

Slavery and colonialism made it possible to reduce the costs of reproducing labour-power in the industrial metropolis: the benefits of this were shared, unequally, between capitalists and (white) workers. For the wage that capital paid the industrial worker, it also purchased the unwaged labour of the slave. So too with the historical organisation of domestic labour, whereby capital harnessed both the ('productive') labour of the man and reproductive labour of his wife for the cost of the (male) wage.

This dynamic of both concealment and dependency reappears in the contemporary racialised organisation of reproduction in which both waged and forms of commodified reproductive labour has dramatically increased and diversified. The low-waged reproductive work performed by migrants – predominantly women of colour – is central to the contemporary maintenance and reproduction of labour-power. Framed another way, the 'middle-class' status of many families and households, whose wages have, in fact, stagnated since the 1970s, is based almost entirely upon the devalued labour of women of colour, on whom they depend on to clean their homes and offices, look after their children and care for their elder relatives.

Notes

1. Silvia Federici, *Caliban and the Witch: Women, the Body and Primitive Accumulation* (New York: Autonomedia, 2004), p. 91.
2. H.J. Spillers, 'Mama's Baby, Papa's Maybe: An American Grammar Book', *Diacritics* 17(2), Culture and Counter Memory: The 'American' Connection (Summer 1987), pp. 65–81.
3. B. Bryan, S. Dadzie and S. Scafe, *The Heart of the Race: Black Women's Lives in Britain* (London: Virago Press, 1985), p. 18.
4. C. Robinson, *Black Marxism: The Making of the Black Radical Tradition* (University of North Carolina Press, 2000 original edition, 1983), p. 81.
5. *Ibid.*
6. E. Williams, *Capitalism and Slavery* (London: Andre Puetsch, 1966, original edition, 1944), p. 52.
7. Federici, *Caliban and the Witch*, p. 103.
8. M. Mies, *Patriarchy and Accumulation on a World Scale* (London: Zed Books, 1998, original edition, 1986).
9. Federici, *Caliban and the Witch*, p. 104.
10. b. hooks, *Ain't I a Woman* (Boston: South End Press), p. 32.
11. A. Davis, *Women, Race & Class* (New York: Random House, 1983, original edition 1981), p. 5.
12. W. Pease cited in D.G. White, 1985. *Ar'n't I a Woman? Female Slaves in the Plantation South* (New York: W.W. Norton, 1985), p. 120.
13. Spiller, *Mama's Baby, Papa's Maybe*, p. 67, emphasis in the original.
14. Davis, *Women, Race & Class*, pp. 5–6.
15. *Ibid.*, p. 12.
16. *Ibid.*, p. 7.
17. Orland Patterson, *The Sociology of Slavery* (London: Magibbon and Kee, 1967), p. 105.
18. Douglas Hall, 'Slaves and slavery in the British West Indies', Social and Economic Studies 11(4), 1962, p. 306, cited in Rhoda E. Reddock, 'Women and slavery in the Caribbean: A Feminist Perspective', *Latin American Perspectives* 12(1), Winter 1985, p. 67.

19. Gwendolyn Midlo Hall, Social Control in Slave Plantation Societies (Baltimore, MD: John Hopkins Press, 1971), p. 26, citied in Rhoda E. Reddock, Women and Slavery in the Caribbean, p. 67.

20. L. Davidoff and C. Hall, *Family Fortunes: Men and Women of the English Middle Class, 1780–1880* (London: Routledge, 1992, original edition, 1987).

21. Federici, *Caliban and the Witch*, p. 88.

22. *Ibid.*, p. 75.

23. L. Davidoff and C. Hall, *Family Fortunes: Men and Women of the English Middle Class, 1780–1880* (London: Routledge, 1992, original edition, 1987).

24. McClintock, Imperial Leather, p. 5.

25. Todd, S., Domestic Service and Class Relations in Britain 1900–1950. *Past and Present* 2009, 203, pp. 182–204.

26. Davis, *Women, Race & Class*, p. 6.

27. *Ibid.*, p. 12.

28. Moynihan, D.P., *The Negro Family: The Case for National Action* (Washington DC: US Department of Labor, 1965).

29. H. Gutman, *The Black Family in Slavery and Freedom, 1750–1925* (New York: Pantheon Books, 1976).

30. P.H. Collins, *Black Feminist Thought: Knowledge, Consciousness, and the Politics of Empowerment* (New York & London: Routledge, 2000; original edition, 1990), p. 55.

31. *Ibid.*, p. 58.

32. *Ibid.*, p. 57.

33. White, *Ar'n't I a Woman?*, p. 98.

34. Gutman, *The Black Family in Slavery and Freedom, 1750–1925*, p. 75.

35. Davis, *Women, Race & Class*, p. 19.

36. *Ibid.*

37. K.C. Larson, *Bound For the Promised Land: Harriet Tubman, Portrait of an American Hero* (New York: Ballantine Book, 2004).

38. White, *Ar'n't I a Woman?*, p. 119.

39. A. Davis, 'Reflections on the Black Woman's Role in the Community of Slaves', *The Massachusetts Review* 3(1–2), 1972, p. 89.

40. Davis, *Women, Race & Class*, pp. 16–17.

41. b. hooks, *Yearning: Race, Gender and Cultural Politics* (Boston, MA: South End Press, 1990), p. 46.

42. Collins, *Black Feminist Thought*, p. 188.

43. *Ibid.*

44. b. hooks, *Yearning*, p. 45.

45. H.V. Carby, 'White Woman Listen! Black Feminism and the Boundaries of Sisterhood'. In Centre for Contemporary Cultural Studies (eds), *The Empire Strikes Back: Race and Sexism in 70s Britain* (London: Hutchinson, 1982), p. 112.

46. b. hooks, *Yearning*, p. 42.

47. *Ibid.*

48. *Ibid.*, p. 41.

49. *Ibid.*, p. 42.

50. *Ibid.*, p. 42.

51. Mohanty, C., 'Under Western Eyes: Feminist Scholarship and Colonial Discourses', *Feminist Review* 30, 1988, pp. 61–88.

14

Along the Fasara – A Short Story

P.M.

Mika, the woolly rhino mother, was devouring bunch after bunch of the tough marsh grass. Her young one, little Nipo, was nibbling at fresher and softer herbs, never more than a few steps away from his mother. It was a peaceful late summer afternoon; one wrote the year 12'967 BCE. Only a few small white clouds were suspended in the deep blue sky. The air in the valley was glimmering because of the heat, countless insects were humming around, and butterflies were dancing along. Their curly dark brown coats protected mother and son against the hungry gnats and horseflies.

Now it was the time to fatten oneself for the harsh winter. So far it had been a good summer, rather short, but lush, humid and hot.

It was quiet in the valley, no dangers.

The lion pride was fast asleep two kilometres further up. Wolves and hyenas didn't dare to attack rhinos. Old Arko, the lone tiger, was far away, too, somewhere on the plateau, probably, stalking a limping deer or a bison calf.

But what? The woolly rhino mother sniffed the air, her left ear twitched.

Humans! Still far away, in the river. Approaching fast.

Mika reacted leisurely and without panicking, moving towards the western wall of the valley, into a rocky bay, grown over by thicker and higher brushwood. No need to take any chances with humans. Best remain unseen.

Mika grunted towards her young one, who followed her obediently.

Magla and Tana were merrily paddling down the river, which they called Fasara in their simple, but melodious language. Their double canoe was made of deer hides – a perfect piece of craftsmanship. They had stowed away their ample luggage under the bow and the stern. They kept their two javelins ready at hand, just in case. Both women had their long black hair plaited and arranged in coils on both sides of their heads – to keep it out of the way. They had fleshy, round faces, an olive-green skin, plump cheeks and they were squinting their dark eyes because of the reflections of the sun in the river. Their bodies were robust and rather short, with a long rump and short legs. Magla's face was triangular with a small, pointed chin; Tana had a double chin and a flatter nose. To appear as unnatural as possible they had painted their lips in red, lined their eyes in black and put a light blue shade on their lids. They were wearing armless vests made of fine, bleached chamois leather, stitched with pearls of mussels and beads of stones in gaily coloured patterns. Both had the same tattoo on their left upper arm: a crow, a bear, a lizard, their taboo animals. They were not allowed to either kill or eat them. No big gastronomic loss.

Magla and Tana were not on a hunt, that's why they were laughing and singing loudly. They were actually announcing their arrival to whoever was present in the valley. They were on their trip to the winter quarters at the South Ocean, a recon team looking for a campsite for the night. They loved this task and volunteered as often as they could. They felt exhilarated to be away for a few hours from the other thirty members of the glorious and proud crow-bear-lizard society, Kagurasifa, in their own language.

They had just eaten fermented hemp cakes and were shouting the stupid song of the clumsy bear, which climbs a tree and falls down on his ass into a thorny bush. Whenever they sang the refrain, they smacked the water with their paddles and laughed out loudly.

There was enough water in the river, which was smooth and without any dangerous rapids. At some places in one of its many bends it enlarged into shallow lakes where they had to paddle to get ahead. The valley was between one and two kilometres wide and lined with high, beige-white rocky walls. High up on the rim the pine forests of the plateau formed a dark green band.

In the blue sky vultures, buzzards and, more rarely, eagles were gliding about, looking out for prey. Swallows had built their nests in the cliffs. Once in a while their screaming swarms dived down to the river to catch insects.

Insects didn't bother Magla and Tana, as they had applied a repellent salve that also smelled pleasantly and had a slightly arousing effect.

Magla was thirsty and scooped up water with her hollow hand, splashing some on Tana, who retaliated by whipping up some water with her paddle. The canoe wavered, almost capsized, but they managed to balance it out. They were experts.

'There!' Magla hissed, pointing her paddle at the eastern shore.

A brown-furred otter was standing on his hind legs and observing the two women intently. His whiskers twitched disapprovingly. Then he dived into the river with an elegant jump. There was no sound and no splash. Another expert.

'Bathing weather,' Tana commented.

'Let's go swimming right now,' Magla suggested.

'The camp site first.'

'It's ideally suited everywhere here.'

They let themselves drift along and sang another song about the clever crow that could read old fairy tales from knots in strings.

Just as they had reached another loop, they heard a terrified scream from the cliff on the left. They looked up and saw an eagle attacking and shredding a crow. Feathers were thrown around, wings slapped against wings. In the end the big eagle carried away the limp crow.

'What a piece of shit!' Magla exclaimed.

The two women were shocked: a really bad omen.

'Look, there!' Tana pointed at one of the balconies in the cliff: a large, brown spot.

'Bura, the she-bear,' she explained, 'with two young ones.'

'She lives there, on the sunny side of the valley, well protected against the wind,' Magla said, a frown on her forehead.

They stopped the canoe with their paddles and let it land on a soft, sandy beach. They climbed out of the boat and pulled it on the beach, half lifting it in order not to damage the skin.

'Bura having young ones is a good omen,' Tana said, 'I hope it evens out the crow's death. All we need now is a message from the lizards.'

'They're all over the place anyway,' Magla answered, 'let's not believe too much in omens. But look at Bura's cave and terrace – hasn't she found a perfect place? Southwesterly oriented, protected against north winds, near the river, but no danger of floods, a lot of game and fish all around here.'

'Are you thinking what I'm thinking? You want to stay here through the winter?'

'It could be possible.'

'And Bura, the she-bear?' Tana objected.

'We'd have to give notice of termination of her lease,' Magla remarked with a cruel smile.

Tana shook her head, as if to shake off a completely unthinkable idea.

'Let's look just for a suitable camp site,' she said, with a sigh.

They were wearing old leather shorts and were barefoot. They carried the canoe further up to the fringe of the sand strip, near the first willow trees. They looked around.

'There,' Tana cried, 'between those alder trees, next to the two rounded rocks!'

She pointed towards a large open sandy area.

'Great,' Magla said, 'soft ground, and good protection against winds. Not too close to the river. You never can tell.'

The first thing they did, was to cut down an alder pole with one of their sharp stone axes. Then they attached the red kid skin pennant of their society to it and rammed it into the sandy beach, as a clearly visible sign for the others.

They fetched their baggage from the canoe: the winter clothes, the mocassins, the fur boots, fur caps, bows and arrows, leather bags, knives, ivory statuettes, angling gear, sewing set, contraceptives, drugs, toys, combs, balms and oils in bone flasks.

They carried the bundles to the campsite and started gathering firewood.

The others would probably arrive in the evening and be grateful for a fire – and some food. So Tana said: 'Let's go fishing!'

They took their fishing gear and walked along the shore, in the direction of the bear cave. They looked up to the rocky wall. There were three balconies about fifty metres upward, wide ledges, caves, bays and smaller holes. To reach the bear's place a wide rubble slope had to be crossed.

'We'd have to make a ladder and to block the access across the rubble,' Magla said.

'You seem to be infatuated with your cliff house.'

Magla insisted: 'We could stay here even in winter. It could be possible.'

'But why? We already have our usual winter camp in the Baka valley.'

'It's nicer here. And there is more game, and more space.'

Tana shook her head.

'You want to put tents on those rock ledges?'

'No tents,' Tana replied, still looking up the cliff dreamily, 'huts, woven walls – real housing.'

'I can't believe it!' Tana exclaimed, 'We've been going down the Fasara for tens of thousands of years. There must be a reason why we've been doing this. But now super-clever Ms. Magla comes and says, let's stay here.'

'You're right: thousands of years is a long time. But things can change. Tents are okay, but here we could live much more comfortably. We could have permanent hearths, sheltered work places, cosy meeting rooms...'

'If Bura lets us,' Tana objected.

'We'll get rid of her. No problem.'

'Whatever. Let's stop this nonsense and catch some trout,' Tana interrupted her friend.

They found some rapids and soon they discovered the gray shadows of the fish. They prepared their baits, wielded their hazel rods. The fish bit. After a short while they walked back to the camp with two dozen trout on a hemp string.

Bura, the she-bear, peeping down out of her cave, hadn't missed any part of the action on the sandy peninsula. The humans had piled up branches and driftwood. A canoe was parked nearby on the sand. Then they had been fishing, a lot of fish in a very short time. Bura was hungry. She had been planning to go fishing herself in the late afternoon and to make her round of the valley. Fishing was part of her age-old programme. Bears had been fishing here for hundreds of thousands of years. You could speak of entitlement. But now – she grunted annoyedly. You had to watch out with humans. They were like hyenas – harmless individually, very dangerous as a pack. If they didn't move on the next day – as they always did – she had to think about moving away. As long as they stayed down at the river, there was no acute danger. Had they discovered her already?

They were very unconcerned. They even took off their coats. They jumped into the water. The two females horsed around in the shallow river, then they swam against the current like beavers or otters. Were they hunting? Presently they disappeared and surfaced some meters downstream. They were like big fish. Maybe it was feasible to kill them – but they were too big!

They were playing!

Bura suddenly felt like bathing, too. She often swam through the river with her young ones, to eat blueberries on the other shore. You could also find rabbits or grouse. Very tasty! But today she'd rather stay in her cave, in spite of the hunger. Bura was worried. The humans had been looking up to her and communicating in an acoustic language in a lively manner, mentioning her name.

Magla and Tana laid their plump, brown bodies on the warm sand of the beach and enjoyed the sun. Agum, the vulture, was circling far above them and wondering whether there were corpses lying there. He dived downwards. Magla chased away a fly with her hand. No cadavers. Live humans, no food. Back to the half-eaten deer skeleton under the crippled fir tree.

Uko, the otter, was swimming by. When he surfaced briefly, he saw the two women lying in the sand. Phew! He had seen them diving – nothing to write home about, mere beginners! Their fishing was world-class, though, respect! Could he get to the trout, while they were asleep? Anyway, it was shameless to lie on the beach without coats. He had to tell Ruva to keep the kids in the burrow. But look now…

A swarm of canoes came down the river, ten, twenty, thirty. A lot of humans! Loud humans, shouting and laughing humans. Wrinkled old ones with grey or white ponytail hair styles, wriggly children in smaller canoes, paddling along wildly, yapping dogs, proud hunters, a merry society. Uko dived away.

Dako, one of the young men, saw the camp sign first, shouting a throaty 'Yahoo!' and steering his canoe, that he shared with his cousin Lasa, to the sand bank. Tana and Magla jumped up, rubbed their eyes, and waved to them. They put on their clothes, took along the trout, and walked over to Dako.

'We're early,' he said, blinking into the sun.

'The camp site is over there,' Tana explained, pointing at the spot behind the alder trees.

'The fish is here.' Magla showed him the trout.

'Great,' he said, 'a perfect place, nice trout, too.'

The canoes went ashore. The first thing was the dogs running around excitedly. Then the children ran after them, screaming. Within a few minutes the beach was filled with canoes, the sandy peninsula the theatre of a busy open-air household. The kids were already in the water with the dogs. The adults carried the baggage to the campsite.

Agu, the oldest member of the society, screened the surroundings and discovered Bura's cave.

'Let's go swimming,' said Fira, his companion.

Agu smiled. 'Good idea, learning from the kids, eh?'

Rather clumsily they peeled themselves out of their clothes. They walked to the beach and swam to the other shore. They went onto the sand bank and walked a few steps into the bushwood.

'Rhinos,' Agu remarked, 'have been drinking here a few hours ago. A mother with her young one. Fresh dung, too.'

'Nice spot,' Fira said, who sat on a flat rock, with her feet in the river.

Agu joined her.

'This ledge up here,' she said, 'three large terraces, neat and dry. A valley with lots of fish, lots of game. Beeches, oaks, all sorts of herbs. A little paradise.'

Agu squinted his eyes.

'What do you mean?'

'Remember Difa? What he told us about the toad-fox-adder people, who build houses with clay and twigs and live therein for many years. It could be done up here very easily. You don't even need roofs.'

Agu nodded and smiled.

'We're a bit tired, aren't we?'

She kissed him lovingly.

'That's not the point,' she said, 'It just seems the time for a fresh start. After these thousands of years.'

'Thousands of years,' he sighed thoughtfully, 'it seems a long time. But if you start every day as a new day, it's nothing. As long as we're happy, nothing must change.'

'Are you happy?'

'Yes, with you I've always been happy.'

'Old toady. One can be happy in many ways.'

'Okay. But Bura isn't stupid. We'll have to winkle her out.'

Fira grinned.

'No problem. Remember Tuka?'

'Oh, Tuka!' he exclaimed with a deep sigh.

Many years ago, this obtrusive, scheming and shameless woman had dared to approach Agu.

Fira had got rid of her successfully – but it was still an open wound, because Agu had been more than flattered.

Now Tuka lived with frog-leech-eel, where she had found a young man stupid enough to cope with her.

In front of their lodge across the river, Uko and Ruva, the otter parents, had been watching the activities on the peninsula. Humans all over the place! And in their river. Some were scooping up water with leather buckets. Two were angling. The kids were everywhere; a dog had tried to hunt Uko down. Others just went back and forth busily.

'There goes the neighborhood,' Uko hissed to his wife.

'And the family values.'

They'd just managed to chase their young ones back into the lodge, when they had discovered that two grey haired humans were making love in the grass, just nearby, in plain sight.

'I hope, they'll move on soon,' Ruva whispered, 'or we will have to pack up.'

There was chaos everywhere. Lizards went hiding under rocks. A dismayed water snake had fled downriver. Ducks flew up. Even Bura looked worried. On top of all they smelled of this awful oil, the stink of their society.

'I've overheard these two shameless individuals talking about staying here,' Ruva reported.

'We'll have to talk to the others,' Uko remarked grimly.

'Talk, talk, – you never really *do* something about anything,' Ruva complained.

'A dog, let's get in!'

And they disappeared.

As the sun set behind the western rim, the air cooled off fast in the valley. Agu, Magla and others observed that the terraces in the cliff just across were still in the sun. They also noticed that the wall of rock was radiating heat through the whole night.

Before nightfall they had put on their long trousers and long-sleeved shirts and they had rubbed perfumed insect-repellent on their bodies. Neatly groomed they sat around two campfires grilling fish, a few rabbits and some ducks. The fires were burning brightly, with much smoke and flames, announcing their presence to all inhabitants of the valley.

Lomo, the oldest lion further up in the valley, expressed his indignation with a bone-shattering roar that ended in a protracted, miserable cough. There was much laughter about the old show-off at the campsite.

When they had eaten, drunk and lit their hemp pipes, the moment for discussions and story telling had come.

Fira, the oldest and most experienced of all women of Kagurasifa, brought up the topic of the rock terrace. Magla had already spoken to her briefly, and Agu, one of the three oldest hunters, was fully informed, too.

At first, the idea was flatly rejected. The tradition of thousands of happy years was evoked, the feasibility questioned, logistical problems mentioned. But most were willing to think about it, with the exception of some young men and women. How could they meet their far-away lovers in other societies, how could they continue their affairs that they had begun last autumn? Their lovers were all waiting for them down in the Baka valley. Furthermore the canoe trip to the ocean had always been great fun – why stop here already?

Fira found out that only two men and one very young woman had such affairs going. They could paddle on in two canoes and inform the other societies about what Kagurasifa were up to. They would worry about them not coming this year. In other years, they would all travel down and up again. This would just become their new permanent base camp for all kinds of trips and expeditions. They wouldn't be stuck here for ever.

'Let's give it a try,' Ukam, one of the bravest hunters in his prime years, exclaimed, 'Let's get us settled here and see, what happens. Game is plentiful around here. We won't starve.'

Tura, another sophisticated hunter and unorthodox trapper, was all for it too. She considered it as a thrilling social experiment, probably the beginning of a new life style with un-thought-of possibilities.

Agu liked this way of thinking.

'I'm the oldest of this association,' he said, 'the keeper of traditions and customs. But I'm looking forward to being involved in a new adventure. Fifty years, just up and down the Fasara, that's enough!'

'Fifty years is a long time!' Tana joked.

'Okay, tomorrow, we'll start building,' stated Duba, Fira's sister and one of the three self-proclaimed wise women of the society.

Now Paka, the intellectual of the society and master of the drum, sang the long ballad of the mythical oak tree, in which the crow, the woodpecker and the owl lived and quarreled until they created a united front against the mean marten. They sang a few shorter songs, scaring sensitive night-active rodents and small predators and fell asleep contentedly.

All those bats, owls, weasels, rats and beavers could finally get down to their respective businesses undisturbed. Even Uko swam out and caught some late supper for his family. A fat eel.

In the next morning Mika, the woolly rhino mother, came to the conclusion that this year it was worse than it had ever been. The humans were louder, more reckless in their amorous and musical activities, and they seemed to make no move to pack up. The sun was already high up over the eastern rim and they were still here. Was it time to abandon this valley definitively, being a responsible rhino mother? To be on the safe side, she ambled further down the valley with her son, getting away from the focus of the disturbance.

Uko didn't have a good morning either. The humans had started to frolick in the river right after sunrise; they communicated in their loud, vulgar language and began to wash their clothes in his drinking water. Ruva, who was nursing their young ones in the lodge, hadn't stopped accusing him of cowardice, inaction and lack of initiative. She even accused him of being a peeping Tom, an anthropophile and a traitor of his species. Uko considered emigration. So far only two canoes had left: were the others planning to stay?

After the morning bath they met for the first strategy discussion.

'Bura usually moves away, when humans stay in her vicinity for too long,' Fira began, 'but that can take days. We should nudge her away a bit. Some of us could climb up to the rim and begin to annoy her. She can't climb up, so she must move to the left or the right on the ledge. Then we must block her access – bears ware very conservative and always return to their lairs. I suggest we close the narrow passage with a big rock.'

'And how are we going to get in then?' Tana asked.

'We'll build ladders.'

'So we need annoyers,' Agu concluded, 'big rock movers and ladder makers.'

The children were recruited as annoyers, putting to use their natural competence. The strongest women and men should find a big rock and set it in place with diverse levers, poles and ropes. The old ones should build wooden ladders.

By around noon, Bura felt uncomfortable and had decided to move. There had been continuous harassment by falling pebbles, pinecones and branches, and she had had to endure incredible obscenities shouted by adolescent rowdies. Of course she was outraged – but what could she do? Her young ones were entitled to a decent education. What they experienced and heard here could damage their psychological health for their whole lives. With her two little ones she walked along the ledge in a southern direction. As soon as she had left the small passage, a huge object came down from above and got crammed in the gap with a loud bang. Bura understood: she would never be able to come back to her favorite terrace. She growled angrily and ambled away: this valley was lost for her. But there were other valleys.

As soon as the big rock was safely in place, the old ones put up one of their ladders and climbed onto the first terrace. There they erected their second ladder and reached the second terrace, and then the third one. They were on the sunniest terrace now.

The initial disappointment was severe: the ground was full of bear shit, bones and rotten debris of all kinds. The caves stank horribly. Then they looked down into the valley. The sight was stunning. They were enthusiastic.

'Okay, that's it,' Fira said, 'let's start the cleaning.'

To the dismay of all later archeologists the society cleaned out the whole terrace and the caves quite thoroughly. They found some human bones and skulls from earlier ages, probably from the 'friendly old ones', as they called them, that had lived there, or whose bones had been dragged there by predators. They threw everything down the cliff. They kept one skull for decorative purposes.

Meno, the old badger, who had dug his burrow near the foot of the wall of rock, wasn't pleased with the new developments.

'They come here and throw all their rubbish in front of our cave and we can't figure out how to deal with it. They're full of their non-patriarchal social structures and their consensus-oriented methods of communication, but they don't show even the most minimal respect for the less privileged ecological stakeholders. At least they could've organised public hearings with us old-established, concerned residents. But no, they just go ahead. It's always the little ones that are hit. They've driven out Bura brutally. I'm being buried in waste. What's next? We're headed towards an ecological catastrophe.'

The floors were wiped with improvised brooms, walls were washed and ceilings scratched. Then Fira lit several fires perfumed with rosemary, sage and rose wood, to burn the stink away.

In the evening a hundred-metre long terrace and five deep caves were cleaned out and smelled inviting.

'So far, so good,' Fira said.

The society returned to their camp, bathed, fished, ate, sang, danced and slept.

Actual building started on the next day. Fira, Agu and Magla (the one with the pointed chin) were the members of the construction committee that defined the locations of the party cave, the various sleeping houses, children's houses, love nests, depots, workshops, kitchens etc.

They drew the plan in the sand and everybody applauded enthusiastically.

'We need a name, before we begin construction,' Duba declared.

The society began to think about suggestions.

'Bura-Bura?'

'Fasarama!'

'Magla-Tana,' Agu exclaimed, 'those two were here first.'

'Maglatana!' everybody shouted, and work began immediately.

The children cut twigs, young men and women fetched clay from the river shore in leather buckets, young trees were felled for beams, rafters and poles, suitable rocks for the hearths were collected.

They secured the edge of the terrace with a thigh-high clay wall and a railing, to make it safe, especially for small children. Behind this they built a veranda, where you could sit in the sun or work. Then they installed the thinner partitions for the various rooms, all with doors and windows. They constructed beds and put in soft twigs and furs. In the centre of the installation, at the entrance of the largest cave, they built a circular room with a hearth and set comfortable deck chairs around it: the party room. They even built a smoke escape. And they put the Neanderthal skull into a niche.

The children began to cover the walls with paintings using the red earth they had found near the river: rhinos, lions, canoes, horses, zigzag lines, hands and spirals.

Yura, the she-eagle, had kept an eye on all these activities from far above and understood perfectly what was happening on the terraces to the south of her aerie. The idea to reinforce a nest with clay and twigs against wind and weather was convincing, but not applicable to her own home. How could she get up enough clay just with her beak? That would take years. Yura admired these featherless bipeds, their imagination and sense of initiative. She would get along with them. There was no conflict of interests. Yura was particularly fascinated by the drawings the children hat painted on the walls. Weren't those spirals aerodynamic patterns of a deep symbolic significance? Hats off!

For two weeks Kagurasifa was busy building Maglatana. As the weather stayed nice, they mostly slept down at the river, where they could fish and relax.

Uko, the otter, was on the edge of a nervous breakdown. His wife had already left him to go back to her mother with the kids. The word divorce had been spoken. Uko himself had scheduled a meeting with beaver master Kero from the upper side valley C5. If he could take over the abandoned lodge there, maybe Ruva would come back.

Finally the day of the grand opening came. The camp on the peninsula was moved. The canoes were stored in a safe place near the foot of the cliff, the baggage lifted to the terrace with a rope and a pulley. Then all of them assembled at the foot of the first ladder. It was Fira's turn to make the speech.

'Magla, Tana, Dako, Agu, Ukam, Paka, Tura, Lasa, Nika, Famo, Rika, Gaba, Deri, Rana, Iti, Setu, Mimo, Lota, Oro, Mea, Limo, Nete, Dona, Koto, Impo, Piga and Dero! Today Kagurasifa moves into Maglatana, our new winter home. Disease, death, cold, fear, hate and hunger – stay away! Health, love, warmth, plenty and happiness – be with us! Long live Maglatana, long live Kagurasifa!'

The good wishes were repeated and underlined by long howls and cheers! Fira cut a garland made of flowers that was hanging across the sturdy ladder. Then they climbed up in the order of their names.

The new home smelled of half-dried clay, aromatic herbs and rosemary fires. They took their personal belongings to the beds and then assembled again on the space in front of the party room, looking down to the valley together. Bison horns filled with honey beer, which Paka had started a week ago, were passed around. More toasts were made, the construction was praised, the local crows, the absent bear and the omnipresent lizards invoked. They lifted their horns together and had a first gulp. Then they sat on the benches and began to eat the grilled meat, the fish and a cold vegetable soup, that somebody called gaspako.

Everyday life began in Maglatana.

Fira had discovered cool and dry caves that could be used as food larders. Ukam was busy setting up his workshop for stone tools and hunting weapons, the best and biggest that had ever existed. Which meant *ever*. Paka was inventing new musical instruments and thinking about a library of knotted strings to collect all the old stories and reports before they were forgotten. Looking at the pictures, abstract figures and squiggles that the children had painted on the walls, another idea to store texts had suddenly hit him. But it seemed so daring to him, that he kept it to himself. First he wanted to solve the problem of suitable materials. Bark? Burned clay tablets? Kidskins?

Lasa and Tura found an ideal cave for their pharmacy. There would be a permanent brewery, a menstruation cave, a leather workshop, a perfumery and a clinic.

Piga, an exceptionally bright girl, approached Agu with some ideas. She had observed that the clay animals, that the children had made, became hard when left in the ambers of the hearth. Using clay, she had made a cup that looked much like the wooden cups they used.

'Couldn't we make them bigger, harden them in a fire and use them as buckets?' she asked Agu. 'And also,' she continued, showing him a handful of grass grains, 'plant these grains and have a ready supply of them every year, as we're now staying here to gather them.'

'Clever girl,' he said and smiled, 'but let's not rush it. Let's first try our new semi-nomadic lifestyle for five thousand years. Then we'll see, what happens next.'

'But *next* is a long time in the future,' Piga protested.

'Okay then,' Agu said, 'choose a suitable patch around here and plant your grains. But now it's already too late. Do it next spring. And go ahead with your pots, if you must.'

'Pots?'

'Forget it,' Agu sighed.

On the plateau there was a lot of game: deer, horses, bisons, pigs and juicy geese. Hunting parties went up there and brought back provisions for the winter. Strips of meat were smoked and safely stored. Herbs and berries were gathered and dried. Fat was rendered and decanted into skins. Oils were made from nuts. Mushrooms with more or less interesting effects, dried. On the southern side they found a rivulet. They built a stone basin underneath so that they could get fresh water without having to go down to the river. They even built a contraption with hollow pieces of wood that Mea called showa.

Kagurasifa had only occupied a small fraction of the terraces suitable for housing. They were planning to invite other societies to join them. Several hundred persons could live here together. Others were not so optimistic. Upa, the manifold rabbit mother, and Lilo, a proud father of many a squirrel, met by accident by a hollow tree trunk in a birch copse.

'You know, mister Lilo,' she chirped, 'these humans here will ruin the ecological equilibrium of this whole valley. Overpopulation, overfishing, overexploitation of fauna and flora. That's what will hit us. For tens of thousands of years they just passed through, making a terrible hullabaloo, but they left us unmolested for the rest of the year. Now suddenly they're getting settled. Who knows why? They're building artificial burrows, putting up ladders, they trample through our territories, and they set dogs on us. Most of us have already left. Or are dead.'

'I see,' the squirrel said, 'I understand your qualms. As for us, we operate on another level.'

'We'll never be successful, if everybody only thinks of his own interests.'

Paka, Tana and Mimo began to create big paintings on the ceiling and walls of the large party cave of Maglatana to remember its first inhabitants: a rhino (aka Magla), a squirrel (Tana), a ring snake (Dako), a bison (Agu), a horse (Ukam), a duck (Duba), etc. The children put clay statuettes of all the animals they encountered in niches. Sometimes they played with them. Dera put together clay discs and twigs and pulled them around with strings. Soon they had filled a ledge with a long procession of these kara'kara, as they called them. Agu frowned, when he observed them.

One morning they were scared out of their beds by a loud roar from above. When they looked they saw the shaggy face of a young lion gazing down in frustration. They laughed at him – he roared again, but he couldn't get down. Shit!

IV

COMMONS

15

The Strategic Horizon of the Commons
Massimo De Angelis

It is clear that the common is not logically antagonistic to capitalism. On the contrary, a necessary condition for the existence of capitalism is the presence of certain kinds of commons. Indeed, without the capacity of capitalists to call upon the mutual aid and class solidarity of other capitalists and to use the communal character of workers to their advantage, capitalism would not have been able survive the shock of class struggle over centuries. Indeed, if capitalism was not a common-pool resource system organized on some levels as common property, then it would never have been able to have become a self-reproducing system, even in the short run. – George Caffentzis

It is almost a law of contemporary society that the more commons are attacked, the more they are celebrated. – Silvia Federici

For three decades, George, Silvia and I have been friends and collaborators, occasionally publishing together and always open to conversation. I first met them one late summer's day in 1989; my then PhD advisor, Harry Cleaver suggested I visit them in Brooklyn and so that's what I did. Since then, on countless occasions – whether in formal meetings or personal encounters, or via email, Skype or phone – we have kept in dialogue, catching up with the latest personal and political news, fine tuning or harmonising our interpretations of the world. It is, without exaggeration, true that I would not have written my last two books without my 'ask the philosopher' emails to George. He helped me untangle many a theoretical knot and provided reassurance that I was moving in the right direction. Equally, I would not have written my last two books without engaging with the deep, passionate discussions of oppression, exploitation and injustice that Silvia brings to life when talking about the many different instances of the work of reproduction. As always, pointing to the crucial strategic weaknesses that make those relations possible, and true to form, always hinting at other possibilities, other movements, other worlds.

So my debt to their friendship and their scholarship is beyond the measure that 6000 words could account for. As a humble gesture, in this essay I investigate three interrelated aspects of their work that were crucial for the architecture of my most recent work.[1] First, the groundbreaking issue by Midnight Notes on *The New Enclosures* helped develop my own thinking on the continuous character of enclosure – and its opposite, the formation of commons. Second, the possibility of *omnia sunt communia* (all things are held in common), sealed for me by George's short but insightful critique of Elinor Ostrom and both George and Silvia's clarity on anti-capitalist commons. Third, the identification of reproduction commoning as the strategic site from which to envision a horizon of emancipation for all; this insight I owe to Silvia's tireless focus on the many, often hidden, forms of reproduction work in contemporary capitalism.

Before addressing these themes, what follows is a brief recollection on the state of anti-capitalist thought, prior to the radical conceptualisation of the commons. It is a short account of some earlier important moments involving George and Silvia that helped move forward our thinking towards understanding commons as systems; and a brief discussion of what is meant by commons as systems.

Prolegomena to the Commons

The radical utilisation of the concept of the 'commons' has only re-emerged recently. Before the Midnight Notes 1990 issue on enclosures,[2] the concept of the enclosures of the commons referred more narrowly to enclosures of common goods (land, forests, etc.) and the expulsion of communities who depended on those resources *at the origin of capitalism*. At times the analysis would be extended to more recent times of colonial invasion. *The New Enclosures* by Midnight Notes, transformed the enclosures into a contemporary problematic – an ongoing, conflicted and live issue. In a similar way, prior to Silvia's numerous writings on the role of women in holding together, through the work of reproduction, the social networks in households, villages and communities, we could not really appreciate the role of reproduction as a cohesive force that held the community together *vis-à-vis* external forces. To indicate what we call today commons, radicals previously used terms as such as self-organisation, self-valorisation, community and autonomy. These are all important foundational features of current understanding of commons, whose systemic character include them all without exhausting them. Yet, a definition without references to the capitalist environment that seeks to enclose, or the problematic of social reproduction through which lives are reproduced through mutual aid networks of support that are the ultimate targets of those enclosures: these terms on their own are only bad abstractions, entities without a social force. Complexity is reduced to radical dogma.

There are three early moments at which I was inspired by and with George and Silvia to start thinking about commons as systems. First, Silvia's political recollections of the Wages for Housework period in New York were not only accounts of women's self-organised political struggles, but also of mutual aid, of women's communities in solidarity with each other, of community centres and communal kitchens. These stories reverberated with my own experiences of social centres and often temporary autonomous zones in 1970s Italy, although I knew she was talking about something more grounded. There were also some hints about what we today call commons in George's and Silvia's accounts of their time in Nigeria in the mid- to late-1980s. Looking back in 2010, George made this explicit. He recalled asking,

> [W]here is the class struggle here? The answer that eventually came was a surprise to me: the commons still existed in Nigeria and made it possible for many who are outside of the waged labor market to have collective access to land and for many waged workers with ties to the village, common land to subsist when on strike. Much of the Nigerian class struggle I observed was a struggle against the police, the oil companies, and the army to prevent the enclosure of the agricultural village common land, forests and waters. In fact, increasingly I began to see Structural Adjustment and neoliberalism – both the theory and practice – as a direct attack on the remaining commons from pre-capitalist times and the new commons that were created by workers' struggles (including our famous 'social and economic rights').[3]

A second early moment that was significant for our commons thinking occurred in the mid-1990s, with the movement of the Zapatistas. Commons presented themselves with a specifically political character: commons 'against and beyond capitalism'. I became closer to George at the Zapatista-organised *encuentro* – 'for humanity and against neoliberalism' – in Chiapas in 1996, along with other friends and comrades, including Harry Cleaver, John Holloway, Gustavo Esteva and Monty Neal. George, Silvia and Harry urged me to attend and, again, I am very grateful for their advice. Zapatista communities welcomed us to the Lacandon jungle, where they had built toilets, *cabañas* for us to sleep in, huts for discussions and seminars, and amazing amphitheatres: 4000 international guests hosted by indigenous communities, who monitored how we washed our plates and gave us an opportunity to cross ideological divides.

Something magical resonated inside us. Neoliberal despair began to give way to a sense of hope. Alternatives and autonomy from capital and the state seemed a little more possible. Yet neither was completely absent:

the Mexican army, for instance, was surrounding the forest where we were staying. Many more orthodox activists could not understand this duplicity: the simultaneous existence of an *outside to capital* in the jungle of Chiapas *and* capital's army at the jungle's boundary. But this coexistence of inside and outside capital – or in, against and beyond – became clearer when I travelled to Spain the following summer for the second *encuentro*. The final slogan, 'one *no*, many *yeses*', precisely evoked this duplicity and made it more complex: a common *no* against neoliberalism; and, at the same time, many heterogeneous, culturally-rooted and situated alternatives to articulate and to explore. Soon after, Midnight Notes published an issue with this very title,[4] confirming for me that my enthusiasm for the experiences of the *encuentros* had a political and theoretical resonance. I started then to think about commons, even if I hesitated to call them that way yet.

The third moment was from the early 2000s. In public meetings, one point Silvia and George made always struck me: 'The World Bank says there are *x* millions of people living on under $1 a day … And yet they live, just think of how that is possible.' Meaning there must be some form of social cooperation that is not accounted for by the monetary measure.[5] The question of social cooperation takes us to the question of systems.

Commons as Social Systems

How can we develop a framework that holds together different strands of thought from the social and political sciences, along with insights from George and Silvia? How can we integrate George's discussions of the 'deal' or the work/energy crisis, say, along with Silvia's emphasis on reproduction, into a coherent understanding of commons and social reproduction? How can we retain the centrality of labour and hence class struggle – so as to not throw the baby out with the dirty water – yet also articulate ideas from the science of complexity, cybernetics and general system theory?

Just as for Marx the commodity is the cell form of the capitalist mode of production, so the common good is the cell form of post-capitalist wealth, wealth-in-common, shared wealth.[6] Yet this formulation does not tell us anything about *how* we share, nor how we produce and reproduce what needs to be shared in different contexts. These questions can be posed within a framework of the commons as social systems.

Commons are social systems comprised of two sets of elements. First, the material and immaterial elements that constitute commons-wealth, what is shared; and second, the social relations among the people within these commons communities, the rules and norms, both formal and informal, they use to coordinate their actions and their social relations. These two fundamental elements are brought together and (re)produced through the activity of *commoning*, of doing in common. Commoning, a term uncovered by another member of the Midnight Notes milieu, historian Peter Linebough, is the life and creative energy of the commons.[7] Through specific forms of commoning, communities not only reproduce the means of their reproduction – their common wealth – they also reproduce particular relational values, or value practices.[8] According to this perspective of commons as systems, commoning not only produces and reproduces commons, it also multiplies commons values – a commons *subjectivity*, opposite from and antagonist to the individual capitalist subject known as *Homo economicus*. Commons are not constrained by the 'bottom line' of capitalist value; rather their dynamic architecture is choreographed, structured and organised by multiple values that allow both individual freedom and coordination.

The importance of conceptualising commons as social systems is twofold. First, it allows us to identify what is internally generated by a self-organised group of people, a community of commoners, working with shared resources through common valuing processes. Thus conceptualising commons as social systems allows us identify and situate the meaning of autonomy. It also allows us to understand autopoiesis, the fact that commoning communities not only produce their own internal relations, but also the material and immaterial components that are necessary for their own (re)production. And it is also only by understanding commons as systems, that we can identify the circuit of commons value production, in turn making intelligible the concept of self-valourisation.

Second, by understanding commons as systems, we can postulate specific environments in which they are located and with which they interact. Indeed, in systems theory, a system is by definition a system-environment unit. The types of relations between commons systems and their environments are of a primary political importance. These relations determine the potential both for recomposition, collaboration and the scaling-up of commons and commoning; but also the threat of enclosure and cooption by the powers of capital and the state, for – as George and Silvia have tirelessly pointed out – state and capital systems are ever-present in the environment of the commons. Thus, our contemporary understanding of (anti-capitalist) commons is rooted in (class) struggle – against capital and against the state.

In the Environment of the Commons: the Enclosing and Coopting Force of Capital and the State

The New Enclosures appeared in 1990. *What the ****?!*, my Marxist background screamed at me: all the classical Marxists I had read until then clearly defined primitive or original accumulation as a distinct and distant phase of capitalism, events that occurred before the beginning of accumulation 'proper'. Two pieces in that that issue of Midnight Notes, one credited to the collective as whole, to which George had made a substantial contribution, and one by Silvia, claimed that neoliberalism represented a new wave of enclosures, of 'original' accumulation. (And this was more than a decade before David Harvey began talking about neoliberalism as 'accumulation by dispossession', an improper term really, since also 'normal' accumulation is based on dispossession of workers' time.) In the following months and years, I started to reread *Capital* with this new obsession in mind, to see with my own eyes how Silvia and George's take on enclosures and primitive accumulation could open a new way to interpret Marx.

In 2001, I published on this in *The Commoner*, a web journal I founded and to which George and Silvia have contributed several times in one way or another.[9] A few years later, I published a second piece, in *Historical Materialism*, in which I outlined a typology of modern neoliberal enclosures: of land and natural resources; social enclosures such as cuts in services that transferred the cost of reproduction to families and communities; of urban design.[10] Adopting this neoliberalism=new enclosures interpretation, I developed a framework that suggested that 'original accumulation' is continuous in capitalism. This means that enclosures are a central aspect of capitalist development. They are especially important in determinate crisis states, when capital needs to lay the basis for a new round of 'proper' accumulation (where 'accumulation proper' refers to the exploitation of labour and its associated 'logics'). But – a point made by George and Silvia – enclosures means the expropriation of resources used by communities to reproduce themselves independently of capital – and this often happens in moments in which capital needs to decompose working-class composition, to reduce class power and to shift the costs of social reproduction back onto the working class, thus boosting profits and initiating a new round of accumulation. Looking back, we suffered so many enclosures through the 1990s – to name just a few: IMF structural adjustment programmes; land grabs; environmental 'externalities'; attacks on 'welfare'; introduction of university tuition fees; and so on and on and on… The articles assembled in *The New Enclosures* were foundational in giving us the tools to appreciate not only this dark side of neoliberal capital, but also to hint at its mirror image. Since there could be no enclosures without something to enclose, Midnight Notes postulated the continuing presence of commons.

The dark side of capitalism includes a dark side to commons, and in several pieces George and Silvia have explored ways in which capital seeks to co-opt commons as part of its wider strategy. For example, in a 2013 article they remind us how the World Bank and United Nations strategise about 'soft privatisation':

For years, part of the capitalist international establishment has been promoting a softer model of privatization, appealing to the principle of the commons as a remedy to the neo-liberal attempt to submit all economic relations to the dictate of the market. It is realized that, carried to an extreme, the logic of the market becomes counterproductive even from the viewpoint of capital accumulation, precluding the cooperation necessary for an efficient system of production.[11]

For George and Silvia, one type of commons stands against capitalist enclosures and the cooptation of commons. This is the only type of commons that matters politically, the type of commons that must be constructed, nurtured and linked to others: the anti-capitalist and beyond-capitalist commons. They provide two interrelated arguments to support this political assertion. First, George assuages any doubts regarding the *technical* possibility of communalisation of any resource (it is only a question of politics and balance of forces). And second, Silvia offers us a strategic point from which to build a strategy of transformation: reproduction. I will discuss these, in turn, in the next two sections.

The Theoretical Roots of 'All in Common'

Radical thinking was taken by surprise, and some degree of enthusiasm, by the awarding, in 2009, of the Nobel Memorial Prize in Economics to Elinor Ostrom, for her life-time work on the commons. Was a section of the establishment pushing its case to make the cooption of commons central to neoliberal strategy in the context of the 'Great Recession'? After all, Ostrom postulated the pacific coexistence of commons, capital and the state; the public choice regarding which to favour depended on their 'effectiveness' in different contexts. Or was this award the symptom of something else, of the beginning of a paradigmatic change in the way capitalism would be managed, the opening of Keynesian deals for the twenty-first century? But deal with whom – and how? While I was wrestling with these possibilities, George sent me a paper, to be published in *The Commoner*.[12] 'A tale of two conferences' included a very simple and effective critique of Ostrom's understanding of commons purely as 'common-pool resources' and this, in turn, put me on the path of thinking commons as social systems no matter the resources that are pooled: a theoretical point reverberating with the political principle of *omnia sunt communia*, all in common.

In Ostrom's understanding, '[t]he term "common-pool resource" refers to a natural or man-made resource system that is sufficiently large as to make it costly (but not impossible) to exclude potential beneficiaries from obtaining benefits from its use ... Examples of resource systems include fishing grounds, groundwater basis, grazing areas, irrigation canals, bridges, parking garages, mainframe computers, and streams, lakes, oceans, and other bodies of water'.[13] George's conceptual critique is simple. If we look at the history of common property regimes it becomes obvious that 'many have been based on non-common-pool resources ... On the basis of the history of common property regimes, it is difficult to decide what types of goods are "conducive" to private property and what kinds of goods are "conducive" to common property'.[14] Indeed there are myriad examples, both historical and contemporary, in which communities communalise resource units into a 'common pot' and then establish rules or customs for its appropriation.

A social centre or neighbourhood association might have a library (resource system) containing books (resource units) brought by the project's various participants. Or it might be tools that are pooled. Fab labs (fabrication laboratories) and communal kitchens operate on the same principle. Friends and family members frequently communalise food items on a shared picnic blanket. In cyberspace P2P (peer-to-peer) production systems, in which individual software developers, with their own computer hardware and their own labour time, contribute to the development of a program, or else build the platform through which P2P file sharing occurs, thus communalising the files for all. Pooling money to buy needed stuff – whether pooling among friends or fundraising from strangers – is another form of aggregating resource units and turning the aggregation into a common pool. Every 'resource unit', or what economists call 'private goods', could in principle be communalised, if it is sensible to do so. Even children can be 'communalised', as when they live in a 'community' with 'many eyes': each child's autonomy and security is enhanced whilst adults'reproduction work is minimised.

We thus have two cases – resource *systems* and the *pooling* of resource units – which between them seem to cover all the types of commonwealth needed to commons. It is also worth noting that a resource system might be 'natural' (a source of fresh water, say) or 'manmade' (such as road infrastructure). Moreover, from an analytical point of view, there is no difference whether such systems were initially constructed by commoners or were instead reclaimed or appropriated from capital – one example is what George, in work on the oil industry, has called the 'hydrocarbons commons'.

One part of George's critique of Ostrom thus categorically opens up commons to a much wider horizon of activities. My approach has built on this. I have also taken on board another part of his critique of Ostrom. This involves shifting our focus from a commons' internal mechanisms to its relationship vis-à-vis its own environment, especially vis-à-vis state and capital systems. He draws a distinction between the approach of Ostrom and her associates and that of Marxists and radicals.[15] In George's words, while Ostrom and her associates 'look to endogenous variables ... to determine why one property regime changes into another', Marxists and radicals emphasise that there are no logical reasons why a social centre, a village commune or an indigenous community that has been managing a common pool resource, sometimes for generations, 'suddenly breaks down even though the logic of the coordination problem had been more or less solved'. While the former 'look to changes in the characteristics of the resource (e.g. whether its value on the Market or the cost of excluding non-commoners has increased) or in the characteristics of the commoners (e.g. the number of commoners has increased) for an explanation of the breakdown',

> ...the anti-capitalist supporters of the commons ... look to the larger class context to determine the dynamics of 'the drama of the commons.' For it is only by determining the class relations and forces within a particular region and stage in capitalist development that will ultimately determine the existence or annihilation of a common-property regime ... For the particular regime that manages a common-pool resource will be determined, e.g. by the labor needs of the dominant capitalist class in the region and by the commoners' solidarity and political-military power to resist the inevitable force that the desirous capitalists deploy.[16]

Such a political reading of context is, for George, essential in assessing the sustainability of commons. He of course sides with,

> ...the anti-capitalist supporters of the commons [who] see the struggle for a commons as an important part of a larger rejection of neoliberal globalising capitalism since it is the commons in the indigenous areas, in the global sense, and in the area of collective intellectual production that is now threatened with enclosure by a capitalism bent on commodifying the planet, its elements, its past and future. Their key issues are how to bring together various aspects of the struggle against commodification and create 'another world' satisfying the needs of global justice.[17]

So we have a tension, between an interpretation of commons as endogenous social systems, on the one hand, and commons as systems influenced by external social forces, on the other. In the first case, the ability of a commons to sustain itself depends on its management principles, even if we are talking about self-management. In the second, this ability depends on power relations vis-à-vis capital (and the state), whether attempting to enclose (and thus destroy) or to co-opt (sucking surplus value by using commons as a way to suppress social wages).

George's scholarship has helped me enormously in confirming my view of the necessity of framing commons as social systems. He is right to draw attention to commons' socio-political context and to see this strategically, as a field of possibilities (where these possibilities could run in favour of state and capital). Yet Ostrom's arguments should not be neglected. In many cases, even in anti-capitalist milieu, commons have been destroyed not through enclosure or cooptation, but due to a deficit of immaterial resources – insufficient coordination skills, a fall in trust, burn-outs, diminished purpose, excessive free-riding, an inability to adapt effectively to a new context. (I have several personal experiences of commons that include one or more of these.) How to work together? How to create a system that is resilient and (re)producible, within a deep democratic structure and with a moderate degree of openness? These are complex issues! In many urban areas, especially in the global North, the culture necessary to sustain communities needs to be recreated anew. Commoning needs to be learned and relearned. These matters are internal to the commons, yet they are as political as the ones posited by George. Healing subjectivities from *detritus* left by capital, dealing with the fear of the other, the xenophobia, racism and sexism embedded in many languages and subcultures ... these are important organisational and political matters.

But once we understand commons as social systems, we realise that tensions between commons' endogenous and exogenous forces is a tension that necessitates productive articulation rather than only categorical differentiation and contraposition. Social systems are *constituted* not only by their internal relations, but also by their relations to their environment. Hence the sustainability of the system is affected by the conditions of both internal and external relations: political recomposition of the commons happens when commoners can create a movement to collectively define their own environment *and* to limit capital's presence, pushing back capital and thus expanding the commons sphere. But a precondition of this, is that commons can be, and indeed are, created in whatever context – George's first insight.

The Strategic Horizon of Reproduction

While George alerts us to the mechanisms of state and capital in the environment of the commons, Silvia helps us to define a horizon of transformation, pinpoint a strategic direction and identify a transformative force: not just commoning, but *reproduction* commoning. Let us explore this in more detail.

For Silvia, the question of reproduction and reproductive labour goes back to the 1970s and her participation in New York's Wages for Housework campaign. That campaign anticipated contemporary radical demands for citizens' income, which in today's condition of generalised precarity, generalise also the claim for a social wage in exchange for our unwaged work in many spheres of life. In more recent work, Silvia locates reproduction as the primary site of social transformation through a critique of discourses on 'the common' upon which the demand for a citizen's income is often founded.[18] The principle of 'the common', according to a post-workerist strand of autonomist Marxism, is based on the idea that production and reproduction work are blurred in contemporary capitalism, thanks to the growth of 'immaterial' and 'affective' labour: informalisation, automation and knowledge work, for instance, produce a form of social cooperation that creates a common space with no hard boundaries of inclusion and exclusion. Such immaterial labour produces 'states of beings' and 'affects' which are therefore no longer the prerogative of reproduction labour. This means the development of the common is an immanent prerogative of contemporary capitalist system; the task of the 'multitude' is simply to prevent capital from capturing wealth from it.

According to Silvia, this strand replicates Marx's own blind spots on both women's unwaged reproductive labour and workers' self-activity that has, throughout capitalism's history, created institutions to limit capital's encroachment into their lives. The idea that capitalism is now grounded on immaterial and affective labour is myopic in two respects. First, it fails to see the ecological and social costs capital imposes in extracting the material resources (mining, energy and so on) necessary to sustain 'immaterial labour'. Second, it is inattentive to the bare materiality and emotional side of reproduction work, irreplaceable by technology, often unwaged or low-waged and executed in increasing isolation – for instance, by migrant mothers forced to leave behind their own children to be cared for by grandmothers or aunts.

Commoning for reproduction becomes here the key feminist insight we must treasure in a new politics, a politics that is developed by taking insights from women's reproduction struggles around the world and for whom the commons are a context of emancipation. First, Silvia identifies reproduction commoning as the process through which collective interest and mutual bonds are generated, a process internal to reproduction commons. Second, reproduction commoning is the first line of resistance against a life of enslavement, wherever this life is located in a patriarchal household, an army, a factory or a brothel. Third, it is a way to delink reproduction from capital's measure of things, from its values, from its line of command. Fourth, by delinking from capital, commoning also facilitates a decoupling from its systems of violence, the prison, the war machine, the custom office, upon which the capitalist market depends. And finally, through reproduction commoning we turn the abstract conception of solidarity into a living collective body, which develops its resilience vis-à-vis capital, better able to endure capital's myriad attacks.

In her path-breaking book *Caliban and the Witch*, Silvia demonstrates how the waves of witch-hunting in Europe and Latin America in the early modern period was an attack on the organic networks of community reproduction created by women and sustained by commoning. An insistence on the importance of organic support networks is a common theme in much of Silvia's writing and today women remain at the forefront of many such networks: communal gardens that spring up in derelict urban spaces; movements that reclaim houses from foreclosing banks (as in Barcelona); communal kitchens (as in numerous parts of Latin America throughout the last three decades). But her work always embeds a crucial tension. On one side are women's collective energies mobilised to the benefit of their communities (communal clinics, creches and kitchens); on the other is an alertness towards the criminality of capital's strategies of enclosures and cooptation (so-called microcredit, for example, where lenders destroy women's cohesion by setting one against the other in the servicing of loans with huge interest rates).

But in the end – to return to a point made near the beginning – if there are enclosures, there must be commons to enclose. In her embrace of both the internal dynamics of reproduction commoning and the struggles against capital in the environment of the commons, Silvia, like George, helped me not only to understand commons as social systems, but also to locate reproduction as the strategic site from which to build and sustain power.

The overall point of reproduction commoning is worth repeating. Silvia provides us with the political ground on which to base our strategies of emancipation from capital. The strategy of reproduction commoning has the potential to produce (and reproduce) relational values that are alternative to the ones synthesised in capital's bottom line of profit maximisation and cost externalisation onto waged and unwaged labour. And as our bodies also exist in relation to ecological systems, reproduction commoning as strategy also responds collectively to the entire matrix of bio-costs imposed by capital on our real bodies and ecological systems.

* * *

There are commons to defend, to strengthen and to expand. The work and reflections of George and of Silvia anticipated by many years of current debates on commons – and on struggles for commons and against enclosures. This work grounded these debates both politically and theoretically and continues to shape them. We are all in their debt.

Notes

1. Massimo De Angelis, *Omnia Sunt Communia. On the Commons and the Transformation to Postcapitalism* (London: Zed, 2017).

2. Midnight Notes, *The New Enclosures* (Jamaica Plain, MA: Midnight Notes, 1990).

3. George Caffentzis, 'Two Themes of Midnight Notes: Work/Refusal of Work and Enclosure/Commons'. In Craig Hughes (ed.), *Towards the Last Jubilee! Midnight Notes at Thirty Years* (New York: Autonomedia, 2010), p. 28.

4. Midnight Notes, *One No, Many Yeses* (Brooklyn, NY: Autonomedia, 1998).

5. See, for example, George Caffentzis, 'Dr. Sachs, Live8 and neoliberalism's "Plan B"', in David Harvie, Keir Milburn, Ben Trott and David Watts (eds), *Shut Them Down! The G8, Gleneagles 2005 and the Movement of Movements* (Leeds: Dissent! and Brooklyn, NY: Autonomedia, 2005), pp. 51–60.

6. See also Nick Dyer-Witheford, 'Commonism', in Turbulence Collective (eds), *What Would it Mean to Win?* (Oakland, CA: PM Press, 2010), pp. 105–12. Also at www.turbulence.org.uk/turbulence-1/commonism/index.html.

7. Peter Linebaugh, *The Magna Carta Manifesto: Liberties and Commons for All* (Berkeley, CA: University of California Press, 2008).

8. Massimo De Angelis, *The Beginning of History: Global Capital and Value Struggles* (London: Pluto, 2007).

9. Massimo De Angelis, 'Marx and primitive accumulation: the continuous character of capital's "enclosures"', *The Commoner*, 2 (September 2001).

10. Massimo De Angelis, 'Separating the doing and the deed: capital and the continuous character of the enclosures', *Historical Materialism*, 12(2), 2004, pp. 57–87.

11. George Caffentzis and Silvia Federici, 'Commons against and beyond capitalism', *Community Development Journal*, 49 (issue supplement 1) (January 2014), p. 197. At http://doi.org/10.1093/cdj/bsu006. First published in *Upping the Anti: A Journal of Theory and Action*, 15 (September 2013).

12. George Caffentzis, 'A tale of two conferences: globalization, the crisis of neoliberalism and question of the commons', *The Commoner* ('other articles in common', 2004).

13. Elinor Ostrom, Governing the Commons: The Evolution of Institutions for Collective Action (Cambridge: Cambridge University Press, 1990), p. 30.

14. George Caffentzis, 'A tale of two conferences', p. 22.

15. George describes the approach of Ostrom and her co-workers 'neo-Hardian', after Garret Hardin, whose (in)famous argument postulated an inevitable 'tragedy of the commons'.

16. George Caffentzis, 'A tale of two conferences', p. 24.

17. *Ibid.*

18. See, for example, the three articles collected together in Part III of Silvia Federici, *Revolution at Point: Housework, Reproduction, and Feminist Struggle* (Oakland, CA: PM Press, 2012).

A Vocabulary of the Commons

Marcela Olivera and Alexander Dwinell

In Cochabamba in 2000, when Bechtel tried to steal our water, it wasn't just SEMAPA (the government-run water utility) that they claimed ownership over, but also the wells and cisterns developed and maintained by neighbourhoods and communities. They even claimed the rain. In some ways it was the scale of their theft that made us remember the ways that we were all connected to and dependent on water.[1]

We have found the research and writing by Silvia Federici and George Caffentzis on the commons and the new enclosures useful in illuminating key aspects of our struggles and providing us with effective theoretical tools for analysing them. Using these tools and the analytic approaches they model, we will examine (1) the structure of the Water War conflict, to reveal how (2) the conflict was not only about water but, above all, was a struggle for something new. We will also examine (3) how the politics of language allows the state to co-opt the idea of the commons. We will also begin (4) to reverse the erasure of the labour of social reproduction (primarily provided by women) enacted by the privatisation of the water and the framing of resistance to that privatisation. It is through the theorisation of the commons that we can assert through our experiences that the commons are not a utopia or an ideal to achieve, but are in constant formation thanks to the struggle between communities, the state and private capital.

The Structure of the Water War

What is commonly referred to as the Water War took place in Cochabamba, Bolivia in 2000. Of course, beginnings and endings are hard to fix and the war started earlier when the national government passed a series of laws which provided the legal structure for the corporation Aguas del Tunari (a subsidiary of Bechtel) to privatise the region's water, which they did at the end of 1999. Through a series of conflicts starting in January 2000 the community came together to contest this privatisation. In April

2000, a major victory occurred when the people's resistance to privatisation drove Bechtel out of the country. While for many this marks the end of the Water War, as this essay will show, the battle over the water is still ongoing.

To understand the Water War it is essential to look at the structure of the conflict and understand who fought it. The organisational base that mobilised against the privatisation and commodification of the water and its supply service, what became known as La Coordinadora, emerged from a variety of community and neighbourhood associations that, before Bechtel's arrival, built and maintained systems that provided irrigation in rural and provincial areas and drinking water in the city. There was a great diversity to these collectives, but one commonality among the various organisations was that they worked to collectively decide issues of access, management, and availability of water. They decided on the service level provided, the design standards of the systems, and their own organisational, structural, and management forms. They developed their own methods of resolving conflicts, usually under a complex framework known as *usos y costumbres* (customs and traditions). These organisations made decisions with and within the community; they were not reliant on the state. In fact, it was from these communities that the demand that Bechtel must go emerged.

New Enclosures, New Commons

When discussing the Water War most people project a state-centered point of view in which the Water War is described as a struggle for citizen rights, where the people took to the streets to demand the right to water, but this is not how it felt on the ground.

In *Feminism and the Politics of the Commons in an Era of Primitive Accumulation* Silvia Federici writes, 'The new enclosures ironically demonstrated that not only commons have not vanished, but new forms of social cooperation are constantly being produced'.[2] This reflects our observations of the Water War. During our struggle, we realised that, although we came together to reject the privatisation of our water, we weren't just fighting to restore what we had, but to form something new. It was this desire that gave us the strength to come together and kick Bechtel out.

Following the war, we realised that what we had been fighting for was not to return the water to the state, (under SEMAPA management), but for greater collective control over the use and distribution of water by ourselves. We tried – and are still trying – a variety of approaches to achieve this. We expanded the board of SEMAPA to include workers and community representatives, we returned the ability to regulate water to the communities and new water committees emerged.

Often times this struggle is most visible in neighbourhood water committees coming together to collectively decide how to address their needs, such as in the San Pedro Magisterio neighbourhood where people came together to build a water treatment plant, or in others where people collectively worked through the question of how best to work together to access water, debating whether to pool resources to build a water tank, to advocate for access to the public water supply, or through some other strategy.

Our approach is to seek to defend and improve the historical regulation of water access under the idea of *usos y costumbres*, an approach that is incompatible with the state and the framework of laws that define its existence.

The Politics of Language

In the introduction to *Midnight Notes 12: One No, Many Yeses*, published in 1998, the authors name the phase of capitalism that emerged after the collapse of the Bretton Wood system and the practices of resistance against it, as the 'new enclosures'.[3] In returning to the period of so-called primitive accumulation in Marx's work, Silvia and George demonstrate the importance of the politics of naming and the struggle over what those names refer to in practice. As a part of the 'return' to the enclosures they have both argued for the centrality of the concept of the commons.

In a 2013 essay, Silvia and George demonstrate how the idea of the commons not only helped a variety of progressive movements understand their political actions during the period of the new enclosures, but also how the World Bank and the UN were trying to claim this language and redirect it towards neoliberal ends.[4] They also draw an important distinction between the commons and the public defining the latter as 'managed by the state and not controlled by us'.[5]

Returning to Bolivia and the Water War, President Evo Morales, Vice-President Alvaro Garcia Linera and the local governments pushed the idea that the public, and by that they mean a public utility regulated by and responsible to the government, was the appropriate body to regulate water usage and access. As Silvia observes,

> There is a crucial difference between the common and the public as the latter is managed by the state and is not controlled by us ... for the sake of the struggle for anti-capitalist commons it is crucial that we do not lose sight of the distinction.[6]

In addition, the government is articulating a rights framework (for instance, Law 071 of the Plurinational State is *Ley de Derechos de la Madre*

Tierra – Law of the Rights of Mother Earth) in which the right to water is bound up with and dependent on the state. The people of Cochabamba did not fight to save the water for capitalism. This is not what we fought for; we are struggling to build a water commons.

Over the past decade we have seen great strides and successful uprisings, from the gas and water wars to the movements of indigenous communities. We have also seen counter movements – conservative, liberal, and even those claiming the mantle of communism – try to reclaim our words and our deeds and use them to maintain, rebuild, and expand the state. In the Water Wars we united around the idea of the defense of water and life, we declared that the water was ours, and by this we meant the people's, to be held in common. Now the state asserts its 'public' identity and claims that it will develop structures to create, regulate, and resolve every aspect of our social life.

We can also observe this attempt to control the frame of the possible by controlling the language in the debate over the various ways the struggles of indigenous people are being reinterpreted. In Bolivia, as throughout South America, indigenous peoples have raised challenging questions that go the heart of the nation-state. In Bolivia the new constitution attempted to resolve these questions by proclaiming itself a 'plurinational' state. This solution raised new questions of autonomy which have since been co-opted by both the state (supposedly leftwing) and the private sector (rightwing). For Morales, Garcia Linera, and the MAS (their party, the Movement Toward Socialism), the main concern is to develop legal structures that defines who belongs to an indigenous 'nation' and then legislate its position within the plurinational state. The right has seized on the question of autonomy and seeks to use it as a weapon against the more progressive elements of the MAS platform by supporting indigenous autonomy in order to declare their own autonomy, with the ultimate goal of opting out of contributing to the general social welfare. In other words, none of these intentions actually seek to weaken the coercive aspect of the state or capitalism.

A Place of Social Reproduction

A politics which sees only what can be codified in law or commodified in the market cannot recognise the commons and renders invisible much of the labour of social reproduction. This historical erasure helps create the conditions under which seven out of ten women in Bolivia have suffered some type of violence and denies the value of the ongoing and everyday work – performed by women for the most part – needed to reproduce our common world. In the Water Wars, recovering traditional structures for managing water for agriculture was important, but no less so than the battle for control over domestic water use.

The privatisation of water directly impeded the ability of people – primarily women – to maintain their family's lives. As Silvia so often does, we seek to make visible how water privatisation affects the labour of social reproduction. We see how women previously had been able to use water domestically to grow food in small garden plots to feed their family and neighbours; in food preparation; in cleaning; and in other ways that maintained the household and allowed for social reproduction. Women were now confronted with a situation where they had to purchase the water as a commodity.

The impact of the privatisation through the increase in water bills – powerfully marked by the public burning of the bills – was registered in its relationship to the wage, but as is so often the case its impact on the unwaged, sustenance work of women remained invisible. The seizure of 'even the rain' attacked precisely the domestic use of water and it was the resistance to this that spurred many women, who in turn inspired their partners, to resist the privatisation.

The economic aspect of the privatisation was devastating, but equally, if not more, important was the under-recognised impact on the collective work of social reproduction. During the months when Bechtel operated in Cochabamba many women could no longer share household duties with their neighbours because of decreased access to water. But while this acted to isolate the women, they were still able to access these existing support networks as they organised against Bechtel.

Women make up more than fifty per cent of the population in Cochabamba and they – not just urban women, but also those from the countryside – were hugely active in the mobilisations during the Water War. The resistance to privatisation required everyone's participation and organisational work, but because of women's central relationship to water and their role in the reproduction of daily life, the construction of a solid movement was only possible with women's participation. In fact, when leaders of 'la Coordinadora' sought to hide from the soldiers in a convent the nuns asked, 'Where is La Coordinadora? She must be a brave woman.' This misrecognition went from being a funny story to an established truth.

Conclusion

The work of Silvia and George in exploring, explaining, and expanding our understanding of the commons has helped us to clarify the practices of resistance in Bolivia outside, against, and in parallel to the state. At the same time, our experience helps to show that the commons is not an ideal to achieve, but a daily practice of communities whose defense and enlarge-ment is, socially and politically, in constant tension with state and other structures of power.

It is thanks to Silvia and George's contribution that we can better ana-lyse and communicate, not only the structure of the conflict in the Water War of Cochabamba, but also, its stakes: that it took place not only to pro-tect water but to create, produce, and generate new and different ways to recuperate and expand the commons and to exercise our power to take decisions over our lives. Their work has reinforced our understanding that many of the recent efforts towards liberation have been recuperated by the state and has shown that we are not alone in this situation. The language that emerged from our struggles is being seized by people in power on both the right and left in an attempt to rebuild and strengthen their political positions and institutions. A right-based discourse implies ownership (a person or country 'has' a right to control such and such to the exclusion of others), and assumes isolated entities in conflict. This makes invisible pre-cisely the kind of labour we are highlighting here, whereas commoning helps us picture the ongoing and everyday work needed to reproduce a shared social sphere. By insisting on making visible the labour of social reproduction, we are better able to see the damage levied by the privatisa-tion of water. As we reflect on the place of the commons in Bolivia we realise that although commoning may not be something we frequently say, it certainly is something that we do.

Notes

1. In Silvia Federici, *Revolution at Point Zero: Housework, Reproduction, and Feminist Struggle* (Oakland, CA: Common Notions/PM Press, 2012) p. 139.
2. Midnight Notes Collective, 'Introduction' to *One No, Many Yeses* (Brooklyn, NY: Autonomedia, 1998).
3. George Caffentzis and Silvia Federici, 'Commons against and beyond capitalism', *Community Development Journal* 49(S1), (January 2014), pp. i92–i105. First pub-lished in *Upping the Anti*, 15 (2013).
4. *Ibid.*, p. i102.
5. *Ibid.*, p. i102.

17

A Bicycling Commons: A Saga of Autonomy, Imagination and Enclosure

Chris Carlsson

> Commons are not given, they are produced. Although we say that commons are all around us – the air we breathe and the languages we use being key examples of shared wealth – it is only through cooperation in the production of our life that we can create them. This is because commons are not essentially material things but are social relations, constitutive social practices... Exclusive reliance on 'immaterial' commons, like the internet, will not do. Water systems, lands, forests, beaches, as well as various forms of urban space, are indispensable to our survival. Here too what counts is the collective nature of the reproductive work and the means of reproduction involved. – George Caffentzis and Silvia Federici[1]

A Bicycling Commons is a curious concept. Rather than referring to a specific land or landscape, it refers to a shared state of mind and a shared set of experiences. What animates the notion of a Bicycling Commons is that so many people who have chosen to bicycle in cities feel they are a part of it. How does this relate to actual political projects to reclaim and reopen commons? When did the Bike Commons emerge? From where? What kinds of political antecedents helped shape this sensibility? And is it an ongoing reality or is it best understood as a passing phenomenon of a very particular transitional period between the twentieth and twenty-first centuries?

The quickest and easiest starting point is Critical Mass, the mass bike ride that began in San Francisco and within a few years had erupted in cities across the planet. Paradoxically, Critical Mass stimulated the rapid expansion of bicycling in hundreds of cities worldwide, but I would argue that the bicycle is an incidental – or accidental – facilitator of an urgent need to address a wide range of issues. At one time or another in our lives, most cyclists came to identify bicycling as a way individually to embrace social change. Perhaps we concluded it was the key to unravelling the dangerous traffic nightmare plaguing most of the world's cities, or to reclaiming a more convivial public space from the domination of private cars. Or we connected bicycling to a refusal to participate in oil wars; or a refusal to accept the mountain of debt associated with car and oil dependency; or a refusal of the massive pollution by fossil fuels that is wreaking havoc with the world's climate.

For most of the bicycling commoners riding through urban space nowadays, it began in childhood. As children we quickly discovered that bicycling unlocked nearby streets and neighbourhoods, and eventually entire cities. Personal mobility, a freedom to move independently through space, is an intoxicating pleasure and is a right of all humans – or should be. This freedom of mobility has been thoroughly colonised by the marketing engineers of the automobile industry for more than 100 years. Bicycling's history stretches back to the late nineteenth century. Bicycling, after a boom in the 1890s, was overrun by automobility in the early twentieth century, but not before nineteenth-century bicyclists had led the charge for good roads covered in asphalt. As cars came to dominate personal transportation, displacing walking, bicycling and streetcars, streets were widened and reorganised to accommodate faster speeds and more parking. Bicycling was redefined as a child's first vehicle on their way to a mature embrace of the car in adulthood. Most people across the planet have been convinced to accept this, or at least they were until about a generation ago.

Starting in 1992 in San Francisco, Critical Mass emerged as a monthly 'organised coincidence' in which first dozens, then hundreds, and eventually thousands of bicyclists took to the streets to 'ride home together'. While cars clogging streets in endless daily traffic jams are treated as inevitable and natural, part of the unavoidable 'weather' of city life, dense masses of bicyclists are anomalous, some kind of strange unnatural aberration, an unexpected emergence of rebellious creativity. Though Critical Mass riders always insisted, *We aren't blocking traffic, we ARE traffic!*, most participants, bystanders and motorists understood that this was something more than mere traffic. I dubbed it a Defiant Celebration.[2] We discovered that by bicycling together in a celebratory mass seizure of the roads we were cracking open the closed public space of city streets, reclaiming it from the decades-long enclosure of our thoroughfares by the forces of 'motordom' and their successful marginalisation of other transit options. We also opened a self-governed space free of commerce, where coming together in conversation and shared activity was a natural experience not requiring permission, licenses or the purchase of products. These experiences helped shape the imaginations of countless thousands. This, in turn, defined the surge of bicycling as participation in the creation of a new kind of commons, explicitly against the aforementioned enclosure of public space ensured by urban design, motordom and bureaucratic inertia.

And, almost by accident, the mobile open space attracted yet more new participants who, once having entered this unexpected social experience, experienced directly the new Bicycle Commons.

By extension, the long-lost awareness that the city's public byways had been conquered and 'enclosed' by the industries that together comprised 'motordom' was suddenly made apparent.

> [I]n North America, the reclamation and commoning of the means of reproduction must necessarily take different forms. But here too, by pooling our resources and re-appropriating the wealth that we have produced, we can begin to de-link our reproduction from the commodity flows that, through the world market, are responsible for the dispossession of millions across the world. We can begin to disentangle our livelihood not only from the world market but also from the war machine and prison system on which the US economy now depends... Indeed, if commoning has any meaning, it must be the production of ourselves as a common subject.[3]

As the original commons was open to all, Critical Mass opened itself to anyone to join, too. As long as you had a bike to ride, you didn't have to buy anything to participate in Critical Mass, neither object nor service, nor an ideology beyond a desire to partake in public life on two wheels. When hundreds and thousands of cyclists seized the streets for a convivial and celebratory use of public space, many of the expectations and rules of modern capitalist society were challenged, at least implicitly. Individual behaviours escaped the logic of buying and selling, if only for a few hours. Once in the street together, unexpected connections emerged, unplanned events occurred, and serendipitous relationships began. Unlike a trip to the mall or the market, the conversations were unburdened by the logic of transactions, of prices and measurements. It was a free exchange among free people. The experience altered one's sense of city life immediately, and more importantly, shifted collective imaginations in ways we only began to grasp.

Critical Mass cyclists, during the event's golden era (the first five years in most cities),[4] found themselves practitioners of a new kind of social conflict. The 'assertive desertion' embodied in bicycling challenged the system of social exploitation organised through private car ownership and the oil industry. And by cycling in urban centers in the Empire, Critical Massers embraced a growing movement around the world that repudiated the social and economic models controlled by multinational capital and modes of life that had been imposed without any form of democratic consent. This mass seizure of the streets by a swarming mob of bicyclists 'without leaders' was precisely the kind of self-directing, networking logic that has been transforming our economic lives and threatening the structure of government, business, and (as more imaginative military strategists were coming to understand) policing and war-making too.

In an essay called 'Bicycling Over the Rainbow: Redesigning Cities and Beyond' (September 1995) that was first distributed as a xerocracy flyer at a San Francisco Critical Mass in September 1995 I wrote:

> We conceived Critical Mass to be a new kind of political space, not about protesting but about celebrating our vision of preferable alternatives, most obviously in this case bicycling over the car culture. Importantly we wanted to build on the strong roots of humor, disdain for authority, decentralization, and self-direction that characterize our local political cultural history. Critical Mass descends from the anti-nuke movement as much as it does from the bicycling initiatives of the past. It is as much street theater as it is a (semi) functional commute, or at least it has been at its best. It is inherently anti-corporate even though there are more uncritical supporters of the American Empire and its monied interests riding along than there are blazing subversives, which is just another of the many pleasant ironies of CM.
>
> The bicycle itself embodies the counter-technological tradition that is the flipside of America's infatuation with technological fixes. Like the pro-solar movement in the 1970s, today's bike advocates tend to view the bicycle as something that is inherently superior, that brings about social changes all by itself, endowing it with causal qualities that ought to be reserved for human beings. I am a daily bike commuter, have been for most of the past 20 years, and am very fond of bicycling in cities. I greatly appreciate the bicycle for its functionality in short-circuiting dominant social relations, but let's not forget that it is merely another tool, and has no will of its own. When I bicycle around town I see things happening and can stop and explore them in depth with no hassles. I also see my friends and acquaintances and can stop and speak with them directly. This, combined with the absence of mass media pumping into my brain in the isolation of my car, sets up organic links and direct channels of human experience and communication. These links are potentially quite subversive to the dominant way of life in modern America, which is one of the reasons I like bicycling.
>
> But bicycling is not an end in itself, just like CM is really about a lot more than just bicycling. Our embrace of bicycling doesn't eliminate an enormous social edifice dedicated to supporting the privately-owned car and oil industries. Similarly, the infrastructure design of our cities and communities is slow to change in the face of our preferential choice of bicycling. Finally, we won't see any real change if we continue to act as isolated consumer/commuters, and in part CM allows us to begin coming together. But CM is far from enough, and until we begin challenging a whole range of technological choices at their roots, our lives and the planetary ecology are likely to continue worsening. Our capitalist society doesn't really care what we buy or which toys we like to play with, as long as we keep working within a system that systematically excludes us from decisions about the shape of our lives or the technologies we must choose.

The space we've opened up in CM is a good beginning. Out of it must grow the organic communities that can envision and then fight for a radically different organization of life itself. We will never shop our way to a liberated society. So questions of utopia lurk beneath the CM experience. What kind of life would you like to live, if you could choose? What of all the work that this society imposes on us, is work worth doing? What kind of technologies do we need? What direction do we want science to go (e.g. do we want to dedicate millions to military 'defense' and a space program, or shall science address the basic research associated with redesigning cities, transit and energy systems, etc.)? Why do we live in a 'democracy' in which serious questions such as these are never discussed, and if they are, only in remote academic journals and around the occasional kitchen table? Why is politics primarily a detached and meaningless ritual of popularity and money?[5]

This essay was translated several times and quickly spread to dozens of other rides in other cities. These kinds of ideas were enthusiastically embraced from Brazil to Italy, though a Bicycle Commons did not prove strong enough to radically alter the dominant culture's priorities. Nevertheless, bicycling has returned to the world's cities in a way no one could have predicted. By 1994 there were many Critical Masses, but even more interesting was that so many people were starting bicycling clubs, bike kitchens, bike ballet groups, bike circuses, midnight rides, bike cafes, and producing an endless stream of zines, hats, stickers, posters, buttons, and a remarkable profusion of bike-related creative expressions. Picking up enthusiasm from a wide swath of the population, literally hundreds of thousands of people are now bicycling every day instead of driving in cars. This is an amazing outcome of a slowly snowballing collective decision to change life that started small in one place, then spread to other places, and eventually led to millions of people in hundreds of the world's cities changing their everyday behaviour.

This surprising turn to bicycling as transportation has been both a successful fruit of the Bicycling Commons experience, and paradoxically, has also been a sign of the rapid decline of the Bicycling Commons. As more and more people choose to bicycle as everyday transportation, fewer experience the euphoria and transformative experience that was once transmitted through the Critical Mass experience. Prior to mass adoption of daily cycling, it was easy to feel connected to other cyclists in various urban environments, as one shared the sense of being a hardy minority, soldiering on in the difficult choice to cycle through social and infrastructural hostility and obstruction. The bicycling culture that gave rise to the sense of a Bicycling Commons started to disintegrate precisely as more and more people were choosing to bicycle as their everyday transportation. As I write in 2017, bicycle culture – and especially the solidarity that bound cyclists together – has practically disappeared (at least in San Francisco).

Curiously, the original pre-Critical Mass bicycling advocates of the late 1980s were largely middle-aged white men who fully embraced the arguments of a Stanford engineering professor named John Forrester, articulated in his book *Effective Cycling*. The main argument of this book was that to be 'effective' a person needed to ride 10,000 hours to gain the proper experience to be able to ride on city streets fully integrated with motorised traffic. The goal was to make cyclists equal users of the road by having them emulate as closely possible automobiles.

In 1994, when Critical Mass was reaching its most dynamic period and thousands of riders were beginning to appear at the monthly rides, San Francisco traffic planners held a public meeting to discuss the Comprehensive Bike Plan that they were starting to work on at the time. While many argued for separate bikeways of the type that is common in Denmark, Holland and Germany, a group of the cleats-and-helmets-with-clip-on-mirrors crowd, all in bright yellow riding clothes (the 'semi-professional' bicyclists that had made up the bulk of advocates during the prior very quiet decade) showed up to denounce any effort to create dedicated bike lanes. Echoing the arrogance of John Forrester's engineering studies, they insisted that anyone in favour of the European model was ignorant, and that the 'proven' solution was the 'effective cycling' programme, which would facilitate cyclists raising their proficiency and speed so they could successfully behave like 'normal traffic' on 'normal streets'. They insisted that the car-dominated streets of the late twentieth century United States were inalterable and permanent, and that any effort to reclaim streets from cars or redesign thoroughfares was just pointless.

This public conflict delayed planning and implementation of bicycle infrastructure improvements for many years (including a three-year hiatus over a lawsuit that stopped all bike improvements). Nowadays, San Francisco has a number of separated bikeways on major thoroughfares, and many more planned. The pace of implementation has been glacially slow, but a quarter century after the first surge of demand for bicycling space emerged, it's beginning to show up in dozens of cities around the world that previously had nothing for bicycles (from Sao Paulo, Brazil to Mexico City, to Milan, Italy and Paris, France, not to mention New York, San Francisco, Chicago, and dozens of US cities).

During this period of history, roughly 1990–2025, the world is transitioning from the twentieth-century commitment to automobiles to a multi-modal approach to urban transportation that foregrounds bicycling and walking, supplemented by public transit. To be sure there are still strong political and economic forces putting up major resistance to this transition, especially given the central role of the automobile and oil industries in most industrialised economies. But literally millions of citizens across the world are 'voting' on this directly by getting on bicycles and changing their daily behaviour. This didn't erupt from a bureaucrat's on-high policy decision, but rather from an urgent need by people in cities everywhere to address the ridiculous irrationality of endless traffic conges- tion, horrible air pollution, catastrophic collisions, neighbourhoods devastated by being engineered to accommodate maximum space for high speed car use and no-speed car parking, perpetual indebtedness to pay for car costs, and so on. As social solidarity has been torn apart in societies everywhere by the horrible consequences of neoliberal capitalism and aus- terity, a new kind of solidarity around the embrace of the bicycle has helped many to find a remarkably joyful connection to their sibling cyclists.

This 'bike culture solidarity' has been largely a middle- and upper-middle- class phenomenon. Poor people have been bicycling through the whole of the twentieth century without making a political or cultural issue of it. Once the bike culture started to catch on during the past generation, it took root among the parts of the population who were perhaps most separated from the kind of everyday solidarity that has always been the hallmark of poorer communities. Social ties and organic communities have been dis- rupted by an economic system that reduces all interaction to commerce and transactions. People who have been too poor or too far from the mod- ernised cities are the ones whose human solidarity has been most resilient. In places like Mexico, it is still not uncommon to hear people dismiss so-called 'backward' small towns as *Pueblos Bicicleteros*, to denote their lack of modernity. But in a delicious turnabout, those towns can now claim to have leapfrogged the stupidity of twentieth-century modernism to embrace a fully modern twenty-first-century sensibility rooted in a shared and eco- logically grounded consciousness, and at ease with self-propelled mobility as a sensible first choice in lieu of oil-and-auto dependency.

Here in San Francisco, bicycling has also boomed since the early 1990s. We've had an enormous increase in daily bicycling trips during this period. As bicycling became normalised for tens of thousands of people, what was once a dynamic bicycling culture has largely disintegrated. Critical Mass still rolls every month but it has been quite a long time since I thought it magical or inspiring. Generally it is a very predictable and rather boring ride these days without much conversation or discussion. The local Bike Kitchen is still going strong, though it is in an expensive space that has thrust a certain degree of normality onto its once intangible essence. Dozens of bike shops are doing well here as small businesses. New sepa- rated, buffered, painted bike lanes are opening here and there though we are far from a comprehensive network of functional bikeways separated from streets dominated by cars.

There are still some independent efforts to use the bicycle in politically interesting ways. The activist group PODER has organised Bicis del

Pueblo, which holds monthly bike-building workshops, organised group rides, and more to serve the largely Latino population of the working-class, southern part of San Francisco. In Los Angeles the Ovarian Psycos are an all-female posse of cyclists who are pushing boundaries of both gender and racial exclusion in the bike scene down there. Bicycles continue to provide a means for social groups to assert their independence, their opposition to the dominant culture, and to enact a partial agenda of urban transformation. But bicycling has been aggressively captured, too, by monied interests committed to the preservation and extension of existing dynamics of power and wealth.

Bicycling and Neoliberalism

The 25-year trajectory of bicycling culture in San Francisco cannot be understood apart from the primary advocacy organisation in the city, the San Francisco Bicycle Coalition (SFBC). When Critical Mass began in 1992 the SFBC was a group of about 15+ volunteers who met once a month in the back of a Chinese restaurant. About a year later they took the leap to renting an office and formalising a paid director and part-time staff. After the police attack on Critical Mass in 1997 the SFBC enjoyed a sudden influx of new recruits and within a year had grown to more than a thousand dues-paying members. By 2000 the new executive director was pushing membership growth as a strategy, while she was damping grassroots activism in favour of a more typical hierarchical organisation. By the mid-2000s the SFBC had surpassed 5000 members and by 2010 it had reached 10,000. The executive director's leadership was rewarded with appointments to representative positions on the SF Municipal Transportation Agency and the Golden Gate Bridge, Highway & Transportation District. The organisation gained financial and political support from foundations, corporations, and governmental agencies and its budget soared to well over a half million dollars a year. Politicians sought its endorsement during each election cycle, and that power-to-endorse became an important arrow in the SFBC's quiver – though we have to say, too, that the politicians that gained support from the Bicycle Coalition have not produced a comprehensive transformation of city streets, or even a significant fraction of them, to accommodate daily cycling.

Over two and a half decades this organisational evolution provides a revealing window into the co-optation of a once-radical movement of bicyclists into a relatively conservative and cautious organisation, run in a strict top-down manner to ensure nothing unpredictable rocks the efforts to normalise and mainstream bicycling. Of course this could only be true in part because there are no other San Francisco organisations of bicyclists to speak of. For a brief time in 1997 and early 1998 a small group called 'Grip' staged some interventions and sought to develop an action-oriented organisation of cyclists committed to engaging in local political fights. But that effort petered out after less than a year. Critical Mass riders have eschewed any organisational efforts *as Critical Mass* because ultimately Critical Mass is an event, not an organisation. Participants have shown little interest in more formal organisations beyond those who have become members of the San Francisco or East Bay Bicycle Coalitions. These days there are fewer regular riders than newbies and visitors, a further structural reason why organisation does not emerge from the event.

The expansive, participatory, and utopian qualities that characterised the first years of Critical Mass rides gave way over time to ossification and repetitiveness within Critical Mass itself. The political space of bicycling outside of Critical Mass has been filled by the SFBC which subsumed 'activism' into free labour for a hierarchical lobbying corporation pushing a 'pro-bike' agenda. Jason Henderson, writing in his excellent book *Streetfight: The Politics of Mobility in San Francisco*, argues:

> The original agenda of the SFBC, closely aligned to the Critical Masses of the 1990s, had its roots in a broad criticism of automobility, but the new SFBC took pains to stress that the majority of its membership owned cars and yet chose to bicycle. The SFBC of the nineties was characterized by a leadership that offered progressive critiques of the geography of capitalism and of a lifestyle centered on unfettered hyperconsumption, the incessant speeding up of everyday life, competition rather than cooperation, and possessive individualism rather than collective action: in other words, a critique of neoliberalism and conservatism.
>
> In 2012 the new SFBC was sponsored by large corporate foundations whose wealth came from capitalist investments, and this included a who's who of San Francisco and Silicon Valley businesses and entrepreneurs. Among them, Google, Microsoft, Pacific Gas & Electric, an array of private transportation, urban planning, and architectural consultants, real estate firms, attorneys, and individual donors connected to software and social networking firms. The organization maintained a very large volunteer base as well, one that provided some sixteen thousand hours of free work, and 26 percent of its income came from the fees of its thousands of progressively inclined individual members... In addition, despite the large corporate and foundation financing, the SFBC relied heavily on in-kind support from hundreds of independent small businesses such as restaurants, bicycle dealers, bars and cafes, and other small-scale retailers.[6]

With this increase in budget and profile, the SFBC earned its money by becoming a meek team player for local interests, hoping for handouts from their benefactors. With regard to a real bicycle agenda, they have acquiesced to a glacial effort to transform bicycling corridors throughout the city (losing the argument for the primary north–south artery on Polk Street to cranky condo residents and car-loving bar owners). The difficulty of crossing the bay by bicycle has been exacerbated by the SFBC and East Bay Bike Coalitions, who both have abdicated to the state's traffic engineers at Caltrans. Caltrans's proposal is for a ten-year project to cost $1 billion that will attach an external dual-use bike and maintenance lane to the west span of the Bay Bridge to connect San Francisco to the middle of the Bay and the other half of the recently built Bay Bridge bike lane. Ignored in this acquiescence is the easy and cheap alternative of having the west span returned to its original six lanes with one reserved for cyclists – for a budget of less than 0.5 per cent of the cost of the other approach. The SFBC and EBBC both ignore the vital history of the San Francisco Freeway Revolt that halted freeway construction through the City in the early 1960s, at the exact time when the Department of Highways (rechristened Caltrans years later) was reconfiguring the Bay Bridge to connect to a high-speed freeway system that was never built.

The San Francisco Bicycle Coalition found supporters among real estate developers who see higher profits in building housing for younger workers that reject car culture (relieving the developers of having to spend money on accommodating automobiles in expensive parking garages). Bicycle advocates in San Francisco, New York, Memphis Tennessee and other cities have turned a blind eye to the resulting displacement of working-class communities and people of colour that big real estate developments have caused, as long as they also included new bicycle infrastructure. Unfortunately many of cycling's most earnest and well-meaning advocates have tunnel vision, seeing only support for bicycling as the issue. This produces a weird 'arms race' for funding and attention at the expense of other issues, and fails to recognise the way bicycling has become co-opted by wealthy interests to reinforce their own power and money. By maintaining a narrow focus on bicycling isolated from other social dynamics, the official proponents have facilitated a depoliticisation of bicycling and helped make it a component of the larger agenda of marketisation and neoliberal reorganisation of urban life. This defensive embrace of the status quo has also exacerbated class and racial dynamics that have given bicycling a reputation as part of a gentrifying culture, something that young white hipsters bring wherever they go. The invisibility of the legions of mostly immigrant workers commuting by bicycle also co-exists with the ever-higher profile of mainstream bicycle advocacy, more grist for the mill of social fragmentation.

This dynamic has complicated the development of proper bicycling infrastructure. Efforts to improve public thoroughfares for uses other than by private autos inevitably produce public opposition. The aforementioned Polk Street debacle has led to partial improvements but falls far short of a truly safe reimagining and redesign of the road, having fallen victim to vociferous opposition from bar owners and local elderly and wealthy residents of condominiums. But the class and ethnic tension provoked by the neoliberal embrace of bicycling has led activists associated with the Mission District's 'Calle 24' Latino commercial district preservation efforts to angrily oppose both the establishment of 'parklets' (where parking spaces are repurposed into small public parks with chairs and tables) and the arrival of the expanded bike-sharing system now branded as 'Ford GoBike'. Part of the Calle 24 opposition stems from longtime Latino small businessses whose clientele has been displaced to the suburbs by gentrification, and can only return to shop by car, hence the insatiable need for parking. Also, anti-gentrification campaigners across the Bay Area have come to identify parklets as emblems of gentrification since few working-class residents have the time or wherewithal to 'hang out' during the sunny afternoons when the (free to the public) parklets are at their best. Instead, white hipsters with laptops, or wealthier mothers with babies tend to be the predominant users of such spaces. Whether parklets *cause* gentrification or are merely easily *made use of* by people deemed gentrifiers doesn't come under much scrutiny. Latino bicycle activists, who often favour public space reconfiguration away from private cars, have generally been drowned out by the avidly pro-car sentiments of the local population. Loudly asserting the necessity of car use, these locals also wrap their dependence on private cars in a cultural enthusiasm (e.g. the 'lowriders') that elides their hidden support to the automobile and oil industries, hardly bastions of Latino cultural pride!

Bicycling: A Window to Larger Changes

In my opinion, bicycling is only an interesting activity worth promoting if it leads to bigger changes than merely getting more people on bicycles. After all, there are cities such as Copenhagen and Amsterdam where nearly half the population use bicycles regularly for transportation, yet these are hardly utopias that have escaped the darker realities facing people across the world. It's great to have fewer cars and many more bicyclists, but not if the society they are bicycling around in is based on the same logic as the one that made cars seem so normal for so long. The problems we face are far greater than what kind of vehicle we use to move from place to place – even if the choice we make about vehicles is *one* important decision among dozens that we face as individuals.

Bicycling fails its potential as a key to unlocking crucial and urgent political and social change if it allows itself to be about merely bicycling. I don't
really care about derailleurs or brake pads or what colour or brand your
bicycle is, whether you like racing bikes, mountain bikes, or folding bikes. It
is not interesting. These are the easy and acceptable obsessions of a consumer society. Your ability to act in the world is channelled into deciding
how to spend money. Buy the good products, don't buy the bad ones, and
you are doing your part. This is wrong. By accepting the logic of a neoliberal
consumer society, in which your political agency is limited to shopping
choices, you lose the ability to change how we live, to change what kind of
world we make together every day with our labour, our activity.

Bicycling, luckily, can be about a lot more than just buying the latest
gear. And it can be about a lot more than just getting some stripes painted
on a busy boulevard, or even new bike highways crisscrossing a country as
some places are now planning. Because if we all got up across the planet
tomorrow and bicycled instead of going in cars, while it would be a good
step in the right direction, we would still be bicycling to jobs that are
producing the world we live in now. We would still be going to banks,
advertising agencies, and real estate offices, buying and selling people's
homes, manipulating currencies, promulgating propaganda for politicians
and products; vast military budgets would go on being spent to control
populations and territories and to make war; borders would still block the
free movement of people while allowing toothpaste, tennis shoes, wheat
and wood to cross the earth, burning fossil fuels along the way.

We cannot shop our way to a sensible world. We have to make it, and
we have to make it together. When we choose to move through cities on
bicycles it's clearly a better choice than using automobiles most of the
time – for us as individuals, and for the larger society we live in. Bicycling
is *doing*, it is an active *production of movement* and as such is a key part of
redesigning life. But politically and philosophically we have to connect
the activity of bicycling to the activity of reinventing life. If we learn to
move around differently by bicycling, we also have to learn how to use
water differently, produce and distribute food differently, build and share
safe and adequate housing for everyone on earth differently. We have to
connect bicycling's rebellious meaning to plans to make sure free communications and free transportation are inviolable human rights alongside
food, water and shelter.

Bicycling is the key to opening a much more complicated conversation
about how different life could be. Riding our bikes is so simple and such a
pleasure and can lead us into a shared Bicycle Commons. That shared,
familiar pleasure is a great place to start thinking critically about the choices

we make about much more than merely how we get around. Bicycling, at its best, should challenge us to change not just how we get from point A to point B, but what we do at point A and what we do at point B. It should help us to ask why we do those things, who decides what is worth doing, how could we make those decisions together – that is, what is democracy now? – and who benefits from the choices we make? Bicycling can unlock much more interesting questions with much more interesting answers than we might think at first thought.

Writing in 'Commons against and beyond capitalism', George Caffentzis and Silvia Federici underscore the dynamics of enclosure that the Bicycling Commons has importantly emerged to confront:

> From New Delhi and New York to Lagos and Los Angeles, urban space is being privatized, street vending, sitting on the sidewalks or stretching on a beach without paying are being forbidden. Rivers are dammed, forests logged, waters and aquifers bottled away and put on the market, traditional knowledge systems are sacked through Intellectual Property Regulations and public schools are turned into for-profit enterprises. This explains why the idea of the commons exercises such an attraction on our collective imagination: their loss is expanding our awareness of the significance of their existence and increasing our desire to learn more about them.[7]

The Bicycle Commons burst into consciousness 25 years ago, primarily through the contagious pleasure that the Critical Mass phenomenon helped spread worldwide, and the opening of the forgotten public space of our shared thoroughfares. But the Commons as an animating force shrinks when the bicycle is merely a practical device, simply a way to get around. When bicycling is fused with a more expansive agenda that challenges the logic of incessant growth, a world based on commodification of humans and their creativity, and the reduction of nature to 'resources', the sense of a Bicycling Commons, based on choosing together to produce a different way to move around and hence a different way to live, thrives. A deeper agenda lurks within our spinning wheels but can slip away quite easily if we defer to the narrow common-sense agenda of those who can't see the forest for the trees, who can't see that bicycling is just a doorway to a much larger transformation of how we make life together.

Notes

1. George Caffentzis and Silvia Federici, 'Commons Against and Beyond Capitalism', *Community Development Journal* 49(S1), (January 2014), p. i101.
2. For the 10th anniversary we published *Critical Mass: Bicycling's Defiant Celebration* (edited by Chris Carlsson; Oakland, CA: AK Press, 2002).

3. Silvia Federici, 'Feminism and the Politics of the Commons', in David Bollier and Silke Helfrich, *The Wealth of the Commons: A World Beyond Market & State* (Amherst, MA: Levellers Press, 2012). At http://wealthofthecommons.org/essay/feminism-and-politics-commons.

4. In *Shift Happens: Critical Mass at 20*, Chris Carlsson, Lisaruth Elliot and Adriana Camarena (eds) (San Francisco, CA: Full Enjoyment Books, 2012), I wrote an essay called 'Ruminations of an Accidental Diplomat' that details some of my experiences in various cities around the world, offering evidence for my assertion of a five-year window in which the best of the experience rises and falls in each locale.

5. The full text is reproduced in *Critical Mass: Bicycling's Defiant Celebration*.

6. Jason Henderson, *Streetfight: The Politics of Mobility in San Francisco* (Ameherst, MA: University of Massachusetts Press, 2013), pp. 133–4.

7. George Caffentzis and Silvia Federici, 'Commons Against and Beyond Capitalism', pp. 94–5.

18

Common Paradoxes

Panagiotis Doulos

In his entry for *Keywords for Radicals*, George Caffentzis outlines the gene-alogical succession of the keyword *commons* in its historically specific forms.[1] He traces this 'family tree' back to the medieval period and the emergence of the word as a legal term defining the field of collective own-ership which belonged to nobody. The commoners had collective usage of the commons, but did not own them. In this type of analysis, as Caffentzis rightly points out, the notion of the commons is neither devoid of history nor is it separated from its social expressions at any given time. By looking into its primary appearance as ancestry, he emphasises its significance and its possibilities in the social antagonism of the present: 'commons are back', as he specifically states. Although Caffentzis acknowledges that the term is vague and is used ambiguously and contradictorily in its different historical manifestations, he does not himself steer clear of the trap of conferring a particular historical interpretation on it. To a certain extent, the historical quest surrounding this concept suggests the existence of a common revolu-tionary essence at its core.

Following Caffentzis's argument, I would like to trace a different line of descent in order to highlight the problematic nature of this specific rea-soning. The concept of the commons appears as a political and philosophical concept already in the world view of ancient Greek symbolism, where it constitutes a specific field of social practices that define social existence itself. The primary appearance of the concept opens up certain paradoxes that are quite significant. To begin with, I will explain why we are all idiots in capitalism, and how the Greek notion of 'idiōtēs' (*ιδιώτης*) relates to the commons.

In Pericles' funeral oration, Thucydides discusses participation in the commons, by which is meant the public affairs of the city (polis) and its citizens (polites), and states: '[We Athenians regard] him who takes no part in these duties, not as unambitious, but as useless'.[2] In its contem-porary use, the word 'idiot' refers to an imbecile or someone who behaves stupidly. Essentially, it does not differ greatly with its ancient Greek denotation. The Greek word idiōtēs literally means a private person, to wit, someone who has retired to the private sphere and is deprived of political rights. In the world view of ancient Greeks during the city-state period, whoever did not participate in the commons, that is, in the Agora and the process of common decision-making on the matters concerning the *polis*, was considered an idiōtēs, that is, someone useless. In this sense, in the contemporary context of the glorification of vulgar individualism, we can all be considered idiots. Furthermore, the ancient Greek meaning of the commons characterised human nature itself, as well as the hierarchisation of human life. Therefore, if one did not participate in the commons, one was considered not only an idiot, but also a non-subject. In other words, one turned into an abject.[3] The first sentences of Aristotle's *Politics* (1999: 3) are quite telling:

> Every state is a community of some kind, and every community is established with a view to some good; for mankind always act in order to obtain that which they think good. But, if all communities aim at some good, the state or political community, which is the highest of all, and which embraces all the rest, aims at good in a greater degree than any other, and at the highest good.[4]

This is what distinguishes man from the animal kingdom. Man is, by nature, a 'political animal'.[5] For that reason, whoever cannot live in society is 'either a beast or a god'.[6] Therefore, whoever is not part of the political community does not pertain to human nature. Human nature can acquire true existence and become materialised only within the context of the 'commons' and participation therein. Animals can create certain forms of community or instances of socialisation through their activities but, as they do not have Speech, they cannot be considered as more than simple nature. Speech expresses the realm of freedom and human nature, which lies at the threshold between beast and god. This link between human nature and the commons presents a paradox of double exclusion both within and outside the sphere of the commons. In the ancient Greek city-state, only free male citizens had access to the commons. Slaves, foreigners and women were excluded. The commons could become materialised only within the symbolic walls of the political community. For that reason, the practice of ostracism[7] was not only a symbolic punishment; it also had a defined and materialised character. The loss of the identity of the free citizen meant the debasement of the subject to a natural state amounting to slavery. The individual enjoyed the realm of freedom and Speech as a subject only when included within the walls. Outside the walls, s/he can only be considered as 'simple nature', a *naked life* in the words of Agamben.[8]

So if, as Silvia Federici rightly pointed out,[9] Marx provides in his *1844 Manuscripts* a clear idea of the relation between alienation and the commons, we must not forget that the distinction between free, conscious and reasonable activity of humans with regards to nature is based on the analysis of Aristotle who, as a ghost, hovers above Marx's head. For the human being, a 'social creature', a 'living species' that is universally free, participation in the community and the commons is a natural condition, one that justifies relations of inclusion–exclusion and power. The commons appear as a neutralised, abstract entity, an essence that characterises human beings and turns into a field of power and command that naturalises existing power relations. The relation of inclusion–exclusion exists within the commons as an active paradox, if we consider that the notion of participation in a common idea and practice is what defines the form of the commons.

Furthermore, if we accept, as Federici argues elsewhere,[10] that the female form is identified with the commons and the sphere of reproduction, we assert the division between production and reproduction, public and private. However, on the basis of the line of descent I have followed, in ancient Greece the commons refer to the public and not the private sphere. That is, in this patriarchal world, the commons appear as the exact opposite of the sphere of reproduction. Tracing the origins of the notion of the commons, as Caffentzis has done, does not help us elevate it to a critical category if we take the earlier ancient Greek understanding as a starting point. Neither does it provide with certainty the possibility of detecting a revolutionary core in commoning practices. For the ancient Greek political community, the commons as a privilege of the public sphere belong exclusively to men: they are the expression of the patriarchal society, of the exclusion of women from the public sphere and their enclosure in the sphere of the idiots.

In this context, the early relations of domination that excluded women from the forms of participation in the commons are a natural condition. It is no coincidence that the word 'common', which referred to the woman that escaped the private sphere, also meant 'prostitute' (common woman: playgirl, prostitute). The ancient Greeks identified woman as a form of reproduction of life, but only within the boundaries of the private sphere. When outside it, when rendered a 'common' woman, she lost the sacred right to the reproduction of life and she turned into an even more inferior being, one for the 'common use' of men. The assertion and reinforcement of the separation between production and reproduction, the public and the private, seems to allow, at least under specific historical conditions, the reinforcement of exclusion.

How much has this symbolic order changed since then? Could it be that this relation and the fragmented language it articulates still echo in today's social organisation? Contemporary theories on the commons seem to turn the meanings and practices of ancient Greece upside down. However, the problem remains that the effort to define the commons through partici- pation or through tracing the lineage of the concept necessarily defines borders and perimeters. More importantly, it defines which subjectivities are included within the symbolic walls of the commons and capable of participating, and which not. In these circumstances, it is not very clear what the difference is between the capitalist and anti-capitalist commons. The constitutive convention of exclusion remains.

Although the first exclusion, within the walls of the commons and out- side them, seems to be lifted for those who participate in them, the reproduction of exclusion within the walls of the commons is not avoided. If, for example, collective ownership is considered a form of commons that abrogates the exclusion of those who do not have access to private owner- ship, how can one challenge the practices of exclusion between the small minority of commoners and the majority of those who do not have access to the property (and who are forced either to work for a wage, or migrate) within the same community? If the commons do not question the very core of the logic of capital and do not push for the abolition of the property- form itself and also the way in which the capitalist barbarity is constituted, there is a real danger that they re-fetishise the logic they are trying to negate. The assertion of reproductive labour does not negate the labour- form. The real question remains: how to abolish the power that labour-form implies? How can we challenge the hierarchies that are being reproduced within one same community? These are problems encountered when we try to fit social practices and ideas within a logical model.

In conclusion, I believe the emergence of these paradoxes runs through commoning discourses. This does not diminish their value within the con- text of social resistance. Under capitalism, the subject is contradictory and schizophrenic anyway. The same goes for the way in which communing discourses expresses their social practices and ideas. The issue is not how to reproduce a non-adulterated theory. Perhaps it is even dangerous for, when unfolded, a 'non-adulterated' theory could lead to the creation of hierar- chies and powers in different forms. The awareness of the contradictions and paradoxes that exist within the way in which we resist and act helps us stand critically against capitalism, but also rethink our own selves. Perhaps that is why social resistances are not fixed forms, but rather verbs and ques- tions in constant movement, change, and transformation.

Notes

1. George Caffentzis, 'Commons', in K. Fritsch, C. O'Connor and A.K. Thompson (eds), *Keywords for Radicals: The Contested Vocabulary of Late-Capitalist Struggle* (Chico, CA: AK Press, 2016), pp. 93–101.
2. Thucydides, *The History of the Peloponnersian War* (DigiReads, 2009), p. 63.

3. For the notion of abject, see Julia Kristeva, *Powers of Horror: An Essay on Abjection* (New York: Columbia University Press, 1982).

4. Aristoteles, *Politics* (Kitschener: Batoche Books, 1999), p. 3.

5. *Ibid.*, p. 5.

6. *Ibid.*, p. 6.

7. Ostracism was a political practice in ancient Athenian democracy, whereby a vote was held – using shells (óstrako) – on whether a citizen considered a threat to the political system should be banished from the city.

8. Giorgio Agamben, *Homo Sacer: Sovereign Power and Bare Life* (Stanford, CA: Stanford University Press, 1998).

9. In, for instance, her 2016 lecture Towards a theory of the commons. Historical trends, ethical and political perspectives, presented in Puebla, Mexico.

10. For example, in 'Feminism and the politics of the common in an era of primitive accumulation', in Team Colors (ed.) *Uses of a Whirlwind: Movement, Movements, and Contemporary Radical Currents in the United States* (Baltimore: AK Press, 2010); republished in *Revolution at Point Zero: Housework, Reproduction, and Feminist Struggle* (New York: PM Press, 2013), pp. 138–48.

19

The Construction of a Conceptual Prison

Edith Gonzalez

Capital separates. Be it the product of our practice, the means of production or the way in which our actions relate to each other, capital constantly repeats the same process of separation that becomes crystallised in the image of a world as something beyond our control. Capital identifies. The economic compulsion that forces us to sell our labour-power in order to survive is the way in which what we do becomes identified with the dynamic of capital and, in consequence, we assume roles that reproduce it. However, the never-ending process of imposition reveals the existence of a remnant that is suppressed by the way in which social relations are organised within capitalism. The working class revolts against exploitation are an example of this remnant that must be crushed. The same can be said of feminist struggles against the sexual division of labour that condemns women to reproductive activities and dependence on the salaries of men. The emancipating content of feminist struggles and those of the working class have remained trapped in the capitalist *form* of law. That is to say, they have remained trapped in the logic of demands that reaffirm the state as the mediator of social conflict.

However, today the capitalist dynamic is much more violent. Political recognition no longer presupposes economic reward. More and more aspects of life are permeated by the *rule of money*. The disaster and the misery that we live are obvious. Reality appears before us as if we were walking between the lines of *Capital*'s chapters on primitive accumulation.[1] Therefore, it is not by chance that we look to the past for answers, or at least some indications that throw light on how we can destroy this dynamic that is propelling us towards our own destruction. In this context, the struggles for the commons seem to fill the void left by the defeat of class struggle and communism as its principal objective. Contrary to the egotism and self-interestedness that characterise the organisation of social relations in capitalism, the commons call upon us to see hope in the multiplicity of rural and urban struggles against the state and against capital.

That is how the commons have become the core of political debate amongst activists that pronounce themselves as anarchists, feminists, autonomists, eco-feminists, indigenous, and so on.[2]

Within this debate, Silvia Federici's criticism of the notion of the commons in Hardt and Negri is notable.[3] For Federici, the image of a capitalism that nourishes itself solely on immaterial labour is questionable and politically limited. The facts demonstrate the persistence of the exploitation of labour-power in the countries of the global south, where capital has moved as a result of the reorganisation of global production in recent years. In other words, Federici's critique argues that the theoretical-political proposal of Hardt and Negri obscures the fact that the pre-eminence of immaterial labour in the 'Global North' has its other side in the intensification of the exploitation of manual labour in the regions of the 'Third World'. For that reason, it is impossible to think of emancipation through immaterial labour as long as there continues to exist a manual labour that sustains it. Nevertheless, if the commons of Hardt and Negri is a version of emancipation from the perspective of the struggles in the Global North, it might well be said that the work of Federici is an inversion of this perspective.

According to Federici the relocation of capital to regions of the Third World has had a disproportionate impact on women.[4] She argues that the massive exodus of men is one of the consequences of the 'new enclosures', war and hunger. This leaves women in more vulnerable conditions, since they have to face the attack on their subsistence economies, accept precarious jobs and suffer the effects of the programmes of structural adjustment. Women who try to combine access to a wage with domestic labour find themselves obliged to accept home-based jobs that end up involving the children as well.

In the light of these conditions, Federici argues, the emphasis on struggles over wages and within formal governmental institutions around the idea of discrimination does not challenge the root causes of women's misery. For her, the cause of women's misery is that 'globalization aims to give corporate capital total control over labor and natural resources'.[5]

In response to capital's aggressive move into the Third World there has been the emergence of a new cycle of struggles that seek to reclaim control of the material conditions of reproduction and impose limits to the commodification of all aspects of life, while at the same time creating new forms of social cooperation and mutual support.[6] These are struggles for the commons which, according to Federici, have contributed to the resignification of reproduction as the core of anti-capitalist struggle, in which women play a central role. This is why she considers the idea of the commons to offer an opportunity to transform and renew the feminist movement which has been divided through the institutionalisation of struggle. The refusal to see the reproduction of lives reduced to labour-power has motivated Federici to construct a theory of the commons from a feminist perspective, one that takes up the question of how 'to reorganize and socialize domestic work and thereby the home' as well as the problem of how to 'revolutionize' reproductive labour.[7]

While she does not espouse a political vision that naturalises femininity or domestic labour as a feminine vocation, it is difficult to suggest that Federici succeeds in avoiding it completely insofar as she definines repro-duction as the terrain of struggle and women as its historical subject. i.e.:

> If the house is the *oikos* on which the economy is built, then it is women, historically the house-workers and house-prisoners, who must take the initi-ative to reclaim the house as a center of collective life.[8]

In the same way that traditional Marxism fetishised the identity of the working class as the privileged subject of revolution, everything seems to indicate that Federici finds in women the historical subject of the commons:

> [T]he body has been for women in capitalist society what the factory has been for male waged workers: the primary ground of their exploitation and resistance, as the female body has been appropriated by the state and men and forced to function as a means for the reproduction and accumulation of labor.[9]

In this way, Federici's theory of the commons recreates the image of a new emancipatory economic model based on reproduction in counterposi-tion to the failed revolutionary goal of the conquest of state power, but without being able to overcome it. Hence the tendency to idealise subsist-ence economies and the different systems of communal property that exist in the Third World in so many places that have been outside capitalism. Or rather, the image of the emergent commons is projected on to the 'ideal communities' described by the utopian socialists to which Federici refers.[10] That is to say, the commons 'connects past, present and future and reminds us of a pre-capitalist world in which it was 'the poorest people's life support system.'[11]

Today financial institutions such as the World Bank and the IMF understand the positive effects of the commons in repairing the social fabric damaged by financial crises and in managing the self-destructive consequences of capitalism. For that reason, these institutions have been promoting the creation of commons that function as a sort of substitute or alternative to the welfare state. Faced with this problem, Caffentzis and Federici argue that anti-capitalist commons do not seek to cushion the destructive impact of neo-liberalism, nor to provide the social services that the state is unable to provide, but to 'transform social relations and create an alternative to capitalism'.[12] But how are we to distinguish capitalist *commons* from anti-capitalist *commons?* On what should one base such a classification?

It is obvious that we have problems if capital's reply to the struggles for *the commons* has been the creation of capitalist commons which seek to avoid its destruction. The separation of two antithetical commons shows a tendency towards convergence. That is to say that that which in the beginning was a movement of the negation of capital – the organisation of human practice that rebels against its domination – draws more and more towards its affirmation. It can be objected that the struggle for the commons is not a struggle for material things but for practices and social relations: that is, commoning as a practice. Nevertheless, the problem is not solved by simply changing nouns for verbs. It is not solved because it does not speak of the content of these relations, of the antagonism that traverses human practice and that, if it does indeed have the potential to create the commons, also has the potential to create its own negation: capital. In that sense, we cannot think of struggle as being external to capital. What we need to think is how to destroy it while part of it, something that implies an implacable critique of our own practices. Thus, the validity of the commons as movement of negation is not to be found in its being an answer to how to destroy capitalism, but in maintaining itself as a constant question.

Notes

1. Karl Marx, Capital, vol. 1 (Penguin Books: London, 1990), Part 8.
2. George Caffentzis, 'Commons', in K. Fritsch, C. O'Connor and A.K. Thompson (eds), *Keywords for Radicals: The Contested Vocabulary of Late-Capitalist Struggle* (Chico, CA: AK Press, 2016), pp. 93–101. Presentation at seminar Revolución Social, Reproducción de la Vida y Producción de lo Común, Puebla, Mexico, 18th October 2016.
3. See, especially, Michael Hardt and Antonio Negri, *Commonwealth* (Cambridge, MA: Harvard University Press, 2009).
4. Silvia Federici, *Revolution at Point Zero. Housework, Reproduction, and Feminist Struggle* (PM Press: New York, 2012).
5. *Ibid.*, p. 86.
6. Land struggles, time-banks, urban gardens, food coops, health clinics, women's organisations against the violence of the state and men, and more.
7. Federici, *Revolution at Point Zero*, p. 145.
8. *Ibid.*, p. 147.
9. Federici, *Caliban and the Witch: Women, the Body and Primitive Accumulation* (Autonomedia, New York, 2004).
10. 'The principle of the commons lived also in the writing and projects of the "utopian socialists", which inspired the formation of dozens of intentional communities,

many of them created in the United States in the period between 1830 and 1870. Marx and Engels objected to the celebration of the commons, as they did not believe the destruction of capitalism could be accomplished through the creation of "ideal" communities'. Silvia Federici, Towards a theory of the commons. Historical trends, ethical and political perspectives. Presentation at seminar, Revolución Social, Reproducción de la Vida y Producción de lo Común, Puebla, México, 20th October 2016.

11. *Ibid.*

12. George Caffentzi and Silvia Federici, 'Commons against and beyond capitalism', *Community Development Journal*, 49, (2014), pp. 192–1105.

V

STRUGGLES

20

In the Realm of the Self-Reproducing Automata

Nick Dyer-Witheford

Introduction

Capital's development of increasingly powerful forms of Artificial Intelligence (AI) promises, or threatens, major social transformations. It also poses a profound challenge to Marxist thought. George Caffentzis is one of the most original and important anti-capitalist theorists on this topic. His analysis, contained in a rich and complex series of essays written from 1980 to 2008, constitutes a sustained critique of the proposition that AI will mark the 'end of work', an idea common amongst both Marxist and non-Marxist thinkers.[1] Here, I discuss the context of George's writings on AI, his main thesis, arguments with other theorists, and the relation he posits between AI, capitalist globalisation and anti-capitalist movements. I then go on to discuss the recent emergence of new forms of AI, and their implications for the arguments of George and his opponents in this debate about AI, capitalism and class struggle.[2]

Automation, AI and Autonomists

In *Capital*, Marx argues that profit arises from the extraction of surplus value in commodity production. A commodity's value is the amount of socially necessary abstract labour time required for its production. Capital pays the worker enough to re-produce her or his labour-power, sufficient to ensure they turn up for work the next day, but claims as its own the additional value imparted to the commodity created by their work. This much – the labour theory of value – is Marx 101. It is also a proposition apparently defied by capitalism's historical tendency to create machines, from the Jacquard Loom to the cloud-based supercomputer, that match or exceed the productive capacity of workers not just in manual toil but, today, in the intellectual tasks whose automation is the mission of AI.

AI was incubated in the laboratories and universities of the US military-industrial complex from the end of World War II, inspired by code-breaking Alan Turing, cyberneticist Norbert Weiner and mathematical genius *cum* nuclear weapons designer John von Neumann: Caffentzis finds in John von Neumann's eerie description of a system of robots capable of manufacturing themselves – 'self-reproducing automata' – a prefiguration of capital's technological ambitions.[3] However, it took decades for such dreams to be even partially actualised. The first major steps were taken during the great late-twentieth century restructuring of advanced capital, in which from the 1970s on it moved from Fordist to post-Fordist production, globalised itself and adopted neoliberal policies. This transformation was a response to worker struggles, a counter-attack against the strike-power of the mass worker of assembly line factories, and to the unrests of students, anti-war protestors and feminists in the broader social factory. An important part of capital's offensive was intensified automation, including robots and early forms of AI; this crisis provided the context for George's initial writings on such machines.

The first industrial robots appeared on the shop floor of a General Motors plant in 1961, but it was not until a decade later that they began to become common in auto factories, first in Japan and then in the United States and Europe. By the 1980s, however, robots had been deployed against restless autoworkers from Ohio to Turin. Too rudimentary to be considered true AI, they were nonetheless a harbinger of wider technological change. The gradual diffusion of personal computers and the Internet from the Pentagon into civilian life was accompanied by a swell of interest in 'expert systems' and 'fifth generation computing' supposedly capable of taking over a wide range of jobs.[4] This fed into futurism about a post-industrial and or information society in which capital would supersede class struggles by means of advanced technologies.

Within the currents of autonomist Marxism that George was involved in there were differing theoretical and political responses to capital's embrace of high-tech, and, as he recounts,[5] their divergence became increasingly apparent in journals such as *Zerowork* and *Midnight Notes*. One line of thought, of which Antonio Negri was the major representative, based itself on Marx's 'Fragment on Machines' in the *Grundrisse*, a text whose translation into French, English and Italian in the early 1970s thrilled the radical left.[6] In the now-famous 'Fragment', Marx extrapolates from the industrial mechanisation of his age to hypothesise eventual near-fully-automated production systems. He suggests that while such automation might seem to mark the defeat of worker struggles, its undermining of the wage relation would actually destroy capital itself.

Negri and other autonomists regarded this passage as clairvoyant; robots and expert systems meant capitalism was already in a phase of technological self-destruction, and had only to be pushed over the brink by a mass 'refusal of work'. Later, Negri and his comrades added the idea that, though automation was eliminating manual work, the 'general intellect' on which capital relied for techno-scientific advance required 'immaterial labour'.[7] Intellectual, communicative and affective work that would empower post-Fordist labour as a new revolutionary subject ('the multitude') capable of re-appropriating high technology. A focus on 'cognitive capitalism' and 'cyborg' workers broadly characterise this 'post-operaismo' tendency.[8]

George acknowledges the excitement created by the discovery of the 'Fragment': 'The old mole had sprung from his hole to become a shining cyborg in the sky with diamonds!'[9] However, he became increasingly critical of Negri's theory about 'the increasing incommensurability of wealth and labor-time'.[10] Like other Marxist scholars, he noticed that the idea of capitalism automating itself out of existence is hardly characteristic of Marx's thought. After its appearance in the unpublished notebooks that constitute *Grundrisse*, this prediction does not reappear in *Capital*. Its place is taken by another idea (also mooted in *Grundrisse*), that of the tendency of the rate of profit to fall.[11] In this thesis, capitalism's automating tendencies decrease the proportion of living labour involved in production relative to machines and raw material, intensifying the 'organic composition' of capital. This diminishes the contribution to commodity production of the real source of value – living labour – and, all else being equal, results in a falling rate of profit (FROP), culminating in stagnation and crisis.

As George observes the FROP theory seems similar to that of the Fragment;[12] both see capital breaking down because of increasing automation. However, FROP logically contradicts the Fragment; the latter proposes the explosion of the labour theory of value, but the latter depends on its continuance to make the increasing organic composition of capital a cause of crisis. Many orthodox Marxists back the FROP against the heterodox 'Fragment'. However, FROP too has its problems, not the least being that Marx proposed a variety of 'counter-tendencies' to the FROP,[13] including the possibility of capital finding new sectors of production with 'low organic composition', a process that could defer crisis for a long time. The originality of George's approach to AI lies in devising an optic that follows neither standard FROP theory nor the Fragment, but rather focuses on the ongoing connection between sectors of capital with low organic composition (many workers, few machines) and high organic composition (many machines, few workers). For this, he draws on the ninth chapter of the third volume of *Capital*, 'Formation of a General Rate of Profit (Average Rate of Profit) and Transformation of Commodity Values into Prices of Production'.[14]

Here Marx suggests that while the profit extracted by capital as a whole depends on the overall amount of surplus value extracted within its entire system, there is no direct correspondence between any individual capitalist's profit and the amount of socially necessary labour they employ. This is because value is not identical with price; in the process of market exchange, surplus value is redistributed amongst competing capital by the operations of the price system. The direction of this transformation is away from capital with a low organic composition towards capital with a high organic composition. By this argument, automation or AI intensive businesses suck up and syphon-off the surplus value generated by labour intensive capital. George calls this 'the law of the increasing dispersion of organic composition', and proposes that 'every increase in the introduction of science and technology ... in one branch of industry ... will lead to an equivalent increase in the introduction of low organic composition production in other branches of industry'.[15]

In George's account, as in Marx's, the analysis of the translation of value into prices of production – 'the transformation problem' – remains at a high level of abstraction: the concrete processes by which the transfer occurs remain opaque. And though George sometimes criticises *Grundrisse*'s 'obscurity and inconsistency'[16] it has to be said that the third book of *Capital* is hardly less problematic: compiled by Engel's after Marx's death, it too is a chaotic, controversial text. As George acknowledges, Chapter 9 in particular has been a target of would-be 'Marx-killers', because of errors in its attempt to provide a mathematical account of the transformation problem.[17] Nonetheless, it gave him a theoretical framework within which to address ugly empirical features of capital's end-of-century restructuring overlooked by both anti-Marxist champions of post-industrial society and the Marxist enthusiasts for general intellect, features to which we will now turn.

Service Work and Sweatshop Labour

The concrete implications of George's position were clear: there would be no automatic end to wage labour, and no shift to high-tech work that was not counterbalanced by an expansion of the most exploitative forms of proletarian labour. He identifies two sources of a new wave of proletarianisation parallel to the advent of robots and computerisation. The first, which, clearly influenced by the work of Silvia Federici and other autonomist Marxist feminists, he analyses from the 1980s on,[18] is the induction into wage employment of a female labour force. Women previously engaged in unwaged household work were being increasingly hired to perform many of the same activities – care of the young, ill and elderly, cooking, hospitality – but now translated into commodity form. Thus within advanced capitalism the emergence of a high-tech economy with a predominantly masculine 'hacker' labour force of programmers and systems administrators is twinned with the emergence of a low-wage service economy, largely based on the female care work in the spheres of social reproduction.

The second source for the continuation and expansion of wage labour George points to is 'globalisation'. His early attention to this process, while it was still largely escaping the attention of many Marxists, is in part attributable to the time he and Silvia spent in Nigeria; the link to AI is made explicit in his 'On Africa and Self-Reproducing Automata'.[19] In this essay he points out that the high-tech deindustrialisation of the global North is simultaneous with a proletarianisation of the global South. Subsistence farming that had for millennia supported the largest part of the planet's population was slowly collapsing under the pressures of the world market, creating a new phase of 'primitive accumulation' – the dispossession and eviction of people from the land that had provided capital's first labour force.[20]

In Asia, Africa and Latin America, migrants streamed into vast new cities to eke out a living in informal economies, attempt further journeys towards the global North (where, as live in-nannies or domestic care workers they often joined the feminised service economy), or else enter the factories of *maquiladoras* and special export zones in Mexico, the Philippines, Malaysia, Thailand, Cambodia and, above all, China, in sweatshop conditions tantamount to a 'renaissance of slavery'. This, George pointed out, was completely contrary to ideas about an end of work. To update the figures he supplies: from 1980 to 2010 capital's planetary labour force expanded from 1.2 billion to approximately 3 billion, an increase that was not just a function of population growth, but also of deepening market penetration of the planet.[21] Capitalism has always drawn on world-wide labours: the slave trade, super-exploited colonial workers, and peasantry of the periphery all attest to this usually brutal truth. But what distinguished this new wave of proletarianisation was its systematic organisation within cybernetically coordinated systems of production and circulation.

The defining form of this 'global labour market' is the supply-chain.[22] In its ur-form, the supply chain headquarters research, design and marketing in the high-wage areas of the global economy, sub-contracts manufacturing, assembly, and back-end office functions to new industrialised territories where they can be rapidly scaled up or down with market fluctuations, and sends mining, waste disposal and other indiscreet activities to abyssal sacrifice areas where they vanish from sight. Supply chains thus characteristically connect moments of low and high organic production within a single, continuous production process. Their operations thus give us some insight into the transfer of surplus value from sectors of low organic composition to high organic composition that George describes theoretically.

Consider for a moment the production of Apple's iPhone, an exemplary device of informational capital. Its fabrication depends on the linkage of Apple's headquarters in Cupertino, California, staffed by a few hundred highly paid software designers working on advanced computer systems, through a series of manufacturing intermediaries in Europe, Korea and Japan, to the vast factories of Taiwanese electronics assembly contractor Foxconn, employing hundreds of thousands of workers under conditions of suicide- and riot-inducing militarised discipline in the industrial plants of China's Pearl River delta. Applied to the iPhone, 'tear down analysis' (a business methodology to analyse costs of production along a supply chain), shows that of an average iPhone price in 2011 of $630, manufacturing costs accounted for no more than $15.[23] The direct labour part of that cost – the part, that is, actually going to the thousands of Chinese workers in Foxconn factories – is tinier still, amounting to less than 2 per cent of the final price. Overall, from all entire supply chain, Apple drew a profit margin of 58 per cent.[24] This demonstrates the 'law of the increasing dispersion of organic composition' in action.

George's criticisms of the end of work thesis thus offered a perspective that recognised the simultaneity and interdependence of robot factories and sweatshops, fifth generation computing and migrant sex slaves. His work, along with that of Silvia and their comrades in *Midnight Notes*, was a vital contribution to understanding the new composition of global capital. It was also crucial to the self-understanding of movements *against* capital. The *alter-globalism* of the 1990s and early 2000s would see tentative alliances between protestors from the de-industrialising North and the newly industrialising South. Hardt and Negri's *Empire*, with its emphasis on rebel high-tech workers, certainly caught the spirit of indy media centres and open-source activism. But what really characterised the moment of the Battle of Seattle and similar rebellions was the paradoxical weaving, via computers and networks, of an 'electronic fabric of struggle' that, however problematically and provisionally, connected summit-busting students with sweatshop labour organisers, environmentalists with mega-dam protestors and hackers with Zapatistas.[25] It is in these 'strange loops' and 'short circuits' between zones of high and low organic composition of capital that George helped activists identify the incipient class composition of a new cycle of struggles.[26]

Machines Learning

George's writings on automata and high-tech capitalism span some 25 years from 1980 onwards. As it turned out, much of the initial promise for capital of technologies such as industrial robotics and expert systems remained unfulfilled. This was not just because of unanticipated technical problems, though there were plenty of those. The cheap labour global supply-chain probably actually deterred designing and adopting real artificial intelligence. Why invest millions on creating stitch-level robot-vision when you can sub-contract hundreds of women and children as textile workers making t-shirts on old sewing machines in Karachi slum basements for a few dollars a day?

However, by the second decade of the twenty-first century rather different forces, both technological and social, were starting to alter the prospects for 'self-reproducing automata'. Technologically, a new round of AI development started up. It was partly made possible simply by the progress of Moore's Law, the prediction that the digital processing capacities available for a given price will double every eighteen months, which by 2010 had held up for nearly half a century. It was also, however, a fruit of the vast streams of data generated by search engines and social media that have appeared since 2004, as Google, Facebook and Twitter became household names.

Although the new AI involved many elements, the major component was 'machine learning'. The basic concept of machine learning is that AI, rather than requiring top-down programming of computers with general rules applicable to a specific situation (as with 'expert systems'), could be acquired bottom-up by machines taught to learn. Algorithmic processing of enormous volumes of data – be it about credit defaults, terrorist attacks, consumer preferences or legal judgements – can enable computers to inductively detect significant patterns, predict outcomes and then recommend or initiate actions to alter those patterns. In his lucid introduction to machine learning, computer scientist Ethem Alpaydin says its key innovation is that 'Data starts to drive the operation; it is not the programmers anymore but the data itself that defines what to do next'.[27]

The drive to machine learning was, however, not just a matter of technological possibility. It directly relates to new social struggles. The 9/11 attacks on the World Trade Center, marking the eruption of a theocratic, reactionary armed struggle against capitalist modernity, not only effectively killed *alter-globalism*, but also propelled a vast US state interest in techniques for surveillance and mass data processing, which then, via the organisations such as the CIA venture capital arm, In-Q-Tel, spilled over into corporate applications.[28] The so-called war on terror drove advances in robotics, drones and data gathering. Elsewhere on the planet, the decomposition of the mass worker in the North was generating fresh arenas of factory struggle. Over a decade, Chinese assembly line wages were driven up ten-fold by Pearl River strike waves. Cheap global labour was no longer so cheap. Inevitably, capital's thoughts turned again to automation. Following the notorious Foxconn protest-suicides of 2010, the company's owner, Terry Gui, promised to replace assembly workers with one million robots; though this promise has so far only been fractionally fulfilled, it shows how resort to intelligent machines is driven by fear of unruly proletarians.

These events catalysed capital's broader concerns in the wake of the 2008 Wall Street crash. Over the last two decades, computers, social media and smart phones have remade everyday life and placed Apple, Alphabet-Google, Microsoft, Facebook and Amazon in the top ten global corporations by market capitalisation.[29] What they have *not* done, except briefly at the end of the 1990s, is generate the productivity increases necessary to stabilise and continue the 1 per-cent's spectacular accumulation of wealth and power.[30] Today's push to AI adoption arises not just from the desire of giant info-corporations to profitably install themselves as producers of the means of production, but from a more general capitalist anxiety to find the engine of a new phase of economic growth. However, achieving this goal requires more proletarian pain, as is made clear by both of the two main-stream hypotheses about AI's likely employment effects: AI-Apocalypse and Business as Usual.

The AI-Apocalypse version, represented by MIT computer scientists Eric Brynjolfsson and Andrew McAfee's *Race against the Machine* (2011) and *The Second Machine Age* (2014), predicts an imminent jobs crisis produced by digital automation and machine learning, extending beyond routine manual work to journalism, advertising, lawyering and other middle-class occupations. This prophecy was corroborated by a study from Oxford economists Carl Frey and Michael Osborne (2013) claiming that 47 per cent of the 702 occupations into which US jobs are conventionally sorted are 'likely to be substituted by computer capital' within the next twenty years. In the same vein, Martin Ford's *Rise of the Robots: Technology and the Threat of a Jobless Future* (2015), surveys the possible consequences of the latest robotics and artificial intelligence in dozens of fields and suggests that their combined and interacting impacts will massively exceed capital's job-generating capacities. This, then, is a revival of the 'end of work' predictions that George contested two decades ago.

Against this, business-as-usual mainstream economists invoke historical precedent to argue automation cheapens commodities, increases sales and hence both boosts human works in un-automated parts of the labour process and generates new sorts of jobs (Autor, 2015). Thus – to cite a common example – although ATMs and online banking reduced banks' need for tellers, lower labour costs lead them to multiply branches and retrain staff for personalised up-selling of financial services; so far, the number of employees remained roughly constant. Business-as-usual analysis also stresses the limits of current AI's, most of whose achievements are in for-malised situations – such as games – rather than uncontrolled environments. The message is that capital should keep calm and carry on, as AI-driven job loss will be limited, and remediable by skills upgrading. However, as the 'usual' in 'business as usual' includes capital's regular cycles of creative destruction, its advocates admit the possibility of a 'difficult transition' (Economist 2016b) and blandly explain 'there will be winners and losers' (Greengard 2015: xv) – never a good sign.

Recent studies often split the difference between apocalyptics and scep-tics, scaling back the percentage of employment at imminent risk but admitting the possibilities of a significant net job loss (Arntz et al. 2016; Economist 2016; LeClair et al. 2016; WES 2016). All these rival predictions are, however, speculative, looking forward between ten and 40 years. Nonetheless, some indications of a new wave of automation are already apparent. In the United States, the threat of new robotisation is being used to quell wage demands: Ed Rensi, a former MacDonald's CEO responded to the 'fight for fifteen' minimum wage campaign by remarking 'It's cheaper to buy a $35,000 robotic arm than it is to hire an employee who's inefficient making $15 an hour bagging French fries' (Rosen 2106). These threats may exceed capital's actual capacities, but not necessarily for long: a burger-flipping robot was introduced in a California fast-food chain in 2017.[31]

Equally apparent now is the connection between artificial intelligence and precarity. It is not just that contingent work is the necessary resort of the technologically unemployed. Forms of labour that atomise and routi-nise tasks stand in a circular relationship to AI, which can first organise those tasks, and then, by machine learning, absorb them. Thus Amazon's Mechanical Turk's distributed downloading of simple cognitive tasks is referred to as 'artificial artificial intelligence'; the irony is 'turkers' train real artificial intelligences that may one day replace them.[32] Similarly, Uber's software automated dispatch and management functions is now revealed as only the first stage of much fuller, driver-replacing automation.[33] Clearly, the AI apocalypse, if it comes, will arrive masked by the gig economy and other forms of precarious work.

The current class implications of AI also, however, extend beyond the workplace. Machine learning and big data yield the algorithmic profiling now ubiquitous in corporate and state decisions on loans, insurance, med-ical claims and job applications. Such machinic decisions, by intention or oversight, persistently discriminate against anyone who – by postal code, ethnicity, gender, credit history – display evidence of penury or precarity.[34] Machine learning has now, in the hands of capital, becomes the means for an ever more rigorous, comprehensive and recursively self-confirming social stratification sifting grades of labour-power and credit risk. This is even without mentioning the national security systems that in the name of fighting terrorism enable the identification, monitoring and prediction of any form of anti-capitalist militancy.

Beyond this, it has to be said, there is great uncertainty.

Apocalypse as Usual?

George's discussion of AI, despite its vigorous defence of the labour theory of value, is, in its long-term horizon, remarkably open. This is especially the case in two of his later essays on 'Turing machines', i.e. computers.[35] He observes that 'As with all machinery, the Turing machine defines a terrain of struggle with its own landmarks and history that are still in formation'.[36] He also remarks that:

> There is a tension between the old and new in our historical condition with respect to science and machines that needs to be isolated and resolved ... the enormous productivity (and violence) brought about by introducing a new order of machines into the work process is putting ... stress onto the categories of capitalist (and anti-capitalist) self-understanding.[37]

Ultimately, he says, computers *do* pose a serious challenge to the labour theory of value, because,

> [A] universal Turing machine can imitate or instantiate any rule-governed act of labour. If there was, therefore, a positive aspect of labor that created value, either individually or collectively, then one can conclude that machines also, at least theoretically, can produce value.[38]

So in this section I will, in frankly speculative mode, take up a question George asks: 'does the Turing machine create the conditions for a new type of conflict between workers and machine *qua* capital?'[39]

Machine learning does not simply promise to significantly enlarge the scope of tasks capital can automate. It also enables machines to produce problem-solving outcomes that are unforeseen and not even well understood by their programmers. This jeopardises the monopoly on creativity that is a last-ditch humanist defense against machinic replacement. Alpaydin suggests 'Intelligence seems not to originate from some outlandish formula, but rather from the patient, almost brute force use of simple, straightforward algorithms' and then remarks 'it will not be surprising if this type of learned intelligence reaches the level of human intelligence some time before this century is over'.[40] Such forecasts have of course been all too frequent in the past. However, in the case of machine learning they do not depend on some moment of mystical 'singularity', in which machines attain self-awareness. On the contrary, the new model of AI points (perhaps more disturbingly) to the 'de-coupling of intelligence from consciousness'.[41]

Recent AI exploits by machine learning AI's, such as the Jeopardy victory of IBM's Watson and the defeat of grandmaster Lee Se-Dol by Google's Alpha Go, have made the hailing of robot overlords a virulent cultural meme. Such fears and hopes may collapse on technological reefs, as previous AI summers have been followed by AI winters. The 'Hype Cycle of Emerging Technologies', plotted by the market research company,[42] places machine learning at a 'Peak of Inflated Expectations' before an anticipated 'Trough of Disillusionment'. Even if this is followed by a renewed climb towards a 'Plateau of Productivity' the ascent may take longer than AI Apocalyptics imagine. Automation is a matter not just of technological capability but of the respective cost to capital of machines and workers. If workers remain weak and disorganised, with wages stagnating or declining, capital's incentive to replace them is low; only if struggles for wage demands intensify, or the state subsidises AI infrastructures, is advance likely to be quick.

Yet even if machine learning's ambitions of are only slowly realised, they may still yield a level of automation beyond that foreseen by most Marxist theorists. George contends AI capital will always be matched with low wage service workers and global proletarianisation in the global south. But both these options are threatened by machine learning technologies that can target, for example both call centre work and garment sewing in South East Asia.[43] Globalisation and automation will certainly continue to proceed side by side (China's capitalist today are both outsourcing to Vietnam and Bangladesh and rapidly adopting industrial robots) but capital may be shifting its weight from one foot to the other. Equally problematic, however, is the *post-operaismo* assumption that, while material work is automated, new strata of immaterial labour will be summoned into existence. It is accountants overtaken by financial algorithms, journalists confronting automated sports reporting, lawyers looking at computerised discovery processes – that are threatened by machine learning. Creating the infrastructures for ubiquitous machine learning will require a large coding workforce but portions of this work too could be up for automation.[44] The prospect of a generalised intellectual workforce may be overtaken by a far more military sense of 'general intellect': automated machinic command.

Ultimately the scope of automation opened by machine learning may not simply involve jobs. It is possible that capital could incrementally replace each stage of the circuit of capital by cybernetic components; robots producing autonomous vehicles, vehicles that then robotically perform the circulation functions of transport and communication, while with a credit card number ordering their own gas, repairs, toll rates, spare parts, the whole ensemble providing the object of algorithmic, high speed financial speculation. This would be the logical fulfillment of von Neumann's world of self-replicating automata.[45]

Unlikely as this may seem, the very genesis of capital lies in an almost comparable convulsion; that of the vast human eviction from the land that goes by the name of primitive accumulation, conducted over some two centuries, accompanied by the 'discovery' and conquest of a 'New World', with all the enslavements and exterminations this entailed. The advent of von Neumann-style machine capitalism, potentially devoid of human bosses or human workers, would surely be a comparably protracted and tumultuous process. But capital may indeed, after successive centuries of primitive accumulation and the formal and real subsumption of labour, shedding labour in favour of machines, autonomising itself from the human. We could call this 'futuristic accumulation' – or 'apocalypse as usual'.

When George concedes that AI's could create value for capital, he falls back to suggest that 'labor's value-creating capacities must lie in its negative capability, that is, its capacity to refuse to be labor' or its 'self-reflexive negativity'.[46] Be that as it may (machines too can 'refuse to work', by 'accidents' that, as interruptions of surplus value extraction, are from capital's point of view, ontologically equivalent to a strike),[47] proletarian hopes for a better world definitely *do* depend on the capacity for refusal. People will get AI that releases them from dangerous and degrading labour, in a context of equality, cooperation and human self-development, only if they can reject the AI that capital wants to give them, which will render humans evermore superfluous and precarious within an increasingly machinic system of production.

In the United States today, the decomposition of the mass worker has resulted in a toxic conjunction, as rage at deindustrialisation's job loss is hijacked by a racist, xenophobic nationalism and directed against foreign workers and immigrants. President Trump as saviour of the working class does not mention automation, though many of the jobs he has so far 'saved' are slated for that fate. His demand that US corporations repatriate production to a deregulated homeland could trigger an orgy of AI automation, aided by the infrastructural programs such as remaking highways for driverless transportation: 'made in America, by robots'. Yet if the fear of the alien immigrant is replaced by confrontation with the alien power of capital incarnate in AI, this will create a new terrain of struggle.

It is possible that in the riots and occupations around the world that followed the Wall Street crash we can see some very faint foreshadowing of struggles against futuristic accumulation; movements of increasingly precarious proletarians and downwardly mobile middle strata, over-matched in the workplace by capital's technologies and global strategies, joined by apprehensive students and militant hacktivists, directly confronting in the streets and squares the state apparatus that protects an order of mounting inequality and inhumanity. To this mix could be added add other elements that have emerged more recently: the post-Snowden opposition to Big Data-culling surveillance; the resistance to police of Black Lives Matter and indigenous activists; the resurfacing of demands for public control of the economy in the new electoral politics of Podemos, Sanders and Corbyn. But, *pace* Marx, and George, the history of struggles against capital's most recent attempt to create a realm of self-reproducing automata is yet to be written 'in letters of blood and fire'.

Notes

1. Caffentzis, 'The end of work or the renaissance of slavery? A critique of Rifkin and Negri', *Common Sense*, 24 (December 1998); revised and reprinted in Werner Bonefeld (ed.) *Revolutionary Writings: Common Sense Essays in Post-Political Politics* (Brooklyn, NY: Autonomedia, 2003). This essay and most of this series are collected in Caffentzis, *In Letters of Blood and Fire: Work, Machines, and the Crisis of Capitalism* (Oakland, CA: PM Press, 2013). An important exception is Caffentzis, 'From the *Grundrisse* to *Capital* and beyond: Then and Now', *Workplace*, 15, 2008, pp. 59–74.

2. This paper draws on conversations and collaborations with James Steinhoff and Atle Kjosen.

3. Caffentzis, *In Letters of Blood and Fire*, p. 127; John von Neumann, 'The General and Logical Theory of Automata', in James Newman (ed.) *The World of Mathematics* (New York: Simon and Schuster, 1956).

4. Pamela McCorduck and Edward A. Feigenbaum, *The Fifth Generation: Artificial Intelligence & Japan's Computer Challenge to the World* (New York: Addison-Wellesly, 1983).

5. Caffentzis, 'From the *Grundrisse* to *Capital* and beyond'.

6. Antonio Negri, *Marx Beyond Marx: Lessons from the Grundrisse* (New York: Autonomedia, 1984); Karl Marx, *Grundrisse* (Harmondsworth: Penguin, 1973 [1857]), pp. 690–712.

7. Michael Hardt and Antonio Negri, *Empire* (Boston: Harvard University Press, 2000), pp. 289–300.

8. Caffentzis, *In Letters of Blood and Fire*, p. 95.

9. Caffentzis, 'From the *Grundrisse* to *Capital* and beyond', p. 68.

10. *Ibid.*, p. 6.

11. Marx, *Grundrisse*, p. 748; *Capital*, vol. 1 (New York: Penguin, 1976), pp. 772–6; *Capital*, vol. 3 (New York: Penguin, 1981), pp. 317–38.

12. Caffentzis, 'From the *Grundrisse* to *Capital* and beyond'.

13. Marx, *Capital*, vol. 3, pp. 339–48.

14. *Ibid.*, pp. 254–73.

15. 'From the *Grundrisse* to *Capital* and beyond', p. 71.

16. *Ibid.*, p. 60.

17. *Ibid.*

18. *In Letters of Blood and Fire*, p. 11.

19. Originally published in Midnight Notes Collective, *The New Enclosures* (Jamaica Plain, MA: Midnight Notes, 1990); reprinted in *In Letters of Blood and Fire*.

20. Marx, *Capital*, vol. 1: 873–95.

21. World Bank, *World Development Report 2013: Jobs* (Washington, DC: World Bank 2013), pp. 3–4.

22. Richard Dobbs et al., 'The World at Work: Jobs, Pay, and Skills for 3.5 Billion People', McKinsey Global Institute, 2012, p. 1. At www.mckinsey.com/insights/employment_and_growth/the_world_at_work.

23. Tim Worstall, 'China Makes Almost Nothing Out of Apple's iPads and iPhones', *Forbes* (accessed 24 December 2011). At www.forbes.com/sites/timworstall/2011/12/24/china-makes-almost-nothing-out-of-apples-ipads-and-i/#76579bf60b4b.

24. Horace Dediu, 'iPhone sine qua non', *Asymco* (accessed 26 February 2012). At www.asymco.com/2012/02/26/iphone-sine-qua-non/.

25. Harry Cleaver, 'The Zapatistas and the Electronic Fabric of Struggle' (1995), at https://webspace.utexas.edu/ hcleaver/www/zaps.html.

26. Midnight Notes Collective, *Midnight Oil: Work, Energy, War, 1973–1992* (New York: Autonomedia, 1992).

27. Ethem Alpaydin, *Machine Learning* (Cambridge, MA: MIT Press, 2016), p. 12.

28. Michael Jablonski and Shawn Powers, *The Real Cyberwar: The Political Economy of Internet Freedom* (Urbana, IL: University of Illinois Press, 2015), p. 80–5.

29. 'Rise of the Superstars', *The Economist* (accessed 17 September 2016). At www.economist.com/news/special-report/21707048-small-group-giant-companiessome-old-some-neware-once-again-dominating-global.

30. Robert J. Gordon, *The Rise and Fall of American Growth: The U.S. Standard of Living Since the Civil War* (Princeton: Princeton University Press, 2016); Doug Henwood, 'Workers: no longer needed?' LBO News (accessed 17 July 2015). At https://lbo-news.com/2015/07/17/workers-no-longer-needed/.

31. Fortune Editors, 'There's Now a Robot That Can Flip Burgers', Fortune.com (accessed 14 March 2017). At http://fortune.com/2017/03/14/miso-robotics-flippy-burger-flipping-robot/.

32. Hope Reese and Nick Heath, 'Inside Amazon's Clickworker Platform: How half a million people are being paid pennies to train AI', *Tech Republic* (2016). At www.techrepublic.com/article/inside-amazons-clickworker-platform-how-half-a-million-people-are-training-ai-for-pennies-per-task/.

33. Paul Mason, 'The battle over Uber and driverless cars is really a debate about the future of humanity', *The Guardian* (accessed 31 October 2016). At www.theguardian.com/commentisfree/2016/oct/31/paul-mason-driverless-cars-uber-artificial-intelligence-unemployment.

34. Cathy O'Neill, *Weapons of Math Destruction: How Big Data Increases Inequality and Threatens Democracy* (New York: Random House, 2016).

35. 'Marx, Turing machines, and the labor of thought' and 'Crystals and analytic engines: historical and conceptual preliminaries to a new theory of machines'. Both in *In Letters of Blood and Fire*.

36. *In Letters of Blood and Fire*, p. 200.

37. *Ibid.*, p. 198.
38. *Ibid.*, p. 181; see also p. 161.
39. *Ibid.*, p. 180.
40. Alpaydin, *Machine Learning* (2016), p. xii.
41. Yuval Noah Harari, *Homo Deus: A Brief History of Tomorrow* (New York: Signal Press, 2016), p. 101.
42. 'Gartner's 2016 Hype Cycle for Emerging Technologies Identifies Three Key Trends That Organizations Must Track to Gain Competitive Advantage' (accessed 16 August 2016). At www.gartner.com/newsroom/id/3412017.
43. Jae-Hee Chang and Phu Huynh 'ASEAN in Transformation: The Future of Jobs at Risk of Automation' International Labour Organisation (accessed July 2016), www.ilo.org/wcmsp5/groups/public/---ed_dialogue/---act_emp/documents/publication/wcms_579554.pdf.
44. Tony Beltramelli, 'pix2code: Generating Code from a Graphical User Interface Screenshot'. Submitted to 31st Conference on Neural Information Processing Systems (NIPS 2017), Long Beach, CA, USA. At https://arxiv.org/abs/1705.07962.
45. See Atle Mikkola Kjøsen, 'Do Androids Dream of Surplus Value?', Conference paper, Mediations 2.5, London, Ontario, 18 January 2013. At www.academia.edu/2455476/Do_Androids_Dream_of_Surplus_Value; Philip Mirowski, *Machine Dreams: Economics Becomes a Cyborg Science* (Cambridge: Cambridge University Press, 2001).
46. *In Letters of Blood and Fire*, p. 181; see also p. 175.
47. I owe this observation to a conversation with Kjosen.

21

Notes from Yesterday: On Subversion and the Elements of Critical Reason

Werner Bonefeld

Subversion and Critique

Subversive thought is none other than the cunning of reason when confronted with a social reality in which the poor and miserable are required to subsidise the financial system for the sake of sustaining the illusion of abstract wealth. Yet, this subsidy is necessary in existing society, to secure its wealth and prevent its implosion. This rational irrationality of a capitalistically organised mode of social reproduction is at the centre of the critique of political economy. The critique of political economy is intransigence towards the existent patterns of the world. It demands that all relations 'in which man is a debased, enslaved, forsaken, despicably being have to be overthrown'.[1] What, therefore, has to be done – how to 'produce revolution'?[2]

The social relations of price and profit cannot be fought in a direct and immediate manner. What really would it mean to struggle against the inflation or deflation of money, oppose the circulation of coins, combat the movement of interest rates or prices, and resist poverty in a mode of social reproduction that entails the dispossessed labourer in its concept of wealth, that is, of money as more money?[3] It is not the independence of economic categories of cash and coin, value and money, as forces over and above, and also in and through the social individuals that requires explanation. Rather, what needs to be explained are the social relations of production, which manifest themselves in the form of a relationship between economic things that assert themselves behind the backs of those same individuals that comprise and sustain society. In capitalism, the social relations of production are fundamentally production relations of abstract wealth, of money as more money. Capitalist society reproduces itself by making money beget more money. Time is money, and money appears to posit itself as more money without certificate of birth. The dispossessed labourer, the history of 'blood and fire'[4] is the hidden secret of capitalist wealth. Anti-capitalism is however neither a fight for economic and social justice nor for benevolent governance of the economic forces. It is a fight for a new mode of production in which wealth is not money but rather freely disposable time.

The mysterious character of an equivalence exchange between unequal values (M...M′) lies in the concept of surplus value, and that is, in the class relationship between the owners of the means of production and the dispossessed producers of surplus value. For the sake of capitalist wealth, the worker personifies not just labour time but fundamentally surplus labour time, which is the time of profit. Critical reason wants to know what profit is. It thus thinks through the category profit to reveal its birth certificate in the surplus labour of a whole class of dispossessed workers. What a perversion! In order to make a living, the dispossessed have to make a profit for the buyers of their labour-power as condition of sustained employment. And sustained employment is necessary for continued wage-based access to the means of subsistence, produced for the capitalist by labour and purchased back from the capitalist with the wage income received as a result of the trade of labour-power. Profitable capitalists buy labour-power; unprofitable ones make labour redundant. How can the dispossessed labourer without employment make a living? What really are the alternatives to wage-labouring in capitalist society? Begging? Kidney sales? Surrogate motherhood? Pornography? Snuff movies? Gangland muscle?

In the harsh reality of a society in which the profitable exploitation of labour determines the conditions of access to means of subsistence on the part of a dispossessed class of surplus-value producers, justice is the civilised category of domination. What is a fair and just wage?[5] Anti-capitalism does not mean struggle for existence. That struggle belongs to capitalism; the class struggle is about access to the means of subsistence. In order to know what capitalism is, one has to look into the economic categories of price and profit to uncover the sheer unrest of life of a whole class of workers that literally works for their supper, day in and day out, struggling to make ends meet. Capitalist wealth, money as more money, does not reveal this struggle for subsistence; instead it presents itself as a system of injustice between the rich and the poor. In capitalism, the demand for justice belongs to its conceptuality of wealth that seems to appear without certificate of birth. Suffering must be recognised as the immanent substance of capitalist wealth. Class struggle is therefore not a positive category of a struggle for justice, formal equality, and rights of participation and voice. Rather, class struggle is a negative category. It belongs to a society in which the class tied to work is under the compulsion to produce surplus value for the buyer of her labour-power as condition of making a living in competition with all other sellers of labour-power on world-market scale.

British jobs for British workers, or American jobs for American workers, expresses the reality of labour-market competition in nativist terms. The racialised and gendered character of labour markets belongs to the concept of wage-slavery. In this context the demand for equal access of all sellers to all labour markets is both progressive and delusional. They are an affront to civilised notions of a universal humanity; and because of this their critique is also delusional. It is not the racialised and gendered character of the labour market that is so offensive. Rather it is the institution of the labour market itself. The trade in labour-power comprises an exchange between the owners of the means of subsistence and the dispossessed producers of surplus value. In class society the appeal to the values of universal humanity masks 'victors', 'justice' – and clearly racialised and gendered markets have to go. The liberal rule of law is preferable to naked oppression and division, nativism and colonialism. In this contradiction, the appeal to justice resides as a civilising force in class society.[6]

Anti-capitalism means the production of an alternative to capitalism so that the muck of ages comes to a standstill. For this production, the idea of regulating capitalism for the benefit of workers posits a fool's paradise.[7] The planned economy of labour is no alternative to the free economy of labour. Anti-capitalism does not mean a rationalised labour economy; it means the end of the labour economy and the beginning of social relations in which wealth is freely disposable time – the time of labour and the time for enjoyment (Marx) belong to entirely different human realities, the one identifies human beings as means, the other recognises humanity as a purpose. In the commune of human purposes, of 'communist individuals' (Marcuse), humanity does not express itself in the form of 'clipped coins' and the law of abstract equality (Caffentzis). It is not a society of human worth (Hobbes). It is rather a society of human dignity (Bloch).[8] Dignity as the basis of society entails the creation of an entirely new form of equality, that is, an equality of human needs.

On Critical Reason: Beyond Personalisation

The idea of socialism as a planned labour economy by and large conceives of Marx's *Capital* as an economic 'text'. This conception recognises the sheer unrest of life in capitalism as an expression of its unplanned economic character. From this, the economic socialist derives his demand for economic planning: rational life is planned life. Unrest is not a category of socialist planning. Rather it presents a bourgeois prejudice that requires elimination for the sake of socialism. In the planned economy everybody knows their place in the social factory and behaves accordingly, internalising the functions of government. Economics is the formula of a quantified world in which the satisfaction of individual human needs is just a side-show. This stance raises the question about the meaning of critique in the critique of political economy. What is criticised? According to Marx, his critique of political economy amounts to a 'critique of economic categories' and he argued that 'the' economists identify the economic categories as natural things.[9] That is, in the hands of the economists the 'law of capitalist accumulation [is] metamorphosed ... into a pretended law of nature'.[10] Nature cannot be revolutionised. Rather, to prevent its destruction, human kind has to adapt to its laws and regulate its natural process, from the cap-italist idea of a free economy to the socialist idea of a planned economy. The simple idea that labour economy comprises definite relations of human social reproduction is anathema to the economist approach to society. In abstraction from society, what is economics?

The critique of political economy focuses on the system of economic inversion and its categories of cash, price and profit to decipher the social relations that vanish in their appearance as personifications of 'particular class-relations and interests'.[11] Just as the critique of religion does not crit-icise God on the basis of God, the critique of political economy does not criticise real economic abstractions on the basis of real economic abstrac-tions, which can lead only to scholastic debates about neoliberal economics and Keynesian alternatives, free markets and economic resource manage-ment, planning for competition (Hayek) or planned labour economy (Lenin). Rather, and continuing with the critique of religion, it deciphers the social relations that assume the form of God and vanish in the idea of God only to reappear as cowed believers in God, mere human derivatives of divine rule. Similarly, the critique of capital is not a critique from the standpoint of some transhistorically-conceived economic nature that assumed the form of capital and might in some future again assume a state socialist form.[12] Like the critique of religion, it too sets out to decipher the social constitution of the mysterious, seemingly extra-mundane economic forces that prevail not only over the social individuals but, also in and through them. The subject of capitalist society is a coined subject, and what is coined is also clipped.[13] To be a free wage labourer is a great misfortune. It is not an historical privilege. The struggle for subsistence is not glorious, it succeeds as survival. It is a struggle for access to basic things. Glorifica-tion of this struggle as an historical privilege is offensive – it celebrates the struggle for subsistence without asking itself what really is there to celebrate?

The point of the critique capitalist society is not to 'make the individual responsible for relations whose creature he socially remains, however much he may subjectively raise himself above them'.[14] It is not sufficient to criti-cise capitalists for their seemingly excessive addiction to profit, nor bankers for pursuing money for the sake of more money. On the pain of ruin, these behaviours manifest the 'objective necessity' of the capitalistically constituted social relations. Neither the capitalist nor the banker, nor indeed the worker can extricate themselves from the reality in which they live and which asserts itself not only over them but also through them, and by means of them. The critique of the banker, or any other politico-economic operative of a system that asserts itself as an independent force over and through the social individuals, misses the object of critique. The critique of political economy is neither a critique of the personifications of economic categories nor does it personalise the critique of capitalism. It does not argue that the economy of labour is corrupted by the private interests of the capitalist and his political friends, from which derives the demand for political action to set things right, ostensibly in the interest of the class that works – the working class. Clearly it is in the interest of the working class that it works; the alternatives are bleak. Yet, what really does it mean to say that work defines the interest of the working class? What would it mean to say that freely disposable time is in the interest of the working class? The critique of the capitalists and the bankers as responsible for the plight of workers leaves capitalism untouched by thought. It is of course the case that the capitalists experience capitalism as a source of great enrichment and immense power. In this context Max Horkheimer and Theodor Adorno have argued that the 'rulers' are safe for as long as the 'ruled' struggle under the spell of the inverted world, in which, say, the cause of financial crisis, economic downturn, and conditions of austerity are attributed to the greedy behaviour of identifiable individuals.[15] A spell-bound critique of capitalism demands more of this and less of that. It apportions blame and proclaims to know 'how to set things right', ostensibly in the interests of the class that works, securing its employment for a fair wage. For the sake of better-paid wage slaves and sound conditions of employment, it is, say, the profit-making consciousness of the capitalist and the greed of the speculator that is criticised, rejected and condemned. That is, the critique of the capitalist manifests itself as a demand for a better capitalism, one that works in the interests of the class that works. Marx's critique of Proudhon focused on this simple point.[16] Proudhon substituted a critique of the capitalist for the critique of capitalism; he sought to free capital from the capitalist so as to utilise the power of capital for the benefit of a well-ordered society, investing in society for the benefit of workers.

The critique of the capitalist leaves the category of capital not only entirely untouched, it also elevates 'capital' as a thing beyond critique. Instead of a critique of capital, it identifies the guilty party, condemns it, and demands state action to sort things out and set things right, for the sake of humanity, justice and equality. It thus attributes capitalist conditions to the conscious activity of some identifiable individuals, who no longer appear as the personification of economic categories but, rather, as the personalised subject of misery. The personalised critique offers scapegoats – it transforms the rightful critique of capitalism into (populist) resentment against the identified wrongdoers.[17] This personalisation of the economic categories entails a number of differentiations, most importantly between the productive or indeed creative capitalist as a 'producer' of 'real' wealth employing a hard-working and creative people, and the financial or indeed parasitic capitalist who makes his fortune by speculating in money to the detriment of industry and workers. Here the distinction between use-value and concrete labour, on the one hand, and exchange value and abstract labour, including the manifestation of value in the form of money, on the other, appears in the forms of distinct personalities – pitting the creative industrialist against the parasitic banker-cum-speculator. There emerges, then, the idea of a capitalism that is corrupted by the financial interests. Finance turns capitalism into a casino that turns the fortune wheel of the world at the expense of national industry, national wealth, national workers, and national harmony. Money as more money does however not corrupt capitalism. It is the principle of capitalist wealth. The nativist critique of capitalist wealth, money as more money, is Trumpean to the core. For purposes of mass entertainment and populist appeal, it criticises Wall Street and pockets the proceeds.

The capital fetish manifests itself in the form of money as a most incomprehensible form of wealth. It also makes it seem as if the movement of money, which suddenly and without warning has the capacity to cut a whole class off from access to the means of subsistence, expresses the conscious activity and the will of bankers, financiers and speculators. That is, a definite form of social relations manifests itself in the form of a movement of money and then, under the spell of this money movement, rebels against the personifications of a world governed by money. The personalised critique of capital identifies the 'wrongdoer' of the wronged society and calls him a merchant of greed. For the sake of employment and industry, something needs to be done. Something can be done! The personalised critique of capitalist social relations is open to abuse from the outset. It thinks akin to a register of blame, and condemns the identified party as cosmopolitan peddlers who, supposedly, hide behind the economic phenomena, sucking the living life out of the national community of hard-working people, wreaking havoc, from foreclosures to privatisation of seeds and destruction of subsistence farming. The contemporary idea that so-called neoliberal capitalism resulted from a Washington-based agreement between money and power, the so-called 'Washington consensus', purports the idea, at least by implications, of a conspiratorial construction of a finance-driven world economy that, buttressed by the political and military might of the United

States, exploits the – original – nations of the world for the sake of financial wealth, that is, parasitic wealth. This critique, too, knows whom to blame and what to do. The critique of financial imperialism entails the idea of anti-imperialism as a progressive, liberating force. The reverse of anti-imperialism is national liberation, by which the dominated national communities defend their identity in opposition to the disintegrating forces of financial globalisation and imperial power. The idea of the nation as a subject of liberation is as irrational as the belief in a national destiny and a national homogeneity of purposes, from the national industry via the national interest to the national history. The idea of the nation as the foundation of being and becoming recognises the terms 'cosmopolitanism' and 'internationalism' as terms of abuse. In their stead, it puts its faith in the imagined nation as some naturally rooted and active thing, which it idolises as the 'spirit of the people' – like Trump's enunciation of the American people who require walls to assure themselves as national friends. The spirit of the people requires the image of the national enemy. In the friend-enemy relationship, the enemy is the most important. It defines the friends under duress since the friends themselves might be classed as enemy should they lack in national resolve. If indeed it is permissible at all to speak about the national spirit of the people, it is a national spirit not by nature, but by history. By reducing history to nature or by reading nature into history, the notion of national greatness, origin and resolve, becomes delusional inasmuch as a people are forced to act as if they really are natural beings that have a national history. This critique of capitalist wealth is entirely regressive and authoritarian to the bone. It does not admit of knowledge. It admits only of acknowledgement.

Notes from Yesterday

The communist individual is not the hidden secret of capitalist social relations. Rather, its hidden secret is the force of the law-making violence of expropriation that divorced the mass of the population from the means of subsistence, cutting the producer of social wealth off from the direct access to the means of life and making her a wage slave at best.[18] The force of law-making violence appears in the form of economic compulsion, which facilitates the selling of labour-power as apparently an act of free will. In this context, the introduction of labour-saving machinery does not create freely disposable time. It rather lengthens the social working day and makes labour redundant, increasing labour-market competition. History does not stand on the side of the oppressed. Nor does it unfold for their benefit. In fact, history does not unfold at all. '*History* does *nothing*, it "possesses *no* immense wealth", it "wages *no* battles". It is *man*, real, living man who does all that, who possesses and fights; "history" is not, as it were, a person apart, using man as a means to achieve *its own* aims; history is *nothing but* the activity of man pursuing his aims'.[19] These aims are not theologically determined, naturally founded, or purposefully active. History neither creates nor burns witches. Mankind does – not as a natural being but as a member of a definite form of society.

The purpose of capitalist society is the profitable accumulation of abstract wealth for its own sake. The commune of human purposes is not an existing human purpose. Its reality is entirely negative. History appears as a linear sequence of events, from one battle to another and from this division of labour to that division of labour, culminating in the present. This appearance is real but by itself, devoid of meaning. What does it really mean to say that history is a sequence of events? Events of what and what was so eventful? With Silvia Federici and George Caffentzis one thus needs to think out of history, out of the battles for freedom, slave insurrections, peasant revolts, the struggles of Les Enragés, working-class strikes, riots, insurrections and revolutions, to appreciate the traditions of the oppressed, recognise the smell of danger and the stench of death, gain a sense of the courage and cunning of a struggle for food, grasp the spirit of sacrifice, comprehend however fleetingly the density of a time at which the progress of the muck of ages almost came to a standstill. History does not lead anywhere; it has no telos, no objectives, no purpose, and it does not take sides. At its worst, it continues on the path of victorious progress under darkened clouds and smoke-filled skies. At best, its progress will be stopped. Such history has not been made yet, though it has often been attempted. In our time, this attempt is called communism – this attempt at negation that seeks to rid the world of 'all the muck of ages'. For Marx, the struggle against oppression is the struggle of the last oppressed class, time and time again. The proletariat is the name of the oppressed class of our time. Marx says that it is the last class. It might not be the last class, though, and if it is not, then the continuum of history will not have been broken.

Class struggle is not about abstract ideas. It is a struggle for access to 'crude and material things'.[20] What then is the working class 'in-itself' struggling for? 'In-itself' it struggles for better wages and conditions, and to defend wage levels and conditions. It struggles against capital's 'werewolf-like hunger for surplus labour'[21] and its destructive conquest for additional atoms of unpaid labour time, and thus against its reduction to a mere time's carcase. It struggles against a life consisting solely of labour-time and thus against a reduction of human life to a mere economic resource. It struggles for respect, education and recognition of human significance. Above all it struggles for food, shelter, clothing, warmth, love, affection, knowledge, time for enjoyment and dignity. Its struggle as a class 'in-itself' really is a struggle 'for-itself': for life, human distinction, life-time, and above all, satisfaction of basic human needs. It does all of this in conditions, in which the increase in material wealth that it has produced, pushes beyond the limits of its capitalist form. Every so-called trickle-down effect that capitalist accumulation might bring forth presupposes a prior and sustained trickle up in the capitalist accumulation of wealth. And then society 'suddenly finds itself put back into a state of momentary barbarism; it appears as if famine, a universal war of devastation had cut off the supply of every means of subsistence'.[22]

The existence of the social individuals as personifications of seemingly self-moving economic forces does not entail the reduction of social consciousness to economic consciousness. It entails the concept of economy as an experienced concept, and economic consciousness as an experienced consciousness. Dispossession, struggle to make ends meet, solidarity and labour market competition, collective organisation and strike breaking, employment and unemployment, destitution and enclosure, time is money and money is money only as more money, are not abstract things. The dispossessed work for profit and a profit needs to be made so that their employment can be sustained. Working for profit is the condition of sustained wage-based subsistence. Capitalist society does not reproduce itself despite the class struggle. Rather, it reproduces itself through the class struggle. The celebration of the class struggle has to stop. It celebrates capitalist society. Still, in present society there is no alternative to class struggle. The working class either struggles for subsistence or does not, in which case naked life beckons. George Caffentzis's question, how to 'produce revolution' really is the question of how to overcome 'dispossession' (Midnight Notes) and constitute a mode of social reproduction of human satisfaction. The contemporary term of the struggle against the antagonist society, supposedly rupturing its dialectic of reproduction, is Commons – unlike the term council communism, which entailed the politicisation of the social labour relations by the direct producers themselves, it is a term of peaceful association in a hostile society. There is as much history as there is struggle to stop its further progress. Communism is the movement of stopping history in its tracks. Let's politicise the Commons. There is no certainty.[23]

Notes

1. Karl Marx, *Contribution to the Critique of Hegel's 'Philosophy of Right'*. Introduction, in Marx and Engels *Collected Works*, vol. 3 (London: Lawrence and Wishart, 1975), p. 182.
2. George Caffentzis, 'Lenin on the Production of Revolution', in Werner Bonefeld and Sergio Tischler (eds), *What is to be Done? Leninism, Anti-Leninist Marxism and the Question of Revolution Today* (Aldershot, 2002), pp. 150–67.

3. On dispossession as the premise of capitalist wealth, see the contributions by the Midnight Notes Collective, Massimo De Angelis, Mariarosa Dalla Costa, George Caffentzis and Werner Bonefeld in *Subverting the Present. Imagining the Future*, edited by Werner Bonefeld (New York: Autonomedia, 2008), and Silvia Federici, *Caliban and the Witch: Women, the Body and Primitive Accumulation* (New York: Autonomedia, 2004). On contemporary forms of primitive accumulation and struggle, see, for example, the contributions by Federici, De Angelis and Raquel Gutiérrez-Aguilar in *Austerity and Revolt*, special issue of *The South Atlantic Quarterly*, edited by Werner Bonefeld and John Holloway (vol. 113, no. 2; Spring 2014).

4. George Caffentzis, *Letters of Blood and Fire: Work, Machines, and the Crisis of Capitalism* (Oakland: PM Press, 2013).

5. Adam Smith makes this point succinctly when he argues that the wage labourer is responsible for her own subsistence, whereas the slave is in the keep of his masters. The slave is thus of 'more expense than the worker' and the 'work of a freeman comes cheaper than that performed by a slave'. Smith, *An Inquiry into the Nature and Causes of the Wealth of Nations* (Indianapolis: Liberty Fund, 1981), p. 87. Or as Marx (*Capital*, vol. 1, London: Penguin, 1990, p. 719), put it, 'The Roman slave was held by chains; the wage-labourer is bound to his owner by invisible threads' inasmuch as her access to the means of subsistence is governed by the rate of accumulation that determines the rate of unemployment and therewith the conditions of the buying and selling of labour-power. In conditions of wage slavery, what is just?

6. On justice movements, see Silvia Federici, 'On capitalism, colonialism, women and food politics' (interviewed by Max Haiven), *Politics and Change*, issue 2 (2009). At https://politicsandculture.org/2009/11/03/silvia-federici-on-capitalism-colonialism-women-and-food-politics/.

7. For an early critique of this post-capitalist idea, see Caffentzis, 'The end of work, or the renaissance of slavery', in Werner Bonefeld (ed.), *Revolutionary Writing: Common Sense Essays in Post-Political Politics* (New York: Autonomedia, 2003).

8. Karl Marx, *Theories of Surplus Value*, vol. 3 (London: Lawrence and Wishart, 1972), p. 252. Herbert Marcuse, *Soviet Marxism: A Critical Analysis* (London: Routledge and Kegan Paul, 1958), p. 127. George Caffentzis, *Clipped Coins, Abused Words and Civil Government: John Locke's Philosophy of Money* (New York: Autonomedia, 1989). Thomas Hobbes, *Leviathan* (Oxford: Oxford University Press, 1996), p. 59. Ernst Bloch, *The Principle of Hope*, three volumes (Cambridge, MA: The MIT Press, 1995).

9. Karl Marx, 'Letter to Lassalle, 22 February 1858', in *MEW*, vol. 29 (Berlin 1963), p. 550. On 'the' economist as a thinker of un-reflected presuppositions, see Karl Marx, 'Letter to Engels, 2 April 1958', in *MEW*, vol. 29 (Berlin 1963), p. 315.

10. Theodor Adorno, *History and Freedom* (Cambridge: Polity, 2006), p. 118.

11. Marx, *Capital*, vol. 1 (London: Penguin, 1990), p. 92.

12. That at least is the political project of Leo Panitch and Alex Callinicos, and other likeminded believers in socialism as a system of (national) economic planning. For a critique see Werner Bonefeld, 'From humanity to nationality to bestiality', *ephemera: Theory and Politics in Organization*, 12(4), 2012, pp. 445–53.

13. See Werner Bonefeld, 'Capital as subject and the existence of labour', in *Emancipating Marx (Open Marxism, vol. III)*, edited by Werner Bonefeld, Richard Gunn, John Holloway and Kosma Psychopedis (London: Pluto Press, 1995), pp. 182–212; and Caffentzis, *Clipped Coins* (1989).

14. Marx, *Capital* (1990), p. 92.

15. Theodor Adorno and Max Horkheimer, *Dialectic of Enlightenment* (London: Verso, 1979), p. 179.

16. Karl Marx, *The Poverty of Philosophy* (Moscow: Progress Publishers, 1955) and Karl Marx, *Grundrisse* (London: Penguin, 1973), pp. 239–89.

17. As Trump has it: keep them out and lock her up! On this, see Werner Bonefeld, 'Authoritarian liberalism: on class and rackets' *Logos*, 16(2) (2017). At http://logos journal.com/2017/authoritarian-liberalism-class-and-rackets/.

18. Midnight Notes Collective, *The New Enclosures* (Jamaica Plain, MA: Midnight Notes, 1990); Silvia Federici, *Caliban and the Witch: Women, the Body and Primitive Accumulation* (New York: Autonomedia, 2004).

19. Marx and Engels, *The Holy Family*, in Marx and Engels *Collected Works*, vol. 4 (London: Lawrence and Wishart, 1975), p. 93.

20. Walter Benjamin, 'Theses on the Philosophy of History', in *Illuminations* (London: Random House, 1999), p. 246.

21. Marx, *Capital*, vol. 1, p. 353.

22. Karl Marx and Friedrich Engels, *The Communist Manifesto* (London: Pluto Press, 1996), p. 18.

23. To embrace communism is to embrace uncertainty. See Werner Bonefeld, 'Uncertainty and Social Autonomy', *The Commoner*, 8 (2004) and Werner Bonefeld, 'Critical Theory, History, and the Question of Revolution', in Shannon Brincat (ed.), *Communism in the 21st Century*, vol. III, pp. 137–61 (Santa Barbara: Praeger, 2014).

22

Sunburnt Country: Australia and the Work/Energy Crisis

Dave Eden

In September 2017 those of us living in Australia were told that we faced an 'energy crisis'. The Australian Energy Market Operator identified looming shortfalls in electricity production, the increased likelihood of blackouts and continuing sharp rises in prices for households and businesses.[1] Also predicated is a shortfall in the supply of gas for the domestic market, meaning both a potential rise in gas costs for households and manufacturing and another force pushing up prices for electricity production.[2] Over the last decade retail power prices have risen 63 per cent higher than inflation.[3] Yet despite concerns about the dwindling supply of energy production it seems very unlikely Australia will reduce carbon emissions to meet the mild targets of the Paris climate agreement.[4] We are stuck facing a scorching summer sweating our arses off as the planet burns up.

What I want to do here is to examine the writings of George Caffentzis on energy and show their power for understanding our predicament. Energy for Caffentzis is never just a scientific or technical question with scientific or technical answers: 'the first thing to note is that the term "energy crisis" is a misnomer. Energy is conserved and quantitatively immense, there can be no lack of it. The true cause of capital's energy crisis in the last decade is work, or more precisely, the struggle against it'.[5] Can this approach be applied to the current energy crisis in Australia?[6]

Energy Crisis and Theoretical Deadlock

What's going on in Australia? At one level the causes of the energy crisis arise from the inability of any fraction of capitalist politics to ensure the reliability and price of energy necessary for capital accumulation in a way that maintains, facilitates and increases the very same accumulation whilst shifting away from the use of fossil fuels towards renewables. Perhaps this is an unsolvable problem for capital.

Energy prices in Australia are a product of a strange dynamic: retail companies push prices as high as they can go whilst renewable technologies threaten to force wholesale prices down – which causes a drop in investment and thus supply and thus soaring prices. Renewables may be be attractive for investment due to their much lower capital and input costs than fossil fuel energy production. But the spread of renewable energy generation threatens the profitability of all energy production and its intermittent nature can cause savage price spikes.[7] This unfolding dynamic, in the context of policy uncertainty, and the general, global malfunction of profitability means capital is mothballing coal-fired plants but not moving with sufficient size or speed into wind and solar. Profit drives investment and thus supply – and profit is in distress. Profit appears to be simply the excess on top of costs.[8] However, its deep origin is the exploitation of labour. The operation of prices and the movement of capital means that where labour is exploited and where profit is realised can be separated by time, space and ownership. A breakdown in profits is a breakdown in capital's ability to accumulate dead labour from living labour at a level that is sufficient for its continual accumulation.

This is not a view that gets any airplay in Australian debates. Both the left and the right share a logical structure to explain and to lay blame: bad people, bad ideas and rent seeking behaviour by certain sectors of the energy industry. For the government, the problem is environmentalism and its hold on the Australian Labor Party, the Greens and influential, but disreputable, sectors of the population who have hobbled the expansion of the coal power generation and gas exploration due to their irrationality. Prime Minister Turnbull typified the South Australian Premier's renewable heavy energy policy as 'ideology and idiocy in equal measure'.[9] For the left it is the alliance of fossil fuel capital, conservative politicians and climate change denialists who have incinerated the world's future by breaking the mechanism that would have placed a price on carbon. In the *Quarterly Essay* Anna Krien writes: 'How has this happened? In part it is because Australia has a political system captured by the fossil-fuel industry. It is a political Stockholm syndrome built on donations, royalties, taxes and threats … parliament has become a transit lounge for politicians and their staffers on the way to fossil-fuel companies and their lobby groups. Inertia is the result'.[10]

Right and left also share a logical structure to their solutions. If only political power can be taken away from their enemies and bad ideas dispelled, then a new wave of investment can be undertaken which would both solve the energy crisis and launch a new frontier of capital accumulation.

Such approaches are deeply flawed and do us damage. Theory isn't everything – but ideas matter.[11] They matter in how we understand the horizon of possibilities and they impact the choices and actions we attempt to make within that horizon. If we can't see the possibility of a way out of capitalism then we must implicitly or explicitly accept the premises and needs of capital and thus are caught discussing other ways of fuelling accumulation.

Writing after the Fukushima disaster, Federici and Caffentzis argue that the critique of nuclear power couldn't simply be contained to the subject of nuclear power; rather it needed to become a more general critique of capitalism for it to even function successfully as a critique of nuclear power. 'What we need is to approach the question of nuclear power as the prism through which to read our present relation to capital and to bring together different struggles and forms of resisting together. Short of that, our political activities will remain powerless, separated and fragmented...' This is because questions of energy production are *not* simply technical questions of energy production. 'Nuclear power is not just an energy form, it is a specific form of capital accumulation and social control...'[12]

The limits of theory are also a limits of *class composition*. Writing in both the late 1970s and early 1990s the Midnight Notes Collective argued that ecological/Green politics which failed to understand the question of energy within the dynamics of capital accumulation and class struggle also failed to link ecological issues with the questions of daily life around energy prices.[13] They took issue with a moralistic lifestylism where people tried to live more simply and austerely.[14] Their retort was such efforts function as a way of developing 'cheap reproduction' of an intellectual segment of proletarians 'for capital'.[15] That is the reduction of the costs of what it took to reproduce the labour-power of a specific group of workers. Such efforts remained the preserve of only a fraction of the working class – those involved in tertiary and intellectual labour and who lived in rural and semi-rural areas. They argued when an ecological movement speaks in the name of the general interest of humanity, or nature, or the earth, or morality, *in practice* it expresses a limited sectional interest.[16] Not connecting to questions of power prices, working conditions and daily life fails to understand the dynamics that propel global capitalism and the struggles that could overcome it. This failure is also the failure to understand the power that holds the possibility of another society. Writing about the struggle of workers at International Paper in Jay, Maine and their support for environmental ordinance, the Midnight Notes Collective write: 'For if one generalises the Jay worker's tactic into a struggle that denied capital the possibility of enclosing and selectively destroying the natural commons gratis, a truly revolutionary crisis would emerge'.[17] This struggle 'fundamentally challenged prevalent green politics. In place of the question of how to clean rivers, for example, they demanded control over the mill'.

The environmental movement can learn an essential lesson from Jay if it accepts some basic realities. First, that virtually all of the land in the country is owned by some sector of capital. Second, that as long as capital owns the land it will also control how the land is used. Third, that the capitalist priorities which generate pollution cannot be effectively challenged without the political power and organised support of the local working class.[18]

In the 1980 essay 'The Work/Energy Crisis and the Apocalypse' Caffentzis makes the following argument: 'Capital's Apocalypse is the inverse image of the struggle against it'. Energy crises – whether they be a shortage of energy, its costs or the ecological damages that arises from it – are responses to the struggles that go on within capitalism. And it is only these struggles themselves that can banish these crises by going another leap further. 'At root all the missiles, bombs, atomic power plants, all the "idols of the theatre" that capital displays so provocatively, is the struggle against capitalist accumulation, against a life dominated by work and exploitation'. Here Caffentzis was taking aim at the nuclear power technocrats and the no-growth steady state puritans. Both 'merely repropose the crisis' they fail to comprehend.[19]

Work/Energy Crises

Caffentzis grasps that questions of energy can only be understood within unfolding dynamics of class struggle and class composition within the capitalist mode of production by grasping the role that prices of production play in funnelling surplus-value from its point of creation to its point of accumulation as profit.

In 'The Work/Energy Crisis and the Apocalypse' Caffentzis explains an energy crisis and the two different sides that have arisen to explain and solve it. In the face of rising electricity costs and increasing awareness of the ecological impacts of energy production Caffentzis typifies the different approaches as 'anti-limitationists' and 'collective interactionists'.[20] Both shared an understanding that the energy crisis (which was expressed in high energy prices) consisted of dwindling finite resource stocks and the destructive impacts of using these fuels. On one side, anti-limitationists, here played by the nuclear physicist and hydrogen-bomb maker Edward Teller, wanted to solve both through a vast expansion of nuclear power and the complete rationalisation of the social body through the expansion of computerisation and technological expertise. On the other side, the interactions, represented by Elizabeth and Howard T. Odum, a sociologist and an ecologist, dreamt of a low-tech future of a steady state of complex, organic, but ultimately stationary societies build on hard work.[21]

Caffentzis critiques their shared commonalities. Both were deeply critical of the social disorder of the 1960s and 1970s, of the manifold rebellions and the popular assertion of pleasure over duty. Both sides saw 'too much "chaos", uncontrolled behaviour, too many demands and not enough work'.[22] Their utopias were built on the reimposition of work discipline – the only difference is whether it was imposed through high or low tech means.

Both sides failed to understand what was causing the crisis of energy. The energy crisis was not due to simply the volume of the stock of resources or their ecological impact: it was a product of a social crisis. Prices were rising not because the world was running short of coal, oil and gas, but rather because the composition of capital was changing as a reaction to the explosion of struggles in the 1960s and 1970s. As capital fled from rebellions and struggles, high energy prices were a result of surplus value being syphoned from its point of origin to energy companies via the tendency of capital to generate an average rate of profit since market prices fluctuate around prices of production.

The social order of the post-war US capitalism was built around two poles: the factory floor as the site of wage-labour and the domestic house as the site of unwaged reproductive labour. Both these poles had been thrown into chaos by struggles on both the molar and molecular level.

If the 'energy crisis' began in 1973, the logical place to look is in the period immediately before. What was happening to work/energy then? A capitalist catastrophe in commodity production and the reproduction of labour-power. Need we take out the old filmstrips? The ghetto riots, the Panthers, campus 'unrest', SDS and the Weatherpersons, a strung-out imperial army, DRUM in Detroit and the West Virginia wildcats, the welfare office sit-ins, the shooting of Andy Warhol, SCUM, the Stonewall blowout, Attica.[23]

Caffentzis cites the drop in the profits in relation to wages and the rise in government spending in total and on social services specifically as measures of this wave of insubordination.[24] Workers demanded more money and less work and struggles across society either demanded increased government spending, or the state attempting to ameliorate them through spending, thus increasing the tax burden on capital. Both were symptoms of a general refusal to work. In response to this, capital moved. It fled from the factory to the nuclear power plant and high-tech industries (as well as to the Global South). As the family fell apart it poured into the commodification of reproductive labour: the service industry.

Core to Caffentzis' explanation is his application of Marx's theorisation of the way the prices and values diverge – the so-called 'transformation' problem. High energy prices, the apparent signal of a shortage of resources, was the mechanism that made energy capital profitable. This worked because prices diverge from values and capital accumulates in relation to the size of its investment. The surplus-value generated through the exploitation of workers in low tech services becomes the profits of high-tech energy firms. Caffentzis can explain this through a *practical* application of Marx's arguments.

Marx knew that on the day-to-day level prices constantly fluctuated with supply and demand. In *Capital*'s first volume Marx argues that in a society where wealth takes the form of commodities prices gravitate around and express the value of a commodity.[25] Value arises as non-commensurable utilities made by non-commensurable labour process are made commensurable through exchange. Value is an abstraction that, given the level of social need and productivity, expresses through money how much abstract socially-necessary labour time is embodied in each type of commodity. As *Capital* unfolds more and more layers are added to this understanding. In Volume 3 Marx unveils a major modification to his theory: prices diverge from values.[26] In the capitalist mode of production firms exist in competition with each other. This competition works as a dynamic that leads to a tendency to establish an average rate of profit where the returns to capital aren't based so much on the exploitation of the workers they directly employ but rather the size of the capital invested. This works via two interrelated dynamics: prices for a type of commodity gravitate around prices of production (the average costs of production plus the average rate of profit) and capital from less profitable spheres moves to more profitable ones.

'What competition brings about, first of all in one sphere, is the establishment of a uniform market value and market price out of the various values of commodities.'[27] In a particular sphere of capitalist industry, firms that produce more inefficiently or expensively than the average in that industry are still compelled to sell at approximately the social average and are thus either driven to the wall or compelled to improve their productive organisations. More productive and cheaper producers reap extra benefits and thus others in the industry chase after them. Between different spheres, capitalism flees from sites of lower profit to high. 'Capital withdraws from a sphere with a low rate of profit and winds its way to others that yield higher profit.'[28] As more firms enter the more profitable industries, the increased crowding of the market forces profits down whilst industries that see capital flee from it see a drop in supply and thus a consequent rise in prices and profits. These very differences force changes in investment and production that create a tendency towards averaging just as they also constantly upset the average.

Caffentzis echoes Marx that this process masks itself to its participants through its very operation.[29]

He does not see it, he does not understand it, and it does not in fact interest him. The actual differences in magnitude between profit and surplus-value in the various spheres of production (and not merely between the rate of profit and the rate of surplus-value) now completely conceals the true nature and origin of profit, not only for the capitalist, who has here a particular interest in deceiving himself, but also from the worker. With the transformation of values into prices of production, the very basis for determining values is now removed from view.[30]

Debates over the transformation problem tend to focus on questions of logical consistency on the level of theory.[31] Caffentzis shows that understanding the dynamics of the average rate of profit and the gravitation of prices around prices of production is key to understanding how capitalism works *in practice* – especially energy capital. In a paper presented to a conference in Japan in 2012 Caffentzis stated:

One of the fundamental aspects of the capitalist mode of production is that the site where workers are exploited (and surplus value is created) is not the place where the surplus value appears as profit, rent or interest This is one reason for the mystifying aspect of the system. If human labour is central to the creation of values, then how could capitalist corporations that sell commodities produced with very little direct labour (like the electricity produced in nuclear power plants) be able to have even average profits? And on the other side, if human labour is central to the creation of values, those corporations that require very little capital and employ many workers to produce commodities (like the uranium mined in Niger) are usually the most exploitative, but often they barely can appropriate even the average rate of profit. At first one asks in wonder, how is this possible? Its answer is another question, imagine if it did not happen? Since capitalists will only invest in or own commodity-producing corporations so that they will accrue at least an average rate of profit, that means that high capital-intensity corporations experiencing profits below the average (sic) rate will find no new investors (who would invest their money in industries they hope will at least give them an average rate). If surplus value equalled (sic) profits, then such corporations would stop producing commodities that might be quite crucial to the whole system of production. And, after all, capitalists are not philanthropic towards each other nor are they willing to sacrifice even a tenth of their profits for the good of the whole capitalist class (as their complaints concerning taxation attest). If so, how do highly capital-intensive industries (like electricity-producing corporations) that are essential to the operation of many other industries because they supply crucial energy inputs not become investment pariahs leading to a whole crucial branch of industry going bankrupt?[32]

Caffentzis makes the same argument in relation to oil.[33] Oil was important to global capitalism in the twentieth century, (its future is contested).

Oil functions as an input into many other commodities. The price of oil plays a central role in the function of prices throughout capitalism. Oil companies make up 'fifteen of the forty largest companies in the world deal in the extraction, transport and, refinement of oil and gas' and the composition of oil industries is one where the ratio of technological investment to labour is incredibly high.[34] Oil companies are profitable because they realise as profit surplus-value that is produced through the pores of the capitalist system as a whole. This is also why oil is a concern for capitalism as a system on a whole: what happens to these profits matters. Will they flow back into capital accumulation or will it be directed elsewhere?

This is exactly why so many 'responsible' capitalists are concerned about the behaviour of OPEC leaders, for in the last two decades too many of these leaders appear to be 'out of control' (from Quaddafi, to Khomeini, to Hussain, to Chavez, to a new generation that might, after a few changes of dress and rhetoric, include Abu Bakr al-Bagdadi). 'Responsible' capitalists can no longer be sure that the surplus value transferred to the Middle East or Venezuela to purchase oil would be dutifully recycled into Swiss, New York or London Banks as it was in the past. Now it might go to Korans for a *madrassa* in Kabil or rocket-propelled grenade launchers for ISIS.[35]

What was so unique about the Midnight Notes Collective's analysis of the first Iraq War (Desert Storm) is that they saw that the real problem for capital was the working class in the Middle East which demand too much of those profits in the form of wages and social spending. It was the oil proletariat, broadly conceived, that needed to be bombed and disciplined to ensure an acceptable level of profit flowed back to the appropriate coffers.[36]

Australia's Price Shock

In his work on energy and energy struggles, Caffentzis uses categories developed by Marx to analyse specific concrete situations. We can use a similar methodological approach to understand the looming energy crisis in Australia. This looming energy crisis isn't a product of technology nor politics – but rather of the dynamics of profit and struggle. The difference is that Caffentzis used Marx's work to explain how energy capital syphoned up surplus-value made elsewhere as profit; here other elements of Marx's work on the average rate of profit are also needed.

What is crucial to grasp about capital's tendency toward an average rate of profit is that it takes place in real time and across a real geography. These movements contain multiple potentials for interruption and malfunctioning. Capital cannot simply teleport from one industry to another fully formed. The two conditions that facilitate it functioning are the mobility of capital and the mobility of labour:

This constant equalisation of the ever-renewed inequalities is accomplished more quickly, (1) the more mobile capital is, i.e. the more easily it can be transferred from one sphere and one place to others; (2) the more rapidly labour-power can be moved from one sphere to another and from one local point of production to another.[37]

The specifics of certain industries and certain capitalist societies retard both. In Australia high energy prices are driven by the tendency towards an average rate of profit via the formation of an average market value and through the flow of capital from one sphere to another – and also by their interruption and retardation.[38]

The Development of Renewables is a Revolution in the Cost of Creating Energy

Generators bid into the market to provide electricity for each five-minute interval of every day. AEMO ranks all bids in order from cheapest to most expensive (the 'bid stack') and dispatches the cheapest set of bids that meets the needs of the system. The prices paid to all generators dispatches is the bid of the last generator needed.[39]

Derivate contracts are used to hedge the price. Renewable energy threatens to drive the prices down. 'Wind and solar have high capital costs but effectively zero marginal costs; once the facility is built, the energy produced is essentially free.'[40] Renewable energy works to force down the price of producing energy through a massive lowering in the required inputs in labour, machinery and resources (variable and constant capital). The changing composition of energy production is changing the price of production.

Paradoxically, this is not leading to an immediate drop in prices but rather is pushing them up by contributing to a drop in supply as fossil fuel production leaves the market but little new investment flows into renewables. Renewable energy means a massive recalculation in the value of energy – one which renders coal and gas generation of electricity increasingly unprofitable. On the other hand, renewable energy generation requires a large initial investment and is intermittent and impacted by weather. In the absence of reliable storage this will lead to spikes in prices as supply fluctuates. Added to this renewable energy generation draws on a clean energy subsidy and policy uncertainty means that this source of income is not guaranteed long term. Thus, we are witnessing a revolution in the production of energy that is making coal fired technology uncompetitive – but changes to the cost price of power are happening in a way that is leading to dwindling supply and thus paradoxically higher prices.

Now it could well be that capital is actually in the process of moving from coal into renewables – yet so far it isn't. But even if it was this would take time – years in fact – and in the intervening period the actual amount of energy produced dwindles and thus prices rise and supply is unreliable. The very processes of moving to create an average rate of profit in real time creates feedback and distortions in and of itself.

On the other side is the retail energy market. In Victoria, the state that most completely privatised energy prices have risen 200 per cent since 2000.[41] The most common explanation is that ecological charges have pushed up costs. This is bullshit. Rather it is the operation of profit within the particular structures of this market, where energy sold by the largest corporations dominate and consumers are trapped. Very few people are going to choose not to have power. In this sense the average rate of profit is deformed. Here, estimated profit margins (revenue minus costs, so not so dissimilar to Marx's notion of the rate of profit) is 14.4 per cent whilst the profit margin for retail generally is around 4 per cent.[42]

Marx argues that in a particular market the regulation of prices has to do with the composition and structure of the firms competing with each other. When a market is dominated by the firms typified by large investment and high ratio of means of production to labour the market price isn't viable for less productive firms and the former 'forcibly makes room for itself'.[43] In retail energy we have a situation where large vertically integrated companies lead the market, charge high prices and make considerable profit, and smaller competitors, that have higher operating costs, try to compete by offering lower prices but then struggle to be viable.[44] The dynamics in wholesale energy production and in retail are pushing prices up.

Can we see in these prices the operation of struggles from below? Caffentzis' and the Midnight Notes Collective's earlier works are able to point to large and complex social movements. In Australia, where the old barometers of struggle such as trade union membership and days lost to industrial action show a depressing droop we need to be more sensitive to Marx's Old Mole.[45]

You can't be too mechanical about these things. Capital, labour and class struggle are global. You don't have to find a struggle in a postcode to try to explain the movements of capital there. We could say the long-term shift to renewable energy, however partial and incomplete, is the product of decades of environmental struggles 'denying capital its "right to shit"'.[46] As the Midnight Notes Collective and Friends write, 'The reduction of the costs of constant capital can lead to an increase in the profit rate, but it crucially depends upon being able to "externalize" the harm it causes'.[47] But more specifically we can see the struggles against coal and gas mining, especially coal seam gas, shutting down fracking in multiple states and sites and delaying the construction of coal mining, have both blocked new investment and also prevented an increase in the supply of inputs for fossil fuel power generation, a corresponding drop in price and thus a rise in profitability for gas and coal powered electricity.

Gas is especially interesting. In 2014–15 gas generated 21 per cent of electricity in Australia.[48] The majority of Australian gas is already committed for international markets.[49] Paradoxically, internationally, there is growing concern of over-supply.[50] In Australia not only are prices threatening profitability but there is a concern that supply will not be met in 2018–19 – this is partially because as coal production of energy reduces, gas is seen as a stop-gap to renewables.[51] Tellingly the federal government is trying to get state governments to over-turn bans on fracking and pressure gas producers to divert supplies to the domestic market.[52] The fact they have failed speaks to the power of the movements more than the clear thinking of state governments.

Conclusion

These struggles against mining, against the ability of capital to both eat and shit, have drawn together a coalition of urban environmentalists, farmers and rural hippies. The technical nature of mining means that small groups of people have been able to be quite effective in disrupting or at least delaying its operations. Yet isn't this again a repeat of the problem that the Midnight Notes Collective identified earlier: a limited class composition that fails to really address the driving force of capital accumulation? The real threat to profitability is the combination of struggles: against the expansion of mining, by workers within mining and the refusal of customers to pay prices that companies demand as just part of the movement of the class. This would terminate the profitability of the sector and thus capital accumulation. But how to do this? Caffentzis' and the Midnight Notes Collective's problem remains our problem. At the end of 'The Work/Energy Crisis and the Apocalypse' Caffentzis argues the only way we can avert apocalypse is to struggle for a better life. 'As Polish workers have shown, the only way to confront the missiles is to demand more and juicier sausages: "Only those who strike eat meat".'[53] A viable future doesn't lie in more work but rather the struggle against it.

Notes

1. Australian Energy Market Operator, Advice to Commonwealth Government on Dispatchable Capability, 2017, Electricity Statement of Opportunities for the National Electricity Market, 2017.
2. Australian Energy Market Operator, *Update To Gas Statement Of Opportunities*, 2017.

3. Kate Griffiths, *Why are our electricity bills so high? The answers may surprise you.* The Grattan Institute (accessed 13 December 2017). Available from https://grattan. edu.au/news/why-are-our-electricity-bills-so-high-the-answers-may- surprise-you/.

4. Rod Campbell, 'Meeting our Paris Commitment', *Climate & Energy*. The Australia Institute, 2017.

5. George Caffentzis, In *Letters of Blood and Fire: Work, Machines and the Crisis of Capitalism* (Oakland, CA: PM Press, 2013), p. 16.

6. Caffentzis, and the Midnight Notes Collective he is part of, take up the claim that class struggle is the motor-force of history but they reject the Italian workerist and postworkerist emphasis on the centrality of the most productive sections of the working class. Rather shaped by the feminist concerns of Wages for Housework they give special attention to those seemingly on the margins of or outside the wage relation. George Caffentzis, 'The End of Work or The Renaissance of Slavery?' In *Revolutionary Writing: Common Sense Essays in Post-Political Politics* edited by Werner Bonefeld (Brooklyn, NY: Autonomedia, 2003), pp. 115–33; Silvia Federici, *Revolution at Point Zero* (Oakland CA: PM Press, 2012); Monty Neill, 'Rethinking Class Composition Analysis in Light of the Zapatistas', in *The Aurora of the Zapatistas: Local & Global Struggles of the Fourth World War* edited by Midnight Notes Collective (Brooklyn, NY: Autonomedia, 2001), pp. 119–43.

7. Tony Wood, David Blowers and Kate Griffiths, *Next Generation: the long-term future of the National Electricity Market* (Grattan Institute, 2017).

8. Karl Marx, *Capital: A Critique of Political Economy*, translated by David Fernbach, vol. 3 (London: Penguin, 1991), p. 127.

9. Nick Harmsen, *Prime Minister attacks South Australia's renewable energy policy at state Liberal Party's AGM*. ABC News (accessed 6 November 2017). Available from www.abc.net.au/news/2017-08-12/pm-attacks-sas-renewable-energy-policy/ 8800782.

10. Anna Krien, 'The long goodbye: Coal, coral and Australia's climate deadlock', *Quarterly Essay* (66), pp. 1–116, 2017; pp. 107–8.

11. Caffentzis has written on Lenin's *What is to Be Done?* [George Caffentzis, 'Lenin on the Production of Revolution', in *What is to be Done? Leninism, anti-Leninist Marxism and the question of revolution today*, edited by Werner Bonefeld and Sergio Tischler (Aldershot: Ashgate, 2002), pp. 150–67]. Whilst he references Lenin's assertion that 'Without a revolutionary theory there can be no revolu- tionary movement' (V.I. Lenin, *What is To Be Done? Burning Questions of Our Movement* [Peking: Foreign Languages Press, 1973], p. 28) the bulk of Caffentzis' essay is in support of the need for structures that can bring together divergent struggles and class compositions: a 'communicative model of revolutionary organ- ization' (George Caffentzis, 'Lenin on the Production of Revolution', p. 162). Caffentzis celebrates 'Lenin's insistence on the need for putting the proletarian body in touch with all its members, actions and powers, and his sober assessment of the need to have activists capable of outwitting a concerted police strategy of illusion-and ignorance-creation has even greater resonance today when revolution must be planetary or nothing' (George Caffentzis, 'Lenin on the Production of Revolution', p. 166).

12. Silvia Federici and George Caffentzis, 'Must We Rebuild Their Anthill', in Silvia Federici; George Caffentzis; Daniel de Roulet; Anne Waldman; Sabu Kohso, *Fukushima Mon Amour* (Brookyln, NY: Autonomedia, 2011), p. 44.

13. Midnight Notes Collective, *Strange Victories: The Anti-Nuclear Movement in the US and Europe* (London: Elephant Editions, 1985), Midnight Notes Collective, 'The New Enclosures', in *Midnight Oil: Work, Energy, War 1973–1992*, edited by Midnight Notes Collective (Brooklyn, NY: Autonomedia, 1992), pp. 317–33.

14. 'Strange Victories' is credited as being written by p.m. in the edited volume of Midnight Notes essays entitled *Midnight Oil* yet was published earlier as being authored by the Midnight Notes Collective in an edition published by insurrectionary anarchist publishers Elephant Editions. As the latter is a longer and I think complete version of the essay this is the one I have cited here (Midnight Notes Collective, *Strange Victories: The Anti-Nuclear Movement in the US and Europe*, p.m., 'Strange Victories', in *Midnight Oil: Work, Energy, War 1973–1992*, edited by Midnight Notes Collective (Brooklyn, NY: Autonomedia, 1992).

15. Midnight Notes Collective, *Strange Victories: The Anti-Nuclear Movement in the US and Europe*, p. 23.

16. Midnight Notes Collective, 'The New Enclosures', pp. 330–1.

17. *Ibid.*, p. 331.

18. David Riker, 'The Struggle Against Enclosures in Jay, Maine: An account of the 1987–1988 strike against International Paper', in Midnight Notes Collective (eds), *The New Enclosures* (Jamaica Plain, MA: Midnight Notes, 1990), p. 51.

19. George Caffentzis, *In Letters of Blood and Fire*, p. 56.

20. *Ibid.*, p. 11.

21. *Ibid.*, pp. 11–19.

22. *Ibid.*, p. 19.

23. *Ibid.*, p. 20.

24. *Ibid.*, pp. 20–1.

25. Karl Marx, *Capital: A Critique of Political Economy*, translated by Ben Fowkes, volume 1 (London, Penguin Classics, 1990).

26. Karl Marx, *Capital*, vol. 3.

27. *Ibid.*, p. 281.

28. *Ibid.*, p. 297.

29. George Caffentzis, 'The Oil Paradox and the Labour Theory of Value', *Minnesota Review*, 87 (2016), p. 164.

30. Karl Marx, *Capital*, vol. 3, p. 268.

31. I generally agree with I I Rubin's description of this (Isaak Illich Rubin, *Essays on Marx's Theory of Value*, translated by Milos Samardzija and Fredy Perlman, Montreal New York: Black Rose Books, 1990). Marx's method proceeds from the concrete to the abstract to the concrete (Karl Marx, *Grundrisse: Foundation of the Critique of Political Economy (Rough Draft)*, London, Penguin Books, 1993, pp. 100–1). His written presentation proceeds from the abstract to the concrete. Vol. III of *Capital* whilst still abstract from a real capitalist society is closer to it, showing the complexity of different forces operating as part of a dynamic totality. Vol. I, especially the opening chapters on the commodity and thus on value, present the basic cells of capitalism in laboratory conditions.

32. George Caffentzis, 'Against Nuclear Exceptionalism with a Coda on the Commons and Nuclear Power.' *Crisis and Commons: PreFigurative Politics After Fukashima*, Tokyo University of Foreign Studies, 2 December 2012, p. 3.

33. George Caffentzis, 'The Oil Paradox and the Labour Theory of Value'.

34. *Ibid.*, p. 163.

35. *Ibid.*, p. 166.

36. Midnight Notes Collective, 'Oil, Guns and Money', in *Midnight Oil: Work Energy, War 1973–1992*, edited by Midnight Notes Collective (Brooklyn, NY: Autonomedia, 1992), pp. 3–22; Midnight Notes Collective, 'Recolonizing the Oil Fields', In *Midnight Oil: Work, Energy, War 1973–1992*, pp. 39–57.

37. Karl Marx, *Capital*, vol. 3, p. 298.

38. To reemphasise the creation of an average rate of profit in the mind of the economists or Marxists is not the same as the actual material tendencies of capitalism's movement towards, and away from, an average rate of profit.

39. Tony Wood, David Blowers and Kate Griffiths, Next Generation: the long-term future of the National Electricity Market: 11.

40. *Ibid.*, p. 16.

41. John Thwaites, Patricia Faulkner and Terry Mulder, Independent Review into the Electricity & Gas Retail Markets in Victoria, 2017, p. viii.

42. Tony Wood, David Blowers, and Greg Moran, *Price Shock: Is the retail electricty market failing consumers?* Grattan Institute, 2017, pp. 17–19.

43. Karl Marx, *Capital*, vol. 3, p. 286.

44. John Thwaites, Patricia Faulkner and Terry Mulder, Independent Review into the Electricity & Gas Retail Markets in Victoria, pp. 24–6.

45. Australian Bureau of Statistics, *6321.0.55.001 – Industrial Disputes, Australia, September 2016*. Australian Bureau of Statistics (cited 1 December 2016). Available from www.abs.gov.au/ausstats/abs@.nsf/mf/6321.0.55.001?OpenDocument.

46. Midnight Notes Collective, 'The New Enclosures', p. 331.

47. Midnight Notes Collective and Friends, *Promissory Notes: From Crisis to Commons*, 2009, p. 5. Available from http://midnightnotes.org/Promissory Notes.pdf.

48. Department of Industry, Innovation and Science, *Australian energy update 2016*. Canberra: September, 2016, p. 3.

49. Australian Energy Market Operator, *Update to Gas Statement of Opportunities*, p. 4.

50. Gas Strategies, *The outlook for LNG in 2016 – supply growth but where is the demand?* Available from: www.gasstrategies.com/sites/default/files/download/outlook_for_2016_-_gas_strategies.pdf.

51. Australian Energy Market Operator, Update to Gas Statement of Opportunities.

52. Phillip Coorey and Angela Macdonald-Smith, 'Gas truce puts states in firing line', *The Australian Financial Review*, Thursday 28 September, 2017, pp. 1, 4, Nicole Hasham, *States reject demands by Malcolm Turnbull for coal seam gas green light*, 2017, Brisbane Times (Accessed 13 December 2017). Available from www.brisbanetimes.com.au/politics/victoria/states-reject-demands-by-malcolm-turnbull-for-coal-seam-gas-green-light-20171005-gyuv2t.html, Angela Macdonald-Smith, 'Turnbull's gas deal may change nothing', *The Australian Finanical Review*, Thursday 28 September, 2017, p. 4.

53. George Caffentzis, *In Letters of Blood and Fire*, p. 57.

23

Commons at Midnight

Olivier de Marcellus

For me, the Midnight Notes Collective[1] has always had two great strengths. First, the capacity to discern a diversity of emerging struggles, the real movements of society, while more orthodox (not to say dogmatic), schools of thought were still blind to them. The Italian Autonomia movement already had this knack, and it has been a hallmark of Midnight Notes' work, no doubt due also to its second strength: the original historical research which underpins their analysis of contemporary struggles.

While always insisting on the workers' role and initiative in shaping history, Midnight Notes pointed to the innumerable varieties of 'workers' and struggles in the world, liquidating the Eurocentric and messianic myths of the traditional Marxist narrative of history and revolution. Commoning has always been practiced and enclosure, domination and exploitation have always threatened.

In this way, Midnight Notes saw the commonalities of the IMF riots long before the Zapatistas gave a conscious identity to the anti-globalisation movement. It celebrated feminist and peasant struggles, squatting or urban gardening decades before they were taken seriously by others, recognising that the revolutionary lead taken by the 'workers of the earth and the human body ... as a sign of a deep recomposition of the working class internationally'.[2] Already in 1990 it had identified apparently separate phenomena as all part of the global process of new enclosures: peasants evicted from their livelihoods in China, Africa or Latin America, homeless in northern cities, victims of the (first) 'Debt crisis', the collapse of state socialism ... and thus also gave a common ground to a diversity of resistances world-wide. With (too much) time, these perspectives have been more and more widely recognised.

Most important perhaps, the commons, which was a quite exotic concept, is emerging everywhere as an essential alternative to the state/market dilemma. A recent example: Blockupy International's call for an anti-G20 summit in Hamburg as a convergence of 'struggles taking place already to defend the commons, social and civil rights'. Even in France the commons have become a central theme. Benjamin Coriat writes of *le retour des communs*,[3] and a recent presentation entitled *Commun. Essai sur la révolution au XXI siècle*,[4] underlines commoning as political activity. One could also cite the extraordinary success of a recent documentary film, *Demain*, which attracted by word of mouth more than a million people and has become a sort of popular reference. Although it did not use the term, the majority of the alternatives which it documented are commons of one sort or another.

Of course this is not all due to the work of Midnight Notes. There has been an historical convergence of influences: the prominence taken since the Zapatistas by the struggles of indigenous communities in defence of traditional commons; resistances to new enclosures (of water, seeds, fish, DNA, the global quota of CO_2, etc.) that illuminated a diversity of commons that had been taken for granted. Perhaps the very extremes of neoliberal individualism finally engendered a renewed appetite for cooperative activity! Nevertheless, the prescience of Midnight Notes enabled it to help name and give coherence to this diversity of practices and struggles.

Activists' interest in the commons is also stronger than ever in Europe because the inadequacy of traditional left perspectives are (finally) becoming tragically evident. After the collapse of socialism, the last illusions of social democracy have also been liquidated and the credibility of political parties and institutions as such is at an all-time low. And as explicitly anti-capitalist positions regain popularity, some reformist proponents of the commons dare imagine 'A World Beyond State and Market'.[5] Better late than never!

In reality, many progressive people had already instinctively drawn those conclusions. Some because they were dismayed not only by institutional politics, but also by the failure of popular mobilisations and resistances to alter the course of the neoliberal offensive. Others because they had a visceral instinct to create concrete alternatives, rather than to make demands on employers or the State. Typical of the squatting movement, many of them have since created commons of one sort or another.

Can this kind of milieu also become a significant political force? Can the 'alternatives' and the 'militants' – back-biting cousins since 1968 – finally come back together? In France (and Geneva) a new network of local initiatives, Alternatiba,[6] has had some success banking on that hypothesis. A call, originating in the Pays Basque, proposed to mobilise on the issue of climate change by bringing together climate activists and every possible kind of local initiative – often commons of sorts – that could be considered positive for the climate (local agriculture, repair cafés, alternative energy and mobility projects, ecoconstruction, cooperative housing projects, alternative health and culture, etc.). Conferences, films and debates on climate change were thus combined with a whole 'village' of alternatives occupying city streets. Alternatibas were organised in more than a hundred cities, and (people being much more interested in concrete proposals than political debate) attracted almost 600,000 people.

Alternatiba's struggle around climate change aims to 'walk on two legs', encouraging alternatives with one leg and organising non-violent civil disobedience with the other – a form of action which seems to me essential at this juncture for the climate movement. With its second leg it mobilised strongly around the international climate change talks, COP21, in Paris in 2015 and has been involved in a series of spectacular actions. The stretch between the legs is a little awkward and has led to some actions being delegated to its sister organisation, Action Non-Violente COP21 (ANV COP21), but both are powered by the same remarkable national network of young activists. They rather astound me by their combination of efficient methodology and horizontal practices, particularly concerning gender issues. Compared to the anti-globalisation generation – not to speak of the leftists of 1968! – the practice of commoning in grass-roots politics has most definitely improved, and that is certainly one of the most important reasons for hope!

Organising Alternatiba Léman in Geneva, I saw the potential and also the difficulties of the project. A majority of the actors of the two hundred associations involved seemed to be convinced that capitalism is 'heading us into the wall', and see their activity as an alternative, although they don't consider themselves activists or doing something political. But can Alternatiba become more than a convenient platform and bring them to appreciate their commonalities? Create a network of shared values and concrete exchanges that could constitute an overarching and more politically ambitious commons? (The 'Léman', a local electronic currency and credit system, launched during Alternatiba could be one material tool for that.) Time will tell, but experiences such as the Cooperativa Integral Catalana[7] keep us dreaming! And in the obviously totally ambiguous and limited context of Swiss capitalism, we must try to apply George's criterion: 'whether a particular commons increases the power of workers to resist capital and to define a non-capitalist future'.[8] Hopefully a little!

For years, the movement has been in search of an alternative political vision. The one 'No!' and many 'Yeses' of the Zapatistas and People's Global Action was not really sufficient. An ecosystem of commons as an alternative to (Welfare) State and market is a more substantive proposal. 'Power to the Commons!' Thanks to Silvia, George and others of Midnight Notes who have done so much to put the proposition back on the table!

Yes but...

'All power to the Commons?' Sounds good ... but also rather utopian if we cannot say how they might get it! If you will allow me, I have some questions.

I agree that it is through the commons and grass roots movements that real community and thus real social and political strength can be rebuilt. But can action on that level be sufficient? Can the world really be changed without taking power?

Capitalism will not let itself be nudged off the scene by commoning. Nor does it even seem to show more than a marginal interest in co-opting it with a 'commons fix'. Don't we more generally see a head-on confrontation, in Africa, for example, with land-grabbing and Bill Gates' grandiose plans for African agriculture? Or in the ambitions of the new wave of free trade treaties?

Could a Neo-Keynesian Green New Deal still divert the neoliberal race to the bottom, as recent converts, like Lawrence Summers,[9] might suggest? But, as *Promissory Notes* pointed out, Roosevelt had organised labour behind him.[10] 'Larry Summers and whose army?' could force a deal on the colossal interests vested in the current course of disaster?

Rising to the Question of Organisation

Above all, what new forms of organisation does the withering away and betrayals of the old left and worker's organisations leave in the field? Myriads of autonomous initiatives and networks and a potential for periodic swarming. But is that enough?

The swarms of the anti-globalisation movement finally stalled WTO. Lately, resistance to the TAFTA and TISA free trade proposals has involved hundreds of thousands of demonstrators, millions of signatures, dozens of cities declared TAFTA free... but on the institutional level it is Trump and Marine Le Pen who are cashing in.

What is it that we have failed to understand and practice concerning the relation between grass roots struggles and institutional politics?

In past decades, autonomist politics contented itself with insisting on the – effectively essential – role of social movements and grassroots political activity; and criticising – totally correctly – the forms and practices of political parties and institutions. But even at the time, this avoided genuinely addressing the whole picture, as in reality our victories could only be given some permanence and solidity through their 'recuperation' by these institutions. The popular power generated by wildcat strikes, squats and popular resistances would have lost steam without those concessions. And indeed it quite generally did, when it started to come up against hard line austerity neoliberalism.[11]

Today, the depth of the capitalist crisis, the dissolution of reformist institutions, the rise of the extreme right, but also the huge potential of subversive disaffection and rage – *Que se vayan todos!* – put us (happily?) in another situation, in which we must take the responsibility of finding new answers to the question of State power and institutions. Globalisation has not reduced the strategic importance of states. As George pointed out in 2009, stronger states (China for instance) seem actually to be winning out.[12] Rather, globalisation is a strategy of states. Defeating that strategy and submitting 'the economy' to society requires some form of political strength at what remains its key locus: the national state level. What have we learned in recent years to enable us to avoid falling into the old institutional traps?

In Latin America, the social movements of Ecuador and Bolivia long avoided all involvement with parties and government, limiting themselves to building grassroots strength and blocking the attacks of the State. Circumstances forced them further after having brought down successive governments, and faced them with the choice between taking power or letting new neoliberal puppets install themselves. In power, the left did not only redistribute. Part of its policies were designed to empower or create new commons. Chavez launched a programme for the creation of cooperatives, and favoured the creation of a whole network of independent local radios, for example. In Brazil, the campaign against hunger was implemented by supplying school lunches through small scale local agriculture. In Argentina, public policies favoured the emergence of a social economy sector. In Bolivia, the government organised the distribution of small farmers' produce at affordable prices. With his 'Communitarian socialism',[13] Alvaro Linera theorises a process by which the 'illusory' commons monopolised by a minority in the old State could be progressively reclaimed by organisations and communities, and by which representative democracy could give way to a more direct variety. The acid test will be to see what resilience these first steps provide to societies again subjected to right wing rule.

Whatever the immediate outcomes, the long-term objective Linera outlines re-joins other visions of the commons. The differences in strategy seem to be the fruit of very different situations. The Zapatistas 'separatist' option constructing a local alternative to the State is no doubt in large part a function of the relation of forces at the national level. As for the European movements which Linera criticises for their long 'abdication' with respect to the question of State power, it seems as though that is beginning to be called into question.

Of course, even when the left stays in power, its exercise also has its dangers and contradictions. Among them is the fact that the social progress these governments have brought can sometimes inordinately strengthen their hand in relation to the social movements that created them. Faced with government policies that in certain regions favour industrial export-oriented agriculture at their expense, an Ecuadorian peasant leader excused the passivity of their organisation, confiding to us, 'We don't really have the choice. Our base supports Correa!'

In Europe, Syriza betrayed the hopes of its supporters even quicker... Will the grassroots allow Podemos to do the same? There is perhaps more hope for Spain, as they have not put all their eggs in one national electoral basket. The movement of 'rebel cities' in particular is at least looking for some new answers. First, they attack State power from the local, municipal level. Second, while accepting the risk and difficulties of participating in their cities' management, they share an ongoing debate around 'munci-palism, self-government and counterpower'.[14] Clearly recognising that 'State structures are designed to concentrate power and not distribute it,' they seek simultaneously to impose real democratic participation 'from outside'. The struggles for the re-municipalisation of water, against corruption, odious debt or expulsions are apparently led at once from 'inside' and 'outside'. What forms of participation can guarantee a permanent popular mobilisation and control does not seem clear, but at least one lesson from social democracy seems to be heeded: never hand over your commons to a bureaucracy!

One can hope that a new kind of 'inside and outside' political animal is evolving there, which will be able to address the levels and problems normally dealt with by parties; struggling in, against and through the State, without compromising the strength of the grassroots networks; with the horizontal practices and the new forms of participation offered by internet, among other tools. One can perhaps also draw hope from the proliferation of 'participatory' mechanisms peddled by the powers that be. They know a dangerous thing when they see it!

Perhaps there are also lessons to be learned from Iceland where mass *cacerolazos* and popular referendums enforced a *que vayan todos* and blocked the bank bailout. It also initiated a promising experience of popular participation with a Constituent Assembly involving citizens chosen by lot, consensus decision making and participation by internet.

A Common(s) Programme?

One step towards organisation would perhaps be for the movement of movements (at whatever level) to go beyond the simple networking of diverse struggles, to explicitly recognise some common principles and general objectives, such as: relocalisation and subsidiarity; the need for more direct and participatory forms of democracy, or the impossibility of infinite growth on a limited planet. That society should control the economy rather than the reverse; reclaiming credit as a common good; maximising cooperation rather than competition. As Massimo De Angelis proposes, the commons could be a basis for 'establishing a new political discourse that builds on and helps to articulate the many existing, often minor struggles, and recognises their power to overcome capitalist society'.[15]

The idea of an emancipatory common program was revitalised in France through an appeal to resist neoliberalism, launched in 2004 by 13 veterans of the Resistance on the 60th anniversary of the publication of *Les Jours Heureux* by the Conseil National de la Résistance. Still clandestine, it had announced a program of 'social and economic democracy' including Social Security, worker's power, and nationalisation of natural resources, credit, the major industries and services – 'returning to the nation ... the fruits of the common efforts'. Last fall, a call using the same name by a hundred movement figures asked presidential candidates to respond to '10 essential measures' such as: a constitution drawn up by citizens chosen by lot (which should include the crime of ecocide and the rights of Nature); a maximum 20 to 1 salary spread in an enterprise; withdrawal from free trade treaties in favour of a 'just trade' proposal; 'democratic governance' of banks to deal with tax evasion, speculation and the debt; phasing out industrial agriculture... The idea – more or less successful – was also to generate popular participation in the debate and pressure the candidates to at least address the real issues.

Melenchon's electoral programme 'L'avenir en commun' has attracted more attention. Also, a collective effort, its 83 points go from general principles to proposed measures on practically every political issue. Positing the ecological transition and social justice as the objective, and developing the necessary means: changing or leaving the EU treaties, audit of public debt, replacing free trade by a 'protectionnisme solidaire' inspired by the Havana Charter of 1944, limiting stock holders' rights, increasing workers' minimum and maximum wages, revocable political mandates, development of the social economy and defence of the commons... Certain key measures, attacked as unrealistic – loans to the State directly from a reclaimed national bank, control of capital flows or reintroduction of protective tariffs, for example – have been successfully practiced in Iceland or Ecuador.[16] It is a credible Neo-Keynesian proposal to put a limit to EU neoliberalism and face the social and environmental challenges. Hopefully the enthusiasm generated (more than a hundred thousand at the latest rally) will survive the election campaign. With a thousand local groups, 300,000 members and a strong programme it could take real roots. In any case, it's an interesting educational tool – and a change from slogans and baby-kissing.[17]

Well, France – with its centralised tradition and much weaker movements – is no doubt less avant-garde than Spain, but on an ideological level, the mere fact that these ideas enter into the electoral debate is a good sign of the times (like Bernie Sanders using the word socialism in the United States) And a simple return to party politics may be an inadequate answer – but its answering a good question!

Organising Globally?

The larger the social organisation, the greater the likelihood that its 'coordination' gives rise to domination. When capital manoeuvres at the global level, can cooperation – commoning – reach that high? Utopian? But can we afford not to try? As *Promissory Notes* remind us, capital knows how to manage – or even pre-empt – its crises. Worse, it now also openly organises pre-emptive revolt with its 'Colour Revolution' techniques.[18] If we don't organise things, they will!

In the heady beginnings of the anti-globalisation movement with Peoples' Global Action, some already felt our communications to be the first stirrings of a sort of 'global brain'. Since then the historic wave of insurrections of the Arab Spring, Greece, M15, Occupy, etc., dwarfed global days of action and made global revolution seem imaginable... Could the 'Chomeurs Diplômés' of the Magreb, and other armies of well-educated youth with no future under capitalism bring subversive commoning to a new level?

Unfortunately, as *Promissory Notes* had foreseen, new levels of violence and war have beaten back that offensive almost everywhere since. The 'War on terrorism' has created hundreds of thousands of refugees, and fertile ground for racism and the extreme right all over Europe. The 'banality of evil' gains ground every day. Marine Le Pen could well join Trump this year. In Latin America, soft coups have rolled back the wave of progressive governments. Sisyphus is at the bottom again, while social and environmental catastrophes develop so rapidly! Can a more effective form of global networking bounce back to challenge capital globally?

The mobilisation for the COP21 in Paris seemed promising, with its general consensus for mass civil disobedience and a convergence towards an anti-systemic analysis of climate, agriculture and trade issues posing for some the possibility/necessity of a more ambitious, global anti-capitalist network and program. But the socialist government's use of 'terrorism' and tight media control effectively blocked the hoped-for 'climate Seattle'.

Our comrade Ramon Duran foresaw a breakup of globalised capitalism, an era of increasingly competing (and authoritarian) capitalist blocs that would themselves implode some time toward 2030 under the combined pressure of energy shortages, environmental collapse and climate change.[19]

Although Ramon may have exaggerated the imminence of peak oil, environmental collapse and climate change are accelerating faster than anticipated.[20] And it looks indeed as though globalised capitalism may be not only fissuring politically, but also receding economically. In recent years multinational firms are making fewer profits, have expanded more slowly than their domestic peers, and are running into increasing political difficulties.[21] Trump is only an ugly sign of the times.

Ramon thought that only after this epochal civilisational collapse (if we have meanwhile done our homework!) would an alternative have a chance to impose itself.[22] But what will be the state of humanity and the planet by then? The Zapatistas who summarised their strategy in the single word 'Resistir!' seem to have a similar perspective. Is that the best we can hope for?

Une autre fin du monde est possible – graffiti from the recent Labour Law mobilisation in France. Or...? 'The light you see at the end of the tunnel is probably the headlight of an approaching train!' – Žižek

Notes

1. I could have said 'Silvia and George' instead of 'Midnight Notes' in various places in this text, but referring to the collective creation of which they have been the heart is perhaps an even better way of recognising their contributions to the common undertaking.
2. Midnight Notes, Auroras of the Zapatistas: Local and Global Struggles of the Fourth World War (Brooklyn, NY: Autonomedia, 2001), p. 11.
3. Coriat, B. (dir.) (2015), *Le Retour des communs. La crise de l'idéologie propriétaire*, Paris: Éditions Les liens qui libèrent, 2015.
4. P. Dardot and C. Laval), *Commun: Essai sur la révolution au XXIe siècle* (Paris: E.ditions La D.couverte, 2015).
5. D. Bollier and S. Helfrich (eds) The Wealth of the Commons: a world beyond market and State (Amherst, MA: Levellers Press, 2012).
6. www.alternatiba.eu.
7. https://cooperativa.cat/es/ (last accessed 6 March 2019).
8. George Caffentzis, 'A tale of two conferences: globalization, the crisis of neoliberalism and question of the commons', The Commoner ('other articles in common', 2004).
9. L.H. Summers and E. Balls, Report of the Commission on Inclusive Prosperity, Center for American Progress, January 2015. At https://cdn.americanprogress.org/wp-content/uploads/2015/01/IPC-PDF-full.pdf (last accessed 6 March 2019).
10. Midnight Notes Collective and Friends, Promissory Notes: From Crisis to Commons, 2009, p. 5. Available from http://midnightnotes.org/Promissory Notes.pdf.
11. Looking back, I find it very humbling to compare our generation's trajectory with that of the pre-war working class, which advanced answers – whatever their shortcomings – at all levels: powerful unions; the commoning of mutual organisations for health, unemployment, etc.; mass political parties; community organising (in Geneva, Boy Scouts, sewing circles, a whole football league, etc., were organised within the communist party community!).

12. Caffentzis, 'Notes on the Financial Crisis', in Team Colors (eds) *Uses of a Whirl-wind: Movement, Movements, and Contemporary Radical Currents in the United States* (Baltimore: AK Press, 2010); republished in *In Letters of Blood and Fire: Work, Machines, and the Crisis of Capitalism* (Oakland CA: PM Press, 2013), pp. 241–51.

13. Álvaro García Linera, Socialismo comunitario: Un horizonte de época (2015); at www.vicepresidencia.gob.bo/IMG/pdf/socialismo_comunitario-2.pdf (last accessed 6 March 2019).

14. See, e.g. http://mac2.uno/en/ejes-de-trabajo/ (last accessed 6 March 2019).

15. 'On the Commons: A Public Interview with Massimo De Angelis and Stavros Stavrides', e-flux Journal 17 (June 2010); at www.e-flux.com/journal/17/67351/on-the-commons-a-public-interview-with-massimo-de-angelis-and-stavros-stavride (last accessed 6 March 2019).

16. Mark Weisbrot, 'Ecuador's left-wing success story', The Nation, 14 February 2017; at www.thenation.com/article/ecuadors-left-wing-success-story/ (last accessed 6 March 2019).

17. Melenchon's programme: https://avenirencommun.fr/avenir-en-commun/ (last accessed 6 March 2019).

18. PONARS Eurasia, After the Color Revolutions: Political Change and Democracy Promotion in Eurasia, July 2010; at http://www.ponarseurasia.org/sites/default/files/policy-perspectives-pdf/PONARS%20Eurasia_After%20the%20Color%20Revolutions_0.pdf

19. Ramón Fernández Durán, The Breakdown of Global Capitalism: 2000-2030 (May 2012); at https://corporateeurope.org/sites/default/files/attachments/breakdown_capitalism_final.pdf.

20. The sudden collapse of the marine ecosystems could well be one of the nastiest surprises.

21. 'The retreat of the global economy', The Economist, 28 January 2017; at www.economist.com/news/briefing/21715653-biggest-business-idea-past-three-decades-deep-trouble-retreat-global (last accessed 6 March 2019).

22. 'Everything indicates that the degrowth between now and 2030 will be chaotic, not ordered and just. Nevertheless, it is essential to cultivate and reinforce the seeds of an ordered, just and sustainable transformation, even in a totally adverse environment, in order to later fortify and generate sufficient critical mass so that the reverse can become true, in future times', Durán, The Breakdown of Global Capitalism, p. 28.

24

Practising Affect as Affective Practice

Marina Sitrin

We sat around a long rectangular wooden table in New York City. Food and wine lay generally untouched. Friends from Japan were sharing the real e/affects of the Fukushima nuclear meltdown. It was March of 2011. The news was not covering the devastation and death that was transpiring. First-hand accounts were harrowing. Everyone in the area, downwind, down water and, we were quick to learn, in the entire region and beyond, even as far as Tokyo 150 miles away, were feeling the effects. Immediate effects. Sandboxes in Tokyo measured high levels of radiation – Giga counters, though, were soon banned. Friends in Japan organised to go into the heart of the affected area to help evacuate people. The Japanese government was revealing few of the dangers. The opposite. The situation was immediately normalised. People were told to stay put. Drink the water. Eat the food. It was the patriotic thing to do. The head of state went on national television, drinking a glass of water allegedly from the most contaminated zone. Within months, the rubble from the area was spread throughout other parts of Japan. Giga counters and other means of measuring contamination were made illegal, as was sharing such information. Women were ostracised from their families for testing food or refusing to use the water for their children's meals. Such acts were seen as unpatriotic and disobedient. And this was just the beginning. These were only the first stories to emerge. We were listening. We were silent.

We looked around the table, at one another, at the untouched food. The silence grew. And Silvia spoke. Tears in her eyes, passion in her voice. Her voice sounded as if it were trembling – capturing the clenched feelings in our hearts, and rage in our chests. George, quiet and reflective, looking at her as she spoke, agreeing with her words and sentiments.

And we began to plan.

This was my first encounter with Silvia Federici and George Caffentzis.

From there we formed *Todo Somos Japon*, a solidarity grouping to support those affected by Fukushima in various ways.[1] George and Silvia wrote and spoke about the dangers of nuclear power, as they had been doing for decades, but what struck me the most – and continues to strike me – was their heart-filled dedication to action – and a particular sort of action. I had known them as scholars, and I had heard they were active, but I'd had no idea that they were first and foremost organisers and militants. A militancy grounded in care, love, and affect. First was the feeling, as they engaged with what was happening and with what could be done to help those on the ground. And then – following the love and the rage – came the theory and reflection. Of course, it is not simple to separate these things, but when I reflect on Silvia and George, what impacts me most, what immediately comes to mind, is their affective practice, their practice based in affect. The way in which they are guided to do what they do, and the way that they do it. It is this depth of care and love that is manifested in the alternatives they write so prolifically about – commoning as commoners.

One of the first things they did was to write a letter to the people of Japan, addressing those we had met in particular.[2] It began…

> Dear comrades,
>   We are writing to express to you our solidarity at a time when the pain for those who have died or have disappeared is still raw, and the task of reshaping of life out of the immense wreckage caused by the earthquake, the tsunami and the nuclear reactor meltdowns must appear unimaginable. We also write to think together with you what this moment marked by the most horrific nuclear disaster yet in history signifies for our future, for the politics of anti-capitalist social movements, as well as the fundamentals of everyday reproduction.

Care. Love. Trust. Affect. These feelings are rarely talked about – and yet they are at the heart of so many people's experiences in movements.[3] Their presence or absence can explain why people become involved, why they remain involved and why they may drop out. Here I do mean *at the heart*, thinking of the heart as the muscle it is, needing to be worked – else it atrophies. Locating it as the Zapatistas do when they describe their forms of organising as, 'from below and to the left, where the heart resides'.

Social movement theorists and activists speak and write often of the political and economic motivations for movement participation, and even of negative emotions, such as anger and rage. But while the importance of social relationships once in movement has been increasingly discussed over the past decades, there is still a general shying away from topics of love and care, trust and support. This misses so much! It ignores emotions or feelings – affects – that influence our day-to-day organising and inform our very desire to make new worlds. Of course the reason for militant organising is not to help the individual organiser 'feel good'. Nevertheless, most of us find that being involved in collective struggle changes how we feel for the better – it makes us feel more confident, more powerful, happier. We neglect these apparently 'subjective' factors – along with questions of how we treat one another, how we care, or do not care, for our comrades – at our peril. We can too quickly fall into the politics of 'after the revolution'. After the revolution we will be 'free' to address and change our feelings and relationships. Let's change the structures of power and then women can throw off the oppressions of patriarchy. Once we have abolished capitalism then workers can claim their dignity. And so on. This is not about overemphasising the individual and their feelings, but about shining light on the importance of the subjective, addressing it together with the structural, so as to prefigure the world we are trying to create – striving to create the future in the present.

George and Silvia encapsulate this approach – and they thus inspire me deeply. Their theories of the 'larger structures' of patriarchy and capitalism are powerful tools – gifts to social movements. Yet they are also able focus on individual humans, with care, with patience and with love. And it is through – or partly through – this focus on the individual that their theories of change emerge. In this sense, their theoretical work is intimately and completely intertwined with their acts, and these acts grounded in care at every level.

Assemblies and Relationships

Revolution in Tunisia and uprising in Egypt; Occupy Wall Street in the United States; the 15M movement in Spain and Nuit Debout in Paris. These recent direct democracy and direct-action-based movements – and others – have made one of their primary foci the changing of social relations – creating democratic and care-based relationships in the present – while at the same time organising for a different type of society. These movements all used direct democracy over representation, they prioritised direct action over demands, and they took the time to make sure all who wanted to participate were able to do so, often with long and sometimes unwieldy assemblies. Rather than pushing through to an end goal as fast as possible, these movements understood process as central to whatever goals were ultimately decided. As part of this, these movements also immediately organised caucuses or working groups based on gender, race, sexual orientation and legal status – striving to ensure that all voices were heard as equally as possible. Each plaza occupation also facilitated different forms of mediation for conflict, appointed 'peace keepers' (or some other form of security) and set up medical and legal groups. The aim was to help participants feel as supported as possible in the process of organising – but these were also attempts to create alternative societies, where care for the other was manifest in the present. The conflict-resolution groupings were new, and faulty, but they were part of a broader path towards the creation of new worlds – as I will discuss later on, in the section on alternative adjudication.

There are numerous historical examples of movements that prioritise social relationships and care-based organising, and the focus on means as inseparable from ends has been seen most notably over the past twenty years. Examples include the Zapatistas in Chiapas Mexico, autonomous Cantons in Rojava, post-2001 horizontal movements in Argentina and the contemporary Movements of the Squares, among many others. What makes these movements particularly novel is their scale: they combine large numbers of people, from different backgrounds, and span diverse geographical spaces. Taken as a whole this is a new phenomenon that represents a break from prior forms of organising.

Another area of novelty is the priority on prefigurative politics, specifically the centering of individuals' voices, subjectivities and feelings. This focus is key. When a participant is taken seriously, when they are heard and *feel* heard – perhaps for the first time in their lives – they begin to feel like a subject, an actor in their own life. This affect can engender a newfound sense of dignity which, in turn, encourages greater participation in assemblies and subsequent actions. The circle is thus a virtuous one and self-reinforcing. Taken together, these affects help create an environment that is more welcoming and open, thus increasing the likelihood that participants remain involved longer and are willing to risk more together.

Yet the opposite is also true. People who feel more open are usually more vulnerable too. In particular they can be more vulnerable to feelings of betrayal and there is a greater risk of their leaving movements because of emotions.

For love to flourish then, there must be affective conflict resolution. Two of the more advanced social movements are those of the Zapatistas in Chiapas, Mexico and that which created the autonomous cantons of Rojava, in the north of Syria. Both have grounded their practice and the construction of their now self-governing societies in attention to care, which has included the development of alternative forms of adjudication. They are not about avoiding conflict – avoiding difficult discussions or disagreements. But when disagreement leads to division, or when harm is done, they are dedicated to resolving these harms and conflicts collectively. Conflict resolution is accomplished differently in the different locations, for both Zapatistas and revolutionaries of Rojava this is an essential part of the new society – not one that can wait until after the construction of autonomy.

New People – New Women and Girls

Unlike Spaniards or the Argentines, the Zapatista movement generally does not use the language of affect. But they do place at the core of their organising the importance of the participation of all people in the communities and they also reflect on changed subjectivities and new dignities based on this participation. Although a large literature exists on the Zapatistas, little of it addresses the role of emotion in participation. But when we reflect on the importance to the construction of new societies of assemblies and community participation and, in particular, on the role of women and young girls, it is impossible not to speak of emotion. The Zapatistas rose up in 1994 – 25 years ago. There is now an entirely new generation who have been born and grown up under these (evolving) processes: new people have been created – and have created themselves! This creation has been grounded in care, structures of community agreements and processes of collective conflict-resolution.

In 2008 I participated in the First Zapatista Women's *Encentro*, which took place in the autonomous community of La Garrucha, Chiapas. There I witnessed this creation first hand: of new people and, in particular, of new girls and women. There were several days of testimonies by women, older women, from the different communities. Each was powerful in its own way. These women told the stories of their transformation from servitude to militancy, from forced marriage to autonomy, from illiteracy to teaching, from exclusion to being part of 'good government'. As these women shared their personal and collective stories, the transformation of the society could be felt with their words. These were words spoken in Spanish, often a second or third language, and, not used to public speaking, and still held by the culture of demure demeanors, most listeners had to strain to hear the women's voices, even with the amplified sound. But it was a huge step that these stories were being told at all. Then Marialinda, nine years old, took the stage.

A voice came over the sound system that was at once loud and youthful. Her voice did not falter as the older women's had. She not only spoke clearly, but looked up, at the hundreds of people in the room, meeting their eyes. Marialinda began,

> I'm going to tell you about my own life and about my rights. As a girl I have the right to do all the things that I want to do. My parents have given me the right to study in the autonomous schools, so that I can learn. They've given

me the right to go out, to play, to sing and to dance because I think it's necessary to have fun.

People applauded at almost every sentence and laughed at the part about
having fun. It was all true, but it was said in such a way and with such
clarity and self-assurance, that the words took on their meaning in a fresh
way. The Zapatistas had created the next generation – and it was beautiful.
Powerful. Free. And in less than 15 years.

Peace and Consensus

More than seven thousand miles away, in Northern Syria, an autonomous
community, not unlike the Zapatistas, has been growing since 2012.[4] Initiated by the Kurdish freedom movement, this community is now comprised
of several million people and is open to all people from the region who
wish to come and participate. This includes war victims and refugees, particularly women fleeing the Islamic State. The territory is called Rojava and
is made up of three Cantons and a number of affiliated autonomous communities, each with their own local autonomy, but connected to the overall
system of municipal governance. Inspired in part by libertarian municipalism – Murray Bookchin's work has been influential – yet made and
grounded by the Kurdish freedom struggle, this struggle shifted away from
building a party and instead focused on the development of local autonomy
and direct democracy.

Women have been at forefront of this struggle and every aspect of society
must have gender parity. This is not merely symbolic, nor is it only a goal to
be striven towards. If any given group or body does not have the necessary
gender balance, meaning at least half of its members being women, then
the group or body and its decisions are not considered legitimate. The result
is that at each and every level of governance, adjudication, education and
the economy women are leading participants and decision-makers. Moreover – and as evidenced by the many images depicting women with
guns – women are a crucial part of the defense of the region. In fact, wom-
en's battalions have been some of the most successful units fighting against
the Islamic State.

We must pause here a moment, and reflect on what's happening here in
the borderlands of northern Syria (and southern Turkey), as well as in the
highlands of Mexico. These are two of the places where women have been
most systematically and culturally oppressed. Yet now it is women who are
leading and facilitating the most inspiring and prefigurative societies in the
world. This phenomenon of women's leadership – along with the subsequent backlashing reaction, mostly from outside in these two cases – is one

that Silvia addresses in much of her work and political action. From the now renowned *Caliban and the Witch*, to her more recent *Witches, Witch-Hunting and Women* and *Re-Enchanting the World: Feminism and the Politics of the Commons*.

Rojava now has an elaborate system of justice in place. This even includes a university to train people in the process, although its curriculum is constantly evolving along with the justice system itself. At the heart of this new system are Peace and Consensus Committees, which in fact have existed in nascent form in many Kurdish communities since the early 1990s if not before. As with so many processes around the globe that seek justice and attempt to heal harm, they were and are led and facilitated largely by women. As with the Zapatistas, communities are self-governing and avoid institutional and state judiciaries. They have thus had to recreate the meaning and practice of justice. Each Peace and Consensus Committee (PCC) is a small group, of between five and nine people, nominated by the People's Councils. As with other formal areas of social organisation, gender parity is enforced. Each commune is comprised of approximately 300 people – between 30 and 150 families or households. Roughly 4000 communes combine to form a district. Decisions at a higher level are made by a People's Council, comprised of two elected co-presidents from each commune.

When conflicts arise the PCC intervenes to facilitate a resolution, where the goal is always to achieve consensus for both or all parties. The PCCs thus strive to create harmony – peace – within the community and society. They can convene anywhere, from organised meetings in a town or neighbourhood, to an impromptu street discussion. There is no explicit set of rules or way in which they must function. Rather the way that PCCs operate – always striving for consensus within their own operation as well as with 'outside' parties – has evolved over time. Each PCC follows a process that is unique – yet these processes have been learned and shared over the years, through a form of oral history. If a PCC cannot resolve any particular dispute, or if the offence is of a more serious sort, such as murder, then the issue goes to a higher level. In cases of forced marriage, dual marriages, patriarchal violence or any other instance of gender-related violence, the the case must be heard and resolved by the Yekitiya Star – the Star Union of Women – a specific all women's Peace and Consensus Committee.

In Rojava, the incidence of crime has declined and is continuing to decline. I have no doubt this is a consequence both of higher levels of self-organization and cooperation, and of the work of the PCCs. Affect and alternative justice complement one another. There is a virtuous circle, a spiral. As the sense of community and consensus develops, so there are more acts of solidarity and more acts of care. This, in turn, engenders the

creation of more cooperatives and the expansion of collective and consensus decision-making processes, thus deepening the desire for yet more
change, more profound consensus, more care, more justice.

Affecting Conflict – the Future in the Present

It is no coincidence that the largest and, in the case of the Zapatistas, longest,
experiences of self-organisation, autonomy and horizontality both place
such importance on care, mutual trust and effective conflict-resolution.
Affect and conflict go together. We can only deepen and expand our care for
one another if we also have practices to address conflict, minimise harm and
heal injury. In the case of both Zapatistas and Rojava, the militants who
contrasted these autonomous societies starting developing and experi-
menting with such tools well before they were able to claim the physical
geographic regions. In this sense, they started with the heart, they started
with affect. This was part of the prefiguration; resolving harm was *part of* the
revolution, not something to be left for *after* the revolution...

... or the strike or the occupation. George and Silvia are not Zapatistas
or revolutionary Rojavans – except, of course, in the sense that *we are all
Zapatistas*. But nevertheless, they have led in this capacity. Over the past
two decades, global movements have increasingly focused on social relationships – on the process of organising – not just the ends desired.
Assemblies are at the core of many movements and the language of prefiguration – manifesting aspects of the desired future in the present – is
central. Many of these movements are located in Latin America and
southern Europe, and I don't think it's a coincidence that these are the
places Silvia and George have chosen to spend so much time. They have
played a crucial role in sharing experiences and circulating struggles,
human conduits of theory and practice. Not only are they collaborators in
the plotting of future plans and paths, but they involve themselves in a way
that is exemplary of the sorts of relationships we desire – full of trust, care
and affect.

Take Occupy Wall Street or Strike Debt!, two recent US-based movements George and Silvia were part of. I will not go into details here, but I
participated with Silvia in one process of mediation, in which we met with
different members of a dysfunctioning group, listening to the personal
accounts of harm, helping individuals understand others' point of view,
helping the group and its members heal – and become functional again.
We have all experienced groupings that have broken down and fallen apart
through a lack of attention to harm, through a lack of care. Every body of
human beings – from the smallest 'affinity group' to the largest 'territory'
of rebellion or revolution – must face this issue – and keep facing it – if it is
to survive and thrive.

Revolutions always start small (although they can sometimes grow rapidly). Revolutions require patience. Not the 'wait-until-after-the-revolution' type of patience, but the patience to start small, to start with process. And then to build, sometimes painfully slowly, with small pieces of these affective foundations, infinitesimally small, but still there.

We can learn and take inspiration from the Zapatistas – from nine-year-old Marialinda (who will now be an adult of 20) and from the other women (and men) who – by putting care at the heart of their practice – have recreated themselves as new girls, new women, new people. We can learn and take inspiration from the autonomous cantons of Rojava – from their Peace and Consensus Committees, as well as other organisational forms, and the women who have been so central in making their new society. And we can learn from and take inspiration from Silvia and George too. Not only for their ability to recognise and help us understand the significance of the 'big' acts – the Zapatistas' revolution or the Rojavan, say. But also, and perhaps more importantly, for their ability to recognise that a 'small' act of mediation amongst a handful of disaffected activists in central Manhattan is no less important, no less revolutionary. And not only to *recognise* this truth. But to *be* the people who step forward – with care and with love – to help perform the act themselves, to help heal the harm, practise the affect.

Notes

1. *Todo Somos Japon* means 'we are all Japan': it borrows from the Zapatistas' 'we are all Zapatistas', 'we are all Marcos' and 'we are all one another and the other is us'.
2. This letter is from *Jfissures* – a website in Japanese and English that was among the many projects to emerge from *Todos Somos Japon*. The full text is here: https://jfissures.wordpress.com/2011/04/22/a-letter-from-silvia-federici-and-george-caffentzis/.
3. My use of affect comes from hearing it in the autonomous movements in Argentina post 2001, *politica afectiva*, and later in Spain in the PAH – the Platform of Mortgage Victims. It is not intended to engage with the growing body of literature on affect. Some of this does deal with feelings of care and love; other contributions are highly academicised conversations of a biological, philosophical and literary nature. I intend it as it sounds, using it to mean more than just love, but positive feelings more expansively as these relate to political motivations and expressions.
4. In 2012 the Syrian government withdrew from the region, however the development of autonomy and direct democracy had been ongoing for over a decade before then.

Contributor Biographies

Camille Barbagallo is a postdoctoral researcher at Leeds University. Her forthcoming book, *Mothers and Others: The Politics of Reproduction in Neoliberal Britain* (Manchester University Press) analyses the political economy of women's work and the history of care work in Britain. With Silvia Federici, she edited the *Care Work and Commons* Vol. 15 Commoner 2012. She is the editor of *Women and the Subversion of the Community: A Mariarosa Dalla Costa Reader* (PM Press 2019). She has worked as a trade union organiser, in radical publishing and higher education for the last ten years. Her essays and articles have appeared in academic journals, Mute Magazine and Novara Media. She is an organiser with the Women's Strike Assembly.

Nicholas Beuret is a lecturer at the University of Essex whose work focuses on environmental politics and science and technology studies, exploring how ecological crises shape, and in turn are shaped by, political action. He has previously been a researcher on climate migration, the politics of the Anthropocene, and green chemistry, and has been an environmental campaigner for Non-Governmental Organisations, a union organiser and political activist across three continents. His research has been published in journals such as Antipode, Science as Culture and South Atlantic Quarterly, as well as numerous political and news outlets.

Werner Bonefeld is professor of politics at the University of York (UK). His *books include (as author) The Strong State and the Free Economy (Rowman & Littlefield 2017) and Critical Theory and the Critique of Political Economy: On subversion and negative reason* (Bloomsbury 2014) and (as editor or coeditor) *Subverting the Present, Imagining the Future: Insurrection, Movement, Commons* (Autonomedia 2008) and *Open Marxism*, 3 vols (Pluto Press 1992 and 1995).

Chris Carlsson, co-director of the multimedia history project Shaping San Francisco, is a writer, publisher, editor, teacher, and community organiser. For the last 25 years, his activities have focused on the underlying themes of horizontal communications, organic communities and public space. He was one of the founders, editors and frequent contributors to the ground-breaking San Francisco magazine *Processed World*. He also helped launch the monthly bike-ins known as Critical Mass that have spread to five continents and over 300 cities. He has edited six books: *Bad Attitude: The Processed World Anthology* (Verso 1990); *Reclaiming San Francisco: History, Politics, Culture* (City Lights 1998, co-edited with James Brook and Nancy J. Peters); *Critical Mass: Bicycling's Defiant Celebration* (AK Press 2002); *The Political Edge* (City Lights Foundation 2004); *Ten Years That Shook the City: San Francisco 1968–78* (City Lights Foundation 2011, with LisaRuth Elliott); and *Shift Happens! Critical Mass at 20* (Full Enjoyment Books 2012, co-edited with LisaRuth Elliott and Adriana Camarena). He published his first novel, *After The Deluge*, in 2004, a story of post-economic San Francisco in the year 2157, and his full-length non-fiction work *Nowtopia* (AK Press) in 2008.

Harry Cleaver is an American scholar, Marxist theoretician, and professor emeritus at the University of Texas at Austin. He is best known as the author of *Reading Capital Politically* (2000), an autonomist reading of Karl Marx's *Capital*, and *Rupturing the Dialectic: The Struggle against Work, Money and Financialization* (2017).

Carla da Cunha Duarte Francisco has written her MA dissertation at the Catholic University of Rio de Janeiro (PUC-Rio) on the dialogue between feminism and Marxism and the work of Silvia Federici. Her research interests also include social reproduction theory, the history of feminism and post-structuralism.

Massimo De Angelis is professor of political economy at University of East London. He founded the web-journal *The Commoner* and is the author of *The Beginning of History: Value Struggles and Global Capitalism* (Pluto 2007) and *Omnia Sunt Communia: on the commons and the transition to postcapitalism* (Zed 2017).

Olivier de Marcellus escaped from the United States and his class some 50 years ago. Since then he has been based in Geneva, where he divided his time more or less equally between research in education and an activism inspired by autonomous Marxism: anti-imperialism, the squatters' movement, direct action against nuclear power... The Zapatista uprising led him to People's Global Action against the WTO and free trade, organising the first global network of resistance to globalisation. Since 2008 he has concentrated his efforts against the most lethal product of capitalism: climate change. All this leaving little time for reflection, he's not much of an intellectual, but he can testify to how useful the writings of George and Silvia have been to illuminate the paths of so many struggles.

Panagiotis Doulos is a PhD candidate in sociology at the Instituto de Ciencias Sociales y Humanidades 'Alfonso Vélez Pliego' of the Benemérita Universidad Autónoma de Puebla (BUAP) in Mexico. His research interests concern issues of violence, social movements, and critical theory. He is coeditor (with John Holloway and Katerina Nasioka) of *Beyond Crisis: After the Collapse of Institutional Hope in Greece, What?* (PM Press 2018).

Nick Dyer-Witheford, an Associate Professor in the Faculty of Information and Media Studies at the University of Western Ontario, is the author of *Cyber-Marx: Cycles and Circuits of Struggle in High Technology Capitalism* (Chicago: University of Illinois 1999) and *Cyber-Proletariat: Global Labour in the Digital Vortex* (London: Pluto Press 2015), and has also written on the video and computer game industry, the uses of the Internet by social movements and theories of technology. Two forthcoming works are coauthorships: with Svitlana Matviyenko, *Cyberwar and Revolution: Digital Subterfuge in Global Capitalism* (University of Minnesota Press 2019), and, with Atle Mikkola Kjøsen and James Steinhoff, *Inhuman Power: Artificial Intelligence and the Future of Capitalism* (Pluto Press 2019).

Alexander Dwinell is Brooklyn-based artist, publisher, editor, and organiser. As part of the South End Press collective he published such authors as Vandana Shiva, Mumia Abu-Jamal, and Oscar Olivera. He has exhibited at venues that include Flux Factory, Smack Mellon, Temporary Agency, and Carriage Trade and his work and writing has appeared in publications such as Community Development Journal, Latin American Perspective, and Celebrate People's History. He has also managed bookstores in the United States and the United Kingdom, toured in punk bands, and is currently organising with Red Bloom Solidarity Network and the New Sanctuary Coalition – NYC.

Dave Eden's research interests circle around the critique of political economy. His research focuses on two threads: one is the study of contemporary Marxian theory with a special focus on the post-workerists, the state debate, value-form theory and crisis theory. The second thread is the application of these approaches to understand the way that social reproduction is being contested by capital and labour in the context of the crisis.

Edith Gonzalez has concluded her master's and doctorate studies in Sociology at the Instituto de Ciencias Sociales y Humanidades \Alfonso Vélez Pliego' of the Benemérita Universidad Autónoma de Puebla (BUAP) in

Mexico. Her research interests concern issues of democracy, social movements and emancipation.

Raquel Gutiérrez Aguilar was born in Mexico. In the 1980s she was one of the founding members of the EGTK (Tupac Katari Guerrilla Army) in Bolivia. She served a prison term in the 1990s, after which she returned to Mexico. She is currently a Professor of Sociology at the Autonomous University of Puebla in Mexico. She is author of *Rhythms of the Pachakuti: Indigenous Uprising and State Power in Bolivia* (Duke University Press 2014).

Paulo Henrique Flores teaches philosophy at Fluminense Federal University (UFF) in Brazil. His work focuses on the thought of Karl Marx and historical materialism. He is a militant in the Popular Communes Movement (MCP).

Viviane Gonik is a long-time feminist activist based in Geneva. Gonik has worked at the Institute of Occupational Health Sciences in Lausanne, and contributed to studies on work related mental health problems. She is co-author of *HommesFemmes: metamorphoses d'un rapport social* (Georg; Geneve 1998). For the last six years she has inspired a monthly cine-club, Metrboulotkino, about work, to encourage political debate on the subject.

Gerald Hanlon is Professor of Organisational Sociology at Queen Mary, University of London. His major examination of the origins of management knowledge and its links to the authoritarianism, violence, and anti-democratic response to the 'Social Crisis of Our Time' (Wilhelm Röepke) was published as *The Dark Side of Management – The Secret History of Management Thought* (Routledge 2015).

Bue Rübner Hansen is a postdoctoral researcher at the University of Aarhus. He is an editor of *Viewpoint Magazine*, and has engaged as an activist researcher in the British student movement, municipalism in Barcelona, and the migrant and refugee solidarity movement. His research focuses on questions of social reproduction, class formation and ideas of the good life in common, and he is beginning to work on ecology. Apart from *Viewpoint* and academic journals, his writing has been published in *Roar, Jacobin, Novara, Mute, OpenDemocracy* and *Diagonal*.

David Harvie lives in Leeds, where he tries to sing new worlds into being with Commoners Choir. He is author (with The Free Association) of *Moments of Excess: Movements, Protest and Everyday Life* (PM Press 2011) and co-editor (with Keir Milburn, Ben Trott and David Watts) of *Shut*

Them Down! Gleneagles 2005, the G8 and the Movement of Movements (Autonomedia/Dissent! 2005); he was also an editor of *Turbulence: Ideas for Movement* (www.turbulence.org.uk). He sells his labour-power to the University of Leicester, UK.

Malav Kanuga is an urban anthropologist and founding editor of Common Notions, an independent book publishing and programming house based at the Interference Archive in Brooklyn, New York. A doctoral candidate at the Graduate Center City University of New York, his activist-scholar research focuses on historical and contemporary struggles around space, culture, and urban life in an international and postcolonial perspective. He has taught at Parsons, The New School, City University of New York, Kamla Raheja Vidyanidhi Institute for Architecture and Environmental Studies, and in a range of autonomous education initiatives.

Peter Linebaugh is an historian who currently resides in the region of the American Great Lakes. As a child of empire he grew up amid the hopes and rubble of post-war London. He was schooled by a wise woman of Appalachia in Cattaraugus, New York, by US Marines in Bonn, Germany, by Anglicans in Karachi, Pakistan, by Quakers at Swarthmore College, Pennsylvania, and by Cold Warriors at Columbia University, New York, before joining E.P. Thompson at the University of Warwick to learn the art and craft of 'people's remembrancing' which has taken printed results in *Albion's Fatal Tree, The London Hanged, The Many-Headed Hydra* (with Marcus Rediker), *Magna Carta Manifesto, Stop, Thief!,* his *May Day* book, and most recently *Red Round Globe Hot Burning.* He has taught at Harvard and the Attica Correctional Facility; New York University and the Federal Penitentiary in Marion, Illinois. He is proud that once as a child Aneurin Bevan patted him on the head. He's also proud of working with SDS and Midnight Notes.

Rodrigo Guimarães Nunes is a lecturer in modern and contemporary philosophy at the the Catholic University of Rio de Janeiro (PUC-Rio). He is the author of *Organisation of the Organisationless. Collective Action After Networks* (Mute/Post-Media Lab Books: 2014) and of several articles that have appeared in such periodicals as *Radical Philosophy, South Atlantic Quarterly, International Journal of Communication* and *Les Temps Modernes.* His new book, *Beyond the Horizontal. Rethinking the Question of Organisation,* is forthcoming with Verso (2019). As an organiser and popular educator, he has been involved in initiatives such as the World Social Forum in Porto Alegre (Brazil) and the Justice for Cleaners campaign in London (UK).

Marcela Olivera is a water commons organiser based in Cochabamba, Bolivia. Since 2004 she has been developing and consolidating an inter-American citizens' network on water justice named Red VIDA as part of her work as the Latin American Coordinator for Food and Water Watch. She is also member of the Platform for Public and Community Partnerships of The Americas, PAPC, an organisation that promotes exchange of knowledge among water utilities based in solidarity and horizontal cooperation.

P.M. studies in Zurich, Paris, New York; linguistics and literature; novelist, pseudonym P.M. (Weltgeist Superstar 1980; Die Schrecken des Jahres 1000, 1999; AKIBA 2008; Manetti lesen 2012); dramatist; books and articles on urbanistic, ecological and political topics (*bolo'bolo*, 1983; *Subcoma*, 2000; *Kartoffeln und Computer*, 2012; '*The Power of Neighbourhood*' *and the Commons*; New York 2014; Die Andere Stadt, 2017); co-founder of housing cooperatives (Karthago, Kraftwerk1, NeNa1); board member of Neustart Schweiz.

Paul Rekret teaches political and social theory at Richmond University, American International University in London. He is author of *Down With Childhood: Popular Music and the Crisis of Innocence* (Repeater 2017) and *Philosophy, Politics, and Polemics: On Derrida and Foucault* (Rowan & Littlefield 2017). He hosts Beholder Halfway, monthly radio essays investigating music politics on Resonance.Extra.

Stevphen Shukaitis is Senior Lecturer at the University of Essex, Centre for Work, Organization, and Society, and a member of the Autonomedia editorial collective. Since 2009 he has coordinated and edited Minor Compositions (www.minorcompositions.info). He is the author of *Imaginal Machines: Autonomy & Self-Organization in the Revolutions of Everyday Day* (2009) and *The Composition of Movements to Come: Aesthetics and Cultural Labor After the Avant-Garde* (2016), and editor (with Erika Biddle and David Graeber) of *Constituent Imagination: Militant Investigations/Collective Theorization* (AK Press 2007). His research focuses on the emergence of collective imagination in social movements and the changing compositions of cultural and artistic labour.

Marina Sitrin is an Assistant Professor of Sociology at SUNY Binghamton. She participates in, and writes about, societies in movement. Her books include *Horizontalism: Voices of Popular Power in Argentina* (AK Press 2006); *Everyday Revolutions: Horizontalism and Autonomy in Argentina*

(Zed Books 2012); and co-authored, *They Can't Represent Us!: Reinventing Democracy from Greece to Occupy* (Verso Books 2014). She is currently writing a book on global societies in movement and non-movements with the University of California Press.

Sian Sullivan is Professor of Environment and Culture at Bath Spa University. Recent articles from her work on value, biodiversity conservation and the anthropology of nature have been published journals such as New Formations, Capitalism Nature Socialism, Journal of Political Ecology, Antipode, Science & Technology Studies and Conservation Biology. She has also published *Valuing Development, Environment and Conservation: Creating Values That Matter* (with Sarah Bracking, Aurora Fredriksen and Phil Woodhouse; Routledge 2018); *Contributions to Law, Philosophy and Ecology: Exploring Re-embodiments* (with Ruth Pellicer-Thomas and Vito De Lucia; Routledge 2016); and *Financialisation, Biodiversity Conservation and Equity: Some Currents and Concerns* (Third World Network 2012). Building on field research since the early 1990s, her current work deploys oral history to explore socio-ecological pasts and diversities in west Namibia (see www.futurepasts.net).

Nic Vas is an artist, teacher, researcher and a drummer in Leicester (UK) based group Anatomy. Nic has contributed in campaigns and organising efforts with many collectives and organisations such as LAWAS (Latin American Workers' Association), Anti Raids Network, the union United Voices of the World among many others. Nic's research is focussed in the use of visuals in radical grassroots and community organising. Nic's collaboration with ACT ESOL – Language Resistance Theatre – to provide support to incorporate Augusto Boal's theatre of the oppressed as a teaching method in ESOL (English for Speakers of Other Languages) classes has been recently published by the Serpentine Gallery. A Downloadable version of that work can be found here: www.serpentinegalleries.org/learn/language-and-power/act-esol-language-resistance-theatre-resource.

Joen Vedel is a visual artist, writer and political organiser, educated at the Royal Danish Academy of Fine Arts and The Whitney Independent Study Program. He has shown his work in a number of big and small institutions in Europe and the United States and organised a long list of seminars, film programmes and exhibition-projects. He is the author of *Sammenbrudstykker*, a diary of his first-hand experiences in the Greek crises, and the editor of *On Reproduction, Intergenerational Solidarity and the Dancing Body*, a collection of texts by Silvia Federici.

Manuela Zechner has recently been doing post-doctoral research projects on commons in Southern Europe (Aristotle University Thessaloniki/ERC) and on European crisis migrations (Humboldt University Berlin). Her PhD is on Care and Precarity movements (Queen Mary University London). She coordinates the Future Archive project, organises workshops and gatherings of all sorts, works on & off with free radio (The Sounds of Movement) and video (Remembering Europe), and (co)edits books on the basis of collective processes, such as the *Nanopolitics Handbook* (Minor Compositions 2013), *Situating Ourselves in Displacement* (Minor Compositions and JOOAP Press 2017) and 'Una Ciudad Muchos Mundos' (Intermediae, 2018). She publishes in journals like *Transversal, Movements, Subjectivities, Emulations, Kulturrisse.*

Index